CONTEXT MATTERS

INTERNATIONAL VOICES IN BIBLICAL STUDIES

Jione Havea, General Editor

Editorial Board:
Jin Young Choi
Gerald O. West

Number 16

CONTEXT MATTERS

Old Testament Essays from Africa and Beyond
Honoring Knut Holter

Edited by

Madipoane Masenya (Ngwan'a Mphahlele),
Marta Høyland Lavik, Ntozakhe Simon Cezula,
and Tina Dykesteen Nilsen

# SBL PRESS
Atlanta

Copyright © 2023 by SBL Press

All rights reserved. No part of this work may be reproduced or transmitted in any form or by any means, electronic or mechanical, including photocopying and recording, or by means of any information storage or retrieval system, except as may be expressly permitted by the 1976 Copyright Act or in writing from the publisher. Requests for permission should be addressed in writing to the Rights and Permissions Office, SBL Press, 825 Houston Mill Road, Atlanta, GA 30329 USA.

Library of Congress Control Number: 2023948033

Electronic open access edition (ISBN 978-1-62837-368-4) available at http://ivbs.sbl-site.org/home.aspx.

Contents

Acknowledgments ix

Abbreviations xi

Introduction 1
    Madipoane Masenya (Ngwan'a Mphahlele), Marta Høyland
    Lavik, Ntozakhe Simon Cezula, and Tina Dykesteen Nilsen

Part 1. The Context of African Biblical Hermeneutics

Context as Genre in African Biblical Hermeneutics 11
    Kenneth N. Ngwa

Bible Translation, Publication, and Utilization in Africa:
A Tribute to Professor Knut Holter 25
    Jesse N. K. Mugambi

Whose Context Matters? Reading the Story of Hagar and
Bilhah (Gen 16; 30) through Woman-as-Tlhatswadirope Lens 37
    Madipoane Masenya (Ngwan'a Mphahlele)

Part 2. Reception in Context

"Blessed Be My People Egypt": Isaiah 19–20 with Special
Reference to Reception by the Coptic Church in Egypt 51
    Grant LeMarquand

The Portrayal of Africa and Africans in the Book of Ezekiel 63
    David Tuesday Adamo†

Text, Context, and Canonical Ecology: The LRA's
Reception of the Ten Commandments..77
    Terje Stordalen

The Origin of the Griqua Prayer of Adam Kok III and
Its Reception..91
    Hendrik L. Bosman

Shembe's Sermon on the Mount: African Reception of the
Bible as African Biblical Hermeneutics...105
    Gerald O. West

Part 3. Justice in Context

Moving beyond the Text as Slogan: Reading Genesis 19 in the
Context of LGBTIQA+ Lived Realities in African Faith Contexts..........123
    Charlene van der Walt

Dining with the Tormentors? A Biblical and Acoli Context-
Sensitive Understanding of Healing and Restoration...............................137
    Helen Nambalirwa Nkabala

Rape As Cultural Violence: A Feminist Cultural
Hermeneutical Reading of Dinah's Story in Genesis 34...........................149
    Funlọla O. Ọlọjẹde

"Is It Good for You to Be Angry?" (Jonah 4:4, 9): Contemplating
Divine and Human Anger in a Context of Injustice..................................163
    L. Juliana Claassens

Part 4. Ecology in Context

A Wandering Aramean and the Wandering Maasai:
An Intercultural, Ecotheological Dialogue 179
    Beth E. Elness-Hanson

From Eurocentrism in South Africa to Ecological Universalism
in Amos: An African Ecological Reading of Amos 9:7 193
    Ntozakhe Simon Cezula and Tina Dykesteen Nilsen

Contents

Part 5. Contexts beyond Africa?

"Our Grandfather Made the Earth for His Grandchildren":
Biblical Scholarship Traveling to the Heart of the Andes;
An Exercise in Intercultural Indigenous Hermeneutics........................209
    Hans de Wit

Reading the Bible in Present-Day Norwegian Contexts:
The Case of Cancer Patients..223
    Marta Høyland Lavik

Part 6. Other Forms of Context

Contextual Interpretation, Then and Now: Overhearing
Inner-Biblical Discourses to Enrich Contemporary
Contextual Interpretations...239
    Louis C. Jonker

The Production and Worship of Idols in Biblical Tradition 253
    Jostein Ådna

Structural Differences between the Source Languages and the
Target Languages in Bible Translation..267
    Magnar Kartveit

Part 7. Context Indeed Matters in Biblical Studies:
The Legacy of Knut Holter

Global Biblical Criticism: Toward a Dialogical Hermeneutics................283
    Fernando F. Segovia

Knut Holter's Life and Work..309

Postscript: A Generous Move 319
    Sigbjørn Sødal

Contributors...321
Author Index..325

Acknowledgments

This volume is a tribute to Professor Knut Holter, whose scholarly works have made and continue to make lasting impacts in the field of biblical studies. The four editors of this volume are very privileged to have Holter as our much-cherished colleague and friend, and our greatest gratitude goes to him.

The volume consists of a series of essays by contributors who all have a long and close relationship with Holter. We would like to thank each of the contributors for their essays and their scholarship. As we first configured this volume, many names came up that we wanted to invite to make a contribution, but we were constrained by space. We do acknowledge that so many other scholars are indebted to Holter in one or more ways or worked with him closely, but if we were to include essays from all of them, we would need several volumes. We express our apologies to all those close colleagues whose voices could not be heard in this collection.

Two institutions have helped to subsidize this publication: VID Specialized University and NLA University College, both in Norway. We are grateful for their substantial financial contributions, without which this project would not have materialized.

We would like to thank the editorial board of the International Voices in Biblical Studies (SBL Press) for approving this volume to be published as part of the series. We also express our appreciation to the anonymous peer reviewers for their feedback on the essays. Lastly, we wish to convey our heartfelt gratitude to Dr. Funlọla O. Ọlọjẹde for her sterling effort in editing.

Madipoane Masenya (Ngwan'a Mphahlele)
Marta Høyland Lavik
Ntozakhe Cezula
Tina Dykesteen Nilsen

Abbreviations

AB	Anchor Bible
ABD	Freedman, David Noel, ed. *Anchor Bible Dictionary*. 6 vols. New York: Doubleday, 1992.
ABS	Archaeology and Biblical Studies
AcT	*Acta Theologica*
AIL	Ancient Israel and Its Literature
AJCR	*African Journal of Conflict Resolution*
AJT	*Asia Journal of Theology*
ANEM	Ancient Near Eastern Monographs
AS	*African Studies*
ATJ	*Africa Theological Journal*
AThR	*Anglican Theological Review*
BBB	Bonner biblische Beiträge
BHS	*Biblia Hebraica Stuttgartensia*
BibInt	Biblical Interpretation
BibInt	*Biblical Interpretation*
BN	*Biblische Notizen*
BOTSA	*Bulletin for Old Testament Studies in Africa*
BT	*The Bible Translator*
BZAW	Beihefte zur Zeitschrift für die alttestamentliche Wissenschaft
CurBR	*Currents in Biblical Research*
DSD	*Dead Sea Discoveries*
FCB	*Feminist Companion to the Bible*
GPBS	Global Perspectives on Biblical Scholarship
HBT	*Horizons in Biblical Theology*
HeBAI	*Hebrew Bible and Ancient Israel*
HS	*Hebrew Studies*
HSM	Harvard Semitic Monographs

HvTSt	*Hervormde Teologiese Studies (HTS Teologiese Studies/HTS Theological Studies)*
IRM	*International Review of Mission*
IVBS	International Voices in Biblical Studies
JANER	*Journal of Ancient Near Eastern Religions*
JBL	*Journal of Biblical Literature*
JETS	*Journal of Evangelical Theological Society*
JPR	*Journal of Peace Research*
JRitSt	*Journal of Ritual Studies*
JSAS	*Journal of Southern African Studies*
JSOT	*Journal for the Study of the Old Testament*
JSOTSup	Journal for the Study of the Old Testament Supplement Series
JTSA	*Journal of Theology for Southern Africa*
KJV	King James Version
LRA	The Lord's Resistance Army
MS	*Mission Studies*
MTSR	*Method and Theory in the Study of Religion*
NA[28]	Nestle-Aland, *Novum Testamentum Graece*, 28th rev. ed.
NAOTS	*Newsletter on African Old Testament Scholarship*
NASB	New American Standard Bible
NETS	Pietersma, Albert, and Benjamin G. Wright, eds. *A New English Translation of the Septuagint*. New York: Oxford University Press, 2007.
NGTT	*Nederduitse Gereformeerde Teologiese Tydskrif*
NICOT	New International Commentary on the Old Testament
NJPS	*Tanakh: The Holy Scriptures: The New JPS Translation according to the Traditional Hebrew Text*
NLA	Norsk Lærerakademi
NRSV	New Revised Standard Version
NTM	*Norsk Tidsskrift for Misjon*
OBO	Orbis Biblicus et Orientalis
OTE	*Old Testament Essays*
OTP	Charlesworth, James H., ed. *Old Testament Pseudepigrapha*. 2 vols. New York: Doubleday, 1983–1985.
R&T	*Religion and Theology*
SAHJ	*South African Historical Journal*

SBLDS	Society of Biblical Literature Dissertation Series
SBT	Studies in Biblical Theology
SemeiaSt	Semeia Studies
SJOT	*Scandinavian Journal of the Old Testament*
StBibLit	Studies in Biblical Literature
STJ	*Stellenbosch Theological Journal*
SymS	Symposium Series
TBT	*The Bible Today*
TDOT	Botterweck, G. Johannes, and Helmer Ringgren, eds. *Theological Dictionary of the Old Testament*. Translated by John T. Willis et al. 8 vols. Grand Rapids: Eerdmans, 1974–2006.
TEV	Today's English Version
TTKi	*Tidsskrift for Teologi og Kirke*
VID	Vitenskapelig Internasjonal Diakonal
VT	*Vetus Testamentum*
VTSup	Vetus Testamentum Supplement
WBC	Word Biblical Commentary
ZABR	*Zeitschrift für altorientalische und biblische Rechtgeschichte*

Introduction

*Madipoane Masenya (Ngwan'a Mphahlele), Marta Høyland Lavik,
Ntozakhe Simon Cezula, and Tina Dykesteen Nilsen*

Western biblical scholarship has placed itself on top of the global interpretative hierarchy and limited the issue of context to the production of the books of the Bible. In the process, the contexts of Bible readers from the geopolitical South (e.g., African contexts, as in the present case) have been marginalized in the hermeneutical endeavors. The present volume thus foregrounds context as a critical hermeneutical lens for the discipline of biblical studies.[1] Context is defined in creative and nonreductive ways, and the volume thus makes an invaluable contribution by highlighting how context, in its multifaceted character, should be a central part of the discourse by the International Voices in Biblical Studies series. Against this background, three important aspects of the work of Professor Knut Holter, the honoree of this volume, are illuminated in this volume.

The first aspect is context. In 2020, a book containing Holter's chapter, "Interpretive Context Matters: Isaiah and the African Context in African Study Bibles," was published. A closer look at some of Holter's writings show that, more than being just a chapter title, this title also mirrors elements of his scholarship. The main title of the chapter, "Interpretive Context Matters," also describes his stance on context in Old Testament scholarship. The second aspect is the African context. Although Holter is Norwegian, the subtitle hints at his relationship with the African continent. One of

---

1. Given the nature of the present volume with its foregrounding of previously marginalized contexts (the African continent being a case in point) and in the interest of diversity and inclusivity as well as the recognition of the roles played by various languages in their own contexts, all words in languages other than English will be captured in the regular font, thus deviating from the standard norm of italicizing such words.

his main focuses is "networking[2] among African Old Testament scholars and analysis of the history (Holter 1996; 2000) and strategy of African Old Testament scholarship" (Holter 2002, 8). Context and Africa, thus, feature strongly in Holter's scholarly work. The third aspect is scholarly internationalization, which is of great importance to Holter. A brief look at his remarks on these elements may be enlightening.

Demonstrating that context seriously matters to him, Holter (2000, 4-5) says: "By studying the relationship between African interpretation of the Old Testament and its interpretive context, I have also learnt something about the relationship between my own Old Testament interpretation and its Western interpretive context." With emphasis on the importance of context, the editors of this Festschrift also argue that Bible interpretation, especially as it is theorized and practiced on the African continent and elsewhere, cannot be detached from the context(s) of present-day Bible readers (cf. Mbuvi 2022; Ngwa 2022). In Bible interpretation, context matters. Andrew Mbuvi (2017, 154) rightly argues that African biblical study "refuses to deal with the Bible simply as an ancient text and demands that it be engaged to deal with present concerns, addressing issues that resonate with African (and world) realities." Holter (2002, 7) averts a possible misunderstanding that emphasizing context is equal to rejecting traditional historical criticism by echoing African scholars who categorically argue that traditional historical critical methodology should be used "in service of a contextualized hermeneutics" (cf. Ntreh 1990; Ukpong 1999).

Concerning Africa and scholarly internationalization, in the introduction of the book titled *Yahweh in Africa: Essays on Africa and Old Testament*, Holter (2000, 1) advocates "the need for closer interaction between Western and African scholars." He admits that the hermeneutical discussion in the book "is mainly an African enterprise" (2000, 2):

> Still, Africa is no island, neither is African interpretation of the Old Testament, and I am sure that also non-African scholars and scholarly communities would benefit from interacting with their African counterparts and participating in this hermeneutical discussion. Actually, I think it is high time that western Old Testament scholars, who generally take for granted that African colleagues are familiar with their positions

---

2. For networking, see Knut Holter,'s tenure as editor of the *Newsletter on African Old Testament Scholarship* (*NAOTS*). In 2000, the newsletter was renamed the *Bulletin for Old Testament Studies in Africa* (*BOTSA*).

and production, allow the influence to go in both directions, and therefore familiarize themselves with some of the contemporary African discussion.³

Holter reasons that "all the politically correct talk about scholarly internationalisation becomes only empty rhetoric if Africa, or for that matter also the rest of the two thirds world, is not included" (2). He bemoans "the global economic and political tension between the North and the South within which biblical scholarship has to work" and exhorts biblical scholars not to accept this tension fatalistically but to do something about it (2).

For several decades, the honoree has been preoccupied with hermeneutics, especially African biblical hermeneutics, and how dialogue between Western and African biblical scholars can be enhanced/encouraged. The essays in this volume engage explicitly with a variety of Holter's publications, particularly those related to African biblical hermeneutics, but also to the honoree's publications on, for example, divine images or translation issues. It contains essays that focus on the issue of context as it relates to the context of the production and translation of biblical texts as well as the notion of context with regard to the Bible readers, whether located on or outside the African continent. In a multifaceted way, the essays engage with the theme that *Context Matters: Old Testament Essays from Africa and Beyond* outlined in seven main parts, as shown below.

Part 1 of this volume, titled "The Context of African Biblical Hermeneutics," sets the stage for the entire collection of essays. It communicates to the reader different perspectives of doing biblical studies in African contexts. The first essay in this part is written by Kenneth N. Ngwa and is titled "Context as Genre in African Biblical Hermeneutics." Ngwa examines the notion of context as genre both in biblical interpretation in general and in African biblical hermeneutics in particular. Deploying these formulations, he shows how context shapes and functions in Ps 1. Following Ngwa's essay is Jesse N. K. Mugambi's "Bible Translation, Publication, and Utilization in Africa: A Tribute to Professor Knut Holter." Mugambi focuses on some challenges that researchers face in translating the original biblical

---

3. On these remarks, it is encouraging to note that he is quoted eight times in a paper titled "Learning from African Theologians and Their Hermeneutics: Some Reflections from a German Evangelical Theologian," by Hans-Georg Wünch (2015) of the Theologisches Seminar Rheinland, Germany.

languages into African languages and in publishing the Bible. Mugambi presents Holter's contributions in the area of training African students and in collaborating with Acton Publishers (Nairobi, Kenya). The final essay in this section is authored by Madipoane Masenya (Ngwan'a Mphahlele) and is titled "Whose Context Matters? Reading the Story of Hagar and Bilhah (Gen 16; 30) through Woman-as-Tlhatswadirope Lens." The essay is a follow-up to Holter's (1996) statement that African Old Testament scholarship is alive. The essay unpacks the question of context and asks whose context matters, particularly where the Bible has, historically and even up till today, wielded power. To that end, it offers a rereading of the narratives of Hagar and Bilhah through the lens of woman as tlhatswadirope, that is, woman as the washer of thighs.

Part 2 of the volume is titled "Reception in Context," opening with an essay written by Grant LeMarquand, "'Blessed Be My People Egypt': Isaiah 19–20 with Special Reference to Reception by the Coptic Church in Egypt." LeMarquand surveys the two-sided image of Egypt in the Old Testament with an emphasis on the oracle about Egypt in Isa 19–20. One of the questions he addressed is whether Egypt is included in the people of God. Furthermore, the essay shows how the Isaiah passage is used in the Coptic church, considering differences in theological themes. The next essay in this section, written by the late David Tuesday Adamo, is titled "The Portrayal of Africa and Africans in the Book of Ezekiel." Besides showing how the book of Ezekiel portrays Africa and Africans, Adamo also calls the attention of African biblical scholars to the issue of identity formation in the African context, which, in his opinion, needs to be seriously addressed—theologically and biblically. In the essay "Text, Context, and Canonical Ecology: Exemplified by the LRA's Reception of the Ten Commandments," Terje Stordalen argues that the Lord's Resistance Army recruited the social dignity that had long been associated with the Ten Commandments. To demonstrate this, he pieces together aspects of what he calls the scriptural ecology of the LRA and elaborates on Holter's insight that the significance of Scripture is not at all defined exclusively by the semantic potential of its text.

Hendrik L. Bosman's essay, "The Origin of the Griqua Prayer of Adam Kok III and Its Reception," focuses on how the Griqua understood prayer amid the pervasive presence of the British Empire and the encroachment of the Free State Republic on Griqua territory in the nineteenth century. It views the Griqua prayer as a form of hybridity and of resistance—relating Christian and Khoi-San religion, while resisting the encroachment of imperial power. The final essay in this section is written by Gerald O. West. His "Shembe's Sermon on the Mount: African Reception of the Bible as African Biblical Hermeneutics" acknowledges Holter's work on African receptions of the Bible by engaging with this dimension of the honoree's work. West offers a historical and hermeneutical analysis of Isaiah Shembe's reception of the rhetorical voice of Jesus in the parables and in the Sermon on the Mount (Matt 5). The essay analyzes Shembe's interpretation of biblical texts, reflecting on why such an analysis is constitutive of African biblical scholarship.

Part 3, "Justice in Context," opens with Charlene van der Walt's "Moving beyond the Text as Slogan: Reading Genesis 19 in the Context of LGBTIQA+ Lived Realities in African Faith Contexts." The essay focuses on the Sodom and Gomorrah narrative in Gen 19, which is often used in contemporary African faith communities to condemn LGBTIQA+ people as an abomination before God and to label same-sex love as unnatural, un-Christian, and un-African. Van der Walt describes the key learnings from the development of the contextual Bible study, fundamentally designed to push beyond the anecdotal judgmental slogans of the interpretation of the text to a critical slow rereading of the narrative. This is in honor of Holter's commitment to reading the Bible with those who are most marginalized and affected by systems of oppression in African contexts. The next essay, written by Helen Nambalirwa Nkabala, is "Dining with the Tormentors? A Biblical and Acoli Context-Sensitive Understanding of Healing and Restoration." This essay examines the period following a ceasefire by the Lord's Resistance Army in Uganda. During the armed activities of the Lord's Resistance Army, the Acoli people of northern Uganda endured great suffering, but the atrocities were justified by using biblical texts. After the ceasefire, Lord's Resistance Army soldiers were integrated into their respective communities. The essay examines the process of healing and restoration after all that happened and suggests that the context of the Bible and of the Lord's Resistance Army be taken seriously in this process.

Funlọla O. Ọlọjẹde's "Rape as Cultural Violence: A Feminist Cultural Hermeneutical Reading of Dinah's Story in Genesis 34" argues that certain cultural elements in the Dinah story suggest that the episodes of violence are in a sense motivated or reinforced by cultural values. Ọlọjẹde argues that Dinah's story calls to mind certain practices in the (South) African context that are attributable to culture. Significantly, the essay shows that cultural issues, as highlighted in the analysis of Dinah's story, sometimes shape the interpretation of the Old Testament in the African context and beyond. The last essay in this part of the book is written by L. Juliana Claassens. Her essay, "'Is It Good for You to Be Angry?' (Jonah 4:4, 9): Contemplating Divine and Human Anger in a Context of Injustice," acknowledges Holter's long-standing commitment to socially engaged biblical scholarship. It considers conceptions of divine and human anger in the book of Jonah, bringing the narrative portrayal of anger in the book into conversation with recent theoretical discussions of the powerful emotion of anger that informed black liberation theology. The essay postulates that Jonah's anger receives new significance when read in the context of injustice, as represented on the African continent in the form of the harm done by imperialism, war, gender-based violence, as well as the structural violence of poverty.

Part 4, "Ecology in Context," is premised on ecology as an analytical tool. Beth E. Elness-Hanson's "A Wandering Aramean and the Wandering Maasai: An Intercultural, Ecotheological Dialogue" foregrounds the context of the Maasai, a pastoralist people group in Kenya and Tanzania in East Africa. Through a dialogical exegesis of Deut 26:1–15, the essay identifies connections between the pastoralists of wandering Aramean descent and the contemporary Maasai. Both share a triangulated ontological worldview of the interdependent relationships of God, humans, and nonhuman creation, which includes the land. The essay thus concludes that the church has a strategic role in the biblically grounded commission of creation care in order to address the ecological challenges of the contemporary pastoralist Maasai. The other essay in this section is coauthored by Ntozakhe Simon Cezula and Tina Dykesteen Nilsen and is titled, "From Eurocentrism in South Africa to Ecological Universalism in Amos: An African Ecological Reading of Amos 9:7." From the perspective of social justice and ecology, this essay challenges the narratives about Israel's special position. Allowing the contemporary South African context and the context of Amos 9:7 to speak to each other, the article explores the connections between ideological centrism, universalism, and ecology—in close conversation with Holter's publications.

Part 5, "Contexts beyond Africa," opens with Hans de Wit's "'Our Grandfather Made the Earth for His Grandchildren': Biblical Scholarship Traveling to the Heart of the Andes; An Exercise in Intercultural Indigenous Hermeneutics." Here, de Wit analyzes a project located within the field of empirical hermeneutics that deals with interpretation processes between marginalized, extremely poor, indigenous communities in Latin and Central America. One of the central concepts continues to be dialogue—not dialogue between biblical scholars or between different forms of biblical scholarship but dialogue and encounter between non-professional readers promoted by biblical scholarship. The second essay in this part is written by Marta Høyland Lavik and is titled "Reading the Bible in Present-Day Norwegian Contexts: The Case of Cancer Patients." Lavik's essay approaches empirical hermeneutics from the perspective of people who know that they are facing death due to critical cancer diagnoses. It analyzes interviews with cancer patients about the significance of the Bible in times of critical illness. The interpretation of the material shows how biblical texts are read existentially in such situations, how the pressing context of a reader influences what is read, and how these texts are experienced.

Part 6, "Other Forms of Context," considers other perspectives and topics with which Holter engages, thereby, expanding the concept of context. The essay by Louis C. Jonker, "Contextual Interpretation, Then and Now: Overhearing Inner-Biblical Discourses to Enrich Contemporary Contextual Interpretations," critically engages Holter's works on Deut 4 and Isa 40–55. Jonker shows how inner-biblical interpretation and hermeneutics pave the way for sensible engagements with the Christian Bible in contemporary African contexts. It also raises the question of the relevance of historical-critical scholarship in Africa. The next essay, Jostein Ådna's "The Production and Worship of Idols in Biblical Tradition," directs the attention of the readers to the first major scholarly contribution made by Holter by examining the fabrication and worship of idols in Second Isaiah and in Paul. Magnar Kartveit's is the final essay in this section. His "Structural Differences between the Source Languages and the Target Languages in Bible Translation" links up with one of the major interests of Holter, namely, Bible translation. The author argues that in Bible translation, a great deal of effort goes into semantic questions. According to Kartveit, this approach may end up in controversy between people who uphold literal translations and those who opt for contextual renderings. He thus highlights the issue of grammatical and structural differences between the source languages and the target languages.

Part 7, "Context Indeed Matters in Biblical Studies: The Legacy of Knut Holter," concludes the collection of essays with the contribution by Fernando F. Segovia, titled "Global Biblical Criticism: Toward a Dialogical Hermeneutics." In a fitting epilogue, Segovia captures a sense of the dynamics and mechanics of Holter's work as conveyed by a number of his key writings and as reflected in the contributions to this volume.

Works Cited

Holter, Knut. 1996. *Tropical Africa and the Old Testament*. New York: Lang.

———. 2000. *Yahweh in Africa: Essays on Africa and Old Testament*. New York: Lang.

———. 2002. *Old Testament Research for Africa: A Critical Analysis and Annotated Bibliography of African Old Testament Dissertations, 1967–2000*. Bible and Theology in Africa 3. New York: Lang.

———. 2020. "Interpretive Context Matters: Isaiah and the African Context in African Study Bibles." Pages 655-69 in *The Oxford Handbook of Isaiah*. Edited by Lena-Sofia Tiemeyer. Oxford: Oxford University Press.

Mbuvi, Andrew M. 2017. "African Biblical Studies: An Introduction to an Emerging Discipline." *CurBR* 15.2:149-78.

———. 2022. *African Biblical Hermeneutics: Unmasking Embessed Racism and Colonialism in Biblical Studies*. London: T&T Clark.

Ngwa, Kenneth N. 2022. *Let My People Live: An Africana Reading of Exodus*. Louisville: Westminster John Knox.

Ntreh, B. A. 1990. "Towards an African Biblical Hermeneutical." *ATJ* 19:247-54.

Ukpong, Justin S. 1999. "Can African Old Testament Scholarship Escape the Historical Critical Approach." *NAOTS* 7:2-5.

Wünch, Hans-Georg. 2015. "Learning from African Theologians and Their Hermeneutics: Some Reflections from a German Evangelical Theologian." *Verbum et Ecclesia* 36:1-9.

Part 1
The Context of African Biblical Hermeneutics

Context as Genre in African Biblical Hermeneutics

Kenneth N. Ngwa

Introduction

I am honored to offer these reflections in recognition of the untiring work of Professor Knut Holter, who has made significant contributions to the central, rather than tangential or incidental, role that context plays in theoretical and methodological work of biblical hermeneutics. That work of contextual analysis continues, for African biblical hermeneutics and beyond. It is multiply framed—around literary, cultural, religious, political, race, gender, ecological, (post)colonial, and global contexts, among others (Mugambi 2009; Matheny 2012; Mitri 2012; Kibobo 2017; Dube, Maseno-Ouma, and Mligo 2018; Smith 2018; Allen and Smith 2020). There is an intersection involved in theorizing and deploying the trope of context. Madipoane Masenya [ngwan'a Mphahlele] (Masenya 1997, 56) identifies four interrelated themes in her examination of Prov 31, including "racism, classism, sexism, and African culture." I will argue that the shift from conceptualizing context as a space-time of application or inculturation to reimagining hermeneutics as incipiently and perennially tied to context means that one could understand context as a category of analyses and exploration of meaning, just as one would consider race, gender, history, ecology, or colonialism.

I will examine Holter's work in my theorizing context that way for two reasons. First, Holter's work has engaged African exegesis and hermeneutics in ways that move beyond understanding context as a receptacle of meaning. Second, the enormity of Africa—literary and artistic, environmental and ecological, historical and cultural, hermeneutical and exegetical, religious and theoretical—means that context itself often shifts and can never be assumed. It is framed as much by internal dynamics of community and identity formation as by external pressures and assumptions about its place in biblical interpretation. That is why the work of African biblical hermeneutics or African biblical studies, as Andrew Mbuvi (2017) has argued, is as much about placing African contexts in conversation with biblical contexts (literary, historical, religious) as it is about theorizing around that contextual work and narrativizing both dimensions (see also Ngwa 2015; Niang 2019). In my reflections, I will examine broadly the notion of context as genre of biblical interpretation broadly and as genre of African biblical hermeneutics in particular. Then, I will deploy those formulations to exegete how context shapes and functions in Ps 1.

Context as a Genre of Interpretation

Genre is, in simplified terms, an acceptable and recognized mode of communication. In biblical studies, genre plays an important role in shaping meaning (Kampen 1995; Boer 2007). Genre-related questions address the final (written) form of a text, or associated form-critical issues, in oral settings. But genre also attends to the social currency of communication: for whom is a particular genre intelligible and why? How do power and authority function in classifications of texts into specific genres? Genre is interested in more than the literary features of a (con)text, the relation between form and content, or the classification of (con)texts (Masenya [Ngwan'a Mphahlele] 2020). This understanding is informed by Carolyn Miller's (1984, 163) article, "Genre as Social Action," in which she argues that genre is how societies develop conventions for acting together; and that this understanding of genre "does not lend itself to taxonomy, for genres change, evolve, and decay; the number of genre current in any society is indeterminate and depends upon the complexity and diversity of the society." Miller provides five features of this understanding of genre: (1) genre as a conventional category of discourse and action that acquires meaning from a situation and the social context in which the situation arose; (2) genre as meaningful action that is interpreted by rules situated at high levels of symbolic meaning; (3) genre as distinct from form and constituted by a fusion of lower-level forms of action within a hierarchy; (4) genre as recurrent patterns of discourse and enablers in the constitution of the substance of cultural life; and (5) genre as a rhetorical means of mediating private intention and social exigence, "connecting the private with the public, the singular with the recurrent" (163). Thomas O. Beebee (1994, 3) has examined these dimensions of genre under four categories, namely, "genre as rules, genre as species, genre as patterns of textual features, and genre as reader conventions."

The goal here is to view context as a genre—as rhetorical and social work or action. If genres change, evolve, and decay, what about contexts? This work includes the social location—temporal and geographical—of the interpreter. African biblical interpreters find themselves at this interface between geographical and social locations and how the mobilization of both locations often impacts the marginalized placement of African biblical hermeneutics in a global space. To argue that context is a genre of interpretation is to forge methodologies that recognize African voices that work to generate interpretive movements (flows of meaning) and that are not subject to the supervision or approval of Western approaches.

To argue that context matters is to move beyond understanding context as a mode of historical (diachronic) or contemporaneous (synchronic) distribution of meaning; it is to move beyond the noun (context) to the adjective (contextual) and understand that move as a trope of interpretation. As Funlọla Ọlọjẹde(2016) has shown in her analysis of the profession, death, and burial of Deborah, contextual analyses can uncover literary discrepancies and show such discrepancies to be based on assumptions and perceptions of social status. I draw here on George J. Brooke's (2010, 388–79) work on the dialectical and unstable nature of genre analyses with regards to the Bible and ancient rabbinic interpretation. Brooke argues that genre makes

> the text present to a particular community, large or small.... The relevance of the text is to be found in the re-presentation. The authenticity of the representation is to be discerned particularly in the contemporary reader's appropriation of the authoritative text through the re-presentation. Since each generation will require the re-presentation to be made afresh for its own particular circumstances, so the genre, like most others, is inherently unstable.

The sort of representation that Brooke describes can, and should, be understood not only as genre work but also as contextual work; the representation itself (not just the meaning derived from such representation) is, and does the work of, context. It simultaneously reflects, creates, and assesses context, not just meaning. Thus, context is as rhetorically, sociologically, and historically charged and unstable (though not necessarily chaotic) as are concepts like the form, structure, or themes of texts. Context matters because, as a genre, it reflects, recreates, and sometimes enhances community and identity in ways that may or may not be equally or easily accessible to all; nevertheless, it functions as an intelligible category of social mobilization, understanding, and assessment around the changes, the evolution, and even the decay of meaning and of communities.

Context, Method, and Genre

Holter's (2000) *Yahweh in Africa* constitutes one of his most prominent explorations of the importance of context for biblical interpretation. The publication of that work in the Peter Lang's series, Bible and Theology in Africa, does some of the framing work that resists seeing context as primarily or solely about inculturation of meaning or the variety of meaning potential.

Holter explores context in two broad categories—methodological and generic. The methodology falls in two parts. First, Holter (2000, 2) frames context as a product of (and response to) demographic shifts that augur significant implications for biblical interpretation and theological institutions: "over time this changing global distribution will obviously influence the foci of Old Testament scholarship." Context is unavoidable and necessary because it shapes individual and structural (institutional) processes of biblical analyses. Second, Holter makes an ethical appeal to Western scholars to give African biblical hermeneutics a hearing: "all the politically correct talk of scholarly internationalisation becomes only empty rhetoric if Africa, or for that matter the rest of the two thirds world, is not included" (2). In these methodological formulations—demographic and ethical— Holter's work contributes to the *how* and *why* of contextual hermeneutics.

Yet Holter's work includes seeing context as a genre itself. The series Bible and Theology in Africa speaks to the work of theorizing context as a genre. As editor, Holter provides the rationale for the series, which "aims at making African theology and biblical interpretation its subject as well as object, as the concerns of African theologians and biblical interpreters will be voiced and critically analyzed."[1] Theologians and biblical interpreters in/on Africa have published works that squarely sit within the spirit of Bible and Theology in Africa (Mbiti 1986; Getui, Holter and Zinkuratire 2001). Other African series contribute to theorizing that lifts context beyond the inculturation or distribution of meaning

---

1. https://www.peterlang.com/view/serial/BTA.

to context as a genre of biblical interpretation (Mbuvi 2017, 157–59). In this mode of *context as a publication series*, context is already and perennially dialectical engagement, not simply location and/or temporality. As a genre, context engages with historical or contemporaneous concerns of writers and interpreters as more than anecdotal or incidental realities animating the writer or informing interpretation. Context is not simply a location, whether literary or sociological; it is a method. To quote Holter's self-reflective words about contextual analyses, "One consequence of this, which eventually will be recognisable also in academic circles, is that even with the power of defining scholarly interpretive contexts and research, political priorities will be *drifting southwards*" (2000, 5, emphasis added).

Here is a concept of context as genre that I find intriguing—context as a drift, informed by what Holter saw as shifts in demographic data and, more importantly, how he reads that shift as programmatic rather than incidental and cursory. Given the lessons of history, demographic numbers will always shift, but the underlying concept of context as drift, as movement, and the associated concept of context as interpretive affiliation with, and reassessment of, movement is solid. That is what makes Holter's (2000, 5) formulation of context accountable rather than simply his own journey as an interpreter, the lessons he learned from that journey in pursuit of contextual analyses other than his, and the interpretative reflective work that such a journey created for his own given context:

> This has been a gradual process, and, as a result, the reader of this essay collection may find examples of inconsistency between the essays; I said things three or four years ago which I now would not say, as I realise that it too much reflects my western context.

The hermeneutical self-editing ("I now would not say") signals another way context may function as a genre of ethical analyses, consistent with ideological criticism's allergic reaction to presumed or assumed sense of singular meaning. Context matters because it deconstructs absolutism, not just for the sake of recognizing plurality but also for the sake of entrenching an ethic of communal interpretation. As genre, context matters because it produces a different kind of interpreter, an interpreter on the move, and a different kind of interpretation—one that turns such movement into more than exotic expedition and curiosity. That is how context emerges as genre.

In 2006, scholars from Europe and Africa met at a conference in Stellenbosch, South Africa. The editors framed the conference (and the publication that proceeded from it) as a discussion of what Europe has to say to Africa, and Africa to Europe, about the Bible (West and de Wit 2008, ix). Holter's formulations in the volume are a response to Maarman Samuel Tshehla's (2008, 347–67) paper on conversion in Sesotho, addressing the cultural and linguistic nuances in the concept of conversion as a theological and cultural concept. The critical methodological points that Tshehla raised were the issue of context, the primary audience of African biblical interpretation, and the challenges of the transferability of one contextual approach to another:

> Western biblical studies' concentration in academic halls is not facilely *transferable* onto the African landscape. Those who study meanings of the bible in Africa cannot but be meaningful participants in the organic life-contexts in which those readings arise as consequential responses. To posit the Euro-American scholar as the primary interlocutor of the African scholar is thus to miss the point of the latter's principle vocation. (349, emphasis added)

The question of the transferability of method between contexts is not theorized as impossible but as challenging. That challenge is connected not just to the question of a primary or a secondary audience in the abstract, but in relation to what Tshehla describes as the "academic halls" of Euro-American scholars and the "landscape" of Africa's "organic life-contexts." There is clearly a discrepancy at work here—between the institutions that trained and sent missionaries to Africa and the absence of equivalent institutions in Africa in the late nineteenth century. But the issue is more than a deficit in equivalent, matching, institutional infrastructure on the continent in the 1880s, as if establishing such equivalence would render contextual analyses irrelevant. The issue is that Tshehla's organic life-context formulation resists notions of transferability of meaning because the African context and interpreter are not a passive receptacle of meaning distilled in the halls of academia—foreign or local. Context is more than location and more than comparative analyses. Context is process. *It is theory about the mobility of meaning and reflection on that mobility.*

In his response to Tshehla's essay, Holter (2008) frames his reflections around fascination and challenge. In terms of fascination in a "typical missionary context," which I read as the context of transferability, "Motaung represents the receiver side and its reflection about the role of Christianity in a traditional context" (368–69). And as for challenge, the issue is whether Motaung's conversion represents his ability to voice the teachings of the missionaries or his ability to "catch a central concept of the missionary theology ('conversion') and thus convert (!) it into a concept expressing a more contextually sensitive Christian identity (*tsokoloho*)" (369). It is here, I believe, that Holter's contextual work signals a move from location to theory—context as theory of biblical interpretation. This movement draws context out of the shadows of a distant past and its institutional apparatus and discrepancies into the challenging space-time of ongoing dialogue. Holter locates the engagement with Tshehla's work in biblical scholarship as well as in institutional history. His home institution, the School of Mission and Theology in Stavanger, Norway, sent missionaries to what was then the mid-nineteenth century Zululand. That inter-contextual framing led to a question around the theory of context—how one expresses a shared faith in one's own language (Holter 369–70).

One, therefore, ought to speak of contexts, not context. It is the multiplicity of contexts, its genre as a dynamic, which compels interpretive attention. In his essay on Jonah, Gerald O. West (2014) speaks to this multiplicity. He invited a student with whom he was working on Jonah to "bring his African *contexts* into dialogue with the text throughout the exegetical process, making overt what is often covert in the gaze of the biblical scholar" (723, emphasis added; see also Mtshiselwa 2015). In pursuing his work, West would draw on a developed (developing) theory about the tri-polar nature of African biblical hermeneutics. This tri-polar heuristic includes the African context, the text, and the ideo-theological engagement that brings context and text together. This happens through distantiation that allows the text to become Other (thus, giving context a quality of thick texture) and the interpretive move from distantiation to critical appropriation (West 2014, 724). The dialogic engagement is more than incidental; it becomes an interpretive trope.

In *The Stolen Bible*, West (2016) provides historical and theological narrative to argue that, before African biblical hermeneutics developed its established credentials in the 1970s, African ordinary readers had already begun doing this kind of dialogic work, which included (and resulted in) wresting the Bible from colonial and imperial hands. The reason context matters is that it is not about, or not *just* about, appropriation. It is about an approach. It is a genre, a mode of communication, of hermeneutics. As West (2014, 727) puts it in his earlier essay, "our African contexts are power-laden and require a commitment to liberation praxis and not only postcolonial dialogue." Furthermore, and more poignant to the goal of this essay, "our African contexts are readily apparent," but "it is not always clear what resources the Bible has to offer to our contexts."

Contextual analyses also become a genre of interpretation. David Tuesday Adamo's edited volume, *Biblical Interpretation in African Perspective* (2006) represents a textual form of communal interpretation, a form of cluster storytelling that intentionally represents the interpretive force and character of multiplicity variously framed. So, too, is the edited volume by Jione Havea, Margaret Aymer, and Steed Davidson, *Islands, Islanders and the Bible: RumInations* (2015), which explores the possibility of reading biblical texts as islands; in fact, as archipelagic and thus inviting reflection on hermeneutics as talanoa—story that is both fiercely independent and yet interdependent on other stories. According to these authors, "biblical texts are like islands, and readers are like islanders. At the underside of our invitation is a double affirmation: islands are like biblical texts and islanders are (like) readers" (Havea, Aymer, and Davidson 2015, 1). These similes between readers and texts and spaces are not simply metaphoric; they have interpretive significance. Interpretation itself is experienced and performed as waves—movements that have direction but also depth and that produce the reader even as they are produced by the reader. And Holter's (2006, 11) edited volume, *Let My People Stay! Researching the Old Testament in Africa*, seeks to develop "a process whose aim is to root African Old Testament studies institutionally in African soil." The hermeneutical metaphor of planting ("rooting") in the soil evokes the simile between the biblical interpreter and a tree planted by waters in Ps 1.

Psalm 1—Translation and Reflections

¹Happy is the one who does not walk in the counsel of the wicked
And does not stand in the way of sinners
And does not dwell in the city² of scoffers
²But in the law/teaching of Yahweh, the one delights
And on God's law/teaching, the one meditates/muses/mutters day and night
³Therefore, the one becomes like a tree planted by channels of water, which

---

2. The Hebrew word מושב may mean territorial residence or even city (see Gen 10:30; 27:39; 36: 43; Exod 10:23; Num 24:21).

Bears fruit at its time
And its leaves do not wither/fall
And all that it/one does prospers
⁴Not so, the wicked one
They are like chaff that the wind blows asunder
⁵Therefore, the wicked shall not rise in judgment
Nor sinners in the congregation of the righteous
⁶For Yahweh knows the way of the righteous
But the way of the wicked shall perish[3]

By virtue of its language, content, and rhetoric, Ps 1 is considered largely a wisdom psalm. Multiple literary and thematic features account for this classification—the opening exclamation, אשרי ("happy," "blessed"); repeated use of "way" (1:1, 6) as a metaphor of human activity and a genre of dissimilarity between the methods of the righteous and the wicked; focus on meditating (הגה, "muttering," "musing on"); and rejoicing in the resulting torah (teaching, law) that unfolds. These literary and thematic features and methods point to the wisdom character of the psalm (Craige 1983, 58). The psalm further shapes its context in community, as it speaks of "counsel" and "scoffers" and of "justice/judgment" and "knowledge"— issues that assume social structure and processes of implementation. All of these terms and concepts, clustered together in narrative and poetic form, resonate with the social and epistemological rhetoric of the book of Proverbs and its busy, perhaps nomadic, communal life (walking, standing, sitting). The literary context shapes social context and does social work. In its epistemological and spatial locations, personified Wisdom speaks, singling out scoffers for particular rebuke (Prov 1:22) but also building a residential house for teaching (Prov 9:7–8).

Psalm 1 deploys this genre to do interpretive work that understands method and context as perennial rather than incidental to happy outcomes. Arthur Walker-Jones (2009, 24) points out that the use of "way/road/path" in verses 1 and 6 indicates that "the metaphor of path brackets the psalm." In this intersection between literary, narrative, environmental, and spatial construction, דרך is not just an epistemological trope. It may also be read as a physical path or road (Prov 7:8; 8:2), even a highway

---

3. My translation. The forward slashes (/) are intended to signify the dynamic movement of meaning that is present in translation. At every turn, multiplicity infuses the work of meaning-making from translation to interpretation.

(Deut 2:27). That is, דרך is the production of pathways/roads that make up the contexts of the psalm. Conversely, navigating the psalm's literary, epistemological, and material pathways/roads intersects with navigating its ecological materiality and its textual interpretive traditions. Second, the metaphor of a tree planted by channels of water is crucial to interpreting the psalm. In ancient near East and biblical mythology, trees were associated with divinity (e.g., the tree of good and evil and the tree of life in Gen 3) and with Wisdom (e.g., Prov 3:18). As Walker-Jones (2009, 28) writes, "Since trees are associated with goddesses and the temple, the identification of the just person with the tree identifies the just person with divinity and the sacred."

The psalm, then, may function as a metaphor for biblical hermeneutics and its theorizing around context as genre. That process is held together on the "outside" (1:1, 6) by social activity (standing, walking, sitting) around its major methodological pathways and held together on the "inside" (1:3) by human ecological activity (tree planting around water channels) amid wind blowing chaffs. In its poetic, material, and epistemological core and range, the psalm makes an argument that is as textual as it is ecological. An understanding of context as genre creates a method by which the righteous person or community, faced with the challenges of political and environmental exile, ought to become (and indeed is becoming) like an evergreen tree planted beside channels of water (1:3). John Kartje (2014, 78–81) calls this the "People are Plants" metaphor, a familiar metaphor in the Psalms (cf. Pss 37:2; 90:6; 82:8; 102:12; 129:6).

In a diasporic setting, an itinerant group reconstituting its genealogical and political identity in the wilderness gathers around food and drink and laughter, while making claims about knowledge (Exod 18:11–12, 16, 20) or the lack thereof (Exod 16:12, 15; 32:1–6). When such ecological diaspora is associated with imperial powers of conquest, trees can be abused and turned into idols (Isa 44), even as a postcolonial imaginary and engagement with trees also represent the hope of communal restoration (Isa 65:22). God's promise is that the community that survives ecological and political erasure under empire can talk back in ways that are analogous to the form and character of trees.

In this regard, Masenya (Ngwan'a Mphahlele)'s (2010) analysis of Job 3 shows that, in the midst of his intense suffering, Job not only challenges traditional wisdom notions of safety and rewards, but also turns to creation itself, subjecting it to demands for human comfort or wishing it into oblivion (Job 3:13–19). For her part, Dorothy Akoto-Abutiate BEA

(2014, 1–5) has developed a hermeneutic of grafting as a way of forging contextual biblical hermeneutics among the Ewe of Ghana. Masenya (2010, 54–55) notes that God's ultimate response to Job's thoroughly anthropocentric laments is centered in nature and the environment itself (Job 38–39), prompting Job to reexamine his "ecologically insensitive view of life." Masenya (Ngwan'a Mphahlele) argues for an eco-bosadi reading that is sensitive not only to "the androcentric elements in the text but also the class, race, and earth-demeaning elements" (56). Eco-bosadi hermeneutics challenges patriarchy's oppression of women and the earth, subjecting both to critical examination in the search for liberating futures (56–57).

The analogy between biblical interpretation as grafting and ecological hermeneutics connecting the interpreter to the subjectivity of the environment helps illumine an understanding of Ps 1 as a genre of contextual hermeneutics. The root meaning of the opening word, אשרי, includes "to go forward," "to walk on," as if conjuring trailblazing endeavor (Terrien 2003, 71). Given the generally topsy-turvy world of the poem, this opening exclamation signals defiance to the social and environmental disaster identified and named in the poem (Ps 1:1, 4, 5, 6b). If the first word of the poem is "happy," the last word is "perish," both words then set the poetic framework of the psalm as one of social and ecological struggle, portending erasure. Here, context is not imagined and portrayed as a fixed reality and not as a perennially positive reality. Instead, context is explored as dynamic and ethically compelling. It requires that one understands the importance of context, not just as a method ("way" Ps 1:1, 6), but also as a generic metaphor (1:3).

Conclusion

Biblical studies has long deployed genre as a category of meaning-making. In biblical hermeneutics specifically, genre studies has helped to develop a method (or methods) of interpretation. Similarly, contextual hermeneutics has developed methods as well as a theory and history of such methods. In this essay, I have argued that contextual hermeneutics ought to be understood as a genre, much like gender, ecology, race, and exile. Psalm 1 functions to signal how methodology and genre come together in contextual form and subjectivity. Holter's work has contributed to this effort in African biblical hermeneutics and, for that, I join in the communal delight and happiness (אשרי?) of Ps 1.

Works Cited

Adamo, David Tuesday. 2006. *Biblical Interpretation in African Perspective*. Lanham, MD: University Press of America.

Akoto-Abutiate, Dorothy BEA. 2014. *Proverbs and the African Tree of Life: Grafting Biblical Proverbs on to Ewe Folk Proverbs*. Leiden: Brill.

Allen, David, and Steve Smith, eds. 2020. *Methodology in the Use of the Old Testament in the New: Context and Criteria*. New York: T&T Clark.

Beebee, Thomas O. 1994. *The Ideology of Genre: A Comparative Study of Generic Instability*. University Park, PA: Pennsylvania State University Press.

Boer, Roland, ed. 2007. *Bakhtin and Genre Theory in Biblical Studies*. SemeiaSt 63. Atlanta: Society of Biblical Literature.

Brooke, George J. 2010. "Genre Theory, Rewritten Bible and Pesher." *DSD* 17:378–79.

Craige, Peter C. 1983. *Psalms 1–50*. WBC 19. Waco, TX: Word.

Dube, Zorodzai, Loreen Maseno-Ouma, and Elia Shabani Mligo, eds. 2018. *The Bible and Sociological Contours: Some African Perspectives; Festschrift for Professor Halvor Moxnes*. New York: Lang.

Getui, Mary, Knut Holter, and Victor Zinkuratire, eds. 2001. *Interpreting the Old Testament in Africa: Papers from the International Symposium on Africa and the Old Testament in Nairobi, October 1999*. New York: Lang.

Havea, Jione, Margaret Aymer, and Steed Davidson, eds. 2015. *Islands, Islanders and the Bible: RumInations*. SemeiaSt 77. Atlanta: SBL Press.

Holter, Knut. 2000. *Yahweh in Africa: Essays on Africa and the Old Testament*. New York: Lang.

———. 2006. *Let My People Stay! Researching the Old Testament in Africa; Report from a Research Project on Africanization of Old Testament Studies*. Nairobi: Acton.

———. 2008. "Fascination and Challenge." Pages 368–70 in *African and European Readers of the Bible: In Quest for a Shared Meaning*. Edited by Gerald O. West and Hans de Wit. Leiden: Brill.

Kampen, John. 1995. "The Genre and Function of Apocalyptic Literature in the African American Experience." Pages 43–65 in *Text and Experience: Towards a Cultural Exegesis of the Bible*. Edited by Daniel Smith-Christopher. Sheffield: Sheffield Academic.

Kartje, John. 2014. *Wisdom Epistemology in the Psalter: A Study of Psalms 1, 73, 90, and 107*. BZAW 472. Berlin: De Gruyter.

Kibobo, Kabamba J. 2017. *Divining the Woman of Endor: African Culture, Postcolonial Hermeneutics and the Politics of Biblical Translation*. New York: Bloomsbury T&T Clark.

Masenya (Ngwan'a Mphahlele), Madipoane. 1997. "Proverbs 31:10–31 in a South African Context: A Reading for the Liberation of African (Northern Sotho) Women." *Semeia* 78:55–68.

———. 2010. "All from the Same Source? Deconstructing a (Male) Anthropocentric Reading of Job (3) through an Eco-*bosadi* Lens." *JTSA* 137:46–60.

———. 2020. "Whose Reading Matters? Rereading Exodus 1 in the Context of African (South African) Women." *Dialog* 59.2:107–14.

Matheny, Paul Duane. 2012. *Contextual Theology: The Drama of Our Times*. Cambridge: James Clarke.

Mbiti, John. 1986. *Bible and Theology in African Christianity*. Oxford: Oxford University Press.

Mbuvi, Andrew M. 2017. "African Biblical Studies: An Introduction to an Emerging Discipline." *CurBR* 15.2:149–78.

Miller, Carolyn R. 1984. "Genre as Social Action." *Quarterly Journal of Speech* 70:151–67.

Mitri, Raheb, ed. 2012. *The Biblical Text in the Context of Occupation: Towards a New Hermeneutics of Liberation*. Bethlehem: Diyar.

Mtshiselwa, Ndikho. 2015. "Context and Context Meet! A Dialogue between the *Sitz-im-leben* of Psalm 23 and the South African Setting." *OTE* 28:704–23.

Mugambi, Jesse N. K., and Michael R. Guy. 2009. *Contextual Theology across Cultures*. Nairobi: Acton.

Ngwa, Kenneth. 2015. "The Making of Gershom's Story: A Cameroonian Postwar Hermeneutics Reading of Exodus 2." *JBL* 134:899–920.

Niang, Aliou Cissé. 2019. *A Poetics of Postcolonial Biblical Criticism: God, Human-Nature Relationship, and Negritude*. Eugene, OR: Cascade.

Ọlọjẹde, Funlọla O. 2016. "The 'First Deborah': Genesis 35:8 in the Literary and Theological Context." *AcT* 36:133–51.

Smith, Mitzi J. 2018. *Womanist Sass and Talk Back: Social (in)justice, Intersectionality, and Biblical Interpretation*. Eugene, OR: Cascade.

Terrien, Samuel. 2003. *The Psalms: Strophic Structure and Theological Commentary*. Grand Rapids: Eerdmans.

Tshehla, Maarman Samuel. 2008. "Isaac A. Motaung: Conversion and Biblical Appropriation in Sesotho." Pages 347–67 in *African and European*

Readers of the Bible: In Quest for a Shared Meaning. Edited by Gerald West and Hans de Wit. Leiden: Brill.

Walker-Jones, Arthur. 2009. *The Green Psalter: Resources for an Ecological Spirituality*. Minneapolis: Fortress.

West, Gerald O. 2014. "Juxtaposing 'Many Cattle' in Biblical Narrative (Jonah 4:11), Imperial Narrative, Neo-Indigenous Narrative." *OTE* 27:722–51.

———. 2016. *The Stolen Bible: From Tool of Imperialism to African Icon*. Pietermaritzburg: Cluster.

West, Gerald O., and Hans de Wit, eds. 2008. *African and European Readers of the Bible: In Quest for a Shared Meaning*. Leiden: Brill.

Bible Translation, Publication, and Utilization in Africa: A Tribute to Professor Knut Holter

Jesse N. K. Mugambi

Introduction

This reflection is in honor of Professor Knut Holter of NLA University College, Bergen, Norway. It focuses on some of the challenges that researchers face in translating and publishing the Bible (both Old and New Testaments) from the original languages into African languages. In his training of African students and collaborating with Acton Publishers, Nairobi, Holter has contributed immensely to this field. For two decades (2000–2020), the collaboration has yielded successful research projects culminating in the publication of five books that focus mainly on Old Testament scholarship (Getui, Holter, and Zinkuratire 2001; Holter 2006, 2007, 2008, 2020). In that period, Holter and his colleagues trained African scholars at postgraduate level, equipping them with requisite academic, research, and authorship skills, applicable in various assignments within their respective careers. Holter's approach to training is based, commendably, on the principle of apprenticeship and partnership.

In that regard, the most memorable, most innovative, and most challenging undertaking was to conduct an online training course designed for African doctoral candidates in various African countries, from Stavanger, Norway (3–5 May 2021). With the assistance of Associate Professor Dr. Beth Elness-Hanson, this initiative included participants from across Africa when the COVID-19 pandemic was at its peak. With the encouragement and mentorship of Holter, more than twenty African-specialist researchers in this field benefited from his wisdom and from the resources he mobilized.

While honoring Holter, it is appropriate to appreciate the contribution of Kenyan professor John S. Mbiti, who died on 5 October 2019 after an extensive vocation of research and teaching on the themes of African Religions and Philosophy, Christian Theology, and Bible translation. Mbiti's (2014) final and most significant accomplishment is his translation of the New Testament into the language of his birth, KiiKamba: *Utiyaniyo wa Mwiyai Yesu Kilisto*. With this achievement, Mbiti established a precedent as the first and only African scholar to translate the entire New Testament from the original Koine Greek and to publish it in Africa through an African publisher. The only other African who approximated such a feat was Samuel Ajayi Crowther, who during the 1840s translated the Bible from the King James English Version of 1611 (London) into his indigenous Nigerian language of Yoruba (Walls n.d.). Obviously, translations from translations differ markedly from those translated from the original biblical languages of Hebrew and Greek.

Knut Holter, the Mentor

Holter, while serving for decades as a professor of Old Testament at the VID Specialized University in Stavanger, Norway, engaged in research, published, and trained many African Christian theologians on the relevance of the Old Testament for African Christianity (Holter 2018). His approach encourages African postgraduate students to interview African Christians in their respective countries, in their own languages, and focus on the impact of specific Old Testament passages and concepts on the religious heritage of specific African communities. The chosen model of collaboration has proven mutually instructive and encouraging. After committing significant periods of time in Stavanger to the acquisition of technical and academic skills, the students returned to east Africa to exercise those skills in applied exegesis and hermeneutics. Since 1999, the collaboration with Holter has been both joyful and mutually instructive. The first book resulting from this collaboration was a collection of papers contributed mainly by African scholars, titled, *Interpreting the Old Testament in Africa* (2001). This volume preceded another, *Interpreting the New Testament in Africa*, with papers by African participants at the Pretoria-Hammanskraal Conference of the Society for New Testament Studies (Robbins 2001).

In response to Holter's invitation, I visited Norway several times, which provided opportunities to interact with both his colleagues and graduate students in Old Testament studies, many of them from Africa. Through my exposure to various expressions of European Christianity, I have learned to appreciate the counterbalancing of biblical hermeneutics with biblical exegesis within particular cultural contexts. The canonical books in both the Old Testament and the New Testament provide insights into the multi-dimensions of the Christian faith, to the extent that some aspects appear contradictory until the respective backgrounds are properly interrogated.

The cultural history of Christianity in Norway, as in other European nations, predates the era of the Holy Roman Empire. Consequently, the liturgical calendar of European Christianity based on the pre-Christian Scandinavian cultural cycle resonated with its four climatic seasons of winter, spring, summer, and autumn. In her several books, Hilda R. Ellis Davidson (1964, 1993) provided an elaborate description of the appropriation and incorporation of pre-Christian Scandinavian beliefs and practices in European Christianity. Hence, the nativity of Jesus coincides with midwinter, crucifixion and resurrection coincide with the beginning of spring, and harvest coincides with summer and autumn. The celebrations of Christmas and Easter, for example, are derived from Nordic mythology and identify "Father Christmas" as the benefactor who comes with gifts in midwinter.

The European liturgical calendar has been transplanted into African Christianity via the various European missionary agencies that introduced their respective denominations in various parts of tropical Africa. The exceptions to this pattern are found in the Coptic Orthodox Church (Egypt), the Orthodox Tewahedo Church (Ethiopia), and the Greek Orthodox Church, all of which predate the modern North Atlantic missionary enterprise in tropical Africa. These European cultural appropriations of the Christian faith raise questions about their cultural relevance and suitability for African churches.

Much remains to be done in rendering African Christianity "joyfully African and truly Christian" (Gatu 2006, 2017). In view of the comparatively short period since Christianity was first introduced, accepted, and internalized in tropical Africa, it would seem imperative that relevant cultural appropriations become normative in African Christianity. Many missionary-established churches in Africa refer to and conform to mother churches in Europe and North America. Their liturgies, vestments, rituals, and symbols remain foreign. The languages used in the training of African Christian theologians also remain foreign—mainly English, French, Portuguese, and, residually, Dutch and German.

Except for the significant pioneer achievement of Mbiti in his translation of the New Testament into KiiKamba, it seems that the African

Reformation is yet to arrive. The cultural contextualization of the Christian liturgical calendar among various European peoples seems to invite African Christians similarly to contextualize the biblical message in their respective cultural contexts. In his book, *Pentecost without Asuza*, Professor Solomon Waigwa (2006) alludes to this possibility.

One of the motivating factors in the formation of African Instituted Churches has been cultural alienation that the missionary enterprise ignited and facilitated (Waigwa 2006). In his book, *Preaching and the Bible in African Churches*, Hilary Mijoga (2001) documents the frequent deployment of biblical references among African Instituted Churches in Malawi. His findings include an observation that references to the Old Testament are more prevalent than references to the New Testament, indicating that African Christians relate more to Old Testament than to New Testament narratives. This finding is corroborated in other African countries (Mojola 2014).

Among African church leaders who strived strenuously for culturally relevant appropriation of the Christian gospel was the Rev. Dr. John G. Gatu. Under his leadership, the Presbyterian church in Kenya chose as its motto "Jitegemea" ("self-reliance"), this in reaction to the dependency syndrome that missionary patronage had for decades inculcated into African converts, paralyzing the capacity for innovation and creativity. Self-reliance did not mean self-isolation. Rather, it demanded genuine partnership in which everyone and every presbytery would take stock of its resources, appropriating external assistance only on the basis of its own established values (Gatu 2006, 2017).

Holter has trained African Old Testament scholars to discern relevant biblical insights in consonance with the cultural contexts of African Christianity. Throughout the twentieth century, it became normative in the training of African clergy and laity to replace African culture with European and North American norms and values, resulting in cultural alienation rather than cultural reaffirmation. Aylward Shorter (1988) was one of the British Catholic missionary advocates of an appropriation project in East Africa that he named "inculturation." That initiative served as an injection of European Christianity into African culture and religious praxis rather than as a creative translation of the biblical message (Gatu 2006, 2017). Laurenti Magesa (2004, 2014) has likewise elaborated on the necessity of rendering the Christian faith culturally at home in Africa. Hopefully, Holter's trainees would have learned from their exposure to Scandinavia's indigenized Christianity how to apply the gospel appropriately to the tropical African context. Ben Knighton (2004) alludes to the inevitability of such indigenization.

For too long, African churches, with roots in the Western missionary enterprise, have looked up to their parent denominations abroad as the norm setters. Today, while Western Christianity is in numerical decline, Christianity in most of tropical Africa is still young and vibrant, engaging with an electronic media that is completely transforming religious expression with the risk that human memory is rendered increasingly redundant, replaced with mobile phones and minicomputers. The high rate of information digitization is at the risk of rendering African Christianity a mirage, visible only when the digital rainbow appears on the screen of a computer or mobile phone.

African converts to various denominations from Europe and North America adapted hymns from European and American hymnals into the respective African languages. They were neither translations nor transliterations; they reflected approximations of the essential doctrines. The use of hymn books is becoming obsolete, especially where places of worship are served with grid electricity. Mobile phones, laptops, and LCD projectors have replaced hymnals, and electronic musical instruments have taken the place of traditional musical instruments (Davidson 1964, 1993).

The sixteenth-century European Reformation accelerated the quest for contextualization and localization of Christianity throughout Europe, to the extent that the Bible was translated into various European languages as one of the outcomes of the Reformation. The Treaty of Westphalia (1648) supported this trend, with the consequence that every language community became a sovereign nation with its own political and linguistic order. The official Christian denominations of the respective imperial powers were imposed on tropical Africa by means of colonialization and related missionary initiatives. This matrix was extended to Africa's post-imperial period and remains largely intact. Thus, in the nations of tropical Africa, the churches with majority adherents are those established during the colonial period. The African Instituted Churches also have significant membership in African nations such as the Democratic Republic of the Congo, Kenya, Nigeria, and South Africa.

Translation of the Bible into African languages has continued as undertakings by foreign Bible societies. In consequence, movement toward locally initiated and locally funded Bible translations has yet to be realized. These constraints translate into the impression and perception of Christianity as a foreign religion. The same impression applies to Islam in Africa.

Cultural Dynamics of Christian Missionary Outreach in Africa

The gospel as "good news" must reach the target population in ways and by means that strengthen rather than disparage and condemn the recipient culture. No culture is perfect; hence, the need is to evangelize in ways that potential converts can experience fulfillment in the gospel rather than denigration. The rise of tens of thousands of African Instituted Churches serves as an indictment of European and North American missionary outreach in Africa. In African churches, the Bible is revered as the inspired word of God, especially when translated into the respective recipient languages. Challenges arise when the potential and actual converts find contradictions between the Word of God in the Bible and the conduct of those who proclaim and claim to abide by it. Secularism, Islam, and other religions have become ideologies that compete with the gospel, especially in urban areas through the digital media. Brands, denominations, or sects of Christianity introduced and patronized by mission agencies from Europe and North America feature designations such as Anglican (English), Catholic (Roman), Lutheran (German and North American), Methodist (English and North American), Orthodox (Greek), Presbyterian (Scottish), and so on. Neo-Pentecostal and charismatic churches suffer similar caricatures, with the consequence that most African churches can be understood as extensions of European and North American denominations with no indigenous identities.

Such convoluted identities have stimulated African believers to form their own sects, often at the risk of personalizing the gospel. In his book *Pentecost without Asuza*, Waigwa (2006) describes the rise of the Akorino Church in Central Kenya during the early 1920s as a reaction against Western missionary initiatives that collaborated with colonial authorities. Denominational and sectarian proliferation and competition pervade African Christianity. These dynamics have been further complicated by competition between Europeans and Americans who give the impression that unity, cooperation, and consensus cannot be achieved across culture, race, and ideology. Since the Peace of Westphalia (1648), Europe maintains denominations with respective national identities, while African Christianity is plagued with denominational and sectarian competition, conflict, and proliferation, largely patronized from abroad.

The ecumenical movement has endeavored to build consensus among a significant segment of Protestant Christians, but critics offer alternatives to ecumenical cooperation with labels such as charismatic, evangelical,

Pentecostal, et cetera. Missionaries from Europe and North America are still coming to Africa to start new churches, ironically, in a continent that in terms of percentage is more Christian than Europe and North America. In recent decades, African preachers have established Christian ministries in Europe and North America, focusing more on biblical instruction than on cultural indoctrination, whereas the Western missionary enterprise in Africa has focused more on cultural indoctrination than on biblical insights (Morier-Genoud 2018). Such cultural emphases were inevitable, given that the Christianization of Africa could not be separated from imperial expansion.

Within Africa, the challenge remains: How can the gospel be rooted in the cultural soil of Africa without the attendant aberrations of Western Christianity? Cross-cultural evangelization remains problematic, especially when it becomes intertwined with ideological propaganda. What would be the ideal cross-cultural approach to spreading the good news that Jesus proclaimed? Perhaps Saint Paul provides a partial clue: "becoming all things to all people, in order by any means to save some" (1 Cor 9:22).

If African traditionalism is destined for conversion to the various brands of Western Christianity, should Africans in return reevangelize the secularists in Europe and North America? And if Western approaches to evangelization are valid, should contextualized African Christianity be exported to Europe and North America through a reverse flow of missionary outreach? If the answers to these questions are negative, what is the justification for the flow of Western missionaries to Africa at the risk of further fragmenting African Christianity? The principle of freedom of worship has become a faith buffet whereby Africans choose whichever Christian denomination or sect seems more appealing to them. Thus, denominations and sects compete for membership, while ecumenical cooperation seems to be in decline.

Since the principle of freedom of worship is considered a democratic norm, would it be appropriate for African denominations to reexport Christianity back to Europe and North America where Christianity is in decline? If the answer to such questions were positive, what would be the ideological implications for African Christian missionary outreach to the West?

All these variants of religiosity in tropical Africa are propagated within the rubric of basic freedoms. Such freedoms are best deployed within the framework of informed consent, which is practically nonexistent and impracticable in Africa where literacy rates are low, per capita income is low, and internet connectivity is poor. All these strands are woven together and thrust on Africans as options.

African youth are exposed to competing theologies and ideologies via the internet and other information media, with few or no resources to critique and make intelligent choices. Television and the internet are flooded with options but offer no ways or means by which to discern truth from falsehood, right from wrong, usefulness from uselessness. As schooling goes online, parental guidance becomes increasingly remote, while the market reigns supreme. Under these circumstances, the youth will be attracted toward the most colorful and most noisy advertisements rather than toward the most useful and the most valuable options. The increasing visibility of advertisements produces a commensurate decline in reason and careful reflection.

In the midst of these complex and also diverse dynamics, Holter has facilitated field research with his East African graduate students at the VID Specialized University, Norway to explore how ordinary people in Kenya and Tanzania are responding to the tensions between traditionalism and modernity, against the backdrop of biblical teachings (DeHaan 2018). Such mentorship is unique and worth emulating (Holter 2006, 2007, 2008). If the pre-Christian European worldview is the bedrock of European Christianity and identity, there is abundant justification for the pre-Christian African worldview to serve as the bedrock for African Christianity. Already the norm seems to be established: Islam in Arabia, Hinduism in India, Buddhism in Japan. Jesus referred to the Hebrew heritage as the foundation upon which to graft the new faith. Martin Luther sparked the European Reformation with the German cultural heritage as the stock on which to graft the Christian faith. If this principle is ignored or overlooked, the resultant Christianity will be superficial and short-lived.

Scandinavian cultural identity has remained largely intact despite the pressures of industrialization, urbanization, and modernization. Technology has served as a tool for the enhancement of Scandinavian cultural and religious values, whereas Christian missions and Western technologies have undermined African cultural and religious identities. Holter's approach brings a ray of hope to Africa, illustrating that it is indeed possible to embrace the Christian faith and at the same time deploy modern technology constructively and progressively. The Bible is the most widely distributed book in Africa, with competing versions and editions and with multiple agencies involved in the distribution of both the Bible and related literature.

Lamentably, only a tiny percentage of such literature has African authorship and an equally tiny portion has been published in Africa. The implication is that Christianity has a long way to go before it can be recognized as *Joyfully Christian, Truly African* (Gatu 2006). Under what circumstances will it become normative for African theological literature to be authored by Africans, published in Africa, and affordably read by Africans? As in the other sectors of the modern economy, Africa remains a continent whose people *consume* what they do not produce and *produce* what they do not consume.

The church, in the broadest meaning of the term, ought to be exemplary. How can the church in Africa serve as salt of the earth if it has no taste? How can it be light of the world if it offers no illumination? How can it bear good fruit if the seedling is from a tasteless variety? Although the African cultural and religious heritage is resilient, the infrastructure for sustaining it remains fragile, having been dismantled during the colonial period and largely overlooked as a nonpriority consideration after the attainment of independent sovereignty. The gospel continues to be proclaimed across tropical Africa, but the countless voices proclaiming it—under the guise of religious freedom—are so many and diverse that potential recipients can hardly discern core truth from falsehood, sincerity from deceit, honesty from exploitation.

The ecumenical movement could have been of assistance, but other initiatives competed for the African soul—evangelical, Pentecostal, charismatic, and so on. Such competition for the African soul exacerbates the tendencies toward secularism and nihilism among the youth. In Africa, many interpretations have been articulated, and many sermons have been preached on the impact of Jesus within and across cultures. Holter insightfully critiques these dynamics in his project entitled *Maasai Encounters with the Bible* (Holter and Justo 2020). More of such research throughout Africa would be insightfully worthwhile. The European Reformation was rooted in localized Bible and ecclesial interpretations through which theologians in various European communities endeavored to interpret the gospel within their local contexts. Christianity in Africa will become fully mature when African theologians take responsibility for interpreting and publishing the gospel among believers in local contexts. Mbiti has already set a precedent, through his translation and publication of the entire New Testament from the original Greek text into Kikamba: *Utianiyo wa Mwiyai Yesu Lilisto* (Nairobi: Kenya Literature Bureau, 2014).

Conclusion

In an article titled "Christianity and Traditional Religions in Africa," published in *The International Review of Mission*, Mbiti (1970, 430–31) cautioned:

> Christianity has Christianized Africa, but Africa has not yet africanized Christianity.... The Church cannot sit back and rest, but evangelization has gained enough momentum to keep it moving with less energy than was necessary at the beginning of this [the twentieth] century. Energy, effort, wisdom and grace should now be concentrated on africanizing Christianity in our continent; for until we do that, we may well have to face the risk of dechristianization if not a near extinction of Christianity in Africa in the next [the twenty-first] century. The Church in Africa has not been sufficiently prophetic to prepare itself for possible situations in the future. There are reasons for this.... We should, as Christian leaders, pastors and educators, smell the spirit of our times, take it seriously, and project our planning, efforts and preparations towards the future as the case might demand.

Through exemplary mentorship, Holter has demonstrated ways and means of modernizing without abandoning core cultural and religious values, being globally conscious while remaining culturally and religiously rooted at home. Scandinavians in general and Norwegians in particular have clearly illustrated how this challenge can be met. They do not live in the most comfortable part of planet earth. But they have made it so homey as to become a role model for tropical Africa. Holter has championed ways and means to achieve reconstructive change toward a more sustainable future. It has been a joy for me to collaborate with him and to interact with some of the African scholars he has mentored. Hopefully African scholars will turn their focus from the West, the North, and the East back to Africa, our home, the home of humankind. The future of African Christianity remains open at this time when collaboration is poised for unprecedented and irreversible technological change.

Works Cited

Davidson, Hilda R. Ellis. 1964. *Gods and Myths of Northern Europe*. New York: Penguin.

———. 1993. *The Lost Beliefs of Northern Europe*. London: Routledge.

DeHaan, Peter. 2018. *Fifty-Two Churches: A Yearlong Journey Encountering God, His Church and Our Common Faith*. Kindle. Spiritually Speaking Publishing.

Gatu, John G. 2006. *Joyfully Christian, Truly African*. Nairobi: Acton.

———. 2017. *Fan into Flame: An Autobiography*. Nairobi: Moran.

Getui, Mary N., Knut Holter, and Victor Zinkuratire, eds. 2001. *Interpreting the Old Testament in Africa*. Biblical Studies in African Scholarship Series. Nairobi: Acton.

Holter, Knut. 2006. *Let My People Stay! Researching the Old Testament in Africa; Report from a Research Project on Africanization of Old Testament Studies*. Nairobi: Acton.

———. 2007. *Interpreting Classical Religious Texts in Contemporary Africa*. Nairobi: Acton.

———. 2008. *Contextualized Old Testament Scholarship in Africa*. Nairobi: Acton.

———. 2018. "Bio." https://tinyurl.com/SBLPress3817a1.

Holter, Knut, and Leburis Justo, eds. 2020. *Maasai Encounters with the Bible*. Nairobi: Acton.

Knighton, Ben. 2004. "Issues in African Theology at the Turn of the Millennium." *Transformation* 21.3:147–61.

Magesa, Laurenti. 2004. *Anatomy of Inculturation: Transforming the Church in Africa*. Maryknoll, NY: Orbis.

———. 2014. *What Is Not Sacred? African Spirituality*. Maryknoll, NY: Orbis; Nairobi: Acton.

Mbiti, John S. 1970. "Christianity and Traditional Religions in Africa." *IRM* 59:430–40.

———. 2014. *Utiyaniyo wa Mwiyai Yesu Kilisto* [John S. Mbiti's Translation of the New Testament from Original Greek Directly into KiiKamba]. Nairobi: Kenya Literature Bureau.

Mijoga, Hilary. 2001. *Preaching and the Bible in African Churches*. Nairobi: Acton.

Mojola, Aloo O. 2014. "Old Testament or Hebrew Bible in Africa: Challenges and Prospects for Interpretation and Translation." *Verbum et Ecclesia* 35.3: art #1307.

Morier-Genoud, Eric. 2018. "'Reverse Mission': A Critical Approach for a Problematic Subject." Pages 169–88 in *Bringing Back the Social into the Sociology of Religion*. Edited by Veronique Altglas and Matthew Wood. Studies in Critical Research on Religion 8. Leiden: Brill.

Robbins, Vernon. 2001. "Why Participate in African Biblical Interpretation?" Pages 275–91 in *Interpreting the New Testament in Africa*. Edited by Mary N. Getui, Knut Holter, and Victor Zinkuratire. Nairobi: Acton.

Shorter, Aylward. 1988. *Toward a Theology of Inculturation*. Maryknoll, NY: Orbis.

Waigwa, Solomon. 2006. "Pentecost without Asuza: An Historical and Theological Analysis of Akorino Church in Kenya." PhD diss., Baylor University, Texas.

Walls, Andrew F. n.d. "Crowther, Samuel Adjayi." *Dictionary of African Christian Biography*. https://tinyurl.com/SBL3817a.

Whose Context Matters?
Reading the Story of Hagar and Bilhah (Gen 16; 30) through Woman-as-Tlhatswadirope Lens

Madipoane Masenya (Ngwan'a Mphahlele)

Our Paths Crossed!

It was at the International Conference on "Reconciliation and Restitution: An Old Testament Perspective," held at Stellenbosch University, that my path first crossed with that of the honoree, Professor Knut Holter. As far as I can recall, both of us, who had never met before, had two things in common at that conference. First, both of us were privileged to be among the plenary speakers at that important Old Testament meeting, held just two years post South Africa's political independence in 1994. The main theme of the conference is a pointer to that important transitional period in South Africa, that is, when the country transitioned from being an apartheid state to a democracy.

Second, both of us delivered papers that brought together two different contexts of scholarship, that is, the African Old Testament and Western Old Testament scholarship, to bear with what we had to say in our papers. The provocative title of the paper that Holter (1998) read then, "It's Not Only a Question of Money! African Old Testament Scholarship between the Myths and Meanings of the South and the Money and Methods of the North!," remained with me from then until today.

Holter's commitment to affirming the presence of African Old Testament scholarship in that paper until today speaks volumes to the kind of generous and open-minded scholar that the honoree is. Little did I know, though, that our very first meeting at the University of Stellenbosch would mark the beginnings of a long-standing partnership between us as scholars and between our institutions. One such partnership, which left a mark on me, especially as the then emerging scholar in the area of the supervision of masters and doctoral students, is what was fondly referred to as the "Sandwich" program.[1] At the end of the program, which was funded by the Norwegian government and for which the University of South Africa provided three academics to offer tuition and guidance to the students, I was privileged to produce, with Holter as copromoter, my first doctoral graduate! It is thus a great honor for me to be able to participate in this important project, which is meant to honor Holter's scholarship.

What Now of the Myths and Meanings of the South?

In the preceding article, one which thankfully introduced me to Holter's scholarship, especially as it pertains to African Old Testament scholarship, one gets the following gist: African Old Testament scholarship, argued Holter to the amazement of many a European peer, is alive. It is present. Its myths and meanings are pointers to its presence. African Old Testament scholarship is present within the social, political, and ecclesiastical context of Africa. The presence of the scholarship often reflects a deliberate will to deal with questions considered relevant to individual believers, church, and society, and it is based on the assumption that there is some correspondence between the African experience and the Old Testament (Holter 1998, 241).

---

1. The program was constituted as follows: The Norwegian government, then in collaboration with the School of Mission and Theology in Norway (now VID Specialized University), provided funding for three African students from Madagascar, Tanzania, and Uganda. The University of South Africa (UNISA) provided the infrastructure in that, once during their doctoral program, the students traveled to South Africa to spend a semester (four months) with their main promoters who were three academics from the Department of Old Testament and Ancient Near Eastern Studies. The copromoter for all the three students was Holter. During one semester in each year, the students would be at the School of Mission and Theology in Norway, attending classes and receiving guidance from Holter. They would still retain contact with their promoters who also got an opportunity on two occasions (two trips) to travel to Norway to be with the students. During other semesters, the students would be at their home institutions. In a period of four years, the three students were able to receive their terminal degrees while the whole team was able to publish fourteen articles in one of the issues of *OTE*, a prestigious journal of the Old Testament Society of Southern Africa. We indeed have reason to celebrate Holter, the teacher and mentor of worth!

Gerald O. West's view seems to resonate with Holter in the preceding regard. What makes African biblical hermeneutics unique, argues West (2009, 40), "are the life interests that African interpreters bring to the text and the prominent role assigned these life interests in African biblical hermeneutics" (see also Mbuvi 2017, 149–78). Holter (1998, 243–44) thus uses the concept of the myths of the South in the context of an assumed religiocultural affinity between the traditional African context and Old Testament Israel, while the concept of meanings speak to those studies which have a sociopolitical focus. He further reveals the economic challenges faced by African Old Testament scholars that hinder them to be present in the northern conferences as well as to keep abreast with developments in the fields ensuing from such discussions. In the latter regard, Ferdinand Deist, with South African Old Testament scholarship in view, would have held a contrary view, a view that advocated for African-conscious Old Testament studies. In my view, Deist (1992, 315–16) rightfully has reasoned:

> However, I must confess that I am sometimes irritated by a certain colonial inferiority complex that still haunts our academic work. This complex is best illustrated by a tendency in our work to accept and follow without due critical assessment every "latest trend" from abroad as gospel for biblical interpretation. We are so busy "keeping up with the Joneses" that we do not consciously ask ourselves whether what we are importing has any relevance whatsoever for our own questions.... Our inferiority complex makes it important for us to be "one up" on our colleagues in the next congress. So we feverishly ride our individually imported hobby horses and memorise the latest jaw-breakers of our theory of biblical interpretation—*only to lose sight of our continent and the contribution we can make from its perspective.* (emphasis added)

I would like to give a nod to the core of Deist's argument above, which may be summarized as follows: Old Testament scholars who are located on the African continent must defeat the temptation to succumb to low self-esteem, one that manifests itself among others, by our tendency to seek validation from the West (read the North), at all costs. The African continent (read: the South) has something to offer; our situated-ness/location on the continent must necessarily produce an Old Testament scholarship that is uniquely African (Deist 1992). The observation that even after three decades since the publication of Deist's article, South African Old Testament scholarship continues to be committed to or rather captured by the money and methods of the North (see Masenya [Ngwan'a Mphahlele] and Ramantswana 2012), rather than the myths and meanings of the South, reveals either how colonized the scholarship remains and/or how committed it is to the North and all its ideologies or the scholarship's commitment to its true identity in terms of its northern ancestry.

Although in the title his article the concept of methods appears to be the prerogative of northern scholars, Holter (1998, 247) admits that African Old Testament scholarship has also focused on methodological questions. One could even add, as it will also be shown here below, that the African holistic outlook on life (cf. also the ancient Israelite one) knows no compartmentalization between the political, religious, and economic spheres of life. The whole is viewed as religious. For example, being an academic who is located in one of the South African universities, I am afforded an opportunity to obtain funding generated by my research outputs from government subsidy. I am thus able to attend international conferences, both on the African continent and in the northern contexts. However, as a "glocal" African Old Testament scholar, there should be a commitment to be informed first and foremost by my local geopolitical Southern context (cf. the myths and meanings of the South) as well as the global context (cf. the money and methods of the North). The global context though, should not be limited to the United States and Europe, as can be implied from the contents of Holter's article. In my case, the (northern) European context is the context of my former colonial masters. Making European Old Testament scholarship to be my main or only northern interlocutor would thus not only contribute to my perpetuation of white supremacy; it would also contribute to a deliberate participation in neocolonialism and its neoliberal ideologies and policies. One should also hasten to mention that the African continent has its various diasporas located also in the geopolitical North. In the preceding case, the northern location of the money and methods of the North may need to be nuanced somehow.

If the situation of my context were to be given as a case in point, all the four main concepts in the title of Holter's article—myths, meanings, money, and methods—would relate well with what one does in scholarship. Thus, like many an African biblical scholar, especially those with an activist stance leaning towards deliberately foregrounding Africa and her people (cf. in particular, African-South African women's experiences), as hermeneutical lenses in my interaction with the biblical text, my preoccupation in the following section may be viewed as entailing all the four concepts, that is, myths, meanings, money and methods. Why? My brief engagement with selected biblical texts below will focus on the traditional or rather the biological role of woman as mother.

To that end, I will deploy the notion of surrogacy informed by the African-South African notion of woman as tlhatswadirope (cleanser/washer of thighs) as a lens to engage selected texts from the book of Genesis. In the Northern Sotho African-South African culture, a woman designated as tlhatswadirope (cleanser of thighs) is one who comes in to salvage a situation, that is, to serve as a surrogate for her sibling who cannot bear children in her marriage. The expression, tlhatswadirope (cleanser of thighs) foregrounds the significance of women's thighs in the processes leading to and of conception (i.e., sexual act, delivery of a baby, as well as the nurturing of a baby who would be breastfed while carried on the mother's laps). In the preceding sense, the thighs are core to what ideal womanhood should be. Womanhood's core business should of necessity entail the ability of a married woman to bear children, especially male babies.

Viewed from the African religiocultural viewpoint, a woman's motherhood role, for example, is sacred, as every newborn child is viewed as an ancestor returned (cf. Mbiti 1969). However, the politics of childbearing and childrearing and the twin sister of the responsibilities (and restriction/confinement) of women as mothers to the traditional private sphere of the home will fall within the category of the political as well. In the preceding case, Holter's concepts of myths and meanings (of the South) will collapse into one category, that is, the religious, the cultural, and the political. The economic aspect (money) can also feature as in the example from the biblical text discussed below. Not every woman can afford to have a surrogate. So, depending on who becomes a surrogate mother, perhaps willingly or unwillingly, and for whom (read: a woman of class), the notion/practice of woman as tlhatswadirope may take effect. The same also applies to the notion of lobola/bride price (money), as it imposes further demands on a married woman's reproductive capacities. In patriarchal biblical and African contexts, the issue of barrenness was/is always linked to the female; hence, the expectation is that Sarai or Rachel would be the one required to provide a surrogate woman to rectify the situation of barrenness, while in the Northern Sotho context, the family that provides tlhatswadirope is necessarily the married woman's natal family.

As for the category of methods, the bosadi (womanhood-redefined) approach (cf. Masenya [Ngwan'a Mphahlele] 1996, 1998, 2004), can be cited as a case in point, not only of African Old Testament scholarship's commitment to methodological issues, but also, to an extent, of our commitment to the decolonization and depatriarchalization of the received theories (meanings?) and methods of the North. Another example that could reveal a collapsing of Holter's categories (money and methods) is noteworthy. My first paper (Masenya [Ngwan'a Mphahlele] 1997, 1998) that engaged the Sarai-Hagar narrative through the lens of woman as tlhatswadirope was read in the North, right at the heart of the empire! It was at the Annual Meeting of the Society of Biblical Literature in San Francisco in 1997. It was curiously in line with Holter's argument in the paper (later published as an article in 1998) and was cited especially by those scholars who set store by their money and methods and choose to arrogantly cling to these. The words of de Wit (2009, 9–10) come to mind here:

> The fascination with history, the idea that texts are stable objects that can be controlled by means of proper instruments and the ultimate meaning which can thus be discovered, historical distance not as a productive and fruitful given but as an obstacle to understanding, the imbalance between reason and spirituality, the history which develop from high to low, from primitive to erudite—all of this will be decisive for Western biblical studies for a long time.

The preceding engagement with the fascinating and informative title of Holter's article can still lead one to ask: which/whose context matters in our theory and praxis of Old Testament scholarship? And in those contexts where the Bible has wielded power historically and continues to do so today, whose/which context matters? For how long will the West continue to pose as the legitimate tlhatswarope to rectify Africa's situation and all that belongs to her (read: her meanings and myths in biblical scholarship)? To that end, we will engage the stories of Hagar and Bilhah in Genesis through the lens of woman as tlhatswadirope.

The Cleanser/Washers of Thighs:
Some Reflections on the Narratives of Hagar and Bilhah

In different African contexts, the possession of many children is still regarded as a sign of approval by the Sacred Other and/or the ancestors. In these contexts, the role of a woman as mother is thus highly celebrated; hence, the Yorùbá proverb, Òrìṣà bí ìyá kò sí. Ìyá là bá má a bọ ("There is no deity like a mother. A mother is worthy of being worshiped") comes close to deifying mothers. The proverb reveals that there is no deity like (a) mother. The Northern Sotho proverb, A ba tswalwe, ba ate, gobane mo-na-le pelo ga a tsebje ("Let them be birthed and increase because the one with a long heart is not known") also celebrates motherhood (see also Oduyoye 1995, 59).

In the following paragraphs, I use the practice of woman-as-tlhatswadirope as a hermeneutical lens to engage the narratives of Hagar and Bilhah in Gen 16 and 30. In the Northern Sotho cultural context, this woman is called tlhatswadirope, that is, the one who cleanses thighs. In African contexts (cf. also the ancient Near Eastern ones), barrenness was viewed as one of those states that disturbed the order, as it was believed to be set out by (the ancestors) and/or the Sacred Other. As the problematic situation needed to be rectified, the affected woman's family had to produce a substitute to act as a surrogate (tlhatswadirope), who in most cases, was the woman's younger sister. What immediately comes to mind are the words of Rachel, a frustrated matriarch in Gen 30:3: "Then she said, 'Here is my maid Bilhah; *go in to her, that she may bear upon my knees* [tlhatswadikhuru or tlhatswadirope?] and that *I too may have children through her*'" (emphasis added). Although Bilhah's relationship to Rachel was not along blood lines, viewed through the preceding African sociocultural lens, Bilhah appears to play the same role as a tlhatswadirope. Bilhah is expected to wash the thighs, not only of a female family member whose advantage over her would have been age, but that of a woman whose apparent advantage over her was her ethnicity, social class, and deity. Rachel's words resonate with the words of Sarai to Abram about her maid-servant, Hagar (Gen 16:2-3):

> And Sarai said to Abram, "*You see that the LORD has prevented me from bearing children; go in to my slave-girl [maid servant]; it may be that I shall obtain children by her.*" And Abram listened to the voice of Sarai. So, after Abram had lived ten years in the land of Canaan, *Sarai, Abram's wife, took Hagar the Egyptian, her slave-girl [maid servant/*שפחה*], and gave her to her husband Abram as a wife.* (emphasis added)

In the Hebrew Scriptures, "to take a wife in marriage" is a common expression used to refer to a legitimately sanctioned form of marriage (Gafney 2010). Sylvia J. Teubal's observation about the dual identity of Hagar as both a maidservant and a wife is instructive. In Gen 16:4, Teubal (1990, 49–62) notes that Hagar is a שפחה who is given to Abram as an אשה. In Genesis, a woman who is given to a man by his own wife for childbearing purpose is always a שפחה and never an אשה. If אמה is a female slave or female servant, then שפחה is something else; different from a slave or a servant. Teubal reasons that the term is best understood as "companion" (62).

What is intriguing about the expectations of the two matriarchs on the expected outcome of the surrogacy is that Rachel, the younger mistress, assumed with definiteness that Jacob's sexual union with Bilhah would necessarily yield the desired result. "Here is my maid Bilhah; go in to her, that she may bear upon my knees [tlhatswadikhuru or tlhatswadirope?] and that *I too may have children through her*" (Gen 30:3). Not so with the older mistress, though, who says: "*it may be* that I shall obtain children by her" (Gen 16:2). Could it be that the age gap between the matriarchs, with old age depicting more maturity, enabled Sarai to be more cautious and thus less certain, less angry, and less demanding than the younger matriarch?

Even the Sarai–Hagar relationship was not along bloodlines. Hagar was this Other in terms of ethnicity, social class, and relationship with the deity. It appears that the deity featured in Gen 16 and 21 had favorites. Some could opine that such a deity who endorses the chasing away of Abram's פלגש by his main wife and who later encourages her to go back to slavery could not be trusted. Danna N. Fewell and David M. Gunn (1993, 51) reason that "for the ethically sensitive reader such response is troubling: a god who shows arbitrary favoritism is a god who cannot be trusted." The deity seems to be inclined to the interests of the haves of the time. They also note, "Sarai 'sees fit' to abuse her (*'nh*), to humble her, *to put her back in her place—as the true outsider. (After all, she is a woman, a foreigner and a servant)*" (46, emphasis added). At face value, a gender-sensitive, women-identified observer and/or reader of the custom of go hlatswa dirope (cleansing/washing of thighs) may be tempted to think that it was only women who were subjected to the kind of pressure that was experienced by botlhatswadirope (thigh washers) then and perhaps even today. It was not gendered as even men in (traditional) African cultures were/are expected to father children. True masculinity was thus also linked to a man's virility.

As we grapple with the identification of womanhood in both the African-South African and biblical contexts, it may be worthwhile to evaluate the identity of tlhatswadirope in light of (re)definitions of womanhood (bosadi) even in our quest for the kind of context that matters.

Conclusion: Woman as Tlhatswadirope and Womanhood (Bosadi)

From the discussion in the preceding section, it is apparent that underlying the custom of woman as tlhatswadirope was/is the important role that women play/played as mothers in African cultures (cf. Masenya [Ngwan'a Mphahlele] 1998, 283–84). The woman who performs the role of tlhatswadirope both in the African and in the ancient Near Eastern sociocultural contexts is not a concubine or a nyatsi (read: illegitimate wife). She is mohumagadi, a wife. Tlhatswadirope is a mother. The latter is a celebrated role, then and today, both in varying African contexts and globally. However, noteworthy is the fact that not every woman will celebrate a woman's motherly and wifely roles. Can women in the preceding categories also be respected as persons in their own right? Yes, they should.

Also, it could be glimpsed that the concept of family in which individuals were inspired by the African corporeal mentality was/is highly esteemed in those contexts; hence, not any woman was called to step in and play the role of tlhatswadirope in a specific context. The preceding arrangement may probably have enabled the surrogate mother not to adopt Hagar's attitude. "He went in to Hagar, and she conceived; and when she saw that she had conceived, she looked with contempt on her mistress" (Gen 16:4). Present day colonized interpreters of African cultures may quickly view the custom of woman-as-tlhatswadirope as oppressive and thus death-dealing to the young female adults involved. Both the family and corporeal mentality displayed by the custom may be assessed through Western eyes. The following question may be posed to such sceptics: Is it fair to judge values and customs practiced in community/family-oriented contexts by the norms and values espoused in contexts driven by individualistic values? How does one draw a boundary between the rights of individuals in community-oriented contexts and the rights of the communities in question? Whose context matters?

Notwithstanding the preceding questions, noteworthy is the harsh reality that in patriarchal community-oriented contexts, the individual rights of women have almost always been subsumed into those of their communities. One can then ask, which impacts may the practice of woman-as-tlhatswadirope have on a woman who would have been coerced into such a practice? Does her specific (individual) context matter? Will the contexts of African biblical scholars who choose not to fit in to the norm of woman-as-mother by rejecting the imposed surrogacy of Western biblical scholarship through its methods and money be allowed to matter?

Reverting to the title of Holter's article, another question may be asked: How will Old Testament scholarship, which deliberately integrates indigenous knowledge systems with biblical hermeneutics, be received especially by those who continue to set great store by the money and methods of the North to the exclusion of the myths and meanings of the South? As Holter (1998, 248) has rightly argued:

> My point is not that a literary approach is better than the historical-critical one, and that the best of all is to let the OT be interpreted by South Africans brought up under the apartheid regime, or Western Africans brought up in a traditional village. My point is rather that OT scholarship should be open to all kinds of approaches to the OT, hence being careful of defining only certain traditional approaches as 'scientific.'

Holter's insistence that it is not the question of money but that all contexts should matter in our theory and praxis of Old Testament scholarship should continue to be cherished by all of us.

Works Cited

Deist, Ferdinand E. 1992. "South African Old Testament Studies and the Future." *OTE* 5:315–16.

Fewell, Danna N., and David M. Gunn. 1993. *Gender, Power and Promise: The Subject of the Bible's First Story.* Nashville: Abingdon.

Gafney, Wil. 2010. "Ruth." Pages 249–54 in *The Africana Bible: Reading Israel's Scriptures from Scriptures and the African Diaspora.* Edited by Hugh Page et al. Minneapolis: Augsburg Fortress.

Holter, Knut. 1998. "It's Not Only a Question of Money! African Old Testament Scholarship between the Myths and Meanings of the South and the Money and Methods of the North!" *OTE* 11:240–54.

Masenya (Ngwan'a Mphahlele), Madipoane. 1996. "Proverbs 31:10–31 in a South African Context: A Bosadi (Womanhood) Perspective." PhD diss., University of South Africa, Pretoria, South Africa.

———. 1997. "A Bosadi (Womanhood) Reading of Genesis 16." Paper read at the Annual Meeting of the Society of Biblical Literature, November 1997. San Francisco.

———. 1998. "A Bosadi (Womanhood) Reading of Genesis 16." *OTE* 11.2:271–87.

———. 2004. *How Worthy Is the Woman of Worth? Rereading Proverbs 31:10–31 in African-South Africa*. New York: Lang.

Masenya (Ngwan'a Mphahlele), Madipoane, and Hulisani Ramantswana. 2012. "Anything New under the Sun of Old Testament Scholarship? African Qoheleths' Review of OTE 1994–2010." *OTE* 25.3:598–637.

Mbiti, John S. 1969. *African Religions and Philosophy*. London: Heinemann.

Mbuvi, Andrew M. 2017. "African Biblical Studies: An Introduction to an Emerging Discipline." *CBR* 15.2:149–78.

Oduyoye, Mercy A. 1995. *Daughters of Anowa: African Women and Patriarchy*. Maryknoll, NY: Orbis.

Teubal, Sylvia J. 1990. *Hagar and the Egyptian: The Lost Tradition of the Matriarchs*. San Francisco, CA: Harper & Row.

West, Gerald O. 2009. "Interrogating the Comparative Paradigm in African Biblical Scholarship." Pages 37–64 in *African and European Readers of the Bible in Dialogue: In Quest for a Shared Meaning*. Edited by Hans de Wit and Gerald O. West. Pietermaritzburg: Cluster.

Wit, Hans de. 2009. "Exegesis and Contextuality: Happy Marriage, Divorce or Living (Apart) Together?" Pages 3–30 in *African and European Readers of the Bible in Dialogue: In Quest for a Shared Meaning*. Edited by Hans de Wit and Gerald O. West. Pietermaritzburg: Cluster.

Part 2
Reception in Context

"Blessed Be My People Egypt": Isaiah 19–20 with Special Reference to Reception by the Coptic Church in Egypt

Grant LeMarquand

Introduction

It has often been noted that the Old Testament presents Egypt as a two-sided image. On the one hand, Egypt is a place of oppression for the people of Israel (Exod 1:8–14). Egypt is the house of bondage, the place from which Israel is delivered in the exodus (Exod 3:7–12) and, later in Israel's history, a place of political power that the prophets declare Israel should not trust (e.g., Isa 20). On the other hand, Egypt is a place of provision in times of famine, as in the story of Abraham in Gen 12:10 and in the Joseph cycle (especially Gen 46–50), and an asylum for political refugees (1 Kgs 11:40; 2 Kgs 25:26). Although the image of Egypt in the book of Exodus is primarily negative, we should keep in mind that the entire canon begins with Genesis, a book that has a predominantly positive view of Egypt.

Knut Holter's (2000) article, "Africa in the Old Testament," draws attention to this double-sided representation of Egypt, as it is presented in each section of the Hebrew canon—in the Pentateuch, the Prophets, and the Writings. Although much of Holter's attention in his publications has been on sub-Saharan Africa, he has noted that Egypt should be part of our assessment of Africa and the Old Testament. Holter cites approvingly an African scholar who argues that Egypt was "to an extent usually not recognised, fundamentally African. The evidence of both language and culture reveals these African roots" (Ehret 1996, 25, in Holter 2000, 96–97). Holter's concern for considering Egypt in discussions of African interpretation is also seen in an article on the subject in a volume he edited (Habtu 2001).

For centuries, the Coptic Orthodox Church of Egypt has stressed the positive image of Egypt as a place of refuge for Jesus and his family (Matt 2:13–23), understanding this to be, as the Gospel of Matthew says, the fulfillment of Hos 11:1 ("Out of Egypt I called my son"). Less well known is that the Coptic Church also understands Egypt as playing a key role in the worldwide mission to the gentiles, as gentile inclusion is predicted in Isa 19. This essay will begin with a brief survey of the image of Egypt in the Old Testament. The oracle concerning Egypt in Isa 19–20 will then be examined in more detail. Finally, the essay will examine the reception of the passage by the Coptic Church.

Egypt as Oppressor

The word *Egypt* appears in the Old Testament approximately seven hundred times. Many of these passages portray Egypt in a negative light. The action of the book of Exodus takes place in Egypt. Throughout that text, Egypt is portrayed as the quintessential land of oppression. The Hebrews suffer unjustly under the harsh hand of an unnamed Pharaoh. In the first chapter, the Egyptians are fearful of the Hebrews (many translations of Exod 1:12 say that the Egyptians were "in dread"), apparently considering the Hebrews' birth rate to be dangerous. The Egyptians worry that such large numbers will lead to the Israelites seeking power, becoming allies of Egypt's enemies, and finally overpowering Egypt. The solution is oppression—Pharaoh decides "to oppress them with forced labor" (Exod 1:11). When Israel "multiplied" and "spread" (Exod 1:12), their affliction is increased, and it explicitly becomes slavery: "The Egyptians became ruthless in imposing tasks on the Israelites and, made their lives bitter with hard service in mortar and brick and in every kind of field labor. They were ruthless in all the tasks that they imposed on them" (Exod 1:13–14).

The drama of the exodus recounts God's "coming down" (Exod 3:8) to deliver Israel from slavery because God is the God who has seen their afflictions, heard their cries, and known their sufferings (Exod 3:7). The ensuing struggle is portrayed as warfare between the God of Israel and Pharaoh and the gods of Egypt: "on all the gods of Egypt I will execute judgments: I am the Lord" (Exod 12:12). In the end, Pharaoh, his magicians, and the gods they represent are powerless against Israel's God.

The psalms and the prophets look back to this deliverance that God won for Israel. Thus, Ps 135 includes these lines:

> He it was who struck down the firstborn of Egypt,
>> both human beings and animals;
> he sent signs and wonders
>> into your midst, O Egypt,
> against Pharaoh and all his servants. (vv. 8–9)

Psalm 136 instructs the people to give thanks to the Lord,

> who struck Egypt through their firstborn,
>> for his steadfast love endures forever;
> and brought Israel out from among them,
>> for his steadfast love endures forever;
> with a strong hand and an outstretched arm,
>> for his steadfast love endures forever;
> who divided the Red Sea in two,
>> for his steadfast love endures forever;
> and made Israel pass through the midst of it,
>> for his steadfast love endures forever;
> but overthrew Pharaoh and his army in the Red Sea,
>> for his steadfast love endures forever;
> who led his people through the wilderness,
>> for his steadfast love endures forever. (vv. 10–16)

Examples could be multiplied. The story of Israel's deliverance from slavery under harsh Egyptian rule was paradigmatic and identity forming for subsequent generations of Israel.

This Israelite identity, as the freed-from-Egypt people, is one of the reasons that later temptations to turn to Egypt for help were disturbing for subsequent Israelite generations. During the period of the divided monarchy, the Assyrian and Babylonian Empires continually threatened Israel. One political option for frightened Israel and Judah was to turn to the other global superpower, Egypt the former oppressor, for military aid. But Isaiah warns against looking to Egypt for help:

> Oh, rebellious children, says the Lord,
> who carry out a plan, but not mine;
> who make an alliance, but against my will,
>> adding sin to sin;
> who set out to go down to Egypt
>> without asking for my counsel,
> to take refuge in the protection of Pharaoh,

> and to seek shelter in the shadow of Egypt;
> Therefore the protection of Pharaoh shall become your shame,
> and the shelter in the shadow of Egypt your humiliation. (Isa 30:1–3)

> Alas for those who go down to Egypt for help
> and who rely on horses,
> who trust in chariots because they are many
> and in horsemen because they are very strong,
> but do not look to the Holy One of Israel
> or consult the Lord! …
> The Egyptians are human, and not God;
> their horses are flesh, and not spirit.
> When the Lord stretches out his hand,
> the helper will stumble, and the one helped will fall,
> and they will all perish together. (Isa 31:1, 3)

Similarly, Ezek 29–32 is an extensive warning and prophecy against Egypt. Egypt is doomed—Babylon will destroy the kingdom of the Egyptians; the idols will be destroyed; the people will be scattered; the Pharaoh will be killed. And, says Ezekiel, all this is because God has come against Egypt in judgment; Babylon is simply God's tool for the job.

Egypt as Refuge

Although the primary image of Egypt is that of oppressor, the idolatrous empire, which cannot be trusted even many generations after the events of the exodus, there are texts that display another side to this African superpower.

The Greek historian Herodotus rightly wrote that "Egypt is the Nile and the Nile is Egypt." Before the annual flooding of the Nile was stopped by the building of the Aswan dam, the repeated annual floods brought nutrients from the heart of Africa to fertilize the Nile valley and delta, making Egypt a place where food was secure. When there was scarcity in other lands, there was still food in Egypt, and Egypt frequently became a place of refuge for those in need.

The first biblical example of Egypt as a place of refuge comes from the life of Abram: "Now there was a famine in the land. So Abram went down to Egypt to reside there as an alien, for the famine was severe in the land" (Gen 12:10). Although God has promised Canaan to Abram (Gen 12:7), a famine diverts him to Egypt. However, the beauty of Abram's wife leads him to worry that the powerful might kill him in order to possess her. So, Abram tries to engage in deception by claiming that Sarai is his sister (a half-truth). Interestingly, when his deception is discovered, Pharaoh is more kind to Abram than one might expect, and Abram and Sarai are sent on their way unharmed.

Later, Egypt becomes the obvious place to turn for Abram's Egyptian concubine Hagar. After she is turned out of Abram's family, she flees, significantly in the direction of Egypt (Gen 16:6–8). Hagar "fled in the direction of Egypt … when the messenger of Yahweh found her near a well and asked where she was going" (Snell 2001, 127).

Genesis 37–50 also recounts Joseph being sold into Egypt as a slave by his brothers and his eventual rise to power as the right-hand man of Pharaoh. Joseph's ability to interpret dreams leads to his being put in charge of arranging for Egypt's survival through a rare period of need in that land of plenty. And because there is still food in Egypt, Jacob's family is saved from starvation. As Garret Galvin (2011, 62–63) says:

> Joseph's ultimately positive experience in Egypt allows him to save the people of Israel from famine. This experience lays the foundation for the biblical motif of Egypt as a place of refuge.… Without Egypt, Israel could not have survived. Egypt becomes one of the places of refuge for Israelites.

The relationship between Egypt and Israel continues throughout Israel's history. The fact that Moses had a Cushite wife (Num 12), as well as a Midianite wife, Zipporah (Exod 2), shows a close relationship between the two nations. According to 1 Kings, Solomon had an Egyptian wife (1 Kgs 3:1; 11:1), a detail which seems to portray the prestige and power of the Solomonic rule. In the ancient Near East, brides were usually sent from the less powerful to the more powerful. "Traffic in brides … was very much a one-way process. The pharaoh was always willing to receive foreign brides … but never countenanced the export of Egyptian princesses" (Bryce 2003, 108–9). That Solomon receives a pharaonic princess implies his superiority over Pharaoh.

The author of 1 Kings tells of several leaders who oppose Solomon's rule. One was named Hadad:

> Then the LORD raised up an adversary against Solomon, Hadad the Edomite; he was of the royal house in Edom … but Hadad fled to Egypt with some Edomites who were servants of his father. He was a young boy at that time. They set out from Midian and came to Paran; they took people

> with them from Paran and came to Egypt, to Pharaoh king of Egypt, who gave him a house, assigned him an allowance of food, and gave him land. Hadad found great favor in the sight of Pharaoh, so that he gave him his sister-in-law for a wife, the sister of Queen Tahpenes.... When Hadad heard in Egypt that David slept with his ancestors ... Hadad said to Pharaoh, "Let me depart, that I may go to my own country." But Pharaoh said to him, "What do you lack with me that you now seek to go to your own country?" And he said, "No, do let me go." (1 Kgs 11:14, 17, 19, 21–22)

Hadad finds welcome in Egypt, receiving not merely food but a house and a wife from Pharaoh. Hadad is a person of status, so it appears to have been politically expedient for Pharaoh to provide for him.

Similarly, Jeroboam, another person of status and influence, finds refuge in Egypt during Solomon's reign. According to 1 Kings, Solomon's fall out of favor stems from his forsaking the Lord by worshiping the gods of the nations and not walking in the Lord's ways. The prophet Ahijah foresees the division of Israel's tribes and the ascension of Jeroboam to the throne of Israel. When Ahijah's prophecy becomes known to Solomon, Jeroboam is forced to flee, naturally, to Egypt, where he is protected by the pharaoh Shishak (see 1 Kgs 11:26–40).

As a divided nation surrounded by powerful neighbors, those Israelites who found themselves out of favor would often look to Egypt for help. Jeremiah reports that he was not the only prophet to speak against the king of Judah during the late seventh century BCE:

> There was another man prophesying in the name of the LORD, Uriah son of Shemaiah from Kiriath-jearim. He prophesied against this city and against this land in words exactly like those of Jeremiah. And when King Jehoiakim, with all his warriors and all the officials, heard his words, the king sought to put him to death; but when Uriah heard of it, he was afraid and fled and escaped to Egypt. Then King Jehoiakim sent Elnathan son of Achbor and men with him to Egypt, and they took Uriah from Egypt and brought him to King Jehoiakim, who struck him down with the sword and threw his dead body into the burial place of the common people. (Jer 26:20–23)

Uriah's flight was ultimately unsuccessful. He was extradited and then executed by Jehoiakim probably because (unlike Hadad and Jeroboam) Uriah was not a person of significant status in the eyes of the pharaoh. Still, it is significant that Egypt was the place that the prophet assumed would be a place of safety.

Finally, the book of Jeremiah records that prophet's own flight to Egypt. Jeremiah's prophecy actually contains more references to Egypt than any book of the Old Testament besides Genesis and Exodus. These references are almost all negative: Egypt is the Lord's enemy; the poems of the book (see especially Jer 46) "consistently mock Egypt.... Egypt cannot be a place of lasting, secure refuge for God's people" (Galvin 2011, 185). Jeremiah's negative portrayal stems from the temptation that some in Israel had succumbed to—looking to Egypt rather than to the Lord. Although Jeremiah depicts Egypt in a negative light, the picture he paints reveals that some in Israel, retained positive memories of Egypt as a place of refuge.

Isaiah 19–20: Eschatological Hope for Egypt

To this double-sided image of Egypt—Egypt the powerful oppressor and Egypt the land of plenty and refuge—must be added a third theme: Egypt as a type for gentile conversion to the worship of the God of Israel. Isaiah 19–20 provokes a theological question: how can gentiles come into a relationship with the God of Israel? Alec J. Motyer (1993, 163) perceptively mentions that, "Isaiah picks on the unlikeliest candidate, Egypt, the first and most memorable adversary of the Lord's people."

Isaiah 19–20 is a unit predicting Egypt's future. The unit forms a sandwich structure with prophecies of Egypt's doom (19:1–15; 20:1–6) forming an *inclusio* around a hopeful center: Egypt's final healing and inclusion. Isaiah does not foresee much short-term hope for the ancient superpower and, clearly, opposes Judah's rebellion against Assyria and alliance with Egypt. Exchanging a relationship with one evil empire for another will not help Israel, especially given that Assyria is clearly the more powerful. Isaiah 19:1–15 describes Egypt's fate as a military, economic, and ecological disaster. Egypt will engage in civil war ("I will stir up Egyptians against Egyptians," 19:2). Commercial enterprises will fail ("The workers in flax will be in despair, and the carvers and those at the loom will grow pale.... Its weavers will be dismayed, and all who work for wages will be grieved," 19:9–10). The Nile, the source of Egypt's life, will fail ("The waters of the Nile will be dried up, and the river will be parched and dry; its canals will become foul.... All that is sown by the Nile will dry up, be driven away, and be no more," 19:5–7). Along with the river, the wisdom of Egypt will also dry up ("the wise counselors of Pharaoh give stupid counsel," 19:11). Egypt's future is dark. Israel must not put its trust in a failed state.

The outside bracket of the *inclusio*, Isa 20:1–6, describes the humiliation of Egypt's empire at the hands of Sargon II of Assyria. The event Isaiah describes in chapter 20 took place in 711 BCE.

> In the year that the commander-in-chief, who was sent by King Sargon of Assyria, came to Ashdod and fought against it and took it—at that time the Lord had spoken to Isaiah son of Amoz, saying, "Go, and loose the sackcloth from your loins and take your sandals off your feet," and he had done so, walking naked and barefoot. Then the Lord said, "Just as my servant Isaiah has walked naked and barefoot for three years as a sign and a portent against Egypt and Ethiopia, so shall the king of Assyria lead away the Egyptians as captives and the Ethiopians as exiles, both the young and the old, naked and barefoot, with buttocks uncovered, to the shame of Egypt. And they shall be dismayed and confounded because of Ethiopia their hope and of Egypt their boast. In that day the inhabitants of this coastland will say, 'See, this is what has happened to those in whom we hoped and to whom we fled for help and deliverance from the king of Assyria! And we, how shall we escape?'"

The mention of Ethiopia (Cush) in 20:3–5 is explained because the Egyptian Empire at this time (the Twenty-Fifth Dynasty) was ruled by Cushites, the people originally from south of the first cataract in Upper Egypt. The fate of the Cushite-led Egyptian Empire is described not just as military defeat but as utter humiliation ("naked and barefoot, with buttocks uncovered, to the shame of Egypt," 20:4).

The meat in Isaiah's Egyptian sandwich, 19:16–25, could not be more dissimilar. In 2:2–4, Isaiah had predicted the conversion of the nations to Israel's God: "All the nations shall flow" to Jerusalem, to the house of the Lord (2:2). "Many peoples" will come to the mountain of the Lord to learn God's ways (2:3). The torah will go out from Zion (2:3), and the result will be peace: "nation shall not lift up sword against nation" (2:4). This pilgrimage-to-Zion motif is echoed throughout the prophets and the psalms. Chapter 19:16–25 functions as "an intertextual extension of 2:2–4" (Childs 2001, 142). It is also a particular application of Isaiah's universal vision for gentile inclusion to Egypt itself (and then also to Assyria). The two most powerful enemies of God's people are somehow to be reconciled with each other, with Israel, and with the creator God. To be sure, even this text prophesies judgment on Egypt ("The Lord will strike Egypt," 19:22), but this judgment has a restorative purpose: "The Lord will strike Egypt, striking and healing; they will return to the Lord, and he will listen to their supplications and heal them" (19:22).

The final verses of chapter 19 are among the most surprising in all of Scripture.

> On that day there will be a highway from Egypt to Assyria, and the Assyrian will come into Egypt, and the Egyptian into Assyria, and the Egyptians will worship with the Assyrians. On that day Israel will be the third with Egypt and Assyria, a blessing in the midst of the earth, whom the Lord of hosts has blessed, saying, "Blessed be Egypt my people, and Assyria the work of my hands, and Israel my heritage." (19:23–25)

"The ancient enmity between Assyria and Egypt [is] dissolved" (Oswalt 1986, 380). Israel does not make a highway to Egypt to escape Assyria. Rather, a highway will connect all three. And more than a highway, the common worship of the God of Israel will unite these former enemies. Verse 25 goes so far as to use language reserved in the rest of the Old Testament for Israel alone and apply it to these pagan nations: "Egypt my people … Assyria the work of my hands." Motyer (1993, 170) says, "In Egypt the word once was 'Let my people go' (Exod 5:1), but now Egypt is my people."

The Coptic Church's Interpretation of Isa 19

The Coptic Orthodox interpretation highlights four themes in Isaiah's text, themes usually overlooked by Old Testament historical critics.

First, Isa 19:1 states, "Behold, the LORD is riding on a swift cloud and comes to Egypt." Reading Isaiah christologically and canonically, Coptic interpreters assume that "the LORD" in this passage is the Lord Jesus. In this, the Copts are, of course, not alone. In much of the New Testament, the word *Lord* often refers to Jesus. The apostle Paul is a prime example of one who used the Greek word χύριος in this way (1 Cor 1:3: "Grace to you and peace from God our Father and the Lord Jesus Christ"; 1 Cor 8:6: "There is one God, the Father, from whom all things exist, and one Lord Jesus Christ). To the Coptic Church, it seems obvious that the Lord coming on a cloud to Egypt should be understood as the coming of the Lord Jesus.

Of course, this was a much easier exegetical move if one is reading Isa 19:1 alongside the story of the sojourn of Jesus and his family in Egypt from Matt 2. The story of the Holy Family in Egypt, that Jesus was received and safe there, has long been a pillar of dignity for the Coptic Church.

A second theme found in Isa 19 is likewise found in 19:1: "the idols of Egypt will tremble at his presence." According to Coptic tradition, the first place that the Holy Family visited in Egypt was the city of Hermopolis. Recounting the visit to Egypt of seven pilgrims in the years 394–395 CE, a work entitled A History of the Monks in Egypt tells of the coming of Jesus's family to Hermopolis:

> We beheld also another holy man named Apollos in the Thebaid, within the limits of Hermopolis, to which the Savior along with Mary and Joseph came fulfilling the prophecy of Isaiah: "Behold the Lord is sitting on a light cloud and is coming to Egypt. The idols of Egypt will be shaken by his presence and will fall on the ground [Isa 19:1]." For there we see the temple where, after the Savior had entered the city, all the idols fell on the ground upon their faces. (Festugière 1971, 41)

Stephen J. Davis (2001, 133–62) notes that this tradition embellishes the Isaiah text slightly. Although Isaiah says that the idols will tremble, the History of the Monks says they will fall on their faces. I suspect that the story in the History of the Monks contains an intertextual echo of the story of Dagon falling on its face before the Ark of the Covenant in 1 Sam 5:4: "When they rose early on the next morning, Dagon had fallen on his face to the ground before the ark of the Lord." In any case, the coincidence of several factors—the fallen idols in Hermopolis, the Matthean witness that (the Lord) Jesus had come to Egypt, and the Isaian prophecy that the idols would tremble at the Lord's presence—were certainly sufficient for the Coptic Church to give credence to this ancient story.

Isaiah 19:19 provides a third important theme for Egyptian Christians: "In that day there will be an altar to the Lord in the midst of Egypt." Although there has been speculation about where Isaiah thought this altar might be (from those who believe that Isaiah was writing a prophecy after the fact) and more speculation from Coptic Christians about the altar's location (various sites have vied for the honor), Pope Shenoude III has provided a theological interpretation. In a sermon from 1981 on the Feast of the Visit of the Holy Family to Egypt, the Patriarch commented that the reference to an altar in the midst of Egypt signifies that "salvation was through the blood of Jesus" and that the prophecy of "an altar in the middle of a country of Gentiles shows that Jesus is the real offering to the world." Shenoude states that Isaiah "foretold salvation through Jesus Christ: 'For

Christ, our Passover lamb, has been sacrificed'" (Hulsman 2001, 124). Here Shenoude seems to be in harmony with Isaiah's purpose in giving the prophecy: Isaiah was prophesying the inclusion of the gentiles into the covenant with Israel's God, Egypt being the type that would find fulfillment in the fulfillment of the promise to Abraham that all nations would be blessed (Gen 12:3).

Shenoude also provides the reading of a fourth theme. As we have seen, Isa 19:25 calls Egypt "my people." This is a shocking use of language since it is the only place in the Old Testament where a group other than Israel is called "my people." According to Shenoude, God first called the people of Israel to him, and they were called "the people of God." But the prophecy of Isa 19 is the turning point because here for the first time Egypt—a nation of gentiles—was called to worship God and God called Egypt "my people," showing that God came not only for the people of Israel but for other people also. Isaiah 19 is therefore a forerunner of the call in the New Testament for witnesses of God "to the ends of the earth" (Hulsman 2001, 124).

There is humility in Shenoude's interpretation. Rather than declaring that Egypt would somehow replace Israel as God's people, Shenoude understands this prophecy about Egypt being "my people" as a prophecy about all gentiles being welcomed into a relationship with God in Christ. Shenoude affirms that this is an unexpected gift: "The people of Egypt did not pray for Jesus to come, and they did not ask for his grace, yet this grace was offered to them" (Hulsman 2001, 124).

Summary

The dominant image of Egypt as the house of bondage is not the only portrayal of that ancient African nation in the Old Testament. Egypt, as noted by Holter, is also spoken of as a place of refuge. Isaiah goes further and expresses a great eschatological hope that Egypt will become part of God's covenant with the nations. The ancient African church, the Coptic Orthodox Church, goes further to show that Egypt was not just a place of refuge for those escaping famine or war; it was the place of refuge for the Son of God himself, according to Matt 2. Building on Matt 2 and Isa 19, the Coptic Church sees Egypt as a type of gentile inclusion. Given the probability that many Bible readers may have a negative view of Egypt based on Exodus, the more positive view of Egypt in Isa 19–20 and especially the Coptic reading of this text may serve to complicate the negative reading and perhaps encourage a more nuanced view.

Works Cited

Bryce, Trevor. 2003. *Letters of the Great Kings of the Ancient Near East: The Royal Correspondence of the Late Bronze Age*. London: Routledge.

Childs, Brevard. 2001. *Isaiah: A Commentary*. OTL. Louisville: Westminster John Knox.

Davis, Stephen J. 2001. "Ancient Sources for the Coptic Tradition." Pages 133–62 in *Be Thou There: The Holy Family's Journey in Egypt*. Edited by Gawdat Gabra. Cairo: The American University in Cairo.

Ehret, Christopher. 1996. "Ancient Egyptian as an African Language, Egypt as an African Culture." Pages 25–27 in *Egypt in Africa*. Edited by Theodore Celenko. Indianapolis: Indiana University Press.

Festugière, A. J., ed. 1971. *History of the Monks in Egypt*. Brussels: Société des Bollandistes.

Galvin, Garrett. 2011. *Egypt as a Place of Refuge*. Tübingen: Mohr Siebeck.

Habtu, Tewoldemedhin. 2001. "The Images of Egypt in the Old Testament: Reflections on African Hermeneutics." Pages 55–64 in *Interpreting the Old Testament in Africa*. Edited by Mary N. Getui, Knut Holter, and Victor Zinkuratire. New York: Lang.

Holter, Knut. 2000. "Africa in the Old Testament." Pages 93–106 in *Yahweh in Africa: Essays on Africa and the Old Testament*. Edited by Knut Holter. New York: Lang.

Hulsman, Cornelis. 2001. "Tracing the Route of the Holy Family Today." Pages 31–132 in *Be Thou There: The Holy Family's Journey in Egypt*. Edited by Gawdat Gabra. Cairo: The American University in Cairo.

Motyer, Alec J. 1993. *The Prophecy of Isaiah*. Downers Grove, IL: InterVarsity Press.

Oswalt, John N. 1986. *The Book of Isaiah, Chapters 1–39*. NICOT. Grand Rapids: Eerdmans.

Snell, Daniel C. 2001. *Flight and Freedom in the Ancient Near East*. Leiden: Brill.

The Portrayal of Africa and Africans in the Book of Ezekiel

David Tuesday Adamo†

Preliminary Remarks

I am grateful to God for the opportunity to write this article in honor of my good friend and colleague, Professor Knut Holter of VID Specialized University, Stavanger, Norway. He has been a long-time faithful friend and colleague since the 1980s. When I wrote my PhD dissertation, I never knew that it would influence any scholar, especially a Western scholar. I never knew that someone was deeply interested in my so-called wild ideas about Africa and Africans in the Bible. I never knew that someone was following me through my dissertation and other publications until I met Holter, who told me of his excitement about my work and had asked his students to write a thesis on the subject.

Since then, Holter has dedicated himself to attending conferences on the continent and presenting papers on Africa and Africans. Holter has not only attended many conferences in Africa; he has also sponsored many of them. In addition, he has supported some academic religious organizations, especially the Nigerian Association for Biblical Studies in Nigeria. I am grateful for his financial support that enabled me to attend the Annual Meetings of the Society of Biblical Literature, and I am happy to write this chapter in his honor. May the Lord grant him long life and peace.

---

† Note from the editors: We were much saddened by the death of our esteemed colleague, Professor Tuesday David Adamo, in 2022. We therefore decided to publish posthumously his essay in the version submitted for peer review with general editorial revisions.

Overview of Ezekiel

The book of Ezekiel is the third of the major prophetic books of the Christian Old Testament canon that follows Isaiah and Jeremiah–Lamentations (McKenzie and Graham 1998, 88). There were some questions concerning its canonicity because some of its teachings are at odds with the Torah.

The principal theme of Ezekiel's message is God's presence, and it appears to have informed his frequent use of the recognition formula, "and they shall know that I am Yahweh," more than eighty times throughout the book. The formula is used as a recurring refrain to manifest his divine power.

Many Old Testament prophets employed different genres to proclaim their message. Some used poetry more than narratives, while others used prose more than narratives, with many figurative speeches and imageries. For example, Ezekiel uses much symbolic imagery to proclaim his message of judgment and hope. That is the reason why many Ezekiel scholars wonder at how beautiful its literary artistry is and agree that Ezekiel's literary architecture is more advanced "than in other prophetical books" (Zimmerli 1979, 1–2). According to Walther Zimmerli (1979, 1–2; cf. Mays 1978, 22; Greenberg 1983, 23; Blenkinsopp 1990, 3), the great order in the book is a surprise. Margaret S. Odell (2003, 165) affirms that "the book of Ezekiel reflects a degree of literary coherence unmatched in the canon of biblical prophets."

The prophet Ezekiel appears to be an international prophet and a priest who is familiar with the surrounding nations of Africa, Tyre, Ammon, Moab, Edom, Philistia, Assyria, and Babylon.

Since the purpose of this essay is to discuss how the book of Ezekiel portrays Africa and Africans, it is important to highlight the names of Africa and Africans that the book specifically mentions. These include Egypt, Pharaoh, Zoan, Cush, Libya, Lud, and Put.[2] In the so-called historical texts of Ezekiel (16, 20, 23), Africa and Africans are mentioned about fifteen times, in the oracles against the nations about forty times,

---

2. Many epigraphic materials have provided clues that the nations listed alongside Egypt were the mercenary troops of Egypt. According to Rassam Cylinder 2.95–96, 111–115, Gyges of Lydia (לוד) was one ally of the African ruler, Psammetichus I, in the seventh century against the Assyrians. When Nebuchadnezzar marched into Egypt, Put seemed to have participated in the battle against Nebuchadnezzar. For a further translation of the Rasam Cylinder, see Luckenbill (1926, 2:297–96).

and four times in the other sections, making a total of fifty-nine times. I consider the book of Ezekiel a remarkable one because it is one of the books of the Bible that mentions Africa and Africans repeatedly. Of all these terms, Egypt was used synonymously with other African countries, and that is why Africa and Egypt are mentioned together most of the time by the prophet Ezekiel. I will therefore use the terms *Africa* and *Egypt* interchangeably for the purpose of the present investigation.

Unfortunately, many Ezekiel scholars did not pay much attention to how the prophet portrays Africa and Africans. Many have focused on the oracles against the nations in the book but not specifically on the portrayal of Africa and Africans (Lee 2016; Crouch 2011; Corral 2002).

One may ask why there is frequent mention of Africa and Africans in the book of Ezekiel. One of the major reasons could be the familiarity with Africa and Africans in the biblical period—the fact that Africa and Africans had some power that was reckoned with. It occasions no wonder that they have been allies and the hope of ancient Israel—militarily, economically, socially, and religiously. This fact will be made clearer below. As already noted, this essay will examine the portrayal of Africa and Africans in the book of Ezekiel.

Ezekielian Scholarship

Like Isaiah and Jeremiah, the book of Ezekiel has gone through various analyses, ranging from those of scholars who argue for the unity of the book in terms of structure and authorship to those who argue that there is very little contribution of the prophet Ezekiel himself in the book and that the book presents diverse voices and incompatible perspectives (Hauser 2008, 61–62).

However, there are dissenting voices. According to Gustav Holscher, only 144 of the book's 1,273 verses were Ezekiel's authentic words (quoted by Zimmerli 1979, 5). Ezekiel's book was also viewed as a pseudo-epigraph that was penned around 230 BCE during the Hellenistic period and was later reworked by the Chronicler's school (Hauser 2008, 65). Rowley believes that the book contains some secondary elements but not in a large quantity and that Ezekiel, a gifted poet, should not be ruled out as the author of the prose passages (cited by Darr 2008, 251).

Zimmerli (1979, 347–48) places Ezekiel's ministry among the Babylonian exiles but argues that he later returned and reworked his book. He praises the prophet's literary artistry, rhetorical strategies, and theological objectives, though Keith W. Carley (1975, 24) and Lawrence Boadt (1978, 489) argue that Ezekiel's words were repetitive and that he was redundant in his technique.

Influences on Ezekiel and His Book

Ezekiel and other biblical literature share some commonalities such as priestly vocabularies, concepts, and Deuteronomistic influence. Boadt (1999, 4) argues that Ezekiel is a victim of hallucination and fantasy rather than sound theology, but Daniel I. Block (1997, 262) maintains the view that the book of Ezekiel represents "a meticulously unified and well-planned agenda reflecting the historical setting of the prophet himself with virtually no text dating" later than 539 BCE.

However, ancient Near Eastern influences are noticeable in the book of Ezekiel. This can be understood because the prophet functioned in the diaspora, although he was familiar with Jerusalem and his environment (McKeating 1993, 44). It is therefore possible that he was influenced by linguistic and cultural factors from the Mesopotamian world (Kohn 2008, 266). The power of God's hand, the stick, as well as prophesying by eating the scroll in the book resemble similar images in the Mari Letters. The sign acts resemble those of the Babylonian exorcism texts.

From Ezekiel's actions, many query his psychological state. According to Edwin C. Broome Jr. (1946), Ezekiel could be diagnosed as a paranoid schizophrenic because of his sign-acts. David J. Halperin states that Ezekiel imagined himself having intercourse. He is far from being a lovable person and he presented himself as an extreme example of morbidity which afflicted society (Halperin 1993, 5). The unconventional behavior of the prophet, which was a result of the sociological events during his adult life, that is, the exile and other traumatic circumstances, explain his absurd behavior due to posttraumatic stress disorder (Kohn 2008, 267). Marvin A. Sweeney (2001, 2–3) thinks that this might have been the reason for the lower level of scholars' interest in his book. Ezekielian sign-acts are an effective technique of nonverbal communication. He is described as a "suasive or interactive communicator who uses non-verbal behavior to communicate graphically specific message contents" (Kohn 2008, 268).

Scholars basically emphasized corporate rather than individual responsibility to God. Later scholars started recognizing Ezekiel's teaching about individual responsibility to Yahweh in chapter 18 (Kohn 2008, 270; Halpern 1991, 14–15). The prophet is concerned about the urgent need to accept responsibility (Joyce 1989, 187). Gordon H. Matties (1990, 150) regards Ezekiel as promoting the concept of "social self" and that an individual and the community are independent as they seek future restoration.

There is little consensus as to whether the vision found in Ezek 40–48 is an apocalyptic or utopian dream or a historical reality. Steven Shawn Tuell (1992, 18), however, found two sources in these chapters; the first being the core vision from Ezekiel himself (40:1–43; 44:1–2; 47:1–12; 48:30–35) and the second source being the legislative layer or law of the temple. The layer is a redaction of a religious polity for the restoration of Judea. However, Ian M. Duguid (1994, 133) sees Ezek 40–48 and the entire book of Ezekiel as coming from a single author of the exile. According to Kalinda Rose Stevenson (1996, xvii), the purpose of the text is to create new geography using a rhetorical analysis alongside the idea of territoriality as espoused by human geographers.

Many Ezekiel scholars have developed new modes of investigation such as gender analysis, the psycho-historical approach, rhetorical criticism, and anthropological studies, and these have brought a new validity and richness to Ezekielian scholarship and the book.

The discussion above has focused on the preoccupation of Ezekiel scholars who forget that the prophet Ezekiel also spent much of his time discussing Africa and Africans. He portrayed them as an arena of salvation, the origin of Israelite idol worship, Israel's outstanding enemy, as proud people and nations, and an outstanding ally and hope of Judah. These points will be argued in the following discussion.

Africa and Africans in Ezekiel

It may be unwise to deal with Africa and Africans in Ezekiel in isolation from the work of previous scholars that could form a useful background to this research. Thus, this essay will shed light on the direction most scholars have followed, neglecting so important a people that Israel respected, and dependent on, for its survival. A review of Ezekielian scholars is therefore necessary to show how necessary and urgent this research is.

Africa and Africans as Arena of Salvation in Ezekiel

The prophet Ezekiel has a great interest in history. This is evident not only in the careful dating of his prophecies, but also in his careful outlines of Israel's history (Luc 1983, 137–43). Although the prophet lived at the time when the Babylonians threatened the survival of Israel and her faith, the exiled Ezekiel was still concerned not only about Israel's past, but also about the foreign nations, especially Africa. Ezekiel's interest in history is found mainly in the so-called historical chapters of the book (Luc 1983, 138).

In the process of narrating the past apostasy of Israel, the prophet cannot forget the memory of the exodus in Egypt where God delivered his people. He says:

> and say to them: 'This is what the Sovereign LORD says: On the day I chose Israel, I swore with uplifted hand to the descendants of Jacob and revealed myself to them in Egypt. With uplifted hand I said to them, "I am the LORD your God." But for the sake of my name, I brought them out of Egypt. I did it to keep my name from being profaned in the eyes of the nations among whom they lived and in whose sight I had revealed myself to the Israelites. (Ezek 20:5, 9 NRSV)

The above text is likely to be an allusion to Exod 3:11–17 and 6:23. Exodus is deemed important because it is the act of salvation for ancient Israel that took place in Africa. It marked the commencement of ancient Israel's nationhood under Yahweh's leadership. It "sets the pattern for God's future relationship with his people" (Adamo 2021, 5). Most of these powerful acts of salvation began and took shape in Africa. It will be very difficult for any honest scholar to take Africa out of this act of salvation.

The prophet Ezekiel acknowledged that Yahweh made Africa the setting of the great salvation wrought during the Exodus deliverance.

Africa and Africans as Origin of Israelite Idol in Ezekiel (Chapter 20)

On the other hand, Ezek 20 records Africa as the very origin of Israelite idolatry with the word גלולים in verses 7 and 8. Israelites worship the Egyptian deities. The term גלולים is peculiar to the book of Ezekiel, such that thirty-nine out of the forty-eight Hebrew Bible occurrences appear in this prophetic book (Zimmerli 1979, 105). It becomes Ezekiel's favorite term to denote the idolatry committed by Israel in the past and in the exilic present. Ezekiel 20, particularly, records Egypt as the very origin of the Israelite idol.

The presentation of the chthonic cedar is probably influenced by the Egyptian association of the cedar tree with the death and resurrection of the god of Osiris (Lee 2016, 123–25).

Africa and Africans as Yahweh's Enemy in Ezekiel

There is a rich tapestry of imagery of foreign nations in Ezek 25–32. In these eight chapters of prophecies, many ancient nations (Ammon, Moab, Edom, Philistia, Tyre, and Egypt) came alive. I find it interesting that Africa is the last foreign nation to receive a diatribe in Ezek 25–32 and the only one to command four chapters of condemnation. It occupies half of the oracles. This might indicate the prophet's special interest in Africa.

This collection of prophecies belongs to the literary terrain of oracles against the nations. These oracles against foreign nations appear within a specific book of Ezekiel, as it does in Isa 13–23, Jer 46–51, Amos 1–2, Zeph 2–3, and Zech 9. The oracles against the nations display diverse structures and forms, such as a proof saying, an invitation to flight, a dirge, or utterance (Lee 2016, 2).

Africa or/and Pharaoh are represented metaphorically by three images. First, they are characterized as being monstrous תנים, which can be translated as either a "crocodile" or a "sea-monster/sea-dragon" (29:3–6a; 32:2–8). Second, the arms of Pharaoh symbolize Africa's might or strength (30:20–26). Third, Africa's might is also portrayed via the monstrously tall cedar tree and its root reaching deep into the waters with its tops rising high above other trees (31:1–9).

In the first and the last of the oracle against Africa in the book of Ezekiel, Pharaoh is like a crocodile or leonine monster stirring up turbulent waters.[3] In the middle of this oracle against Egypt, Pharaoh is also compared to a cedar that grows monstrously high and becomes "haughty in its loftiness" (31:10); Yahweh finally broke its arms, condemned it to Sheol, and slew it by the sword as Yahweh's enemy.

The cosmological mythological motifs in the Ezekielian oracles against the nations are related to the theological threat to Yahweh's status posed by the military defeat of Judah. The mythological imagery, identifying Egypt and Tyre as chaotic forces and describing their defeat by Yahweh, was used by Ezekiel as a means of affirming Yahweh's power as a divine king and creator (Crouch 2011, 482).

Africa sprawled amid its watery abode, the Nile. The accusation levied against Africa is that they claimed that "my Nile is mine, and I made it/me"

---

3. Indeed, several Pharaohs are described in the reliefs found in ancient Egypt as a "victorious lion," "a fierce-eyed lion," one who "fought like a lion," or "the lion with a deep roar upon the mountaintops" (Crouch 2011, 479–80).

(29:3). This statement in contrast to the repeated statement in the book of Ezekiel, "I am Yahweh," constitutes a direct challenge to Yahweh's claim as the creator.

Chapter 30 is dominated by the judgment against Egypt, Zoan, and Kush. According to Ezekiel, Yahweh will "set fire" on Egypt (Crouch 2011, 481) because of its theological threat to Yahweh's status posed by the military defeat of Judah. The mythological imagery, identifying Egypt and Tyre as chaotic forces and describing their defeat by Yahweh, was used by Ezekiel as a means of affirming Yahweh's power as a divine king and creator (Crouch 2011, 482).

Africa and Africans as a Broken Arm in Ezekiel

Africa and Africans are seen as a broken arm (29:1–6; 32:1–8; 30:20–26). The metaphor refers to the rivalry between Yahweh and Pharaoh. The prophecy that began in chapter 30 can be dated to "eleventh year in the first month, on the eleventh day of the month," which is about three months after the prophecy in 29:1–16. It is believed that it must have been the time that Pharaoh Apries sought to relieve Judah from the siege of Jerusalem by Nebuchadnezzar, king of Babylon (Block 1997, 23). The prophet Ezekiel responded to this situation by using the imagery of a broken arm in Ezek 30:21.

The use of the singular Hebrew arm זרוע and its plural form זרעות arms, which appears six times in the six verses, is remarkable. Ezekiel does not only depict Pharaoh as having a broken arm, but also assigns the breaking of Pharaoh's arm to Yahweh (30:21–22). The cataclysmic catastrophe imagined in this passage shows that Egypt is not only a political power; she also plays the role of a cosmological power in the reality of the exile.

Africa and Africans as Judah's Ally in Ezekiel

There is an intricate connection between Africa and Judah; that is, oracles against Egypt share so many things in common with Judah's oracles in Ezekiel. For example, the use of דליות "branches" in the oracles against Judah (17:6) and "among the interwoven foliage" (29:12; 30:23, 26; 32:9, 11:17; 20:34, 41; 28:25; 34:13; 36:24; 37:21). The most explicit reference to the "house of Israel" as an African/Egyptian ally is in Ezek 29:6–9. There are multiple references to Pharaoh and other consorts—Cush, Put, Libya, and the people of the covenant land who will fall by the sword. These divine castigations are addressed not only to Egypt, but also to the accompanying multitudes (31:2, 18; 32:18, 20, 31, 32) and to "his helpers" (32:21).

Judah's familiarity is expressed in Ezek 31 by the fact that the image of Judah is embedded and repetitively alluded to in a series of oracles against Egypt. One peculiarity about both is the large entourage that accompanies Egypt, so many of which were destroyed, slaughtered, and annihilated. These include fish of the Nile branches (Ezek 29:4), Cush, Put, Lud, and all the mixed multitude who accompanied Egypt to face the divine judgment. There are expressions common to both Egypt and Judah oracles in Ezekiel, which are not accidental or coincidental.

The text describing Judah as African/Egyptian allies contains a proof saying as the reason for judgment. It is headed by the word "because," continues with "therefore," and ends with a recognition formula וידעו כי אני יהוה ("And they shall know that I am Yahweh") (Lee 2016, 153–54).

Judah among Egypt's allies can be sought in the use of the term המון (multitude) in Ezek 29–32. It is significant that of the eighty-six occurrences of המון in the Hebrew Bible, nearly one-third is found in Ezekiel (Lee 2016, 154). With thirteen occurrences, the term primarily characterizes Egypt (Lee 2016, 154). Most of these occurrences appear in chapter 32. This term also characterizes Judah five times, and the rest of the occurrences in Ezekiel are used in association with other foreign nations. Based on this statistical consideration, the term is rightly identified as an important term in Ezekiel, especially in the African/Egyptian oracles (Lee 2016, 154). The meaning of המון is helpfully classified by Daniel Bodi (1991, 26) into three categories. The word carries three basic meanings: (1) "noise, sound, rush, roar, murmur"; (2) "multitude, troops, crowd, horde, abundance, wealth"; (3) "tumult, chaos, pomp, or arrogance." Ezekiel uses the word twenty-seven times (Baumann 1975, 414–18).

Perhaps the common language that Egypt's and Judah's oracle shared is the similarity between Israel and Egypt in terms of their moral failure and the judgment that falls upon them together. The political alliance of Egypt and Judah is further justified by the mention of the list of names of the Egyptian cities in 30:13–39. These names allude to the possibility of the presence of the Judahites seeking political refuge during the rise of the power of the Babylonians. In 30:13, Yahweh vows to annihilate all the dung and empty gods, which shows that the relationship is not only political but also military. The term גלולים is distinctively Ezekielian, to the extent that thirty-nine out of forty-eight occurrences in the Hebrew Bible appear in Ezekiel.

Africa and Africans as the Hope of Judah in Ezekiel

From the above discussion of Africa as Judah's ally, one is certain that Africa is depicted as the hope of Judah. The reed imagery shows that Africa is Judah's ally.[4] The prophet Isaiah and the book of Kings made references to the futility of Judah's hope of seeking political assistance from Egypt (Isa 36:6; 2 Kgs 18:21). The verbal root שען usually conveys a sense of politico-military reliance in the book of Isaiah (Isa 10:20; 30:12; 31:1; cf. 2 Chr 16:7–8; Isa 36:6). Here, the root appears in the form of the expression קנה משענת ("broken reed"). In the parallel passage in 2 Kgs 18, the expression also appears elsewhere in Ezek 29:6b. All these passages have the extremely rare expression קנה משענת combined with the verbal root רצץ, which means "to break, to crush," and with a similar phrase conveying the act of leaning on (Lee 2016, 56).

Africa and Africans as a Restored Community like Judah in Ezekiel

Africa was treated in a similar way as Judah by the prophet Ezekiel. They were to suffer annihilation or destruction, exile, and restoration. In Ezek 29:13–16, Egypt will be restored after forty years of exile among the nations. Yahweh himself will gather the Egyptians from the peoples (v. 13), turn their fortunes (v. 14), restore her kingdom (vv. 14–15), and they will eventually recognize Yahweh as God (v. 16). This portrayal of Africa as restored nations as Israel and other foreign nations confirms the apparent similarity between Israel and Egypt.

There is a contrast in the restoration of Africa with the fates of the other foreign nations appearing in Ezek 25–28. Egypt is the only one that received a restoration that is not assigned to Tyre, Ammon, Moab, Edom, and Philistia. The surrounding nations of Judah end with a note of destruction.

The level of intimacy with Africa seems to mean that Yahweh is ready to place both Egypt and Judah at par in the future restoration. Taken as a whole, the first and last chapters of the Egypt oracles form an inclusio, such that the African oracles begin and end with the comparison of Pharaoh to the תנים.

---

4. The Hebrew Bible often speaks of "the reed" (קנה) in connection with Egypt. For example, in Job 40:15–24, the plant provides cover for the hippopotamus, which was once widespread along the Nile region.

Conclusion

The book of Ezekiel is theocentric, as there is an extraordinary emphasis on God. At its beginning, center, and end, God is present (Moskala 2016, 105). The book portrays Africa and Africans as the arena of salvation through the remembrance of the Exodus event, the origin of Israel's idols, Yahweh's enemy, a broken arm, the hope of Judah, and the restored community.

Ezekiel 29–32 discusses the intimate relationship between Africa and Judah although Africa is first and foremost Yahweh's enemy. In Ezek 29–32, there are allusions to Africa as one of the strongest alliances with Judah. Both Africa and Judah received sentences of exile and the destruction of death judgment. Later, in 29:13–16, the prophecy of restoration, which was denied to other foreign nations, is announced.

God's dealing with Africa and Africans in the same way as with Israel places Africa and Africans in a privileged place on a par with Israel. Egypt will be restored to its original land Pathros, Southland (29:14), as Judah will.

This essay has helped to address not only the presence of Africa and Africans in the book of Ezekiel, but also the African identity formation that needs to be attended to seriously in both theological and biblical ways by African scholars.

Due to the frequency of references to Africa and Africans not only in the book of Ezekiel, but also in the entire Bible (1,417 times), Christianity is at home in Africa. Some scholars have argued that Christianity indeed is an indisputably African religion (Mbuvi 2017, 149–78). This has a great implication for Christianity in Africa, as African anti-colonialists tag Christianity as a foreign religion.

Finally, perhaps, if Western racists have known that the Bible, especially the book of Ezekiel, recognized and respected Africa and Africans, they would have not forced them into slavery or thought that they are half or inferior human beings.[5] Perhaps, the inferiority complex that is still prevalent among African/black people all over the world would have been avoided.

---

5. In 1789, the American Constitution counted black slaves as three-fifths of a free person (Johnstone 1980, 218).

Works Cited

Adamo, David Tuesday. 2021. "The Portrayal of Africa and Africans in the Book of Psalms." *Black Theology*:1–19.

Baumann, W. "המה." *TDOT* 3:414–18.

Blenkinsopp, Joseph. 1990. *Ezekiel*. International Bible Commentaries. Louisville: John Knox.

Block, Daniel I. 1997. *The Book of Ezekiel: Chapters 1–24*. Grand Rapids: Eerdmans.

Boadt, Lawrence. 1978. "Textual Problems in Ezekiel and Poetic Analysis of Paired Words." *JBL* 97:489–99.

———. 1999. "A New Look at the Book of Ezekiel." *TBT* 37:4–9.

Bodi, Daniel. 1991. *The Book of Ezekiel and the Poem of Erra*. OBO 104. Göttingen: Vandenhoek & Ruprecht.

Broome, Edwin C, Jr. 1946. "Ezekiel's Abnormal Personality." *JBL* 65:277–92.

Carley, Keith W. 1975. *Ezekiel among the Prophets: A Study of Ezekiel's Place in Prophetic Tradition*. SBT 2/31. London: SCM.

Corral, Martin Alonso. 2002. *Ezekiel Oracle against Tyre: Historical Reality and Motivation*. Rome: Pontifical Biblical Institute.

Crouch, C. L. 2011. "Ezekiel's Oracles against the Nations in Light of the Royal Ideology of Warfare." *JBL* 130:473–92.

Darr, Katheryn P. 2008. "Ezekiel among the Critics." Pages 249–59 in *Recent Research on the Major Prophets*. Edited by Alan J. Hauser. Sheffield: Sheffield Phoenix.

Duguid, Ian M. 1994. *Ezekiel and the Elders of Israel*. VTSup 56. Leiden: Brill.

Halperin, David J. 1993. *Seeking Ezekiel: Text and Psychology*. University Park: Pennsylvania University Press.

Halpern, Baruch. 1991. "Jerusalem and the Lineages in the Seventh Century BCE: Kinship and the Rise of Individual Moral Liability." Pages 11–107 in *Law and Ideology in Monarchic Israel*. Edited by Baruch Halpern and Deborah Whitney Hobson. JSOTSup 124. Sheffield: Sheffield Academic.

Hauser, Alan J. 2008. "Introduction and Overview." Pages 1–77 in *Recent Research on Major Prophets*. Edited by Alan J. Hauser. Sheffield: Sheffield Phoenix.

Greenberg, Moshe. 1983. *Ezekiel 1–20: A New Translation with Introduction and Commentary*. AB 22. New York: Doubleday.

Johnstone, Ronald L. 1980. *Religion and Society in Interaction: The Sociology of Religion.* Englewood Cliffs, NJ: Prentice-Hall.

Joyce, Paul M. 1989. *Divine Initiative and Human Response in Ezekiel.* JSOTSup 51. Sheffield: JSOT Press.

Kohn, Risa Levitt. 2008. "Ezekiel at the Turn of the Century." Pages 260–72 in *Recent Research on the Major Prophets.* Edited by Alan J. Hauser. Sheffield: Sheffield Phoenix.

Lee, Lydia. 2016. *Mapping Judah's Fate in Ezekiel's Oracles against the Nations.* ANEM 15. Atlanta: SBL Press.

Luc, Alex. 1983. "A Theology of Ezekiel: God's Name and Israel's History." *JETS* 26:137–43.

Luckenbill, Daniel David. 1926. *Ancient Records of Assyria and Babylonia.* 2 vols. Chicago: University of Chicago Press.

Matties, Gordon H. 1990. *Ezekiel 18 and the Rhetoric of Moral Discourse.* SBLDS 126. Atlanta: Scholars Press.

Mays, James Luther. 1978. *Ezekiel, Second Isaiah.* Proclamation Commentaries: The Old Testament Witnesses for Preaching. Philadelphia: Fortress.

Mbuvi, Andrew M. 2017. "African Biblical Studies: An Introduction to an Emerging Discipline." *CurBR* 15.2:149–78.

McKeating, Henry. 1993. *Ezekiel.* Old Testament Guides. Sheffield: Sheffield Academic.

McKenzie, Steven L., and M. Patrick Graham, eds. 1998. *The Hebrew Bible Today: An Introduction to Critical Issues.* Louisville: Westminster John Knox.

Moskala, Jiří. 2016. "Notes on the Literary Structure of the Book of Ezekiel." *Faculty Publications, Andrews University* 200:102–10.

Odell, Margaret S. 2003. "Ezekiel Saw What He Said He Saw: Genres, Forms, and the Vision of Ezekiel 1." Pages 163–67 in *The Changing Face of Forms Criticism.* Edited by Marvin A. Sweeney and Ehud Ben Zvi. Grand Rapids: Eerdmans.

Stevenson, Kalinda Rose. 1996. *The Vision of Transformation: The Territorial Rhetoric of Ezekiel 40–48.* SBLDS 154. Atlanta: Scholars Press.

Sweeney, Marvin A. 2001. "Ezekiel: Zadokite Priest and Visionary Prophet of the Exile." *Occasional Paper of the Institute for Antiquity and Christianity* 41:1–24.

Tuell, Steven Shawn. 1992. *The Law of the Temple in Ezekiel 40–48.* HSM 49. Atlanta: Scholars Press.

Zimmerli, Walther. 1979. *Ezekiel 1: A Commentary on the Book of the Prophet Ezekiel, Chapters 1–24*. Translated by R. E. Clements. Hermeneia. Philadelphia: Fortress.

Text, Context, and Canonical Ecology: The LRA's Reception of the Ten Commandments

Terje Stordalen

Introduction

Knut Holter (2019) offers an intriguing analysis of the use of the Ten Commandments by the Lord's Resistance Army (LRA) in Uganda. The LRA military and spiritual leader Joseph Kony was able to formulate entirely new stipulations—such as the prohibition to smoke—and make his followers to accept them as part of the Ten Commandments. In Holter's analysis, based on the fieldwork by Helen N. Nkabala (2012), the use of Kony's formulation shows that the *concept* of the Ten Commandments existed independently from the actual *text* of the commandments. While most scholars (and certainly churches) are likely to see the LRA's use of the Ten Commandments as unorthodox, the case illustrates important aspects of the social production of scriptural authority, opening up an opportunity to reflect on the significance of African biblical studies for the development of a cultural theory of reception. Although invited to honor Holter, I cannot contribute the kind of knowledge of African cultural practices that shines through in Nkabala's and Holter's works. Instead, I will continue my long-standing conversation with the honoree on hermeneutical and cultural theory, hoping that this would open a discursive space for other voices, better versed in actual African cultural practices, to join the interpretive discourse. Perhaps, in a lucky strike, this could prepare for a dialogue between mostly North Atlantic critical theory scholarship and African biblical scholarship.

From a theoretical point of view, the LRA's reception of the Ten Commandments poses several challenges. First, there is the relation between writing and power. Secondly, there is the paradox of stability and change of the Ten Commandments. Lastly, there is the issue of one group using the canon of another group, while launching a revolution against that group. Each of these are complex, requiring more than one theoretical perspective. I shall argue that the LRA recruited social dignity that had long been associated with the Ten Commandments. To see how this was possible, I piece together a theory of what I call the scriptural ecology of the LRA. This will elaborate on Holter's insight that the significance of Scripture is not at all defined exclusively by the semantic potential of its text.

Context

The LRA appeared in Uganda in the late 1980s as a guerrilla army emerging from the Acoli nation. According to a resolution by the United Nations Security Council (2016):

> [The LRA had] engaged in the abduction, killing, and mutilation of thousands of civilians across central Africa. Under increasing military pressure, Joseph Kony, the LRA leader, ordered the army to withdraw from Uganda in 2005 and 2006. Since then, the LRA had been operating in the Democratic Republic of the Congo (DRC), CAR [the Central African Republic], South Sudan and reportedly Sudan.

It is difficult to identify any consistent political target of the LRA, but the organization repeatedly asserts that it aims to rule society according to the Ten Commandments. It is estimated that the LRA had as many as three thousand soldiers in 2007. In 2005, Kony was charged by the International Criminal Court, and the LRA was later pursued by the military African Union Regional Task Force. Today, some experts claim that the army consists of some one hundred soldiers—but it is still deadly active. A 2017 news article from Uganda by Al Jazeera reporter Natalia Ojewska reports that the LRA had killed over one hundred thousand people to date and forced nearly two million to flee their homes. However, "the most distressing characteristic of the conflict was the fact that the LRA filled 90 percent of its ranks through the systematic forced-conscription of children" (Ojewska 2017).

This was the political and military context for Nkabala's fieldwork in 2008–2010 on the early years of the LRA. The general social and political context need not be detailed here with postcolonial processes rolling across the continent, tribal and nationalist conflicts playing out on several levels, and economic conditions (positive as well as negative) posing challenges to many African states. The overall religious context of the central parts of Africa is characterized by a millennium of Islamic presence in the north, centuries of (originally colonial) Christian presence in the south, and with interwoven indigenous religious traditions. One specific point in this connection is the frequently recurring motif of the biblical Moses as an iconic freedom fighter (Nkabala 2012, 63–64). The dignity thus ascribed to Moses would be the result of generations of cultural production performed by now anonymous agents on different levels of society and almost certainly with mutually irreconcilable interests and agendas—colonial and postcolonial alike. So, paradoxically, many would recognize the importance of Moses (and his commandments) and yet disagree on the precise social and political ramifications of this cultural icon.

Nkabala (2012, 70–91) conducted interviews that show that members of the LRA saw Kony as Moses—a liberator, a lawgiver, and a prophet. Her analyses also reveal how Kony modeled himself after portrayals of Moses in certain biblical Hebrew Bible passages (105–80).

Canons and the Production of Power: An Everyday View

The role of any scripture in the production of social power is a pressing issue. Today, throughout the Christian and Islamic worlds, Scripture is evoked to generate political momentum. There is nothing natural about this role of Scripture. It is the result of social and political struggles and processes starting already in antiquity, including the process whereby the Christian Bible became the charter for the early church (Horsfield 2015). It shows, to put it in the words of Wilfred C. Smith (1993, 18), how "Scripture is human activity." Mainstream biblical scholarship does not address the social production of scriptural authority with much theoretical depth. However, a few scholars have applied the critical theory of Pierre Bourdieu to the analysis of religion and scripture (Bourdieu 1977, 1990; cf. Urban 2003; Verter 2003). As argued by Jacques Berlinerblau (1999, 193–94), one advantage of Bourdieu's theory is that it goes beyond a "voluntaristic" concept of power, that is, the view that social power is generated by human intentions, so that a biblical author's *intention* to sanction a certain practice automatically *gave* popular legitimacy to that practice.

Berlinerblau (1999, 200) argues that human consciousness is not always aware of its own political interests. Bourdieu's (1977) concept of *doxa* describes the taken-for-granted presumptions that underpin everyday practice, what everyone knows without being conscious of it. Scripture becomes a conserving power reflecting and confirming common views on morals, social hierarchies, economy, and so forth. The social order supported by a canonical text is, therefore, rarely explicit in the semantics of that text; it resides in the implicit presumptions for using the text as Scripture. Applying this to the case of the LRA reveals the presence of cultural patterns that support Kony's claim that he should be seen as a Moses (Nkabala 2012, 63–64) or that the Ten Commandments should be seen as social foundation (Holter 2019). It also suggests that these patterns reflected and sanctioned social practices, hierarchies, and politics dominating the habitus in Kony's cultural context. One avenue for future research would be to identify and analyze such social practices in detail. Most of these would, of course, be classified as oral practices. These would contribute to cementing the *status* of Scripture, while keeping the perception of its content somewhat flexible.

Bourdieu's (1977, 1990) theory was based on observations of everyday practices within the Algerian tribe of the Kabyle and is useful for interpreting socially stabilizing roles of Scripture. However, it does not explain why it is possible to use an established Scripture to support a revolutionary movement. Paradoxically, the everyday theory also fails to explain the extreme durability of, for instance, the concept (not the text) of the Ten Commandments. After all, the social *doxa* across central parts of Africa changed dramatically over the last few centuries, but the dignity of the Ten Commandments seems to have remained. So, Bourdieu's everyday theory must be supplemented, first, with theories explaining extreme scriptural durability *and* change.

Durability and Change: Scripture as Cultural Strategy

In the introduction to the volume *Kanon und Zensur*, Aleida and Jan Assmann (1987) gave full attention to the *resilience* of canonical literature. They explained it as a product of three interconnected institutional strategies, namely, censorship (*Zensur*), curation of the text (*Textpflege*), and curation of textual sense (*Sinnpflege*). *Zensur* relates to the selection of certain texts as superb. *Textpflege* secures the verbatim preservation of that text, while *Sinnpflege* secures its continued relevance through constant reinterpretation. Canonicity reflects the continued, institutionalized collective *remembering* of the past.

The Assmanns have refined and elaborated on this theory several times (see J. Assmann and Hölscher 1988; J. Assmann 1992, 1995, 2000, 2015; A. Assmann 1999). The theory provides an attractive analysis of the social and institutional dynamics in one canonical community. It may explain both the endurance of the cultural icon of the Ten Commandments *and* the ability of their actual wording to change. This theory, though, does not explain why a competing social formation would take over the canonical scriptures of their enemies.

The cultural anthropologist Michael Carrithers (1992) argues that human cultural development tends to integrate the cultural production of preceding generations in its continued evolution, which explains why humans, who are biologically very similar, have developed vastly different cultures. In a related argument, the anthropological archaeologist Ian Hodder (2014, 2016) analyzed human dependence on *things*, arguing that physical items and the way humans use them, create path-dependency. Once an artifact is implemented as part of a cultural strategy, it tends to remain. According to Hodder (2012, 169, 105–12), "the tendency is always to find solutions that work within what we have."

Scripture could be seen as a cultural strategy in this sense (cf. Stordalen 2021). The cultural strategy of Scripture spanned millennia in the making. It required the invention of writing, the emergence of scribal culture, and the establishment of a market for written material. It required the socialization of individual agents (authors, editors, patrons of literature, text reciters), institutional agents, (schools, archives, libraries), and nonhuman agents (writing materials, spaces for consuming literature).[1] Since the majority of people were nonliterate (Schmidt 2015; cf. Rollston 2010), the function of writings as tools for social and cultural cohesion further required the emergence of oral practices and popular avenues that allowed the majority to be involved in doing the scriptures. Formats for such participation needed to be culturally crafted, socially rehearsed, and individually internalized. All these human, institutional, and nonhuman agents did not start interacting overnight. This cultural strategy emerged and transformed through slow processes with an inner dynamic, as is the pattern for cultural products (cf. Bennett 2010, 108–9).

The resultant complexity of the scriptural strategy worked towards new generations and subsequent cultures adapting rather than discarding

---

1. For all these, see Carr (2011, 45–46) and Van der Toorn (2007, 237–47).

it. This strategy of using written canons as a means for generating social identity originated in the Eastern Mediterranean from the second millennium BCE through the first millennium CE, spreading from Egyptian and Mesopotamian cultures via Greek and Hebrew societies to Christian, Manichean, and eventually Islamic religions. It kept transforming in the second millennium, for instance in Sikhism, Baha'i, or Mormonism (Stordalen 2021, 332–40). A similar slow buildup and transformation of the scriptural paradigm must have occurred in Africa—inspired first by the Qur'an and then the Christian Bible. By the time of the LRA, Scripture—once the cultural instrument of Islamic and Christian conquerors—had long been a natural, indigenous cultural strategy also in Africa.

Adaption and Ambiguity: Scripture as Cultural Icon

In the case of the LRA, it is relevant to consider the role of Scripture as *cultural icon* for exploring its ability for adaption. Theoretical approaches to cultural icons and iconicity seem to be currently underdeveloped (Parker 2012, 52–68). While there has been some research on the topic of iconic scriptures (cf. Watts 2013), a generally acceptable definition still seems to be lacking. It will suffice here to use the preliminary definition employed by a scholar of communication theory, Emily Truman (2017, 830). She defines a cultural icon as an item serving as a repository of shared values, an item with strong presence in popular culture, rooted in social contexts that contributed to its iconicity.

Truman describes cultural icons in terms of their form, function, and location. "[Cultural] icons are conceived of as 'things' that 'perform actions' in particular 'arenas'" (840). The precise significance of cultural icons tends to be assumed rather than explicitly defined (830–31), which leaves space for an ambiguity of sense. The ability of cultural icons to "change and shift with cultural context … enables them to embody anxieties and tensions about collective values, attitudes, and emotions in the contemporary moment" (843). Therefore, the precise significance of cultural icons is often contested.

Mechanics of Durability, Resilience, and Change: Canonical Ecologies

Taken together, the theoretical aspects above offer sufficiently complex perceptions of the mechanics of scriptural status, resilience, and change to interpret the case of the Ten Commandments in the LRA. To integrate these different perspectives into one coherent view of a particular scriptural moment, I employ the heuristic model of the *ecology* of canonical scriptures (Stordalen 2015, 2021; Stordalen and Naguib 2015, 28–37). The concept of ecology is used in a broad, symbolic sense (cf. Bal 2002). The point is to portray how different elements interplay and influence one another in the production of canonical authority—whether they be scriptural canons or canons of nontextual media (paintings, music, habits, etc.). Here is a list of items, institutions, and roles likely to appear in a canonical ecology:

First is *the canonical collection*. This formally recognized collection may be more or less closed. In addition, there is usually an *actual canon*, what people actually use and revere. As discussed by several contributions in Watts (2013), canonical collections, or parts thereof, may emerge as cultural icons.

Second are the canonical *media*. Formal canons usually come in some form of writ. Popular canons are often oral. Most actual Christian canons are made up of both, including traditions of what the Bible says, but also of rituals, morals, habits, and so on.

Third are canonical *agents* such as *authors*, the *canonical community* using the collection, and *canonical experts* (curators, commentators, interpreters). The agency and power of such experts is often hidden, since canonical discourse usually focuses on (the formal) canon.

Fourth, canonical experts are often associated with canonical *institutions*, and these may have their own agenda.

Fifth, *spaces* and *purposes for doing the canon* also play a role. Mainstream scholarship tends to see canons simply as texts and the use of canon as a matter of public or private reading for informational purposes. In that case, it makes little difference in what setting the canon is consumed. As opposed to this, theories of canonical performance are keenly aware of spaces of consumption. It makes a huge difference whether one hears the canon of classical music at home or at the opera. The space of the opera disciplines the audience with rules and tradition on how to listen, enriching them with communal musical experience—all of which are lacking in the home stereo experience. Similarly, reading or hearing Scripture in solitude is different from experiencing it in specific cultic settings or doing it in a social space.

Sixth, *ways of doing the canon*, the implementation of the canon, involves media like clothing, food, and social and moral action. These can be seen as secondary canonical media holding an augmented body of canonical knowledge and habitus, a pragmatic canonical commentary. To an audience that lives mostly in an oral world, these would be the *only* media in which people could do their scripture. Without these media, the canon would hardly be an authority for the populace. This is the part of the theory that has potential for further development in an African context. All kinds of popular practices, habits, memories, and sentiments—all usually neglected by conventional biblical scholarship—participate in the production of scriptural authority. In the case of the early LRA, these practices were not and can no longer be documented—and perhaps that is also less relevant now. But, as a case study, the use of the Ten Commandments in the LRA indicates the significance of popular practices for the production of scriptural authority.

Not all elements mentioned here will occur in all cases; every canonical ecology is unique, conditioned by spatial affordances, historical conditions, and traditions. Different instances in the ecology may employ different strategies.

Production of Power in the LRA Scriptural Ecology

I cannot offer an empirically based analysis of the production of power in the LRA scriptural ecology. Instead, I will sketch some theoretical perspectives presenting themselves in the aftermath of Nkabala's and Holter's analyses.

The *canonical society* of the LRA was in many ways extreme. It was an army with a large majority of children and teenagers and a few militant adult leaders. It was a community in sharp military engagement, which would strengthen a sense of in-group belonging and interdependence. It was a social formation of individuals likely to have been traumatized by experiences of combat and atrocities—before and during their life in the LRA. Again, this was a fairly small community, with no established civil institutions and little group tradition. All references to, say, religious tradition would involve traditions that belonged also to the enemies, which rendered the *interpretation* of religious heritage critically important. There were no independent religious experts to challenge Kony. Since many members were young and vulnerable, one must assume that there also was not much religious autonomy among lay members. All in all, this social formation offered an unusually potent opportunity for domination by a strong leader.

Since the production of canonical power is rarely "voluntaristic" (Berlinerblau 1999), the canonical ecology of the LRA need not have been premeditated by Kony and his sergeants. It may have emerged rather accidentally and been inspired, perhaps, by the spiritual predecessor Alice Lakwena. The LRA's scriptural strategy would have adapted and developed as the process went forth. Judging from Nkabala (2012, 70–91), the LRA's canonical ecology became rather untypical. The *canonical collection* was multimedial and never entirely closed. It included Kony's prophetic messages as well as biblical writ. The *canonical icon* of the LRA would appear to have been the Ten Commandments, but this was not simply a *text*. The LRA's "ten commandments" included the running religious and military instruction that Kony as lawgiver would receive from the spirit, but also the military and everyday practices that LRA soldiers would perform as a result. The main aim of the LRA was obedience. Anyone that did not follow or believe (this version of) the commandments would die or be destroyed (Nkabala 2012, 78–85). Nkabala does not indicate the existence of any specifically religious institution, but several ritual gatherings seem to have combined religious and military activities. Kony was able to occupy the roles of both author and chief interpreter of the canon. Subordinate religious experts were his military sergeants, again with Kony in a supreme position through his military rank and his prophetic ability to foresee what would happen in the battlefield.

Nkabala's material holds examples of LRA (ex-)leaders and soldiers performing the kind of reinterpretative and harmonizing *Textpflege* that the Assmanns refer to. But a more substantial strategy mirrored in her material is the use of the Ten Commandments as (an already existing) cultural icon—embodying "anxieties and tensions about collective values, attitudes, and emotions in the contemporary moment" (Truman 2017, 843). The LRA shared with neighboring religious communities the taken-for-granted assumption that there exists a set of divine commandments that could guide individuals as well as nations. The obvious assumption would be that the LRA adapted this icon from Christian tradition. But it is worth noting that the idea of a charter text revealed to Kony in the role of Moses, might also have collected dignity from Islamic notions of Moses as receiver of holy writ (Q2, 87, 136; Q6, 91, 154; Q19, 51). Once implemented, one must assume that the canonical ecology built up around this icon kept generating social credibility for the social *doxa* of the army.

As discussed by Holter (2019, see also 2003, 14–19, 85–92), already in the biblical sources, the concept of Ten Commandments was capable of accommodating textual variations—Exod 20, Deut 5, and the Samaritan versions of these passages are all somewhat different. Strictly speaking, none of them holds exactly ten "commandments" (or "words," as in the Hebrew text), but they are all presented as if they did so. The ambiguity of the actual text of the commandments would be represented in African societies not only by these different canonical versions, but also, by conflicting Pentecostal/Reformed versus Roman Catholic/Lutheran ways of ordering and counting the commandments. It is tempting to speculate that the number of commandments in the Ten Commandments in the Hebrew Bible reflected an oral mnemonic strategy corresponding to the number of human fingers. An oral setting would explain the tolerance for textual variation. Could it be that a similar status of the commandments in the oral-written continuum existed also in the African heritage and that this—along with Kony's claim to be a divine lawgiver—provided some sense of legitimacy to the altering of the commandments without disturbing their status as cultural icon? This seems to be a question worth exploring in future fieldwork!

Especially in the earliest years, identifying Kony as a Mosaic liberator gave the LRA social standing in the Acoli nation. This illustrates Assmanns' theory of Scripture being redefined through collective remembering. The construction of the religious leader as canonical *author* is uncommon in traditional Christian religion, but it resembles a typical strategy in revolutionary religious movements like Mormonism, Baha'i, or the Unification movement. The same strategy was used by the Prophet in Islam, and it was applied to Paul in early Christianity. Characteristically, the LRA kept claiming authority for a cultural icon that simultaneously supported the churches to which their military opponents adhered. Revolutions and new religions usually commence with the abolition of the core icons of the old regime. This move (which, again, need not have been premeditated) would deserve further investigation. Does it suggest we should see the LRA more like a reform than a revolution, attempting to appropriate structures of legitimation already present in society?

The most important area of further investigation would be a study of how the LRA canonical ecology worked for individual lay members in the canonical ecology. Nkabala (2012, 78–80) shows that there were ritual sessions organized around Kony's interaction with the spirit. In her 2009 article, Birgit Meyer argues that the experience of sharing significant events contributes to the making of social formation. In other words, the act of collective reception has a social performative dimension. Taking part in these sessions must have built a sense of togetherness also for the young soldiers of the LRA.

More dramatic performative aspects of social reception also relate to a point mentioned by both Nkabala (2012, 86) and Holter (2019, 4). The strict enforcement of Kony's instructions could mean the difference between life and death for young soldiers in the field. For instance, the commandment against smoking was very advantageous for guerilla warfare. This indicates that the soldiers of the LRA would be doing the canon of their ten commandments while fighting in the field—much like mainstream Christians are doing their versions of the canon when behaving according to specific morals or clothing in specific ways. Warfare was a *canonical medium*. In this ecology, abiding by Kony's ten commandments was a matter of life and death!

Most importantly, one should explore how the social production of everyday space (see Lefebvre 1991) contributed to confirming the status of the Ten Commandments. The abovementioned theories offer little in this respect, and they need to be supplemented as we move the focus away from the conventional media and ideologies towards the analysis of Scripture as human activity (Smith 1993).

Conclusion

Holter (2019) set out to demonstrate how a cultural *concept* may influence the reception of a text claiming to mediate that concept. This argument reflected an insight running throughout Holter's authorship, that is, the Bible is a phenomenon of the present as much as of the past, and a discipline naming itself biblical studies needs to take account of this. In so doing, the (past or present) semantics of the biblical text are not as all important as is usually taken for granted in the discipline.

This essay attempts to elaborate on that insight by arguing that the study of canonical texts, in actual use, needs to abandon both the conventional definition of canon as static and the conventional voluntaristic view of textual authority. Canons are much more than frozen collections of text, and canonical authority is not defined by scribal intentions. One must develop cultural as well as social categories for the analysis of canonicity. (This, I would argue, should be no less important for reading early Hebrew Scriptures than it is for the analysis of the Bible in Africa today, but that is a different discussion.)

Common perceptions and social enactment of the significance of Scripture precondition the perception of a text's cultural and social agency. Patterns of social hierarchy and domination are mirrored and reproduced as members of the scriptural ecology carry on doing the canon in their daily lives. Therefore, the above analysis did not explore specific concepts enshrined in the semantics of a given text. Rather, it pointed to the importance of the, mostly unconscious and nonthematized, presumptions about the world and human life that this version of the cultural icon was perceived to charter. An LRA believer might have thought that faith is warfare based on divine instruction. Obviously, the morally adequate response to such a conviction is not a lecture on the real contents of the biblical Decalogue. Hence, the role of biblical studies cannot be limited to exploring semantic and inner-literary dynamics of a text. Scholars need to understand the cultural dynamics of the Bible—past and present.

Works Cited

Assmann, Aleida. 1999. *Zeit und Tradition: Kulturelle Strategien der Dauer*. Köln: Böhlau.

Assmann, Aleida, and Jan Assmann. 1987. "Kanon und Zensur als kultursoziologische Kategorien." Pages 7–27 in *Kanon und Zensur*. Edited by Aleida Assmann and Jan Assmann. Munich: Fink.

Assmann, Jan. 1992. *Das kulturelle Gedächtnis: Schrift, Erinnerung und politische Identität in frühen Hochkulturen*. Munich: Beck.

———. 1995. "Text und Kommentar. Einführung." Pages 9–33 in *Text und Kommentar*. Edited by Jan Assmann and Burkhard Gladigow. Munich: Fink.

———. 2000. *Religion und kulturelles Gedächtnis: Zehn Studien*. Munich: Beck.

———. 2015. "Tradition, Writing, and Canonization: Structural Changes of Cultural Memory." Pages 115–32 in *The Formative Past and the Formation of the Future*. Edited by Terje Stordalen and Saphinaz-Amal Naguib. Oslo: Novus.

Assmann, Jan, and Tonio Hölscher. 1988. *Kultur und Gedächtnis*. Frankfurt: Suhrkamp.

Bal, Mieke. 2002. *Travelling Concepts in the Humanities: A Rough Guide*. Toronto: Toronto University Press.

Bennett, Jane. 2010. *Vibrant Matter: A Political Ecology of Things*. Durham, NC: Duke University Press.

Berlinerblau, Jacques. 1999. "Ideology, Pierre Bourdieu's Doxa, and the Hebrew Bible." *Semeia* 87:193–214.

Bourdieu, Pierre. 1977. *Outline of a Theory of Practice*. Cambridge: Cambridge University Press.

———. 1990. *The Logic of Practice*. Cambridge: Polity.

Carr, David M. 2011. *The Formation of the Hebrew Bible: A New Reconstruction*. Oxford: Oxford University Press.

Carrithers, Michael. 1992. *Why Humans Have Cultures: Explaining Anthropology and Social Diversity*. Oxford: Oxford University Press.

Hodder, Ian. 2012. *Entangled: An Archaeology of the Relationships between Humans and Things*. Chichester: Wiley-Blackwell.

———. 2014. "The Entanglements of Humans and Things: A Long-Term View." *New Literary History* 45:19–36.

———. 2016. *Studies in Human-Thing Entanglement*. Open Access. http://www.ian-hodder.com/books/studies-human-thing-entanglement.

Holter, Knut. 2019. "Thou Shalt Not Smoke: Content and Context in the Lord's Resistance Army's Concept of the Ten Commandments." *HvTSt* 75.3:art. 4997. https://doi.org/10.4102/hts.v75i3.4997.

Horsfield, Peter. 2015. *From Jesus to the Internet: A History of Christianity and Media*. Chichester: John Wiley & Sons.

Lefebvre, H. 1991. *The Production of Space*. Oxford: Blackwell.

Meyer, Birgit. 2009. "From Imagined Communities to Aesthetic Formations: Religious Mediations, Sensational Forms, and Styles of Binding." Pages 1–28 in *Aesthetic Formations: Media, Religion, and the Senses*. Edited by Birgit Meyer. New York: Palgrave Macmillan.

Nkabala, Helen N. 2012. *"There Is No Difference between Moses and Kony": A Critical Analysis of the Contextual Use of Some Old Testament Texts and Motifs in the Early Years of the Lord's Resistance Army*. PhD diss., School of Mission and Theology, Stavanger, Norway.

Ojewska, Natalia. 2017. "Can Ugandans Overcome Trauma of LRA's Violent Crimes?" *Al Jazeera*. 25 September. https://tinyurl.com/SBL3817b.

Parker, Mike. 2012. *Cultural Icons: A Case Study Analysis of Their Formation and Reception*. PhD diss., University of Lancashire, Preston.

Rollston, Christopher A. 2010. *Writing and Literacy in the World of Ancient Israel: Epigraphic Evidence from the Iron Age*. ABS 11. Atlanta: Society of Biblical Literature.

Schmidt, Brian B., ed. 2015. *Contextualizing Israel's Sacred Writings: Ancient Literacy, Orality, and Literary Production*. AIL 22. Atlanta: SBL Press.

Smith, Wilfred C. 1993. *What Is Scripture? A Comparative Approach*. London: SCM.

Stordalen, Terje. 2015. "Canon and Canonical Commentary: Comparative Perspectives on Canonical Ecologies." Pages 133–60 in *The Formative Past and the Formation of the Future: Collective Remembering and Identity Formation*. Edited by Terje Stordalen and Saphinaz-Amal Naguib. Oslo: Novus.

———. 2021. "The Production of Authority in Canonical Ecologies: A Cultural Paradigm and Accumulative Cultural Production." Pages 322–72 in *Levantine Entanglements: Cultural Productions, Long-term Changes and Globalizations in the Eastern Mediterranean*. Edited by Terje Stordalen and Øystein Sakala LaBianca. London: Equinox.

Stordalen, Terje, and Saphinaz-Amal Naguib. 2015. "Time, Media, Space: Perspectives on the Ecology of Collective Remembering." Pages 17–37 in *The Formative Past and the Formation of the Future: Collective Remembering and Identity Formation*. Edited by Terje Stordalen and Saphinaz-Amal Naguib. Oslo: Novus.

Toorn, Karel van der. 2007. *Scribal Culture and the Making of the Hebrew Bible*. Cambridge: Harvard University Press.

Truman, Emily. 2017. "Rethinking the Cultural Icon: Its Use and Function in Popular Culture." *Canadian Journal of Communication* 42:829–49.

United Nations Security Council. "Lord's Resistance Army." 7 March 2016. https://tinyurl.com/SBL3817c.

Urban, Hugh B. 2003. "Sacred Capital: Pierre Bourdieu and the Study of Religion." *MTSR* 15:354–89.

Verter, Bradford. 2003. "Spiritual Capital: Theorizing Religion with Bourdieu against Bourdieu." *Sociological Theory* 21.2:150–74.

Watts, James W., ed. 2013. *Iconic Books and Texts*. Sheffield: Equinox.

The Origin of the Griqua Prayer of Adam Kok III and Its Reception

Hendrik L. Bosman

Introduction

This contribution focuses on the religious and political contexts of the so-called Griqua Prayer—a contextual concern that resonates with the work of Knut Holter and with the title of this Festschrift. In his book *Contextualized Old Testament Scholarship in Africa*, Holter (2008, 11) describes the response of African Old Testament scholars to their interpretative context as the development of "a contextually sensitive scholarship which deliberately proceeds from and responds to the experiences and concerns of the African interpretative context." This contribution to honor Holter, a dear friend and an excellent colleague, sets out to describe the interpretative context of the Griqua Prayer when it was first recorded at the funeral of Adam Kok III in 1874. The essay also highlights the remarkable reception of this prayer by General Jan Smuts during the negotiation of the peace in the Palace of Versailles in 1919 after World War I and in 1940 during World War II when it was still uncertain whether the United States of America would join the Allied Forces against Germany.

The interpretative context pertinent to the Griqua Prayer consists of both the pervasive presence of the British Empire and the gradual encroachment of the Free State Republic on the Griqua settlement in Philippolis during the nineteenth century. Attention will also be paid to a second aspect of this interpretative context, that is, the appropriation of Christianity among the Griquas, as reflected in their church music and congregational life. In the conclusion, the reception of the Griqua Prayer by Smuts will be discussed in terms of his religious life as well as the context of the Versailles Peace negotiations in 1919. It will also be viewed in the context of the time of uncertainty of the 1940s' World War II, when Smuts was deeply worried whether the United States would join the Allies in their war against Germany.

Political Context of the Griqua Prayer

It is difficult to define who the Griqua were and how they came into being. Linda Waldman (2006, 176) points out that the name *Griqua* refers to "the indigenous Khoi residents of the Cape Colony in the 17th century called '#Karixurikwa' or 'Chariguriqua.'"

The missionary John Campbell (1815, 252–58) notes that, in August 1813, the inhabitants of Klaarwater (later renamed Griquatown), "being of mixed race, went by the name of Bastards, but having represented to the principal persons the offensiveness of the word to an English or Dutch ear, they resolved hereafter to be called 'Griquas' because they descended (for a part) from the Charniqua tribe." According to Karel Schoeman (1997, 18) "the Griqua proper, defined as the adherents to the Kok family, were favourable towards Cape Colony … and at best, neutral to the missionaries," while "the Khoi incomers, or Basters, as the group gradually came to be known, were loyal to the LMS (London Missionary Society) and not well disposed to the Colony, where they had experienced a good deal of discrimination."

The missionaries played a complex role in the political development and administration of the Griquas. Coenraad de Buys, a notorious adventurer, cautioned the Griqua in 1820 "to be aware of the Missionaries, for when they have brought you a little into their manners, they will send for more of their countrymen to take the rule over you" (Schoeman 1997, 98). On another occasion, De Buys warned the Griqua "that Missionaries only came to seek their property" (103).

The ambiguity of missionary influence in Griqua politics can be depicted as follows: Campbell commented in 1820 that, on the one hand, missionaries had to interfere as little as possible with the government of the Griqua (Schoeman 1997, 105–6). On the other hand, Dr. John Philip deliberately influenced the politics of the Griqua captaincies for more than two decades "to form a bulwark on the northern frontier, protecting the tribes of the interior against the incursions of the white farmers from the south while simultaneously guarding the Cape Colony against possible attack … from the north" (Schoeman 1997, 20–21).

In 1822, Philippolis was established as a mission station for the San people by Dr. John Philip of the LMS. After Adam Kok II was elected

"Kaptyn" of the Griqua in 1825, permission was granted in 1826 for the Griqua to settle in Philippolis. The pastoral and seminomadic Griqua were expected to settle down near the mission station and become agriculturalists who would contribute to the livelihood of the residents of the mission station (Schoeman 1997, 21–22).

As with many other frontiers, the Transgariep frontier (area to the north of the Orange River) between the different Griqua groups, that is, the British Empire, which governed the Cape Colony and the Boer settlers, was very unstable. After Adam Kok III was elected Kaptyn in 1837, a Griqua civil war broke out in 1838, but with British assistance, Philippolis was protected. Eventually, hostilities also broke out between the British and the Boer settlers, and with substantial assistance from the Griqua, the British defeated the Boers during the battle of Swartkoppies (April 1845) and the battle of Boomplaats (August 1848).

In the middle of the nineteenth century, the balance of power changed in the Transgariep. The Griqua Captaincy diminished, as the death of missionaries Philip and Wright led to the LMS losing much of its influence with the British authorities and with the Boer settlers gradually organizing themselves into an autonomous state (Schoeman 1997, 21). On February 23, 1854, the Bloemfontein Convention was signed by both the Boers of the Transgariep and the British Government. The preceding exercise led to the withdrawal of the British sovereignty from the area as well as the establishment of the Republic of the Orange Free State (Schoeman 1996, 279).

Serious attempts were made to maintain good relationships with the Republic of the Orange Free State. A case in point is the treaty between Captain Adam Kok III and President N. J. Boshof in 1856 that promised cooperation regarding the upholding of the law, the maintenance of order, peace and protection, and the promotion of commerce and religion with the goal of "the improvement and civilisation of both peoples" (Schoeman 1996, 279). An alarming increase in stock theft and property disputes between the Boers and the Griqua led to the decision to look for an unoccupied territory. Consequently, in 1859, Adam Kok III set out on an exploratory expedition ("Kommissietrek") to ascertain what route the Griqua should take to journey toward "Nomansland," which eventually became known as "Griqualand East."

On his return from the expedition to Nomansland, Adam Kok III called a meeting of his followers at the beginning of 1860 and gave a favorable report about the prospects of the unoccupied territory: "there were plenty of water [sic]. A good country to live in.... I said to my people if they will agree to it, I shall trek. The majority agreed to it" (Schoeman 2002, 236–37). It took more than one year to prepare for the migration from Philippolis to Nomansland because it is estimated that in 1861, "nearly half a million acres of land" were in Griqua possession and were to be sold according to its market value (Schoeman 2002, 238). Shortly before his death in 1875 in Griqualand East, Adam Kok III wrote that he "felt compelled to leave Philippolis" in 1861 due to the encroachment of the Republic of the Orange Free State to the north, that is, "the Boers," and being "surrounded by white men"; by the latter, he referred to the British in the Cape Colony to the south (Boezak 2019, 19):

> My reason for coming to this country (Nomansland) was that I saw no chance of me being able to stand as a Native against the Boers. I was surrounded by white men, and after long consideration I came to this conclusion: It was no longer right for me to remain where I was in that situation.

According to Samuel James Halford (1949, 99), it is estimated that about 2,000 Griqua left Philippolis with approximately 300 wagons and more than 20,000 herds of livestock. When one looks at the arduous route the Griqua took to Nomansland, one may well ask why the exploratory expedition recommended it. Halford explains that the Griqua chose the route over the steep Drakensberg Mountains to avoid passing through British territory and to avoid paying grazing and watering charges from local landowners.

Those who participated in this Griqua migration not only endured physical hardship due to extreme weather conditions like drought and harsh cold weather conditions, but also were continually harassed by cattle raiders like Nehemiah, one of the sons of Moshoeshoe I, king of the Basotho (Halford 1949, 100–101). It is possible that the Griqua Prayer was prayed before a skirmish between the Griqua under Adam Kok III and the Basotho cattle raider, Nehemiah, when the Griqua were in crisis, as they suffered a harsh winter season in the Drakensberg in 1862. There is no clear documentary evidence, but strong circumstantial evidence suggests that the Griqua Prayer originated during the 1862 migration to Nomansland because "little is recorded of the actual journey itself" (99). The severe winter conditions and the hostile encounters with the Basotho caused the Griqua to suffer tremendously and established a context that resonated well with the wording and the rhetoric of the Griqua Prayer (Ross 1976, 103). No other event during Adam Kok III's leadership was as traumatic as the agonizing trek from Philippolis across the unchartered Drakensberg Mountains, ending in Nomansland (Griqualand East).

When the Griqua eventually settled in Nomansland at the foot of Mont Currie, they built "a long narrow building, about 8 feet high, with sod walls and roof of thatch, unglazed openings for windows, and a door made of packing-cases." This building served as "a citadel, a place of assembly ... a day-school house ... a kraal for town-goats," and it was here that the Griqua "met for worship, conducted by lay officers of the church, from 1862 to 1869" (Halford 1949, 103). Willa Boezak (2007, 59) explains that the first building erected in Kokstad by the Griqua functioned both as a fort and as a church building, due to their "love for the Christian faith."

The death of Adam Kok III on December 30, 1875 "marked the end of the last independent Griqua community who was gradually pushed off their land until they had to accept the annexation of Griqualand East by the Cape Government" (Dedering 2010, 124; Boezak 2019, 37–38). During the funeral of Adam Kok III on January 2, 1876, his cousin Adam "Eta" Kok spoke the following telling words (Ross 1976, 133):

> We have laid in the grave a man you all knew and loved.... Take a good look into that grave. You will never look into the grave of another of our race.... There lie the remains of the one South African chief who never lifted arms nor fired a shot at a British soldier, though sometimes provoked beyond human endurance.

Religious Context of the Griqua Prayer

The unexpected death of the Philippolis missionary Peter Wright in 1843 led to a unique correspondence between the women of the Philippolis congregation and their sisters in Griquatown. In a letter dated May 20, 1843, the Griquatown women reached out to their counterparts in Philippolis and concluded their communication of sympathy and support with the quotation of a hymn by C. M. Hawes, with the heading "The duty of resignation" (Schoeman 2002, 174–75):

> We have right then to mourn over our loss as the children of Israel mourned the loss of their leader; but we have no right to murmur; we dare not find fault or say, Lord, why hast Thou done this? But may this be the language of each one's heart:

> 'Submission to the will, o God!
> We all to Thee resign,
>> Bowing before thy chastening rod
>> We mourn but not repine.
> It is the Lord should we distrust
>> Or contradict his will,
>> Who cannot do but what is just,
>> And must be righteous still.

It is significant that this hymn focused on submission to the will of God. Advocating resignation amid suffering and adversity played an important role in the communication between the two groups of Griqua women in the middle of the nineteenth century. Since theology and anthropology often form mirror images of each other, one could speculate that such an image of God would resonate within a patriarchal context where the submission of wives to husbands was taken for granted.

After being intimidated by Sir Harry Smith (then governor of the Cape Colony and former military commander in India) to make certain changes to the existing Maitland Treaty between the British and the Griqua, Adam Kok III wrote a letter to Dr. John Philip (LMS) and John Fairburn (journalist) in which he clearly saturates his rhetoric with nineteenth century missionary theology that provides evidence of his Christian education (Schoeman 1996, 121):

> Highly respected Sirs!—Whatever may have been the conduct of our forefathers in the government of this country, since I took the reins of government I have tried to maintain and promote peace. I owe this feeling not merely to my own disposition, but also to the Word of God, in which I had been educated from my youth, and which I trust has not only become the power of God unto salvation, but the rule of my conduct.... As a nation we owe almost everything to the Gospel and the efforts of the London Missionary Society for our present position and blessings, it may be said that we are what we are not by might or by power, but by the goodness of God.

After more than three decades, in 1855 the LMS withdrew from their mission station in Philippolis. The Griqua settlement became an independent Congregational Church with its own minister. It was soon able to manage its own church affairs and became financially self-sufficient (Schoeman 2002, 224). According to Robert Ross (1976, 76–77), the financial flourishing of the Griqua in Philippolis during the 1850s was due to the introduction of the merino breed into sheep farming. The new project enabled the production of quality wool that fetched high prices. It is indicative of a certain religious ethos that the increase in Griqua prosperity was utilized to become self-supporting as a congregation.

After almost two years of migration, the Griqua reached the foothills of the Drakensberg, close to Nomansland. It is recorded that they offered "prayers of thanksgiving" when they saw the "abundance of water and grass" (Halford 1949, 102).

In a pioneering study of Khoi-San religion, Boezak (2017b, 9; 2017c, 319) argues that the Khoi-San in South Africa "easily accepted Christianity" in view of an existing well-developed faith in God: "Jesus's miracles and virgin birth sounded like Heitsi-Eibib's," and "the power of the Holy Spirit" reminded them of the power ("n/um") that shamans received from the "Supreme Being" as a result of the dance of healing.

The notion of God-as-Father played a significant role in Khoi-San religion. It is also of special importance when interpreting the Griqua Prayer in its cultural context. The Khoisan believed that God (Tsui // Goab) will provide for all their needs, and this is clearly reflected in prayers for rain that formed part of the annual rainmaking ceremony, the "*guri#ab*" (Boezak 2017c, 106–10). One of the best examples of prayer for rain is the following prayer by a Nama shepherd recorded in 1881 by Theophilus Hahn (see Hahn 2000, 58–59):

> You, oh Tsui // Goab!
> Father of our forefather,
> Our Father!
> Let the raincloud stream
> Let our flock live
> Let us also live, please;
> For I am weak
> Of thirst
> Of hunger …
> Let me eat the fruits of the veld.
> Are you not our Father?
> Father of our forefathers
> You. Tsui // Goab?
> That we may worship You
> That we may honour You
> You, Father of our forefathers,
> You, our Lord—
> You, Tsui // Goab!

The Griqua National Anthem (originally in Dutch) resembles an evangelical church hymn from the nineteenth century in which the saving of the Fatherland is foremost. Worth noting is that it is combined with the joining of the (Griqua) people and the (British) sovereign in love—a telling example of an attempt to establish a hybrid identity between the Griqua people and the British sovereign (Hymn 1 in the *Songbook of Griqua National Church*):

God, eternally great and good,	*God eeuwig groot en goed*
We beseech thee, save	*Wij smeekend U behoedt*
Our Fatherland!	*Ons Vaderland*
Let the people and sovereign,	*Laat Volk en Zouwerein*
In love be joined;	*In liefd', verbonden zijn;*
O, bless big and small,	*O, zegen groot en klein,*
With generous hand.	*Met milde hand.*

In his discussion of the cultural heritage of the Khoisan, Boezak (2017a, 270) alludes to this hybrid and resistant religious identity: "Although the majority of Khoisan people today are devout Christians, many seem to long for earlier times when they could still freely practice their ancient religion."

Reception of the Griqua Prayer

Ross (1976, 138) and Boezak (2019, 38) cite what is possibly the earliest version of the Griqua Prayer:

Lord, save thy people.
Lord, we are lost unless thou savest us.
Lord, this is no work for children.
It is not enough this time to send thy son.
Lord, thou must come thyself.

Although Ross provides no specific context for the Griqua Prayer, he considers it significant enough to end his monograph on *Adam Kok's Griquas* with this prayer. The position of the prayer at the end of his book follows directly in the same paragraph after the poignant and prophetic eulogy at Adam Kok III's funeral by his cousin Adam "Eta" Kok (cited above). Boezak (2019, 38) also links the prayer with the funeral of Adam Kok III and adds that "they prayed in desperation."

The references above remain circumstantial evidence. Therefore, the initial context and circumstances of the Griqua Prayer are uncertain. Either it refers to the precarious position of the followers of Adam Kok III in Griqualand East in 1876, or it echoes a prayer delivered by Adam Kok III during a previous hazardous situation—of which there were many during the migration of 1862!

At least two receptions of the Griqua Prayer are quoted by Smuts, as noted by his biographer, Sir W. Keith Hancock (1962, 521), who says that throughout his life, that is, when the future looked hopeless, Smuts would then point out that it was time for the Griqua Prayer.

The first reception of the prayer by Smuts took place during the Peace Conference at the Palace of Versailles in 1919 after the conclusion of World War I. The two accounts of his reference to the Griqua Prayer are available. To comprehend what dire circumstances triggered Smuts's reference to the Griqua Prayer, some background information is required.

When World War I ended, a tense peace conference was held at the royal palace of Versailles, and Smuts played a prominent role in the difficult negotiations leading up to a peace treaty (Lentin 2010, 64–92). The victorious British and French suffered much during the war and wanted vengeance by squeezing as much reparation from the vanquished Germany as possible, while Smuts advocated a much more conciliatory formulation that would allow Germany's economy to be rebuilt (Cameron 1994, 80). One of Britain's top economists, John Maynard Keynes, agreed with Smuts, and they were both deeply worried by the formulation of the peace treaty, which, in their view, "breathes a poisonous spirit of revenge" (Steyn 2015, 96). During an after-dinner conversation with Keynes amid the deadlock between the Allies and Germany, Smuts told him that it was time for the Griqua Prayer and then gave a shortened version of it, asking "the Lord to come himself and not send his Son, as this is not a time for children" (Hancock 1962, 521; Skidelsky 1983, 373).

Unfortunately, even Sir Keith Hancock (1962, 521), the major biographer of Smuts, provides no great detail about the historical circumstances of this prayer other than: "He had once heard the story of an old Griqua chief who saw his tribe beset by great dangers and prayed," and in a footnote he provided the formulation of the complete prayer that corresponds exactly with the words of the prayer at the end of Adam Kok III's funeral. The brief description of the context, though, seems to allude to earlier traumatic events.

The second reception of Smuts's reference to the Griqua Prayer during the peace conference at Versailles in 1919 is found in an unlikely source.

Mary Hastings Bradley records the events of her 1921 safari to search for gorilla specimens. The latter were to be exhibited in the Africa Hall of the American Museum of Natural History in New York. During a meeting with Smuts, he told her about the difficult negotiations at the Paris Peace Conference in 1919 and at a certain point, Smuts again declared: "Now is the time for the Griqua prayer." According to Bradley (1922, 20–23), Smuts continued in a manner that provides more information than the recollections of Keynes and Hancock:

> Now there was a battle between the Griqua and the blacks ... and the Griqua came to God in prayer... in broken Dutch.... Blood will flow.... It will be a terrible thing. Now God, you be there. Come yourself. Do not send your Son. This is no place for children. Come yourself.

In the first volume of the diaries that she kept during World War II, another biographer of Smuts, Sarah Gertrude Millin (1944, 269) describes the following encounter in September 1940 with Smuts, who was the then Prime Minister of South Africa and later became a member of Winston Churchill's war cabinet:

> She [USA] will come in [join the Allies against Germany], believe me.... The war remains a serious affair.... Did I tell you the prayer of Adam Kok, of the Griquas? He said "God, in spite of all our prayers, we keep on losing battles. Tomorrow we are fighting a big battle. We need help badly, God, and there is something I must say to you: the battle tomorrow will be a most serious affair. It will be no place, I can tell you, for children. I ask you, therefore God, not to send your Son to help us. Come yourself!"

This third reception relates the Griqua Prayer to Adam Kok III and adds to the older version of the prayer that several battles were lost despite previous prayers. This addition was probably precipitated by Smuts's own war context in 1940 when the Allied forces suffered one defeat after the other and were desperate to see the United States of America join the battle against Germany.

Despite a concerted effort to establish how Smuts came across the Griqua Prayer, no clear evidence has been found to clarify the matter. It could be that the remarkable Griqua leader, Abraham AS Le Fleur I, had contact with Smuts during the first few decades of the twentieth century. Le Fleur was well known as a prolific writer of letters and petitions to British royalty and to political leaders in South Africa and Britain to further the Griqua cause (Dedering 2010, 122; Boezak 2019, 96–102).

The last issue that requires more attention is why Smuts chose to quote the Griqua Prayer when the future looked bleak. Since Smuts seldom attended church services, many people, especially his political opponents, criticized him for being irreligious. Piet Beukes, who knew Smuts well, did extensive research on his religious convictions, and his comments are pertinent to this study. According to Beukes (1994, 9), Smuts "was deeply religious and saw and experienced the hand of God in his own life and in the destiny of mankind [sic] as a whole…. Wherever he went the small Greek New Testament could be found on his bedside table." Furthermore, he concluded that Smuts's religion was embedded in "an inner conviction," as well as his "personal contact with God through thought and prayer, but with little formality or dogma" (24).

Conclusion

This essay focuses on the African interpretative context, an important aspect of Holter's research for several decades. The subheadings have referred to both the political and the religious African contexts of the Griqua Prayer, thus acknowledging Holter's concern with context.

The history of the Griqua is riddled with tragic examples due to the expansion of the British Empire and the establishment of the Orange Free State Republic in the middle of the nineteenth century. Edmund Gibbon was correct with his declaration that the "history of empires is the history of human misery"—all possible contexts within which the Griqua Prayer would be most appropriate (see Brendon 2007, xix).

During the nineteenth century, being a Griqua "was also about being Christian," in close conjunction with "recognition by the Colonial authorities," feeding their pervasive ambiguous identity (Waldman 2007, 23). This ambiguous cultural and religious identity seems to be illustrated when the Griqua Prayer is interpreted within both its Christian and Khoisan contexts (Besten 2006). In postcolonial terminology, one could interpret the Griqua Prayer as a form of hybridity and of resistance—relating Christian and Khoisan religion, while resisting the encroachment of imperial power.

The remarkable reception history of the Griqua Prayer, manifested by the frequent references to it by Smuts, is an indication of how the plight of a marginalized group in South Africa had an impact on the frame of reference of an international statesman to serve as an example of perseverance amidst seemingly hopeless conditions. Due to Smuts's enigmatic relationship with religion and the uncertainty of how he came across the prayer, the jury is still out on the appropriateness of his making repeated references to the prayer in dire circumstances. The fact remains, however, that the Griqua Prayer made an indelible impression on Smuts.

To gain insight into the bigger picture of how Christianity was enculturated within an empire, we are well served to study smaller snapshots of how marginalized religious communities such as the Griqua endured, suffered, and survived through prayer and Bible reading. The discussion of the Griqua Prayer did not only attempt to explain the origin and the reception of the prayer, but it must also be seen as an acknowledgment of the ongoing suffering of the Griqua due to Boer expansionism and British imperialism that triggered the prayer. This contribution attempted to do some justice to Holter's required "contextually sensitive scholarship" by taking much-neglected Griqua interpretative contextual concerns seriously (Holter 2008,11).

Works Cited

Beukes, Piet. 1994. *The Religious Smuts*. Cape Town: Human & Rousseau.
Besten, Michael P. 2006. "Transformation and Restitution of Khoe-San Identities: AAS Le Fleur I. Griqua Identities and Post-Apartheid Khoe-San Revivalism (1894–2004)." PhD diss., Universiteit Leiden.
Boezak, Willa. 2007. *So Glo Ons! Die Khoe-San van Suid-Afrika*. Kimberley: ProPrint.
———. 2017a. "The Cultural Heritage of South Africa's Khoisan." Pages 251–71 in *Indigenous Cultural Heritage: Rights, Debates and Challenges*. Edited by Alexandra Xanthaki et al. Leiden: Brill.
———. 2017b. "Die Gewonde God: 'n Teologie-etiese Besinning, Veral vanuit Khoisan-Perspektief." *HvTSt* 73.4:1–12.
———. 2017c. *Struggle of an Ancient Faith: The Khoi-San of South Africa*. Cape Town: Bidvest Data.
———. 2019. *Griqua Hero: The Remarkable Life of AAS Le Fleur*. Cape Town: Bidvest Data.
Bradley, Mary H. 1922. *On the Gorilla Trail*. New York: Appleton.
Brendon, Piers. 2007. *The Decline and the Fall of the British Empire, 1781–1997*. New York: Knopf.

Cameron, Trewhella. 1994. *Jan Smuts: An Illustrated Biography*. Cape Town: Human & Rousseau.
Campbell, John. 1815. *Travels in South Africa, Undertaken at the Request of the Missionary Society*. 3rd ed. London: Black & Parry.
Dedering, Tilman. 2010. "'We Are Only Humble People and Poor': AAS le Fleur and the Power of Petitions." *SAHJ* 62:121–42.
Hahn, Theophilus. 2000. *Tsui-Goam: The Supreme Being of the Khoi-khoi*. Repr., London: Trübner.
Halford, Samuel James. 1949. *The Griquas of Griqualand: A Historical Narrative of the Griqua People: Their Rise, Progress and Decline*. Cape Town: Juta.
Hancock, W. Keith. 1962. *Smuts: The Sanguine Years 1870–1919*. Cambridge: Cambridge University Press.
Holter, Knut. 2008. *Contextualized Old Testament Scholarship in Africa*. Nairobi: Acton.
Lentin, Antony. 2010. *General Smuts South Africa: The Peace Conferences of 1919–23 and Their Aftermath*. London: Haus.
Millin, Sarah Gertrude. 1944. *World Blackout: War Diaries 1939–1940*. London: Faber & Faber.
Ross, Robert. 1976. *Adam Kok's Griquas: A Study in the Development of Stratification in South Africa*. Cambridge: Cambridge University Press.
Schoeman, Karel, ed. 1996. *Griqua Records: The Philippolis Captaincy, 1825–1861*. Cape Town: Van Riebeeck Society.
———. 1997. *The Mission at Griquatown 1801–1821*. Griquatown: Griekwastad Toerisme Vereniging.
———. 2002. *The Griqua Captaincy of Philippolis, 1826–1861*. Pretoria: Protea Book House.
Skidelsky, Robert J. A. 1983. *John Maynard Keynes: Hopes Betrayed 1883–1920*. London: Picador.
Steyn, Richard. 2015. *Jan Smuts: Unafraid of Greatness*. Johannesburg: Jonathan Ball.
Waldman, Linda. 2006. "Klaar gesnap as Kleurling: The Attempted Making and Remaking of the Griqua People." *AS* 65:175–200.
———. 2007. *The Griqua Conundrum: Political and Socio-cultural Identity in the Northern Cape, South Africa*. Bern: Lang.

Shembe's Sermon on the Mount: African Reception of the Bible as African Biblical Hermeneutics

Gerald O. West

Introduction

Ubusisiwe onesihawu ngoba naye uyohawukelwa mhlazane ehlelwa usizi, ngoba usizi akusilo olwamunye olwabo bonke abaphansi komthunzi welanga. Noma usakhululekile namuhla osizini kusasa uzokubhajwa nawe njengoba bebanjwe izolo.
Blessed is he who shows pity because he too will be pitied on his day of sorrow, because misfortune is not something for one person alone but for everyone under the sun. Even if you are content today, tomorrow misfortune will bog you down, just as others were yesterday.
—Elizabeth Gunner, *The Man of Heaven and the Beautiful Ones of God*

Even the marginally biblically literate will hear the resonance between the words of Isaiah Shembe quoted above and Matthew's "Sermon on the Mount" (Matt 5:1–11): "Ba busisiwe aba nesihau, ngokuba baya kuhaukelwa" (IBaible 1893); "Blessed are the merciful, for they shall receive mercy" (5:7 NASB). The attentive Bible reader/hearer will also note that Shembe is doing something different here. Shembe begins this "izeluleko" (counsel/advice) with the fifth beatitude, not the first, and he elaborates on this beatitude extensively, establishing intratextual biblical connections with other parts of the Sermon on the Mount and other biblical texts. Yet Shembe is clearly invoking the nine "busisiwe's" (blessed's) of Matt 5:3–11, for he, too, has a sequence of nine "ubusisiwe's" in his "counsel ... at Ekuphakameni" ("the place of spiritual upliftment," and the name of Shembe's headquarters of the Nazareth Baptist Church in about 1916), on the March

4, 1932. Shembe is invoking, adopting, and adapting the voice of Jesus, as he hears it in Matthew's version of the Sermon on the Mount.

"The Words of Counsel of Shembe at Ekuphakameni, March 4, 1932" is recorded in the notebooks of the faithful amaNazaretha, encouraged by Shembe to harness the colonizers regime of writing for their own resisting purposes (Gunner 2002, 22). The original isiZulu has been translated and published in Irving Hexham's (1994, 34–36) *The Scriptures of the amaNazaretha of EkuphaKameni* and in Elizabeth Gunner's (2002, 98–103) *The Man of Heaven and the Beautiful Ones of God*.

As I have analyzed Shembe's biblical hermeneutics in some detail already (West 2016, 244–317), this essay only reflects on how Shembe's version of Jesus's Sermon on the Mount in Matthew contributes further to our understanding of Shembe's biblical hermeneutics. It also assists us in understanding how this particular neoindigenous interpretive instance contributes to African biblical hermeneutics more generally. What is particularly significant about the hermeneutics is that it is an early colonial era form of African biblical hermeneutics. Shembe offers us insights into what it means, as Tinyiko Maluleke (1997, 15) prompts us to ask, for Africans "to have" the Bible. Taking the well-known African anecdote about African land[1] as an incisive and summative account of missionary-colonialism, what it means for Africans to have the Bible remains an instructive question. Early African receptions of the Bible offer analytical insights into the historical and sociophenomenological trajectories of what it means for Africans to have the Bible.

My own work on Shembe locates him as a particular prophetic manifestation of "a whole network of African evangelical activity existing outside or on the very edge of the mission churches," shaped by "whole corridors of influence, based on language corridors—Sotho in this case—sweeping down from the Transvaal, deep into the Orange River Colony, and bypassing formally or hegemonically instituted associations and power structures" (Gunner 2002, 21). Shembe's response, argues Gunner, to "the radical dislocation of the early twentieth-century city, from which many who joined his church in the second decade of the century were seeking respite" was "to recreate the social group and to resituate its mental and

---

1. The anecdote says, "When White people came to our country they had the Bible and we (Africans) had the land. They (Whites) said, 'let us pray,' and we (Africans) closed our eyes to pray. At the end of the prayer, they (Whites) had the land and we (Africans) had the Bible" (Maluleke 1997, 15).

material spaces" (23). Within an unstable context constituted by sustained transactions between traditional Nguni culture, European colonialism, missionary Christianity, and an emerging industrial capitalism—over whose political and economic dimensions Shembe and his followers exercised little control—Shembe constructed and attempted to control the religio-cultural dimension and in so doing, tried to reassert some sense of religio-cultural and political-economic integrity (and so identity) (Muller 1999, 26–53). Put differently, he was forced "to create his own world and to inhabit it" (Vilakazi, Mthethwa, and Mpanza 1986, 10). He constructed this world, in Carol Muller's (1994, 19) analysis, by combining "his deep knowledge of the mission Bible with his respect for Nguni traditional ways, and with some knowledge of commodity capitalism." Reconfiguring these resources, she continues, "he constituted a new and hybrid regime of religious truth … in competition with ideologies of the state and the Christian mission."

Our colleague Knut Holter, whose work we honor in this collection of essays, has made a substantial contribution to our understanding of African biblical scholarship. For example, he has provided detailed analytical archives of established and emerging African biblical scholarship (Holter 1996, 2000a, 2002). Holter (2000b, 2008) has shared his own understandings of the relationship between Africa and the Old Testament. He has also made a way for others through a variety of edited projects. In the latter, he has made it easier for African biblical and theological scholars' voices to be heard more widely (Getui, Holter, and Zinkuratire 1999; Holter 2006). Ever attentive to the agenda of African biblical scholarship rather than following in the more familiar footsteps of his Northern/European colleagues, Holter has been a servant of African biblical scholarship. Discerning our African biblical landscape alongside us, Holter has also journeyed with us into the early reception of the Bible by African interpreters in his recent work. Holter offers us a careful analysis of how Africans in the South African colony transacted with missionary-colonialism, particularly the Norwegian missionary component (Holter 2009). In his most recent published work on "the encounter between the Norwegian missionaries and the Zulus," Holter (2020, 41) gives special attention to how missionary-colonial processes of "scripturalisation" and "Bible translation" reflect "a democratizing process, allowing the founding texts of the church to be read by ordinary readers outside the control of missionaries and other religious specialists." It is this work of his that summons me to return to Shembe.

My essay follows a three-part argument. First, I argue that Shembe's biblical hermeneutics is a reciprocal hermeneutics of reception in which the Bible becomes African, while Shembe becomes biblical. Second, I analyze the hermeneutical contours of Shembe's appropriation of the voice of Jesus in Matthew, alongside his more familiar appropriation of the voices of Moses, David/the Psalmist, and Paul. Third, I offer some reflections on how Shembe's "sermon-on-the-mount izeluleko" contributes to African biblical scholarship.

A Reciprocal Hermeneutics of Reception

In his remarkably detailed account of *Religious Encounter and the Making of the Yoruba*, J. D. Y. Peel Peel (2000) provides a perceptive analysis of African appropriations of Christianity (and Islam). "The challenge of producing a cogent account of religious change in any part of Africa over the last two centuries," he argues, "lies in how to blend the three narrative themes which are pertinent to it: missionary endeavor, colonization, and the endogenous development of African societies" (2).

Like Peel, my own work has emphasized the third narrative, the endogenous development of African societies, arguing that neoindigenous African biblical reception should be "conceived of less as the outcome of an encounter between two cultures or religions than as a matter of cognitive and practical adjustment to changes in social experience, within the terms of an existing [African] paradigm" (Peel 2000, 3; see West 2016, 7–8). However, following Peel, I have also recognized that this emphasis on the African narrative strand should not neglect the narrative power of Christianity and the Bible, both "vehicles of trans-historical memory" (Peel 2000, 9).

Among the resources Shembe uses to reconstruct African community amid the ravages of colonialism is the Bible he steals from those who stole African cattle (Hexham and Oosthuizen 1996, 224–28; West 2016, 252–60). And among the biblical resources Shembe uses is the rhetorical voice of Jesus, appropriated together with other biblical voices in order to build his community, Ibandla lamaNazaretha (the church/congregation/community of the Nazarites). In so doing, Shembe himself is reciprocally appropriated by the voice of Jesus. Shembe appropriates and he is appropriated by the rhetorical contours of Jesus's voice. Shembe hears the Bible. Not only has Southern African neoindigenous aural-oral culture prepared Shembe to be attentive to the aural-oral dimensions of biblical texts

(Draper 1996, 2002), Shembe's particular gift is his remarkable capacity to "hear" and appropriate the rhetorical shape of biblical voices.

As I have noted (West 2016, 243), Shembe resembles other neoindigenous African biblical interpreters, such as the West African William Wade "Prophet" Harris (1865–1929) of Liberia. He is "a trail-blazer and a new kind of religious personage on the African scene, the first independent African Christian prophet" (Bediako 1995, 91). The preceding quotation comes from Kwame Bediako, an African theologian, who is ever attentive to the intersection between the indigenous and the Christian. Prophet Harris is significant for Bediako because, like Shembe, he is "a paradigm of both a non-Western and essentially primal apprehension of the Gospel and also of a settled self-consciousness as African Christian, which is uncluttered by Western missionary controls" (91–92). Speaking of Prophet Harris's appropriation of the Bible, Bediako draws on the work of David Shank, who suggests that Prophet Harris was not so much concerned about "belief in" the truth of the Bible, but "participation in" the truth of the Bible. It was not so much "a question of what Moses saw, or what Elijah did, or the words and works of Jesus as reported in the Bible"; it was more "a question of involvement—as with the ancestors, the living dead—with Moses, with Elijah, with the Archangel Gabriel, and supremely with Jesus Christ" (Shank 1980, 466; cited in Bediako 1995, 104).

Shembe locates himself, as I have argued (West 2016, 297–298, 301, 307), alongside the biblical Moses, David (the Psalmist), and Paul. Moses and Paul are particularly important in Shembe's project of community construction. In his teachings, Shembe appropriates the didactic rhetoric and so the authority of Moses the lawgiver addressing the people of Israel (in the Pentateuch), but he also appropriates the rhetoric and so the authority of Paul the apostle addressing the churches he has established (in the epistles, both Pauline and Deutero-Pauline). In each case, Shembe, like Prophet Harris, engages with these biblical ancestors with whom he shares the task of rebuilding community. Neither traditional African tribal authorities nor missionary Christianity were able, in his view, to construct a "moral ethnicity" for African peoples (Cabrita 2008). It is the Bible and its ancestral figures that provided Shembe with potentially resonant neo-indigenous interpretive resources for constructing both a "virtuous polity" and a "theological nationalism," "a discourse that, to legitimate itself, posited national unity on ideas of virtue, healing, peacefulness, repentance and submission to Jehovah's dictates" (Cabrita 2009, 609, 618, 620–24). As Joel Cabrita goes on to argue, "Shembe's ministry was preoccupied with both 'mourning for [his] scattered nation' (Papini and Hexham 2002, 62) and working tirelessly to re-found it upon the new social possibilities exemplified by his Nazaretha communities" (625).

In this essay, I add the ancestral figure and the ancestral voice of Jesus to those of Moses, David (the psalmist), and Paul. With respect to Jesus, by far the most common aural form heard and appropriated by Shembe is the parable genre of Jesus, though he does also adopt and adapt the sayings form, of which Shembe's "sermon on the mount" is an extended example. As with Moses and Paul, Shembe appropriates primarily the rhetorical form itself rather than the didactic-theological content within this form. I use the term *didactic-theological* because it accurately reflects Shembe's emphasis on teaching/instructing/giving advice within a theological frame. While the rhetorical framing is biblical, the didactic-theological content is a sacred hybrid of the neoindigenous and the biblical, a blend unique to the congregation-community building project of Isaiah Shembe.

The Rhetorical Contours of Jesus's Voice

While Shembe's community is attentive to the gospel genre in its many rhetorical elements—recounting stories of Isaiah Shembe (and the later Johannes Galilee Shembe and Amos Shembe) (Hexham and Oosthuizen 2001) that include Jesus-like birth stories, call stories, angelic visitation stories, vision stories, healing stories, and death stories (Mdluli n.d.; Mpanza n.d.; Hexham and Oosthuizen 1996; Gunner 2002, 24–26, 56–63, 139–203; Papini and Hexham 2002, 179–220), it is the rhetorical voice of Jesus which is most fully appropriated by Shembe himself.

The parable form is the most evident voice-of-Jesus-related genre among the oral history sources attributed to Isaiah Shembe. After Shembe's death in 1935, his son, Johannes Galilee Shembe, appointed Petros Musawenkosi Dhlomo to become the congregation's recorder-archivist, concerned as he was "to collect all kinds of testimonies about the work of his father" (Becken 1996, xi). This Dhlomo did collecting, collating, and typing oral and written testimony from 1949 onwards (Becken 1996, xi–xiv; Gunner 2002, xii, 27–28). Included in the manuscript collations of Dhlomo are a series of parables told by Shembe. In my book *The Stolen Bible*, the title of which is borrowed from Shembe's "The Parable of the Liberating Bible," I offer a detailed analysis of Shembe's parable form and its didactic-theological content (West 2016, 252–60). My emphasis here is on the other rhetorically recognizable genre used by Jesus that Shembe appropriates, namely, the saying form in its most memorable example, the Beatitudes. The so-called Sermon on the Mount is the focus of this section of my essay. In this case, we are fortunate that Gunner has preserved what is probably the original isiZulu version translated by Londa Shembe (Hexham 1994, 34–36, §20) and by Gunner herself (Gunner 2002, 98–103). As already indicated, the isiZulu version allows us to hear, with Shembe, the resonances with Matthew's Sermon on the Mount.

Shembe is attentive to the larger literary unit initiated by the Beatitudes (Matt 5:3–12), followed by other forms of didactic discourse (5:13–7:27), collectively known as the Sermon on the Mount (Waetjen 2017, 58–103). As my analysis will show,[2] it is likely that Shembe's "sermon-on-the-mount izeluleko" echoes Matthew more than Luke, though there may be Lukan elements in it. While it is unlikely that Shembe would have been familiar with the designation Sermon on the Mount, the spatial setting of Jesus with which the biblical text begins (Matt 5:1–2), stating that Jesus "went up on the mountain," may well have resonated with Shembe's own mountain, "the holy mountain of Nhlangakazi in Ndwedwe, northwest of Durban," where "from 1915 onwards, members of the AmaNazaretha gathered in pilgrimage every January to pray, to dance in worship, to listen to Shembe and his ministers and to be healed" (Gunner 2002, 23). Shembe may well have expected those he addressed to make the spatial connection.

Like Matthew's Jesus, Shembe begins his discourse with the beatitudes, the blessings. Like Matthew's Jesus, Shembe uses the third person form of address (not Luke's second person). Eight of Matthew's nine Beatitudes are formulated in the third person plural; only the ninth uses the second person plural (Waetjen 2017, 60). All nine of Shembe's are third person singular: "ubusisiwe o-" (Gunner 2002, 98, §§1–9). Given that Shembe is addressing a congregation, it is somewhat strange that he adapts the plural of the biblical text: "Ba busisiwe aba-" (IBaible 1974), choosing to use the singular instead. It should be stated, though, that Shembe's language is gender-neutral, so translations that use "he" are thus inaccurate and unfortunate. Clearly Shembe's addressee is the individual member, for following the pronouncement of blessing in the third person singu-

---

2. I here acknowledge the contributions of the students who reflected on this example of Shembe's biblical hermeneutics with me: Njabulo Sandile, Patrick Makhanya, Linda Mathutha, Mduduzi Mkhize, Simphiwe Thokozani Mthembu, Khanyisani Charles Mthethwa, Sabelo Mthimkhulu, and Simlindele Qotoyi.

lar + causal conjunction formula (in most cases), Shembe goes on (again in most cases) to address the individual member directly, in the second person singular (as is the case in the example cited at the beginning of this essay). Scholars have perhaps overstated Shembe's communal orientation and, in so doing, failed to recognize what members themselves consider to be a significant emphasis on the life of faith of the individual member of iBandla lamaNazretha (West 2015).

In summary, the nine beatitudes of Shembe (plus a later tenth) begin formulaically like Matthew, but then go on in all but two cases to elaborate the causal connection with a focus on the kind of reciprocity required of those who are "blessed." I have used Gunner's (2002, 98–101) isiZulu version, followed by her translation:

1. Ubusiswe onesihawu.
Blessed is he who shows pity.

2. Ubusiswe ongahambi emikhondweni yababi.
Blessed is he who does not walk on the paths of the wicked.

3. Ubusiswe obopha amaxeba abalimele.
Blessed is he who binds the wounds of the injured.

4. Ubusiswe osula izinyembezi zabadabukileyo.
Blessed is he who wipes away tears of the sorrowful.

5. Ubusisiwe lowo ongahloli izono zabanye.
Blessed is he who does not pry into the sins of others.

6. Ubusisiwe lowo ongabeki indlebe yakhe kwabahlebayo.
Blessed is he who does not tune his ears into malicious gossip.

7. Ubusisiwe ohamba emgwaqweni engayicijisile inhliziyo yakhe, ukulalela okubi kwabanye.
Blessed is he who travels the road and does not make his heart razor sharp by taking in the evil ways of others.

8. Ubusisiwe ofisa ukuthethelela, kunolahlayo.
Blessed is he who seeks forgiveness rather than gives up.

9. Ngisho lokhu ukuthi ubusisiswe umuntu oqoqa izoni ekonakaleni kwazo.

I say this, blessed is the person who gathers up sinners in their sinful state.

10. Ubusisiwe onenkolo ebekezelayo.
Blessed is he who has a patient faith.

Herman Waetjen (2017, 60), commenting on Matthew's Beatitudes, offers an insightful analysis of what Jesus and, in part, Shembe are doing with the Beatitudes and the discourse that follows them. Comparing Matthew's Beatitudes with the Old Testament/Hebrew Bible tradition of beatitudes, Waetjen argues that "in contrast to the makarisms of the Old Testament, he does not pronounce blessedness on the experience of God's benevolence [e.g., Ps 32:1–2] or on the benefits of divine grace [e.g., Ps 40:4]," nor are his Beatitudes "requirements for entry into 'the kingdom of God.'" Instead, continues Waetjen, "Jesus' Beatitudes affirm his disciples in their spiritual and psychological state of being and acting by assuring them that they are divinely privileged in their active participation in God's Reign. Each beatitude enunciates a blessedness for this life here and now." What Shembe makes even more apparent, for it is implicit in Matthew's Sermon on the Mount, is that participation in God's (and Shembe's) congregation-community requires reciprocity. Each of Shembe's beatitudes includes an explicit element about the importance of reciprocity. While addressed to the individual, the individual is summoned to participate in the building of the congregation-community through reciprocity.

The first beatitude, cited at the beginning of this essay is a clear example, as is the summative statement in the penultimate section of Shembe's "sermon-on-the-mount izeluleko" (Gunner 2002, 102–3):

28. Ukuthanda kwenhliziyo yakho kugcinele umzalwane wakho. Ngokuba uma uthi uthanda uNkulunkhulu, uzonde umzalwane wakho, uyazihleba. Ungamthanda kanjani uNkulukulu ungazange umbone kodwa ube uzonda ombonayo? (1 Johani 4 v 20).
28. Let your loving heart focus itself on your neighbour. Because if you say you love God and you hate your neighbour, you are simply backbiting yourself. How can you love God whom you have never seen, but you hate the one whom you have seen? (1 John 4 v 20).

Here Shembe provides his disciples with a biblical warrant for faithful reciprocity. Earlier in the "sermon-on-the-mount izeluleko," he offers his disciples a local African warrant. The context is the ninth beatitude, following which Shembe affirms the person who in the midst of personal adversity, nevertheless, seeks out "abadukileyo emkhondweni wokulunga bedukele ebubini. Uyathokoza kakhulu uNkulunkulu ngomuntu onjalo" ("those who have strayed from the path of righteousness and strayed into wickedness. Such a person always pleases God greatly"; Gunner 2002, 35, §10). Immediately following this declaration of the ninth beatitude, Shembe continues to elaborate, this time using images from their common cultural context (Gunner 2002, 98–99):

> 11. Udumo lwenyanga yokwelapha, alukho kwabaphilayo, lukulabo abagulayo ebasindisileyo ngokwelapha uyobongwa izihlobo zalowo obegula.
> 11. A doctor's fame as a healer does not come from the healthy, it comes from those sick whom he has rescued and cured; it is the friends of the sick who will praise him.

However, though the image of the "inyanga" is drawn from the local religio-cultural context, the theological logic hearkens back to Jesus, who rebukes the Pharisees (in Matthew's version, but see also Mark 2:17 and Luke 5:31) when they criticize Jesus's disciples for eating "with the tax collectors and sinners" (Matt 9:11). In his rebuke, Jesus invokes the image of the "physician" (Greek ἰατρός); inyanga (isiZulu) [IBaible 1974]): "But when Jesus heard this, he said, 'It is not those who are healthy who need a physician, but those who are sick'" (Matt 9:12). Shembe does not stop here. He continues, immediately, to establish a theological logic of reciprocity (Gunner 2002, 98–101):

> 12. Kunjalo-ke kumuntu obutha izoni, azigone esandleni sakhe. Ngakho-ke ngathi yisoni kanye nazo sezisindile ezonweni, uyabongwa uNkulunkulu lowo muntu, azuze umqhele ongabuniyo.
> 12. So it is for a person who gathers up sinners and cradles them in his hand. He is a sinner like those he has saved from sin—and such a person will be praised by God, having earned the crown of glory.

> 13. Njengenyanga yokwelapha, abanini bomuntu ogulayo bayiholela genhliziyo emhlophe, ngokuba isindisile isihlobo sabo. Yiba nesihawu nawe uzohawukelwa ngomuso.
> 13. Just as it [is] for a doctor that heals, the relatives of the sick person pay him gladly because their relative is cured. You must show compassion so that they are merciful to you on the morrow.

Resistant Reciprocity

Having heard the voice of Jesus, it becomes clear now why Shembe begins his beatitudes by adapting the order of Matthew's Jesus. Shembe begins with the fifth beatitude (Matt 5:7): "Blessed are the merciful, for they shall receive mercy"/ "Ba busisiwe aba nesihau, ngokuba baya kuhaukelwa" (IBaible 1974). The theological logic of reciprocity implied by this beatitude is then elaborated by Shembe in his "sermon-on-the-mount izeluleko."

The Beatitudes of Jesus are not elaborations of each other, except in the case of the eighth and ninth. Shembe takes up the reiterative rhetorical device of Jesus evident in how the ninth beatitude elaborates on and, so reiterates, the eighth (Matt 5:10–12) and extends this rhetorical device so that his entire "sermon-on-the-mount izeluleko" could be understood as an elaboration on his reordered first beatitude, as Shembe slowly constructs a didactic-theological argument concerning reciprocity. Shembe appropriates the rhetorical formula of Matthew's Jesus, using it to draw out a particular theological ethic. What is one aspect of Jesus's didactic-theological argument becomes for Shembe an extended didactic-theological emphasis.

Shembe makes a theological argument in his "sermon-on-the-mount izeluleko" for "a patient faith" / "onenkolo ebekezelayo" (see above), with each person contributing to the building of a resilient congregation-community shaped by reciprocity. Such a person is blessed indeed and so is the congregation-community they constitute.

Re-membering African Biblical Studies

Not only has Shembe, like many other Africans (including the Norwegian missionary baptized "Isak" fifty years later), seized and appropriated reading and writing from their would-be masters (Holter 2020, 45–47); Shembe has also stolen their Bible. Having stolen the Bible from those who stole African cattle, as his "The Parable of the Liberating Bible" narrates (Hexham and Oosthuizen 1996, 224–28; West 2016, 316), Shembe re-members the Bible, using the missionary-colonial tools of reading and writing (Gunner 2002, 17, 22; West 2016, 249–50), guided by the rhetorical voices of the Bible's great teachers, whether Moses, David (the psalmist), Paul, or Jesus.

My analysis of Shembe's re-membering of the voice of Jesus, whether the parables or the sayings, confirms the various elements of Shembe's biblical hermeneutics I have previously identified (West 2016, 244–317). What Shembe's appropriation of the voice of Jesus adds to our understanding—and more work needs to be done—is a clear recognition of a spirituality of resistance within an African colonial context.

Shembe hears Jesus speaking specifically to his disciples, ensuring that each of them understands the kind of congregation-community that is being built. Shembe's "sermon-on-the-mount izeluleko" is a remarkable piece of reiterative rhetoric, re-membering, reminding, and reconstituting, as it unfolds. Significantly, in his "sermon-on-the-mount izeluleko," Shembe overtly cites (in terms of biblical book, chapter, and verse) a number of the other major voices of the Bible besides Jesus's, including David's (the psalmist) and Paul's, as well as a number of other minor voices, including Job, Solomon (Proverbs), and John (1 John). Using the summative voice of Jesus, Shembe weaves these biblical voices into a clear and coherent summons to a spirituality of reciprocity, which is also, of course, a politics of reciprocity within a colonial context.

Postcolonial African biblical scholarship, including my own, has perhaps been too adamant about the sociopolitical dimension of African colonial era interpretation, neglecting its spirituality of resilience and/as resistance (see the perspective of Nkosinathi Sithole, cited in West 2015). There can be no doubt, as Holter (2020, 49–50) confirms, that Shembe's biblical hermeneutics is a resistance hermeneutics. However, what is also clear is that Shembe's stealing and appropriation of the missionary-colonial Bible is more than an instrumentalist use of the Bible as an anticolonial strategy; Shembe and his congregation-community recognize within the ancestral voices of the Bible not only resources with which to negotiate the missionary-colonial reconfiguration of African society but also substantive spiritual resources with which to reassemble a resilient and/as a resistant *African* community.

African biblical scholarship, Shembe reminds us African biblical scholars, must be partially constituted—re-membered—by the lived faith of the communities of African Bible users we serve. While much of Western biblical scholarship may bracket the lived faith of those who use the Bible in their contexts (though Holter is not among them), African biblical scholarship must not.

Works Cited

Becken, Hans-Jürgen. 1996. "The Oral History of the Ibandla lamaNazaretha." Pages ix–xxii in *The Story of Isaiah Shembe: History and Traditions Centered on Ekuphakameni and Mount Nhlangakazi*. Edited by Irving Hexham and G. C. Oosthuizen. Lewiston, NY: Mellen.

Bediako, Kwame. 1995. *Christianity in Africa: The Renewal of a Non-Western Religion*. Edinburgh: Edinburgh University Press; Maryknoll, NY: Orbis.

Cabrita, Joel M. 2008. "A Theological Biography of Isaiah Shembe, c.1870–1935." PhD diss., Faculty of Divinity, University of Cambridge.

———. 2009. "Isaiah Shembe's Theological Nationalism, 1920s–1935." *JSAS* 35:609–25.

Draper, Jonathan A. 1996. "Confessional Western Text-Centred Biblical Interpretation and an Oral or Residual-Oral Context." *Semeia* 73:59–77.

———. 2002. "'Less Literate Are Safer': The Politics of Orality and Literacy in Biblical Interpretation." *AThR* 84:303–18.

Getui, Mary N., Knut Holter, and Victor Zinkuratire, eds. 2001. *Interpreting the Old Testament in Africa: Papers from the International Symposium on Africa and the Old Testament in Nairobi, October 1999*. New York: Lang.

Gunner, Elizabeth. 2002. *The Man of Heaven and the Beautiful Ones of God: Writings from Ibandla lamaNazaretha, a South African Church*. Leiden: Brill.

Hexham, Irving. 1994. *The Scriptures of the amaNazaretha of EKuphaKameni: Selected Writings of the Zulu Prophets Isaiah and Londa Shembe*. Translated by Londa Shembe and Hans-Jürgen Becken. Calgary: University of Calgary Press.

Hexham, Irving, and G. C. Oosthuizen, eds. 1996. *The Story of Isaiah Shembe: History and Traditions Centered on Ekuphakameni and Mount Nhlangakazi*. Vol. 1. Sacred History and Traditions of the Amanazaretha. Lewiston, NY: Mellen.

———, eds. 2001. *The Story of Isaiah Shembe: The Continuing Story of the Sun and the Moon*. Vol. 3. Lewiston, NY: Mellen.

Holter, Knut. 1996. *Tropical Africa and the Old Testament*. Oslo: University of Olso.

———. 2000a. "Old Testament Scholarship in Sub-Saharan African North of the Limpopo River." Pages 54–71 in *The Bible in Africa: Transac-

tions, Trajectories, and Trends. Edited by Gerald O. West and Musa W. Dube. Leiden: Brill.

———. 2000b. *Yahweh in Africa: Essays on Africa and Old Testament*. New York: Lang.

———. 2002. *Old Testament Research for Africa: A Critical Analysis and Annotated Bibliography of African Old Testament Dissertations, 1967–2000*. New York: Lang.

———. 2006. *Let My People Stay! Researching the Old Testament in Africa; Report from a Research Project on Africanization of Old Testament Studies*. Nairobi: Acton.

———. 2008. *Contextualized Old Testament Scholarship in Africa*. Nairobi: Acton.

———. 2009. "Did Prince Cetshwayo Read the Old Testament in 1859? The Role of the Bible and the Art of Reading in the Interaction between Norwegian Missionaries and the Zulu Elite in the Mid-Nineteenth Century." *OTE* 22.3:580–88.

———. 2020. "Isak—the Son of the Rainmaker—and the Bible: An Example of Resistance Hermeneutics in Zululand around 1870." *JTSA* 166:41–51.

IBaible. 1974. *IBaible eli iNgcwele*. Repr., Cape Town: Bible Society of South Africa.

Maluleke, Tinyiko S. 1997. "Half a Century of African Christian Theologies: Elements of the Emerging Agenda for the Twenty-First Century." *JTSA* 99:4–23.

Mdluli, S. n.d. *Umlando kaIsaiah Shembe*. Inanda, Durban.

Mpanza, Mthembeni. n.d. *UShembe NobuNazaretha*. Inanda, Durban.

Muller, Carol Ann. 1994. "Nazarite Song, Dance and Dreams: The Sacralization of Time, Space and the Female Body in South Africa." PhD diss., University of New York.

———. 1999. *Rituals of Fertility and the Sacrifice of Desire: Nazarite Women's Performance in South Africa*. Chicago: University of Chicago Press.

Papini, Robert, and Irving Hexham, eds. 2002. *The Catechism of the Nazarites and Related Writings*. Vol. 4. Lewiston, NY: Mellen.

Peel, J. D. Y. 2000. *Religious Encounter and the Making of the Yoruba*. Bloomington: Indiana University Press.

Shank, David. 1980. "A Prophet for Modern Times: The Thought of William Wade Harris, West African Precursor of the Reign of Christ." PhD diss., University of Aberdeen.

Vilakazi, Absalom, Bongani Mthethwa, and Mthembeni Mpanza. 1986. *Shembe: The Revitalization of African Society*. Johannesburg: Skotaville.

Waetjen, Herman C. 2017. *Matthew's Theology of Fulfillment, Its Universality and Its Ethnicity: God's New Israel as the Pioneer of God's New Humanity*. London: Bloomsbury T&T Clark.

West, Gerald O. 2015. "Layers of Reception of Jephthah's Daughter (Judges 11) among the AmaNazaretha: From the Early 1900s to Today." Pages 185–98 in *Reception History and Biblical Studies: Theory and Practice*. Edited by William John Lyons and Emma England. London: Bloomsburg T&T Clark.

———. 2016. *The Stolen Bible: From Tool of Imperialism to African Icon*. Pietermaritzburg: Cluster.

Part 3
Justice in Context

Moving beyond the Text as Slogan: Reading Gen 19 in the Context of LGBTIQA+ Lived Realities in African Faith Contexts

Charlene van der Walt

Encountering the Text as Slogan and the Reality It Informs

The Gen 19 Sodom and Gomorrah narrative, as it is commonly referred to, is often used in contemporary African faith communities to condemn LGBTIQA+ people as an abomination before God. The narrative is also used to label same-sex love as unnatural, un-Christian, and un-African. Although I employ the term *African* throughout the essay to broadly situate the argument contextually, I do not mean by this that I consider Africa to be a homogeneous context or landscape. In line with the deeply contextual work developed by the scholar honored in this volume, Knut Holter, I am deeply aware of the rich and diverse sociocultural, political, and religious differences across African societies and that the statuses of African peoples differ based on gender, class, race, ethnicity, religion, age, and sexual orientation. More specifically, most of the work described in the essay refers to East African and Southern African contexts.

Within the preceding context, Gen 19 is often drawn on anecdotally within ethical debates and discussions in African faith communities as a clear textual example of God's negative judgment of LGBTIQA+ people and those who navigate gender, desire, and love outside of the hetero-patriarchal binary directive:

"It is about homosexuality."
"It is about how homosexual acts are an abomination that will be punished by God."
"It shows you why God hates gays."

"It is about this thing that should not happen between men, and God hates it."

The above are but some of the standard answers to the foundational question that is used by the Ujamaa Centre when appropriating a contextual Bible study methodology that aims to guide those engaging the biblical text in the process of moving from social-consciousness to critical-consciousness (or text-consciousness), namely: "What is this text about?"[1]

In this contribution, I aim to reflect on the ongoing process of the Ujamaa Centre in collaboration with a number of faith, civil society, and NGO partners to develop contextual Bible study resources.[2] These body of theology resources aim to capacitate African faith leaders and LGBTIQA+ believers and activists to assist African faith communities to become spaces of radical hospitality and inclusion to all those in the African context known by the derogatory term Izitabane.[3]

Hanzline Davids, Abongile Matyila, Sindi Sithole, and Charlene van der Walt (2019, 10) appropriate queer methodology to unpack the

---

1. The Ujamaa Centre for Biblical and Theological Community Development and Research at the School of Religion, Philosophy, and Classics at the University of KwaZulu-Natal regularly conducts workshops on an invitational basis on the African continent. The thematic areas addressed in these workshops are determined by the communities inviting the Ujamaa Centre, and the aim is always to employ contextual Bible study resources to foster greater conscientizing, transformation, and liberation of the poorest or marginalized.

2. When it comes to developing resources to address the intersection of faith, gender, and religion in the African context, some of our key civil society or NGO partners are Inclusive and Affirming Ministries (IAM), Gay and Lesbian Network Pietermaritzburg (GLN), The Other Foundation, Global Interfaith Network (GIN), and ACT Ubumbano. For more information on IAM and the resources that they have developed, see https://iam.org.za/ For more on GLN, see https://gaylesbian.org.za/. For more on The Other Foundation and the resources that they have produced, see http://theotherfoundation.org/. For more on the GIN, see https://gin-ssogie.org/ For more on ACT Ubumbano, see https://www.actubumbano.org/.

3. The Ujamaa Centre has five thematic areas: body theology, which explores issues related to embodiment; bread theology, which reflects on socioeconomic issues; earth theology, which focuses on environmental justice; people's theology, which engages community activism; and public theology, which reflects on the public role of faith and religion. The praxis reflection offered in this contribution aims to contribute to ongoing work in the area of body theology.

process of reappropriating terms such as Izitabane.[4] The harsh and derogatory term is used in the African context to name and shame LGBTIQA+ people and in the process leads to stigmatization, exclusion, and violence committed against queer African bodies. The authors reflect on how terminology employed in African settings to describe or name LGBTIQA+ people illustrates something of the sense-making and meaning-making process used in local communities when trying to grapple with a phenomenon or reality that is outside or counter the dominant ideal, construction, or understanding. They also show how the stability of constructions of normalcy is maintained through derogatory naming and terminology that strip the Other of humanity. To reflect on the precarity of African Izitabane in a comprehensive way, it is important to reflect on the dominant ideological underpinning that informs normative constructions of sexuality and gender and how these constructions remain stable through acts of surveillance, othering, exclusion, and discrimination.

The foundational ideology on which dominant notations of normalcy are based is heteropatriarchy. Heteropatriarchy derives from the conceptual combination of two foundational societal ideologies, namely, compulsory heterosexuality or heteronormativity and patriarchy. Heteronormative discourse describes reality primarily and exclusively from the position of the heterosexual. Within the heteronormative, there is only space for heterosexual experiences, constructions, and realities. Consequently, no other alternatives are tolerated.

Heteronormativity strategically combines with patriarchy to form heteropatriarchy. Feminist theorists termed the system of male dominance, patriarchy, to conceptually frame how men benefit from their "privilege, power and authority [that] are invested in masculinity and the cultural, economic and/or social positions" (Cranny-Francis et al., 2003, 15; Thatcher 2011, 26).

Within this system, bodies are divided into the strict binary of male versus female based on essentialist biological sex characteristics. Through customs and belief systems, bodies are sexed and gendered into the dominant and normal sexual orientations, and what these bodies ought to

---

4. We deliberately choose to reappropriate a term used to describe and shame LGBTIQA+ people in the African context to reshape the meaning and intent of terminology born in an African setting. We believe that this approach contributes to the development of indigenous terminologies and theoretical frames to speak to the lived reality of sexual and gender diverse African people.

desire is strictly prescribed. Izitabane bodies experience violence because they embody sex, gender, and sexuality differently from the prescribed heteropatriarchal norm. They counter the heteronormative insistence that biological sex, gender expression, and sexual orientation should align.

To maintain and protect the stability of heteronormativity, those who are gender nonconforming or who somehow do not fit the bill prescribed by the framework of heteronormativity have to be policed, put under scrutinizing surveillance, or at its most extreme, corrected or annihilated. In South Africa, homophobic rape is one of the most violent acts perpetrated against queer bodies in general and black lesbians in particular in an attempt to maintain heteronormative stability. Heteropatriarchy further informs dominant ideas about masculinity, family, marriage, and citizenship, and it often functions as a stimulus for social exclusion and discrimination discourse on LGBTIQA+ in an African faith context.

Religious communities in Africa play a significant role in maintaining heteropatriarchy, and faith often does violence against LGBTIQA+ bodies (West, Van der Walt, and Kaoma 2016, 1–8). The intersection of static notions of African culture and exclusivist religious positionalities, deeply informed by uncritical biblical appropriations, foundationally informs the exclusion of Izitabane in the African context. Culture and religion, which are deeply informed by sacred scriptural engagement, maintain the seeming stability and normalcy of fixed binary gender and sexuality constructions, and continue to stabilize heteropatriarchy. Sanctioned heteropatriarchy is based on how the Christian Bible is read and interpreted. Heteropatriarchy is often informed by exclusivist practices of biblical interpretation and finds expression in citing proof texts that often lead to exclusion, discrimination, and violence (Van der Walt 2017a, 20). The Bible is often employed as an external source document that somehow contains answers or rules and prescriptions that inform correct ethical behavior as well as right contemporary conduct. This approach ignores the lived contextual reality of contemporary interpreters and makes light of the contextual gap between the world of and behind the text and the complex reality that interpreters currently navigate. Much of Holter's work, as an Old Testament scholar, focuses on the African contextual landscape and explores the gap between the world of the biblical text and the interpretative landscape of contemporary African interpreters (e.g., Holter 2006, 377–92). Informed by foundational insights from Latin American liberation theology and underpinnings from feminist theory, contextual

Bible study, as a methodology employed by the Ujamaa Centre, appropriates a deeply contextual see-judge-act methodology.

Theoretical Underpinnings Informing Life-Affirming Interventions

Although religion and biblical interpretation profoundly form part of the strands of oppression of LGBTIQA+ in the African context, as shown in the argument above, we are also deeply aware of the liberating potential that responsible and accountable Bible engagement and religious communities of care hold for the poor and marginalized (Schüssler Fiorenza 1988, 3–17; West 2006, 307–36). Holter's (2016, 209–21) reflection on the notion of the poor in ancient Israel and contemporary African contexts has enhanced ongoing related work being developed at the Ujamaa Centre. The position of faith and religion concerning sexual reproductive health and rights is contested.

In the next part of this contribution, I reflect on some of the foundational theoretical underpinnings and key leanings that inform the contextual Bible study methodology and approach, as championed by the Ujamaa Centre. I will further narrow the focus of the argument by reflecting on the implication of drawing on this methodology in the context of LGBTIQA+ lived realities at the intersection of gender, sexuality, culture, and religion in Africa. In the final part of the essay, these discussions will lead to a reflection on a Bible study that remains under continued development through the process of ongoing praxis reflection by the Ujamaa Centre. The latter endeavors to engage the Bible beyond remembered or politicized slogans to deep critical contextual engagement that is aimed at conscientization, liberation, and transformation.

See-judge-act is the praxis cycle employed by the Ujamaa Centre (West 2016b, 135–47). The lived reality of a particular marginalized community or population, as they understand it, is the starting point of the "see" moment of the praxis cycle, and it informs the epistemological orientation of the approach. The approach takes seriously the embodied contextual lived reality of those often deliberately silenced or preferably who should be unheard.[5] It is important to note that the experiential and thematic agenda is not determined primarily by the socially engaged biblical

---

5. Arundhati Roy makes the poignant observation that there is indeed no such entity as the voiceless but systemic power dynamics that rather deliberately silences or preferably shuts out the cries of the poor and marginalized. Roy made this distinction

scholar or critical readers of the Bible. The impetus for a contextual Bible study process develops rather organically from the needs of communities most affected and impacted by situations of injustice. When engaging LGBTIQA+ lived realities in the "see" part of the praxis cycle, the aim is to reflect on the embodied lived realities of LGBTIQA+ in a diversity of African settings. Thus, the texture of work done in the South African context differs dramatically from that done in other African countries where same-sex sexuality remains criminalized. I am, however, not arguing that South African Izitabane navigate a carefree existence due to constitutional protection. It is indeed well known that the South African constitution takes a progressive stance on gender, sex, and sexual orientation, and this finds pertinent expression in the Bill of Rights.[6] However, the Izitabane in South Africa experience prejudice and sexual discrimination based on their expression of gender identity and sexuality. There is a far-reaching disconnect between the South African constitutional position on sexual diversity and the embodied lived reality of LGBTIQA+ people in the African context (Van der Walt 2019, 221). As already noted though, the reality in other parts of the African continent remains more dismal where same-sex sexuality is criminalized. Those suspected of same-sex intimacy are victimized, ostracized, and often left vulnerable and destitute in the face of blackmail, manipulation, fear, and violence.

The "see" or community consciousness moment in a contextual Bible study process encourages those participating to engage critically with violence, injustice, and dehumanization within their local embodied context. Rather than focusing on homosexuality as an issue, the "see" moment aims to animate and amplify LGBTIQA+ people's narratives and reflect on the embodied lived realities navigated by African Izitabane. The insistence on drawing on narrative is informed by insights developed from partnering with African feminist scholars and those associated with the work of the Circle of Concerned African Women Theologians.

Where it is possible and safe to do so, we invite African Izitabane to share their narratives or experiences in such a way as to give body, name, and face to what remains a mere topic of discussion for many within African faith communities. Despite positive experiences of support and solidarity voiced by LGBTIQA+ who share their narratives during a contextual

---

during her acceptance speech of the Sydney Peace Prize in 2004. For a full version of the speech, see the *Sydney Morning Herald*: https://tinyurl.com/SBL3817d.

6. Section 9, Bill of Rights in the South African Constitution.

Bible study process, the complexity of representation remains an issue that warrants ongoing critical reflection. To my mind, it cannot be the task or responsibility of African LGBTIQA+ people who are already situated in a precarious position to educate or move those not willing to engage sexual and gender diversity by performing their pain in story form. Setting up brave spaces for mutual vulnerability and sharing remains imperative as we journey with faith communities to greater inclusion.[7] Rather than constructing LGBTIQA+ sexuality as an issue of concern or topic for discussion for African church leaders and faith communities, the greater imperative seems to be developing spaces and vocabulary to enable faith communities to grapple with the embodied reality of sexuality and sexual-reproductive health rights in general. Rather than being a burden, it seems LGBTIQA+ people are a gift to African faith communities when cracking open space for conversation that will allow more bodies to matter.

After an in-depth contextual engagement, the praxis cycle moves on to the "judge" or critical-consciousness moment where interpretative communities slowly and deliberatively engage the biblical text. The contextual Bible study process aims to slow down the textual engagement by having those participating read and, carefully and collectively, reread the biblical text. Unlike contemporary notions of speed and productivity that are so often praised and sought, the contextual Bible study process deliberately slows the process down. In that way, readers are allowed to truly encounter one another and the text as they are guided through a process that enables interpretative communities to grapple with contemporary questions and ethical concerns, while they navigate the intricacies and nuances of the biblical text. This phase draws on insights from biblical scholarship by using both literary-narrative and sociohistorical modes of analysis to identify and read with marginalized voices in, under, above, and behind biblical texts. In line with these insights, Holter (2011, 377–89) makes a compelling argument about the importance of historical critical scholarship for African interpretative communities. These ancient biblical voices become the dialogue partners for contemporary marginalized communities, as the text functions as a dynamic reflective surface (Van der Walt 2015, 57–75; 2017b, 117–132; 2018, 170–86; Van der Walt and Terblanche 2016, 176–94). The interaction between the ancient text and

---

7. Boonzaaier and Van der Walt (2019, 95–110) explore the contours and complexities of co-creating transformative spaces through dialogue.

contemporary reader creates space for the development of moral imagination, as Martha Nussbaum (1999) has proposed.

Dynamic and often uncomfortable spaces are constructed with care to facilitate a dynamic engagement where the first reality of life is brought into dialogue with the second reality of biblical texts, as argued above. Fundamentally, the first two movements of the praxis cycle aim to empower communities to "act" collaboratively and with imagination to address situations of injustice, marginalization, and violence. However, a central philosophy of the Ujamaa Centre is that change is a process, not an event, and therefore, however costly, hard, or complicated the thematic area or complex the community that we partner with, we remain committed to the process and open to its surprising unfolding. I hope to illustrate something of this commitment in the final part of this contribution where I offer the contextual Bible study of Gen 19 as an example of the Ujamaa Centre's work on LGBTIQA+ lived realities in the African context and part of an ongoing dynamic praxis reflection process (West and Van der Walt 2019, 109–18; West, Van der Walt and Zwane 2021, 5–23).

Developing Faith Resources to Address Homophobia and Hate Crimes in the African Context

As stated at the outset of this contribution, the reception history of Gen 19 in African contexts is often considered straightforward. According to many, discussion is unnecessary, as Gen 19 is about God's condemnation of homosexuality. The Ujamaa Centre began using Gen 19 as a focus text as part of its work in the area of gender-based violence in the late 1990s. Work that developed into the so-called Tamar Campaign started from reading the story of the rape of Tamar in 1996 (West and Zondi-Mabizela 2004, 4–12). The focus on gender-based violence led to the development of contextual Bible study resources exploring several intersectional areas of interest, including the rape of men (West 2015, 235–61). Genesis 19 was chosen because it named the reality of male rape and because it was so widely accepted as an anti-homosexuality source text. It was hoped that in the process of engaging with the passage, it would be possible to have broader discussions on LGBTIQA+ lived realities, especially when contrasting queer love and desire with homophobic violence and male rape.

The Gen 19 Bible study has undergone numerous revisions considering these shifts in focus and aim. In a workshop conducted in Kenya in November 2019, as part of a three-stage training process funded by the

Arcus Foundation in which we worked with pairings of local LGBTIQA+ activists and church leaders from five African countries (South Africa, Kenya, Tanzania, Mozambique, and the Democratic Republic of Congo), we used the following version to enable conversations about the difference between contemporary understandings of consensual same-sex love and intimacy and sex as violence.[184]

Practically, a contextual Bible study-facilitated process implies a movement between small group reflections and engagement and plenary discussion that enables collective reflection. Ideal small groups consist of between five–seven participants who engage the questions, as outlined below, in a facilitated process to read and reread the biblical text slowly. The contextual Bible study questions are constructed to guide contemporary readers through the see-judge-act movement, as outlined above. The following questions enable this movement when reading Gen 19:

1. Listen to Gen 19:1–13. This story has often been used to address the issue of homosexuality. In groups of two, share how this story has been used to speak about homosexuality in your context.
2. Let us study the story more carefully. This story is part of a larger story that begins in Gen 18. The story begins with three men visiting Abraham. Read Gen 18:1–8. How does Abraham receive these strangers?
3. On the same day, in the evening, two of these strangers leave Abraham's home and journey toward Sodom (18:16). Reread Gen 19:1–3. How does Lot receive these same strangers (now referred to as angels) who were earlier received by Abraham?
4. Reread Gen 18:1–8 and Gen 19:1–3. Compare these texts. In what ways is the hospitality that Abraham and Lot offer similar?
5. The men of Sodom, in contrast to both Abraham and Lot, do not receive the strangers/angels with hospitality. Instead of offering hos-

---

8. Compare this most recent version with the earlier versions of the Bible study to see some of the results of continuous collective critical praxis reflection. West (2016a, 186–88) shares some critical reflections on earlier versions, and West, Van der Walt, and Zwane (2021, 5–23) illustrate the benefits to the interpretative process when expanding the narrative frame to include Gen 18 as part of the contextual Bible study process. These processes of revision illustrate something of the organic collaboration between readers with a diversity of interpretative resources. Revisions and adjustments are not only the work of trained readers or biblical scholars, but they are the collective labor of those who join the interpretative process.

pitality, they offer violence. Reread 19:4–5. Why do they choose to receive these strangers by knowing/raping them?
6. What is Lot's status in the city of Sodom? Reread 19:9. What does his status among the men of Sodom tell us about why the men of Sodom threatened to rape him?
7. In Gen 18, the hospitality of Abraham causes the visitors to include Sarah in the blessing (18:9–10). In Gen 19, the hospitality of Lot causes the visitors to protect Lot and his daughters from being raped by the men of Sodom (19:8–11). Lot offers his daughters to the men of Sodom because he knows that most of the men of Sodom are heterosexuals. While Lot's treatment of his daughters as his property is unacceptable to us, it is clear that Lot recognizes that the men of Sodom want to use sex to abuse, humiliate, and dominate both his visitors and him. This is a story about power expressed in a sexual way as rape. In what situations in our societies do men rape men? Why do men rape other men? (Are men who rape men homosexuals?)
8. It is important to recognize that this story is not interpreted as a story about homosexuality in other parts of the Bible. How do other Old Testament texts characterize this story? See Isa 1:7–17; Ezek 16:49–50. How does Jesus characterize this story? See Luke 10:10–12 // Matt 10:14--15. What is the sin of Sodom according to these biblical texts?
9. Why is it important to reread this story by beginning in Gen 18? What have you learned by rereading this story?
10. What will you now do to help others in your church or community understand that this is a story about hospitality, not homosexuality?

The most recent version of the Gen 19 contextual Bible study holds many possibilities for critical praxis reflection, especially when drawing on the insights of queer, gender critical, feminist, and African biblical hermeneutics. To conclude, I will limit myself to three brief observations. I hope that these short reflections will link to the overarching commitment of this volume to reflect on the various ways in which context matters and to celebrate a dear friend of the Ujamaa Centre, Holter, for whom African faith communities matter deeply.

First, the broadening of the narrative frame to include Gen 18 and the insistence on reading Gen 19 in conjunction with the Old and New Testament reception of the original narrative make it almost impossible not to grasp the centrality of hospitality as a key thematic underpinning for the Gen 19 narrative. Once this broader context is taken into critical consideration, it seems no longer possible for contemporary interpreters to declare merely that this text is about homosexuality. Inter-text and narrative context therefore clearly matter. A second dimension of the Gen 19 narrative that generates rich reflection is the consideration of Lot's status among the men of Sodom. The migrant/outsider status of Lot and the subsequent vulnerabilities that it produces resonate deeply with those who call the African continent home, where so many are forced into precarious motion due to climate realities, violence, hunger, socioeconomic challenges, and conflict. Learning from relatable contextual settings clearly matters in the interpretation process. Finally, at first glance, question 7 might seem particularly provocative when reflecting on the sexual orientation of the men of Sodom. The formulation of the question, however, draws from insights developed by critical gender and gender-based violence scholars. Question 7 captures key learning about how rape and the threat of rape are used as tools for social control, disciplining, and humiliation. Question 7 enables faith communities to grapple with the complex reality that rape has less to do with sex and desire than with power and control. Rather than appropriating this text to illustrate same-sex desire, the Gen 19 contextual Bible study allows African faith communities to grapple with the pervasive, punitive, and dehumanizing reality of gender-based violence and homophobic hate crime as a form of punitive control and punishment. Considering the staggering embodied and contextual reality of gender-based violence and homophobic hate crime, and how it profoundly affects African communities, the context simply has to matter more. It is imperative that African faith communities pay urgent attention, get involved, act in solidarity with those called Izitabane, and, in the process, restore our common humanity.

Works Cited

Boonzaaier, Michelle, and Charlene van der Walt. 2019. "Co-creating Transformative Spaces through Dialogue." Pages 95–111 in *Teaching for Change: Essays on Pedagogy, Gender, and Theology in Africa*. Edited by L. Juliana Claassens, Charlene van der Walt, and Funlọla O. Ọlọjẹde. Cape Town: Sun.

Cranny-Francis, Anne, Wendy Waring, Pam Stavropoulos, and Joan Kirkby. 2003. *Gender Studies: Terms and Debates*. New York: Palgrave.

Davids, Hanzline, Abongile Matyila, Sindi Sithole, and Charlene van der Walt. 2019. *Stabanisation: A Discussion Paper about Disrupting Back-*

lash by Reclaiming LGBTIQA+ Voices in the African Church Landscape. Johannesburg: The Other Foundation.

Holter, Knut. 2006. "Let My People Stay! Introduction to a Research Project on Africanization of Old Testament Studies." *OTE* 19:377–92.

———. 2011. "The Role of Historical-Critical Methodology in African Old Testament Studies." *OTE* 24:377–89.

———. 2016. "The 'Poor' in Ancient Israel—and in Contemporary African Biblical Studies." *Mission Studies* 33:209–21.

Nussbaum, Martha C. 1999. *Sex and Social Justice.* New York: Oxford University Press.

Schüssler Fiorenza, Elisabeth. 1988. "The Ethics of Biblical Interpretation: Decentering Biblical Scholarship." *JBL* 107:3–17.

Thatcher, Adrian. 2011. *God, Sex, and Gender: An Introduction.* New Jersey: Wiley & Sons.

Van der Walt, Charlene. 2015. "'It's the Price I Guess for the Lies I've Told That the Truth It No Longer Thrills Me…': Reading Queer Lies to Reveal Straight Truth in Genesis 38." Pages 57–75 in *Restorative Readings: The Old Testament, Ethics, and Human Dignity.* Edited by L. Juliana Claassens and Bruce C. Birch. Portland, OR: Wipf & Stock.

———. 2017a. "'But He Refused to Listen to Her…' Developing a Safe Communal Space Where Marginal Voices Can Be Heard." *JTSA* 159:5–21.

———. 2017b. "Is There a Man Here? The Iron Fist in the Velvet Glove in Judges 4." Pages 117–32 in *Feminist Frameworks and the Bible: Power, Ambiguity, and Intersectionality.* Edited by L. Juliana Claassens and Carolyn J. Sharp. London: Bloomsbury T&T Clark.

———. 2018. "'To the Wonder': Finding God in the Most Unexpected Places." Pages 170–86 in *Considering Compassion: Global Ethics, Human Dignity, and the Compassionate God.* Edited by L. Juliana Claassens and Fritz De Lang. Portland, OR: Wipf & Stock.

———. 2019. "Mind the Gap." Pages 221–38 in *Freedom of Religion at Stake: Competing Claims among Faith Traditions, States, and Persons.* Edited by Dion A. Forster, Elisabeth Gerle, and Goran Gunner. Portland, OR: Wipf & Stock.

Van der Walt, Charlene, and Judith Terblanche. 2016. "Reimagining a Solitary Landscape: Tracing Communities of Care in Exodus 1–2 and the Film Shirley Adams." *OTE* 29:176–94.

West, Gerald O. 2006. "The Vocation of an African Biblical Scholar on the Margins of Biblical Scholarship." *OTE* 19:307–36.

———. 2015. "Reading the Bible with the Marginalised: The Value/s of Contextual Bible Reading." *STJ* 1:235–61.

———. 2016a. "Reconfiguring a Biblical Story (Genesis 19) in the Context of South African Discussions about Homosexuality." Pages 186–88 in *Christianity and Controversies over Homosexuality in Contemporary Africa*. Edited by Ezra Chitando and Adriaan van Klinken. Oxford: Routledge.

———. 2016b. "Recovering the Biblical Story of Tamar: Training for Transformation, Doing Development." Pages 135–47 in *For Better, for Worse: The Role of Religion in Development Cooperation*. Edited by Robert Odén. Halmstad: Swedish Mission Council.

West, Gerald O., and Charlene van der Walt. 2019. "A Queer (Beginning to the) Bible." *Concilium* 5:109–18.

West, Gerald O., Charlene van der Walt, and Kapja J. Kaoma. 2016. "When Faith Does Violence: Reimagining Engagement between Churches and LGBTIQA+ Groups on Homophobia in Africa." *HvTSt* 72:1–8.

West, Gerald O., Charlene van der Walt, and Sithembiso Zwane. 2021. "From Homosexuality to Hospitality: From Exclusion to Inclusion; from Genesis 19 to Genesis 18." *JTSA* 168 :5–23.

West, Gerald O., and Phumzile Zondi-Mabizela. 2004. "The Bible Story That Became a Campaign: The Tamar Campaign in South Africa (and Beyond)." *Ministerial Formation* 103:4–12.

Dining with the Tormentors? A Biblical and Acoli Context-Sensitive Understanding of Healing and Restoration

Helen Nambalirwa Nkabala

Introduction

The surrender of Dominic Ongwen, one of the most notorious leaders of the Lord's Resistance Army (LRA)[1] on 6 January 2015 and his consequent committal to the International Criminal Court at The Hague have brought fresh memories of pain and suffering to some people in Uganda, in particular in northern Uganda.[2] While the International Criminal Court is of the view that, for justice to prevail, Ongwen must be tried and brought to justice, it is contestable whether the justice of that court alone can really bring total healing and restoration to the people of northern Uganda.

Traditionally and from time immemorial, the Acoli have had their own mechanisms of subjecting culprits to a justice system, which is acceptable to the society. These are in the form of rituals. With the LRA ravaged northern Uganda for over twenty years, it was natural to offer a solution that would ensure forgiveness and reconciliation with a view to promoting healing and restoration. Using reintegration rituals, the Acoli practice mechanisms that ensure that those returning home are welcomed by the community.

This essay highlights some of the ritual experiences and practices that soldiers such as Ongwen are subjected to in order to make them welcome and reintegrate into the Acoli society after engaging in war. The essay

---

1. For more information on LRA, see Nkabala 2021.
2. Ongwen was convicted on 21 May 2021 and sentenced to twenty-five years in prison.

shows how the Acoli rituals can be used as an interpretative lens to view the rituals in the Bible and as the basis for restoring cohesion in Acoli land. While the Acoli may not see any connection between the rituals and their Christian faith, the fact that they practice both opens a window for researchers like myself to explore the relationship between the two. My aim is to show how the Bible makes meaning to the Acoli in the midst of the challenges they face as they try to return to normalcy after decades of war. This essay therefore is a dialogue between the Bible and African experiences. It further contributes to the discussion of how ancient texts can be approached from contemporary African perspectives (Holter 2002, 114).

Methodologically, I build on qualitative interviews done with former LRA soldiers. The analysis also employs a biblical exegetical approach. Structurally, I start by briefly exposing the Acoli cultural context as an interpretative context. I then highlight the importance of rituals in the healing and restoration of the former LRA combatants. I present an interaction between the Bible and the Acoli context before the conclusion.

Acoli Cultural Context as an Interpretive Lens?

For a long time, the Bible was read and interpreted through Western lenses. However, the 1990s saw a paradigm shift on the African continent with the emphasis on the role of the ordinary reader (Holter 2006, 388). Knut Holter (2002, 1; 2006, 389) opines that "the Old Testament has become an African book and it is therefore to be read from the perspectives of African experiences and concerns." This essay is an attempt to respond to this call to read texts with sensitivity to the challenges that are prevalent on the continent. It will therefore explore ways in which the Bible can be read in light of Acoli traditional rituals in order to contribute to the healing and restoration of the society after decades of war in northern Uganda.

Acoli Traditional Rituals for Reintegrating Former LRA Fighters

Rituals are fully embedded in the Acoli culture, and in this section, I explore voices of the Acoli's view of reintegration rituals. The presence of the term kwer (ritual) in Acoli vocabulary confirms that rituals have been part and parcel of the Acoli traditional beliefs and practices from time immemorial. Believed to have been handed to them by Jok-kene (God-alone), the Acoli perform these rituals for several reasons but with the main aim of keeping the community together in peace and harmony.

Historically, rituals were performed to appease the gods, ask for favors, avert impending calamity, cleanse returning soldiers from war, or purify a person who returned home after a long time. It is therefore not surprising that when people, male and female alike, returned from the battlefield of the LRA, they were subjected to certain rituals. These cultural tools are instrumental to the reintegration process (Shanahan and Veale 2009). The Acoli believe that soldiers at the warfront were exposed to many things that made them impure. The impurities always manifested in diseases and calamities (Harlacher et al. 2006, 54; Baines 2005, 11). The situation was worse if a person killed others while on the battlefield. Such a person had to confess publicly and ask for forgiveness, then would undergo special rituals to ensure that there was peace in society or the person would be haunted by the spirits of the dead. It was believed that, if not cleansed, such a person could be trailed by a spirit of bad luck, which would bring misfortune to the person and his or her family, or clan (Harlacher et al. 2006, 62). As observed by Alicinda Honwana (2006, 6), those who have engaged in war are not easily accepted back into society, for they are considered to be polluted by the wrongdoings from the war; they are contaminated by the spirits of the dead and the carriers of their anger. Therefore, taking into consideration the view that context matters, it becomes clear here that the Acoli have exploited the existence of their rich cultural beliefs and practices to put behind them war traumas and open the way to reconciliation and peace (105). I also argue that an interaction between the biblical and the Acoli contexts exemplifies what J. Wentzel Van Huyssteen (1999, 113) refers to as a post foundational theology, which is described as a theology that fully acknowledges the role of context, the epistemically crucial role of interpreted experience, and the role of tradition in shaping religious values. The Acoli ritual beliefs and practices have indeed remained a crucial part of shaping theological reflections in northern Uganda after the LRA war. To use the words of Christoffel H. Thesnaar (2014, 5), this essay also illuminates the plausible form of cross-contextual and interdisciplinary conversation between the Old Testament and the Acoli society.

Importance of Rituals to Reintegrating Former Combatants to the Community

In this section, I present some of the perceptions and views about the meaning of rituals especially for the reintegration of female ex-LRA soldiers in northern Uganda. I am aware of the limitations of rituals, but from my understanding, which is shaped by my research in northern Uganda, the role of rituals in promoting healing and restoration within societies cannot be underestimated. Through rituals, members of a particular community are in a position to remember and share meanings collectively, and this, in turn, revitalizes the community (cf. McGuire 2002, 17). Meredith B. McGuire's view is confirmed by Ritah, a former LRA soldier, who relates that, "when I had just returned from the bush, no one wanted to sit close to me or to talk to me. However, after going through the ritual, they started to accept me."[3] Ritah's voice represents those of many other former soldiers with similar experiences. In this case, we see an example of a strengthened bond between Ritah and the community. Catherine Bell (1997, 29)stresses that "rituals are social mechanisms with a particularly vital role to play in maintaining the system."

Additionally, one elder explained that, when rituals were performed on the former LRA soldiers in the presence of the communities, they offered a platform for them to seek forgiveness, especially for atrocities such as killing, which presumably they committed against their will. He further explained that, even when it is almost impossible in some cases to reconcile with the dead, through these rituals one was able to make peace with the dead and his/her family members.[4] In a follow up conversation with Mego Christine,[5] who emphasized the importance of appeasing the dead and promoting peace among the living and the dead, rituals are described as the only vehicle through which the dead and the living can make peace. This view resonates with Ferdinand Okwaro's (2010, 57) observation that rituals are developed to address clients' problems as well as help people to adapt to changing circumstances. Similarly, Mego Christine's views are echoed by Erin Baines (2005, 45), who explains that after undergoing the rituals, "former LRA soldiers who were solitary prior to the ceremony were now more sociable, they were better able to converse in a 'normal' manner, and aggressive behavior tended to reduce or disappear."

Many of the former LRA soldiers I interviewed confirmed the scholar's view that they felt better placed in the society after undergoing the rituals because the community members were more receptive toward them. Even

---

3. Interview with Ritah, a former LRA member, conducted at Acholi Inn on 20 April 2021.

4. Telephone interview with Acoli chief (elder), conducted on 18 May 2021.

5. Mego is a title given to an elderly woman by the Acoli, but this and all names used in this article are fictitious.

those who had experienced demonic attacks before undergoing the rituals confessed that they lived a normal life without attacks after going through various rituals. In my view, this shows that the use of the Acoli rituals in the reintegration of former LRA soldiers was helpful because they made the former LRA soldiers feel accepted in the communities, implying that the rituals contributed to the healing and restoration in the region.

Speaking about the role of rituals in Acoli culture and their impact on those who have benefitted from them, an Anglican reverend argues that the Bible is also full of rituals. In his view, rituals, on their own, pose no problem; problems arise when people slide into witchcraft. On whether he supports the rituals, he explains that as religious leaders, they do participate in the rituals, as they emphasize the Christian rituals as well as the traditional ones.[6] The voice of the reverend represents many other Christians in Acoliland who believe that as Christians they still desire to promote their culture. As Peter, a Pentecostal church pastor, also argues, even Jesus had a culture that he practiced, and it did not make him less the Christ.[7] While these sound more like popular voices, as Holter (2008, 12) warns, they should be taken as more than just an echo of an ordinary reader's context. In the discussion in the subsequent section, I will show how context is deliberately activated in the act of interpretation (Holter 2008, 11), by offering insights into the interaction between the Acoli rituals and some biblical views of healing and restoration.

Selected Biblical Texts on Forgiveness and Reconciliation and the Acoli Rituals

As Holter (2002, 114) has rightly observed, the future of African Old Testament scholarship lies with letting the Bible interact with the different African experiences and concerns. In this section, I explore the biblical teachings on forgiveness and reconciliation, and show how these interact with the Acoli beliefs and practices. This section addresses questions about the role of the Bible in Acoliland even after decades of war and given that the Bible is the main reference point for the LRA fighters. Forgiveness in the biblical sense refers to the restoration to former favor (Exod 35:15).[8] The Bible notes that forgiveness enables the nation to receive relief

---

6. Rev. Simon, in a telephone interview on 13 May 2021.
7. Peter, in a telephone conversation on 16 May 2021.
8. All biblical texts in this essay are in accordance with the African Bible.

from the hardships caused by their sin (Sproul 2015, 646). For instance, the promise of forgiveness in 2 Chr 7:14 (ESV) meant the restoration of a community after the Babylonian exile (Sproul 2015, 646). So, through forgiveness, sin is forgotten or not reckoned against the sinner. Forgiveness signifies remission of the punishment due to sinful conduct and the divine deliverance of the sinner from the penalty (Vine and Bruce 1981, 122). The process of forgiveness is preceded by humility and trust in God, who offers forgiveness as a free gift to all who repent and turn back to God. It is evident that one receives forgiveness depending on how one perceives God's mercy. W. E. Vine and F. F. Bruce (1981, 123) also state that forgiveness, as translated in the New Testament, denotes dismissal, release, or remission of sins and therefore passing over just penalty (see Mark 3:29; Eph 1:7; Col 1:14).

In the Old Testament, Yahweh's forgiving character is conceived in anthropomorphic terms (cf. Gen 50:17; Isa 15:25; 25:28), and prayers for forgiveness are also common (cf. Exod 10:17; 32:32; 34:9; Ps 25:11–22). The Bible records that there is forgiveness with God who restores his people so that they might honor him (cf. Ps 130:4). Commenting on Ps 130:3–4, 7–8, Gary M. Burge and Andrew E. Hill (2012, 531) submit that God graciously sets people free from their sins by his merciful forgiveness. Often, Yahweh is asked to forgive according to his great covenant love (Num 14:9) and once, rather pathetically, to forgive Jacob because Jacob is so small (Amos 7:2). Additionally, the conditions for forgiveness explicitly mentioned in Hos 14:3 are confession of sin and prayer for forgiveness. The conditions for forgiveness include humility, prayer, and seeking God's face by the people of God (Burge and Hill 2012, 379). Such conditions reflect what is expected in Acoli rituals. Once a person has confessed her/his sin publicly and undergone the rituals, that person is deemed worthy of forgiveness.

In her article, "Christian Identity and Ethnicity in Africa," Philomena N. Mwaura (2010, 134) notes that practicing forgiveness is vital to the work of reconciliation, and when humans promote integral development, it will always enhance social justice, common good, and social responsibility. It should be appreciated that the process of forgiveness precedes reconciliation and the latter will encourage dialogue and mutual listening, which are necessary for peaceful coexistence in a community with diverse cultural rituals and religious challenges. It is also argued that human forgiveness is to be strictly analogous to divine forgiveness, and if certain conditions such as repentance and confession are fulfilled, then, there is no limitation (Vine and Bruce 1981, 122). This is biblical, as revealed in Matt 6:12, 18:21, 22, and Luke 17:3. Mwaura (2010, 136) stresses that forgiving others, though difficult, should be part of the reconciliation process. Forgiveness must thus carry something of the boundless grace that God gives.

Köhler argues that in Old Testament theology, Yahweh is revealed as one full of compassion and grace (cf. Exod 34:6; Josh 24:19), a God of justice and recompense (cf. Isa 45:21; Köhler 1957, 47–48). According to his gracious character, it is also possible that Yahweh will forgive a guilty group because of the righteousness of some members of the group. For instance, in Gen 18:26–32, Abraham asks the forgiveness of Yahweh for Sodom and Gomorrah if as few as ten righteous men are found in those cities. Further, as recorded in Jer 5:1, Yahweh himself asks Jeremiah whether even one righteous person can be found in Jerusalem for whose sake he might forgive or pardon the city. Scholars such as Chris Sugden (2000, 36) have also commented on the possibility of God forgiving, restoring, and atoning a community in response to intercessions made by his people. The compassion and faithfulness of God make it possible for him to restore his people. Commenting on the compassion and goodness of God in *Biblical Christianity in African Perspective*, Wilbur O'Donovan (2009, 62) argues that the compassion of God makes it possible for him to embrace his people. It can be argued, therefore, that the character of his goodness and compassion are the ingredients for restoration and reconciliation of humankind to himself.

However, sometimes, Yahweh is said not to forgive. In such passages, the absence of the conditions mentioned is implied or expressly stated (Hos 1:6). Yahweh will not forgive Judah because of its pride (Isa 2:9), because it has renounced Yahweh for other gods (Deut 29:19; Jer 5:7) or because of its obduracy in evil (2 Kgs 24:4). In Num 15:30–31, one who sins deliberately has despised the word of Yahweh and broken his command. Such a person must be entirely outlawed, since his/her sin is inseparable from Yahweh. This means that in such a case of deliberate sinning, forgiveness appears to be impossible. Other examples where Yahweh is said not to forgive due to breaking his law are the incidents of rejecting Saul in 1 Sam 15:25 and the damnation brought upon King David in 2 Sam 12:11–18.

Similarly, among the Acoli, there was no ritual or provision for deliberate killing. A deliberate sin brought the wrath of condemnation from the elders who would banish the culprit from the village or even put the person to death to avoid the contamination of the rest of the community.

To avoid a situation where one would sin deliberately, the Israelites were to wear tassels on the hem of their garments and a violet cord on the tassel. On seeing the tassels, the children of Israel would be reminded of all the commands of Yahweh (cf. Num 15:37–39). The affixed items were to help them stay in obedience to God's commandments. Biblically, the garments held divine significance. A case in point is that of a woman who suffered from bleeding for twelve years and who decided to touch the garment of Jesus and was made well (cf. Matt 9:20). Although garments had the purpose of setting people apart for God, Jesus himself practiced observing the law as instructed in the Old Testament passages (cf. Exod 13:9, 16; Deut 6:8). However, he condemned the exaggeration that often went with it by the Pharisees (cf. Matt 23:5).

Although some biblical narratives depict Yahweh as not forgiving, we learn in 2 Sam 12:24–25 that David slept with Bathsheba, who conceived and gave birth to a son whom he named Solomon—derived from the Hebrew word for peace and compensation, literally, meaning "beloved of Yahweh" (Sproul 2015, 470). Yahweh had instructed the prophet Nathan to name the child "Jedidah," which confirms that Yahweh loved him. The preceding ritual also shows that God had forgiven David for having Uriah killed and taking Bathsheba, his wife (2 Sam 12:25). It should be observed that the same prophet communicated Yahweh's anger and rejection to David for the sin he committed (2 Sam 12:5–10). In pursuit of forgiveness, David repented and was forgiven by Yahweh who spared him but killed the son who was the product of the act that enraged Yahweh (2 Sam 12:13–19). In other situations, the sinner recognizes and accepts sprinkling as an effective means of cleansing when he/she asks God to purify him/her with a hyssop that is used for sprinkling in purification (cf. Lev 14:4; Num 19:18). It is by this ritual of sprinkling (with water) that the sinner will be made clean and will be washed until he/she is whiter than snow (Ps 51:7; cf. Job 9:30; Isa 1:18; Ezek 36:25; Heb 9:13–14). The practice of sprinkling, especially either for purification purposes or as a blessing, is entrenched in African beliefs and practices. Among the Acoli, as in many other African societies, water is life, and it is believed that water washes away all sins. For cleansing purposes, the elders use a special grass called ajuu, which they dip into a calabash of water and sprinkle. Similarly, if anyone was going on a mission (either hunting or war), they were blessed. Water is poured into a calabash, and an elder would use the stem of a tree called obololwedo to sprinkle the water on the person. The act of sprinkling for either blessing or cleansing is still practiced in many communities.

Going back to the Old Testament, after the death of the child, David stopped fasting and changed his clothes. He was restored to his normal self and relationship with God. David was encouraged to go and worship Yahweh because he knew his own sin was forgiven (cf. Burge and Hill 2012, 300). What happens in David's life clearly resonates with what we find in the Acoli culture. After confessing one's sin and undergoing a cleansing process, the sinner is restored to good health, with the belief that his/her sins are no longer counted against him or her. Such a person lives in freedom henceforth. Already in the Old Testament, God had prefigured the reconciliation of humankind to himself by not ceasing to offer pardon. He reveals himself as the God of tenderness and of compassion (Exod 34:6), who freely retains "the ardor of his wrath" (Ps 85:4; cf. Ps 103:8–12) and speaks peaceably unto his people (Ps 85:9). It is indeed reconciliation—even if the word (reconciliation) is not used—which Yahweh proposes to his unfaithful spouse in Hos 2:16–22 and to his rebellious children in Ezek 18:31–32.

All the rites of expiation in the Mosaic ritual, ordered purification from all kinds of imperfections, point ultimately to the reconciliation of people with Yahweh. In Leviticus, different sacrifices were offered with specific objectives. For instance, in Lev 4:16, the "sacrifice for sin" expiates ritual faults in which the offended person is God. In Lev 5:14–26, the "sacrifice of reparation" (guilt offering) deals with infringements of rights either of God or of neighbor, be it the living dead or those who are still alive. The imposition of hands makes the victim and the offeror one (Lev 16:21–22), and the scapegoat is then sent into the desert bearing all the faults. This may be compared with the goat and the sheep used in the Acoli ritual of lakerket. As seen above, the goat becomes the bearer of the sin and is pierced. It is also a ritual that symbolizes the washing away of sin using the blood of animals. The sacrifice for sin in Leviticus had the greatest prominence, and so it was given a new significance in the books of Chronicles and eventually the New Testament. It overshadows Christ who becomes the lamb whose blood is shed for the ransom of many or for the forgiveness of many. This is the blood that reconciles the people of the new covenant with God (cf. Lev 4:16; Exod 32).

According to Maccabees, the time has not yet arrived for the complete remission of sins, and the faithful servants of the true God remain in expectation of something better through which God would reconcile with his people (2 Macc 1:5; 7:33; 8:29). For the Maccabees to reconcile with God, they had to pray so that Yahweh would open their hearts to his law in order to do his will (2 Macc 1:5). To do this, they returned the booty on the eve of the Sabbath so that they could celebrate the Sabbath with heartfelt praise and thanks to the Lord, who had reserved that day for distilling on them the first dew of his mercy (2 Macc 8:27–29). After receiving the first dew of God's mercy, they distributed the booty among the victims of the persecution—widows and orphans—and the rest to themselves and their children. They then joined in public supplication, imploring the merciful Lord to be fully reconciled with his servants (2 Macc 8:29). Reading this, and other previously discussed texts within the Acoli context would open up an understanding of this complete reconciliation as that which ends with the sharing of a meal as a sign of total forgiveness and reconciliation. It exhibits a similar sense as the ultimate Acoli ritual of mato-oput, which involves the drinking of the bitter herb from the oput tree and at the end of which the elders serve a meal that is shared by the participants, including perpetrators and victims. Moreover, the offenders and the offended tend to coexist harmoniously after the ritual, thus promoting healing and restoration within the community.

Conclusion

To conclude, the study of rituals requires that one examines the context in which they are practiced. First, I have shown that the Acoli exploit the beliefs and practices in their context to promote healing and restoration. A discussion of the interaction between the Acoli rituals and biblical notions of forgiveness and reconciliation has also showed that the different practices and beliefs of the Acoli resonate with those of the Bible. The conversations with the community members and former LRA members have shown that, though the LRA uses the Bible to justify atrocities committed in northern Uganda and beyond, the Acoli people have not ceased to believe in the Bible. Based on this background, I suggest that theologians and biblical scholars explore how to use connections between Acoli beliefs and practices and the Bible to promote restoration in communities. In my opinion, it is important to refer to cultural contexts and religious texts when examining relationship models for healing and restoration of communities. This can enable the former LRA members, now reintegrated into their communities, to relate with those who suffered the brutality of the LRA war.

Finally, now that Dominic Ongwen, a former LRA commander, has been convicted by the International Criminal Court, it seems to me that there is a missing link. As the people of his community have argued, it is important for him and the Acoli community that he undergoes the rituals for his own healing and restoration and for the healing of the community members who suffered as a result of the activities he commanded. With these rituals, coupled with a heavily Christian community, which believes in forgiveness and restoration, using acceptable means from both its culture and the Bible, the story of Dominic Ongwen's acceptance in the community may be concluded, paving a way for him to dine with the same people he earlier tormented.

Works Cited

Baines, Erin. 2005. *RocoWat 1, Acoli: Restoring Relationships in Acoli-Land; Traditional Approaches to Justice and Reintegration*. Vancouver: Liu Institute for Global Issues.

Bell, Catherine. 1997. *Ritual: Perspectives and Dimensions*. New York: Oxford University Press.

Burge, Gary M. and Andrew E. Hill. 2012. *The Baker Illustrated Bible Commentary*. Grand Rapids: Baker.

Harlacher, Thomas, et al., eds. 2006. *Traditional Ways of Coping in Acoli: Cultural Provisions for Reconciliation and Healing from War*. Kampala: Intersoft Business Service.

Holter, Knut. 2002. *Old Testament Research for Africa: A Critical Analysis and Annotated Bibliography of African Old Testament Dissertations, 1967–2000*. Bible and Theology in Africa 3. New York: Lang.

———. 2006. "Let My People Stay! Introduction to a Research Project on Africanization of Old Testament Studies." *OTE* 19:377–92.

———. 2008. *Contextualized Old Testament Scholarship in Africa*. Nairobi: Acton.

Honwana, Alcinda. 2006. *Child Soldiers in Africa*. Philadelphia: University of Pennsylvania Press.

Köhler, Ludwig. 1957. *Old Testament Theology*. Maryknoll, NY: Orbis.

McGuire, Meredith B. 2002. *Religion: The Social Context*. Vol. 5. Belmont, CA: Wadsworth.

Mwaura, Philomena N. 2010. "Christian Identity and Ethnicity in Africa: Reflections on the 'Gospel of Reconciliation.'" Pages 128–38 in *African Theology on the Way: Current Conversations*. Edited by Diane Stinton. London: SPCK.

Nkabala, Helen Nambalirwa. 2021. *Kony as Moses: Old Testament Texts and Motifs in the Early Years of the Lord's Resistance Army, Uganda.* Bible and Theology in Africa 31. New York: Lang

O'Donovan, Wilbur. 2009. *Biblical Christianity in African Perspective.* Milton Keynes: Paternoster.

Okwaro, Ferdinand. 2010. "Modernity and Efficacy in Kenyan Ritual Healing." *JRitSt* 24.2:57–79.

Shanahan, Fiona, and Angela Veale. 2010. "The Girl Is the Core of Life: Social Reintegration, Communal Violence, and the Sacred in Northern Uganda." Pages 115–32 in *Culture, Religion, and the Reintegration of Female Child Soldiers in Northern Uganda.* Edited by Bård Mæland. New York: Lang.

Sproul, R. C. 2015. *The Reformation Study Bible.* Orlando: Reformation Trust.

Sugden, Chris. 2000. *Gospel, Culture and Transformation.* Oxford: Regnum Books International.

Thesnaar, Christoffel H. 2014. "Seeking Feasible Reconciliation: A Transdisciplinary Contextual Approach to Reconciliation." *HvTSt* 70(2): art. #1364. http://dx.doi.org/10.4102/hts.v70i2.1364.

Van Huyssteen, J. Wentzel. 1999. *The Shaping of Rationality: Toward Interdisciplinarity in Theology and Science.* Grand Rapids: Eerdmans.

Vine, W. E., and F. F. Bruce. 1981. *Vine's Expository Dictionary of Old and New Testament Words.* Vol. 2. Old Tappan, NJ: Revell.

Rape As Cultural Violence: A Feminist Cultural Hermeneutical Reading of Dinah's Story in Genesis 34

Funlọla O. Ọlọjẹde

Introduction

Among other things, feminist cultural hermeneutics challenges cultural practices that debase or marginalize women and that are supported by or presumed in the biblical text. From the perspective of African feminist cultural hermeneutics as a dialogue between biblical and African contexts through the topos of abduction-rape, this essay argues that certain cultural elements in the Dinah story suggest that the episodes of violence are in a sense motivated or reinforced by cultural values. Such a perspective is consonant with Knut Holter's (2008, 11–52) description of "contextually sensitive Old Testament scholarship," which in the context of African biblical hermeneutics promotes an interaction between the Old Testament and Africa. Specifically, Dinah's story calls to mind certain practices in the (South) African context that are attributable to culture. The power dynamics at play in an act of rape is often rooted clearly in patriarchal and cultural norms that support male dominance of women who are expected to be passive and submissive to a gender hierarchical order that subordinates them to men and portrays them as sexual objects. What happened to Dinah after the horrific incident in Shechem is undocumented. But it is not difficult to imagine that her life would be similar to Tamar's who "remained desolate in her brother Absalom's house" after being raped by her brother Amnon (2 Sam 13:20). Importantly, the essay shows that cultural issues, as highlighted in the analysis of Dinah's story, at times shape the interpretation of the Old Testament in Africa and beyond and confirm that context matters indeed. The rape of Dinah therefore recalls the practice of rape abduction called ukuthwala in some parts of South Africa.

In the story of Dinah's rape, whose centrality several translations downplay and subtitle as the Treachery of Jacob's Sons (NAS), Jacob's Children (KJV), Dinah and the Shechemites (NET), among others, we encounter Dinah, Jacob's only daughter by Leah, as a young virgin girl who grew up in a household that was predominated by male siblings. Dinah could be mistaken for an adventurous soul who mingled freely with the youth of the land where her family had recently settled, but the likelihood was that, being an only daughter among several sons, Dinah craved the company of other girls of her age. In the course of interacting with the daughters of the land, Shechem the son of Hamor met and became infatuated with her. So, he grabbed her one day and raped her.

Although some commentators try to downplay Shechem's action by portraying it as consensual sex between two youngsters rather than rape (Betchel 1994, 19–36), the text is explicit enough about the nature of the encounter—it was a violent one. Shechem lay with Dinah by force (v. 2), and the act was seen as defilement (v. 5) and a disgraceful thing in Israel (v. 7). It is noteworthy that the narrative repeated several times (vv. 2, 5, 13, 27) that Dinah was defiled (טמא) and the act led to the massacre of the men of Shechem. Dinah's brothers, Simeon and Levi, described the act as treating their sister as a harlot (v. 31). This argument is supported by Richard M. Davidson (2011, 139–40) who, following Mishael Maswari Caspi (1985), investigates the grammar of the narrative and, comparing it to that of the Tamar story (2 Sam 14), persuasively demonstrates that the incident was an act of rape and not of consent as some critics have argued. He notes that the succession of the three verbs in "he took her," "he laid her," and "he violated her" shows that Dinah was forcibly taken.[1]

Notwithstanding, Shechem offered to make reparations. He would marry Dinah (vv. 4, 12). His parents then approached Dinah's aggrieved family to ask for her hand in marriage through intercultural marriage between the two clans. Jacob's sons agreed on the condition that every male in Shechem be circumcised. But this was a ruse, as the reader would soon realize. The men of Shechem indeed submitted themselves to circumcision, but on the third day, while still sore, they were all murdered in cold blood by Simeon and Levi.

---

1. See Scholz's (2000) argument that Dinah's ordeal was clearly a case of rape.

Two clear incidents of violence are reported in the story. First, Shechem forcefully had sexual intercourse with Dinah, and second, Jacob's sons brutally massacred the men of Shechem and pillaged their city. In this essay, I shall argue that certain cultural elements in this story suggest that the violent rape of Dinah in a sense is motivated or reinforced by cultural values. Presumably, notions of what constitute violence differ from one culture or context to another; thus, Sally Engle Merry (2009, 4) sees violence as a social construct, which is often "very much shaped by cultural meanings" and which may differ from one society or cultural group to another (Hoffman and McKendrick 1990, 3). This study accepts a broad definition of violence as the use of force or coercion to cause injury or pain to a person, group of persons, or the personal space of another in a way that results in the violation of that individual, group, or space. The analysis of the episodes of violence in Gen 34 via a cultural lens would help to clarify the link between culture and violence.

Culture of Violence or Cultural Violence?

In a recent publication, I clarified the distinction between a *culture of violence* and *cultural violence*, terms which are sometimes used interchangeably in literature (Ọlọjẹde 2018, 247–67). A culture of violence is said to develop in a context where the protracted use of violence has become an acceptable means of resolving conflicts and consolidated itself into a culture (Pandey 2012, 143, 137). A culture of violence is one in which violence is an accepted way of life and in which a particular subcultural group (e.g., a gang) sees violence and aggression as a normal way of resolving issues (Levinson 1989, 16). Van der Merwe (2013, 74), however, seems to use the term culture of violence to refer to both culture of violence and cultural violence. To him, violence serves both a practical (instrumental) and a social function; it is an effective language of communication, of sending specific messages. The author interchanges the culture of violence with cultural violence, noting that what he calls culture of violence is what Johan Galtung (1990, 291) refers to as cultural violence, namely, "any aspect of a culture that can be used to legitimize violence in its direct or structural form." I have argued however that a careful consideration of Galtung's term shows that 'culture of violence' should be differentiated from 'cultural violence' (Ọlọjẹde 2018).

This contribution employs Galtung's definition of cultural violence as aspects of norms and values of a particular culture that are used to justify violence. Whereas cultural violence, which Galtung classifies as an overarching category of violence, implies that certain cultural forces and elements shape and legitimize the use of violence in a society, in a culture of violence, violence has become customary and a legitimate way of resolving issues. This is not to say that in a culture of violence, cultural norms and values do not surface since the violence itself could affect and shape such norms and values. The emphasis here is on cultural violence, and I shall reread Gen 34 with the assumption that Dinah's violation is motivated largely by cultural violence.

Elements of Culture in Gen 34

This essay posits that the cultural elements in Gen 34 could help us see more clearly women's situation not only in the biblical world but also in a modern African setting. The story of Dinah's rape is set in what appears to be two conflicting cultures—Israelite and Shechemite—which also share certain practices such as men holding court by the city gate (v. 20; cf. 23:18; Ruth 4:1–2) or offering dowry and gift (v. 12; cf. Gen 24:53; 29:18–20). In both cultures also, parents negotiated for wives for their sons just as Samson's parents did on his behalf (vv. 4, 6, 8; cf. Judg 14:1–10; Gen 21:21; 24:3, 51; 38:6–10), and marriage was deemed a contract between two families both among these Hivites and the children of Israel. "Marriage arrangements were customarily negotiated by a parent on behalf of the son" (Sarna 2001, 234). Genesis 34 also alludes to the custom of paying a fine or compensation as reparation in the case of the sexual violation of an unbetrothed virgin (vv. 11–12; cf. Exod 22:16–17; Deut 22:28–29; 1 Sam 18:25; Sarna 2001, 235).

Some other cultural practices and customs were at variance in both cultures. For example, at that point in the world of Genesis, the practice of male circumcision (vv. 14–17, 22, 24) was already normative among the Israelites. As a symbol of YHWH's covenant, the circumcision of Abraham's male descendants eight days after birth was mandatory (Gen 17:9–14). When Jacob's sons learnt of what Shechem had done to their sister, they felt that he had "wrought folly" or caused disgrace in Israel (v. 7). They informed his father Hamor that their culture forbade them to give their sister to an uncircumcised fellow (v. 14; cf. Samson's parents' dismay when he indicated interest in a Philistine girl in Judg 14:3). The sons of Israel were not ready to compromise the custom of circumcision, which was central to their identity. Remarkably, the Shechemites did not realize that their uncircumcision was also a custom and that no culture was superior to the other. They had no objection to intercultural or exogamous marriage and were ready to undergo circumcision to compromise their own custom.

Furthermore, the culture of patriarchy is strongly portrayed in this narrative where Dinah, the primary victim and central figure, is rendered speechless and voiceless throughout, while her brothers and father as well as other males in the story determined the direction of her life. Paul Hamilton (1995, 372) identifies six conversation scenes in the chapter—Shechem to Hamor (v. 4); Hamor to Jacob's sons (vv. 8–12); Jacob's to Hamor and Shechem (vv. 14–17); Hamor and Shechem to their townsmen (vv. 21–23); Jacob to Simeon and Levi (v. 30), and Simeon and Levi to Jacob (v. 31). None of these feature Dinah. It is apparent that culturally, and at that time, it was inappropriate for Dinah to talk in the circumstances. Hamilton (1995, 372) asserts that, "throughout all of this violence and vendetta, not one word has been heard from Dinah. She is abused, avenged, spoken about, delivered, but she never talked." Should her silence not be considered a cultural silence? A young woman dared not talk when men talked. But perhaps she was also too traumatized to speak, as victims of rape often are. Her pain was too deep to put into words.

Equally remarkable is that both Dinah's and Shechem's mothers are missing in the story. They seemingly had no say in the matter because, in their context, they did not matter. One would have thought that at least Dinah's mother would be visible in a serious matter such as the rape of her only daughter, but no—it was a man's world. Mothers were invisible. Perhaps the presence of both Dinah's and Shechem's mothers in the negotiations would have made a difference in the outcome. Noteworthy also, Dinah's potential to become a mother herself seems to have been eroded by the violence done to her. Although she is listed as one of the children who went down to Egypt with their father Israel (Gen 46:15), nothing is ever said of Dinah again. There is no mention of a husband[2] or of progeny. Like Tamar (2 Sam 13:20), she also must have remained desolate in her

---

2. Niditch (2012, 40, 41) notes that Dinah "seems to fade out after her brothers retrieve her" and that, "like a prostitute, she has become a person of outsider status, unfit to be a bride.... Once raped, however, Dinah is so consigned to the background of the story that the issue that emerges is less her status as a sufferer than the status of the men who control her sexuality."

father's house—a victim of cultural violence and stigma; a monument of sorrow and conflict, with no memorial.

Genesis 34 and Cultural Violence

The first of the two incidents of direct and physical violence reported in Gen 34, Dinah's rape by Shechem, is what would be regarded today as an instance of gender-based violence, which is carried out by an individual (v. 2). The other, the invasion of Shechem, which resulted in the slaughter of the men of the city and the abduction of their wives and children by Simeon and Levi, is a group violence directed at others outside the society of the aggressors (vv. 25–29).

In the first episode, the reader is not told how Shechem and Dinah met. Was he the brother of one of Dinah's friends or just a dashing young prince who randomly spotted Dinah in town and became infatuated with her? No one knows. But Shechem took (seized or grabbed) her and raped her. After all, if they so desired, princes could have their way with girls, as Amnon later did with Tamar (2 Sam 13). Without doubt, Shechem's rape of Dinah was an act of violence—a violation of her personhood, her dignity, her sanctity. But he did not stop there. Despite or because of his professed love for Dinah and not having paid a dowry yet or formally married her, Shechem abducted and detained her after the horrific encounter (vv. 17, 26). Incidentally, we are never told that Dinah loved Shechem. How could she love her abuser and abductor? Although interpreters easily compare Dinah's rape to Tamar's rape, what is easily ignored is the perpetrator's reaction to the victim in the two stories. Whereas Shechem continued to profess love for Dinah after her abduction, Ammon, we are told, hated Tamar exceedingly after violating her, such that the hatred with which he hated her was greater than the love with which he first loved her (2 Sam 13:15).[3]

While in custody, Dinah must have endured physical pain besides unspeakable emotional and mental agony. She was violated by a man driven by passion, power, and a sense of impunity. Shechem took and lay with Dinah simply because he could. In the world of Genesis, it was not strange that a man would take a woman. It was culture. Did the Pharaoh

---

3. At least Ammon was unpretentious about his emotion after Tamar's ordeal. As Scholz (1998, 171) has rightly pointed out, rape and love do not go together.

and Abimelech not *take* Sarah (12:10–20; 20:1–18), and did Abimelech and the men of the land not covet Rebekah (26:6–11)? The men of Sodom also demanded to *take* Lot's guests, but he offered that they *take* his daughters instead. For the Canaanites, taking a woman was a cultural norm; hence, Hamor was not appalled by his son's crime, which to him must have been a simple misdemeanor on the part of an exuberant youth. It is also ironic that Shechem, who committed this dishonorable act, is described as more honorable than all his father's house (v. 19). His act of violence against an innocent young maiden was legitimized by a culture of impunity that called evil good. In the patriarchal culture of the sexually degraded people of Canaan, a woman's body could and should be taken by a man. Such violence was culturally acceptable, and if any party was aggrieved, a gift should be enough to pacify it.

But the sons of Israel would have none of that; their cultural orientation did not accommodate the violence against their sister. Such was not done in Israel, and Dinah's brothers would not be appeased with a dowry or gift. Their father's reaction to Dinah's violation, however, appears to be pacifist. He exercised restraint, and like his later offspring, David, who did nothing on hearing that Ammon raped his sister Tamar (2 Sam 13:21), Jacob also said nothing, did nothing. He was concerned only about what the people of the land could do to him and his household (v. 30). So, he chose the path of least resistance. In contrast, when his sons heard of their sister's rape, they played along with the Shechemites, offering that Dinah could marry Shechem only if the entire male population of the city underwent circumcision. But it was a ploy to "immobilize the males" (Sarna 2001, 236). Motivated not only by Shechem's love for Dinah, but also by greed, both Shechem and his father persuaded their fellows that Israel's cattle and substance would become theirs if they consented to the proposition by Jacob's sons (v. 23). The men were swayed and went under the knife. But three days after the surgery, when the circumcision pain was most intense (vv. 25–26), Simeon and Levi went on a rampage, responding to Shechem's violence with rage and aggravated violence (vv. 7, 25–29). They slew all the men of the city including Hamor and Shechem, plundered their goods, and captured their women and children (vv. 26–29).

Susan Niditch (2012, 41) compares Dinah's story to that of Samson and the Timnites (Judg 14–15) because it is "a feud between two groups of men over ownership of one group's woman." The massacre of the men of Shechem by Jacob's sons also seemed to be motivated by a culture of honor and shame rooted in ethnocentrism. Shechem had treated Dinah in a most abominable and dishonorable way, bringing shame to her family and clan (v. 7). For Niditch (2012, 41):

> The rape lowers Dinah's status but also that of her father, and brothers, and it is their status that most occupies the author.... Their status is raised in turn by the success of their plan and the theft of other women, while Dinah's lowered status remain.

Her brothers spoke of the reproach that Dinah's marriage to an uncircumcised would bring to their family (v. 14), stressing that their sister had been treated as a harlot (v. 31). In an act that smacked of cultural arrogance and supremacy, they lured the men of Shechem into a trap of circumcision. In their view, the only way they could defend their family honor and dignity was to take revenge and respond with greater violence. Indeed, the blood of virginity of an innocent girl was spilled, but shedding the blood of all the men of Shechem, who all were innocent except Shechem, amounted to an overkill. The entire adult male population was murdered because of one man's crime. Even Jacob admitted that his sons went too far. They had made his breath to stink before the inhabitants of the land (v. 30). Many years later, on his deathbed, Jacob condemned the move by his two sons as cruel (Gen 49:5, 7), and he distanced his own honor from his sons' definition of family honor (49:6). The unjustifiable assassination of innocent men was carried out in a kind of "rage that reached unto heaven" (cf. 2 Chr 28:9). Their wrath was cruel, and though carried out under the guise of culture, the violence was no less despicable. Even at that time, their action was seen as ethically unacceptable, for the text itself clearly resists it.

Cultural Violence and the African Context

On several levels, Dinah's rape calls to mind certain practices and violent acts that are attributable to culture in the African context. For example, the practice of circumcision mentioned in Gen 34 finds resonance in many African communities where circumcision is regarded as a rite of passage into adulthood. The idea of offering a dowry and gifts to the parents of an unbetrothed virgin who has been violated is also not uncommon, particularly in South Africa. For instance, among the Nguni groups, the parents of a girl who is pregnant outside wedlock are obliged to claim compensation in the form of an agreed number of cows from the father of the unborn child for the damage done to their daughter. This practice is an offshoot of the lobola negotiation that takes place when a young girl is about to marry.[4] The insinuation is that the violator is paying for the dowry that the girl's parents would have received at her wedding.

Dinah's abduction is also reminiscent of the cultural practice of ukuthwala in which a young girl is abducted for marriage among the amaXhosa in some rural parts of the former Transkei (now Eastern Cape) or among the amaZulu of South Africa.[5] Ukuthwala, also known as abduction marriage or forced marriage (literally, "to carry"), refers to a form of marriage in which a man (or with the help of his friends) abducts a young girl he wishes to marry. The girl is ambushed and carried forcefully by known or unknown assailant(s) to the man's house or hideout where she is eventually forced to marry her abductor (Karimakwenda 2018, 145).[6] Ethnographic studies confirm that such abductions involve the use of force including grabbing, dragging, and carrying of the young woman (Rice 2014, 388–89; 2016, 394–411).[7] While some parents disapprove of the abduction and demand the return of their daughter, others consent to the arrangement and receive the lobola tokens, which the abductor and his parents subsequently offer. However, in South Africa, where rape is categorized as a priority crime, such abductions are inevitably accompanied by the rape, including sometimes the gang rape, of the victim (Rice 2014, 163). One of the motivations behind rape is to compel the girl's family to consent to lobola negotiations for her marriage (388–89).

Certainly, rape is an act of direct violence, but, to the extent that certain cultural forces contribute to its perpetration, it can be regarded also as

---

4. According to Rice (2014, 387), "lobola involves the transfer of wealth in the form of cow—or more commonly today, their cash-value equivalent—from the groom or his family to the bride's parents. This exchange formally transfers any children born of the union from the bride's lineage to the groom's, legitimises the marriage, [and] compensates the bride's family for the loss of their daughter's (re)productive labour."

5. Compare variations of this practice across South Africa among speakers of tshiVenda, siSwati, xiTsonga, sePedi, and IsiNdebele, and other language groups (Karimakwenda 2018, 121).

6. For more on ukuthwala and its various nuances, see Rice (2014, 388–89); Karimakwenda (2018, 127–128). Studies at times distinguish between coercive and violent ukuthwala and a more benign (traditional) form that assumes that there is some degree of consent between the parties involved.

7. Some cases of ukuthwala occur when the couple tries to avoid elopement and, instead, stages an abduction to circumvent the social stigma that would have accompanied elopement (Rice 2014, 389).

cultural violence, as in the practice of ukuthwala described above. Aspects of culture are used to justify rape and sexual assault, but the cultural presumption in some circles is that these are normal male behaviors and should not be taken too seriously because, after all, "boys will be boys." However, this study does not presuppose that all acts of rape are culturally motivated but highlights forms of rape, specifically of females, that base their expression on cultural sanctions because of their prevalence in our contemporary settings and as an illustration of cultural violence.

Whether Dinah was a minor or not, we may never know. However, in South Africa, for instance, the increase in the rape of children and infants has been blamed on a cultural myth that claims that men can be cured of HIV if they have sex with a young virgin (Rice 2014, 389).

Another element of culture that helps to legitimize sexual violence against women in some parts of the country is the belief that young boys who undergo initiation rites through circumcision are obliged to assert their masculinity and establish their new status in society by engaging in sex with females. This is the inverse of the Dinah episode, in which Shechem was eager to undergo circumcision in order to legitimize his act of sexual violence. The practice of ukuthwala is also undoubtedly a cultural phenomenon, and because it invariably entails the sexual violation of the abducted bride, it is classifiable as cultural violence. In these scenarios, sexual violence is ritualized. However, research has shown that ukuthwala is a harmful cultural practice (cf. Karimakwenda 2018, 127).

Again, the power dynamics at play in an act of rape is often firmly rooted in patriarchal and cultural norms that support female subjugation. Such norms encourage men to assert the power bestowed on them by culture sexually and, if necessary, in a physically violent way. However, problems arise when cultural elements are used to sanction ethically unsound practices, which could plunge society into moral atrophy and ethical bankruptcy. Of course, it is easy to assume that, because rape does not occur in a cultural vacuum and cultural elements could be employed to legitimize its manifestation, then, most members of the society are complicit. On the contrary, perpetrators merely exploit weak and unquestioned misogynistic norms to legitimize their heinous deeds in the name of patriarchal power and authority. Their actions do not represent societal ethos but are products of a violent subculture.

Of the second act of violence, namely, the slaughter of the Shechemites, Niditch (2012, 41) says, "It is an act that evens the score but also serves as a reminder that wife stealing and rape were regularly associated with war in ancient Israel, even when the reason for war had nothing to do with the ownership of the women." I would reckon, however, that it is the ownership of women and the contestation for their bodies that sometimes ensue in war—as in the case of Samson, the Timnite and the Philistines (Judg 15:1–17), or of the Levite, his concubine, and the Benjamites (Judg 19–20). Notably, however, ukuthwala is not the result of conflict but it could lead to one.

Final Remarks

I have shown that corresponding elements of culture in an African context are relatable to the cultural elements in the Dinah narrative, especially in the violent acts. However, rather than responding to violence with more violence, as Simeon and Levi did, an ethical response to the social challenge of violence and criminality would be the way to go. Thus, it is incumbent on society to reformulate and reinforce communal ethos in order to counteract the existing negative norms that are being sustained by few at the expense of the many members of society who are daily traumatized by violent crimes. Fostering an ethics of care and of communality would be an appropriate step to take in these critical times and the roles of mothers, especially of (potential) perpetrators, could be critical in promoting such ethos.

Although Dinah's story and the practice of ukuthwala highlight the powerlessness of women in these ancient and modern cultures, acts of resistance on the part of women in South Africa have also gained momentum in recent times, causing the government of South Africa to respond with three new laws aimed at strengthening efforts to end gender-based violence. These laws, the Criminal Law (Sexual Offences and Related Matters) Amendment Act, the Criminal and Related Matters Amendment Act and the Domestic Violence Amendment Act, were signed on 28 January 2022. No doubt, reenvisioning a future and a present in which mothers, and women in general, resist the very practice of ukuthwala on communal and policy levels will continue to be critical to the discourse of cultural violence against women and girls.

The story of Dinah demonstrates that the feminist hermeneut ought to pay more critical attention to elements of culture in the reading of Hebrew Bible narratives. And in the African context where many readers of the text tend to put on cultural lens anyway, the findings definitely throw more light on the ancient Israelite cultural milieu and the driving force behind some events in the text that shock the modern reader. Further, the elements of culture in the text that resonate with African cultural elements also help the reader to appreciate the sociocultural context of the text more vividly and why the people of old acted in some of the ways they did.

This contribution, with its strong emphasis on the African context, serves as a tribute to, and upholds the works of Holter, an Africanized European whose Africentered readings of the Old Testament in the last three decades have made indelible footprints on the African sands of time.

Works Cited

Betchel, Lyn M. 1994. "What If Dinah Is Not Raped? Genesis 34." *JSOT* 19:19–36.

Caspi, Mishael Maswari. 1985. "The Story of the Rape of Dinah: The Narrator and the Reader." *HS* 26:25–45.

Davidson, Richard M. 2011. "Sexual Abuse in the Old Testament: An Overview of Laws, Narratives, and Oracles." Pages 134–54 in *The Long Journey Home: Understanding and Ministering to the Sexually Abused*. Edited by Andrew J. Schmutzer. Eugene, OR: Wipf & Stock.

Galtung, Johan. 1990. "Cultural Violence." *JPR* 27.3:291–305.

Hamilton, Victor Paul. 1995. *The Book of Genesis: Chapters 18–50*. NICOT. Grand Rapids: Eerdmans.

Hoffman, Wilma, and Brian W. McKendrick. 1990. "The Nature of Violence." Pages 2–35 in *People and Violence in South Africa*. Edited by Brian McKendrick and Wilma Hoffman. Cape Town: Oxford University Press.

Holter, Knut. 2008. *Contextualized Old Testament Scholarship in Africa*. Nairobi: Acton.

Karimakwenda, Nyasha. 2018. "Where Rape Does Not Exist: Tracing the Unsettled Position of Marital Rape in South Africa through Women's Recourse-Seeking Journeys." PhD diss., University of Cape Town.

Levinson, David. 1989. *Family Violence in Cross-Cultural Perspective*. Frontiers of Anthropology 1. Newbury Park, CA: Sage.

Merry, Sally Engle. 2009. *Gender Violence: A Cultural Perspective*. West Sussex: Wiley-Blackwell.

Niditch, Susan. 2012. "Genesis." Pages 27–45 in *Women's Bible Commentary*. Edited by Carol A. Newsom, Sharon H. Ringe, and Jacqueline E. Lapsley. 20th anniv. ed. Louisville: Westminster John Knox.

Ọlọjẹde, Funlọla O. 2018. "Cultural Violence or a Culture of Violence? An Ethical Unmasking of (Sexual) Violence in South Africa." Pages 247–67 in *Ethics and Justice: Challenging Perspectives from South Africa*. Edited by Chris Jones. Cape Town: AOSIS.

Pandey, Vimal Nayan. 2012. "Political Mobilisation and Rise of the Culture of Violence in South Africa Exploring the Root Causes." *Insight on Africa* 4.2:137–52.

Rice, Kathleen. 2014. "*Ukuthwala* in Rural South Africa: Abduction Marriage as a Site of Negotiation about Gender, Rights and Generational Authority among the Xhosa." *JSAS* 40.2:381–99.

———. 2016. "Understanding *Ukuthwala*: Bride Abduction in the Rural Eastern Cape, South Africa." *AS* 77.3:394–411.

Sarna, Nahum M. 2001. *Genesis*. JPS Torah Commentary Series 1. Philadelphia: Jewish Publication Society.

Scholz, Susanne. 1998. "Through Whose Eyes? A 'Right' Reading of Genesis 34." Pages 150–71 in *Genesis: A Feminist Companion to the Bible*. Edited by A. Brenner. FCB. Sheffield: Sheffield Academic.

———. 2000. *Rape Plots: A Feminist Cultural Study of Genesis 34*. New York: Lang.

Van der Merwe, Hugo. 2013. "Violence as a Form of Communication: Making Sense of Violence in South Africa." *AJCR* 13.3:65–82.

"Is It Good for You to Be Angry?" (Jonah 4:4, 9): Contemplating Divine and Human Anger in a Context of Injustice

L. Juliana Claassens

Anger incites people into action.
Anger frustrates the status quo.
Anger motivates people to change.
—Xolani Kacela, "Towards a More Liberating Black Liberation Theology"

Introduction

In his article on the poor in ancient Israel and contemporary African biblical scholarship, Knut Holter (2016, 210) considers the notion of "socially concerned biblical scholars," who "claim a right to participate, with the insights and tools of their particular academic discipline, in the contemporary struggle for justice and human dignity." No longer satisfied to be part of "a discipline whose practitioners perform their sterile textual science totally detached from their own socio-cultural contexts and interests," such (African) biblical scholars increasingly are concerned about issues such as poverty, injustice, and famine, not only in the biblical text, but also in the respective contexts in which they read and write.[1]

---

1. Holter (2016, 213–18) further offers an insightful analysis of three African biblical scholars: Zamani Buki Kafang, from Nigeria, who completed a doctoral thesis on the concept of the poor in the Psalms at Trinity Evangelical Divinity School, Deerfield, USA in 1993; Robert Wafawanaka, from Zimbabwe, who completed a doctoral thesis on the problem of poverty in Africa and ancient Israel at Boston University in 1997; and Lechion Peter Kimilike, from Tanzania, who completed a doctoral thesis on Afri-

Today, in many a context, to be socially concerned means to be angry. In South Africa, we have seen this vividly illustrated in some of the violent scenes associated with student protests in 2016–2017 with what started as #RhodesMustFall at the University of Cape Town, soon spreading to other campuses across the country in the form of #OpenStellenbosch, #FeesMustFall, and #EndRapeCulture. It is estimated that the anger of these students resulted in property damages of over ZAR800 million, with the University of the Northwest hardest hit, followed by University of Johannesburg and University of KwaZulu-Natal (Dentliger 2018).

Also in the United States, proponents and allies of #BlackLivesMatter responded in anger to yet another senseless killing of an innocent man in May 2020. This time, George Floyd's name became fixed in our minds by way of a terrifying eight-minute video clip of police brutality in Minneapolis in which a man, on camera, lost his life.[2] Floyd's last words, "I can't breathe," became a battle cry for so many men and women who find themselves in situations of oppression due to systemic racism, sexism, and homophobia, as well as the slow violence of poverty.

In this essay that seeks to honor the longstanding commitment to socially concerned biblical scholarship by Holter (1998, 2006a, 2006b, 2008), I will consider conceptions of divine and human anger as represented in the book of Jonah. The narrative portrayal of anger in the book of Jonah will be brought into conversation with recent theoretical analyses of the powerful emotion of anger that informs black liberation theology, considering the notion of a productive nature of anger to, in terms of Kacela's (2005, 202) quote at the beginning of this essay, "incite[s] people into action," "frustrate[s] the status quo," and "motivate[s] people to change." I argue that Jonah's anger receives new significance when read in a context of injustice as represented on the African continent in the form of the harm done by imperialism, war, and gender-based violence, as well as the structural violence of poverty.

---

can perspectives on proverbs pertaining to poverty in the book of Proverbs at UNISA in 2006.

2. George Floyd is linked to two more victims of police brutality, Breonna Taylor and Ahmaud Arbery, who together with Trayvon Martin, Michael Brown, and Eric Garner, tragically, have become household names and played a central role in the establishment of the grassroots movement #BlackLivesMatter in 2013–2014. See in this regard Anderson's (2016) insightful analysis of the early roots of this powerful movement.

On Anger

In his article, "Towards a More Liberating Black Liberation Theology," Xolani Kacela (2005, 200) makes a case for the productive use of anger in black liberation theology that may unleash its liberative potential for the black church. Given the dire psychological and physiological consequences associated with the failure to express one's anger, Kacela contends that black liberation theology must become better at appropriating anger (203). The latter, in his view, is a central aspect of the human condition that encompasses the whole range of human emotions including an honest expression of pain and suffering.

According to Kacela, such an appropriation of anger includes not being afraid of making use of the rich biblical traditions about anger in the face of injustice (210–11). In the spirit of the biblical prophets, simply to name anger evoked by injustice and oppression, constitutes a powerful act that may result in much needed change. Moreover, drawing on the work of Marjorie Proctor-Smith, Kacela highlights the importance of, and even the "obligation" to remain angry, thus, tapping into the transformative power of anger (212).

The emphasis on a productive expression of anger in terms of black liberation theology has received new significance in the context of protest movements such as #BlackLivesMatter and, in my context, #RhodesMustFall, #OpenStellenbosch, and #FeesMustFall. In her response to #BlackLivesMatter and the legacy of Martin Luther King on the role of "constructive rage" and "righteous anger" (which may be regarded as the driving forces behind these movements), Yolanda Pierce (2018) reflects on the famous quote by African American writer and activist Audre Lorde (1981) on anger:

> Every woman has a well-stocked arsenal of anger potentially useful against those oppressions, personal and institutional, which brought that anger into being. Focused with precision it can become a powerful source of energy serving progress and change. I am speaking of a basic and radical alteration in those assumptions underlying our lives. Anger is loaded with information and energy.

Pierce (2018) continues to offer examples from African American history in which these sociopolitical movements were propelled forward because of "righteous anger," "prophetic rage," and "holy indignation." As she writes,

"In the 1950s and 1960s, lunch counters, voting booths, church basements, bus depots, public schools, and public streets all became sites in which to deploy an arsenal of anger as demonstrators sang 'We Shall not Be Moved,' along with 'We Shall Overcome.'"

This obligation to remain angry is also at the heart of the #BlackLivesMatter movement that according to Pierce (2018), emphasizes the importance of attending to the question at the heart of contemplating black humanity: "Do black lives matter?" With the unequivocal response that "made in the imago dei, the image and likeness of God, Black lives matter as distinct individuals and in the interconnectedness of all humanity."

Also in black liberation theology in South Africa, anger has and continues to play an important role. Jakub Urbaniak (2017, 102) describes how Tinyiko Maluleke (2015, 35) draws upon the satirical play *Woza Albert!* (written by M. Ngema, P. Mtwa, and B. Simon in 1981), which portrays Jesus as returning to a township in South Africa at the height of Apartheid in order to offer a theological response to the question of righteous anger in the context of poverty and injustice. According to Maluleke, Jesus in *Woza Albert!* returns to a context that faces grave challenges in the form of poverty, unemployment, and inequality, as well as corruption and leadership crisis. As a result, Jesus responds in outrage to "the poverty, the hunger, the corruption and deceit that reign while the innocent suffer." Maluleke (2015, 35–36) writes:

> Such is his shock at this situation of dehumanisation, he not only joins the people in their struggle but ends up getting arrested like so many others at the time.... The play ends with Jesus calling the great heroes of liberation—Albert Luthuli, Steve Biko, Lillian Ngoyi, Robert Sobukwe and many others—back to life, resurrecting them one by one.

According to Urbaniak (2017, 102), black theology offers Maluleke theological resources to make sense of the righteous anger of those caught in the grips of poverty and inequality. Urbaniak argues that "as he takes the side of the vulnerable and the sinned against, Jesus simply shares their anger." And as the so-called Fallist movements in South Africa have clearly shown, students, in particular, are angry. A quote from a *Daily Maverick* article, cited by Urbaniak (2017, 90), is worth noting:

> "We can't breathe" is a phrase often cited by students. Black students have to struggle or be extremely lucky to get into university and face family financial pressures or be lumped with future debt. By their nature,

universities reproduce past knowledge systems before they create new thoughts, meaning Black students are not only usually taught by Whites but taught White. To breathe, or to survive, under financial constraints and repeated cultural domination seems impossible, or at least only tolerable to pay back, pay forward, family investment. (Nicolson 2016)

In light of this productive role of anger in black liberation theology, that is, to raise awareness and to bring about change in response to the experience of being physically and metaphorically suffocating in communities near and far outlined above, let us now turn to a profound biblical expression of an angry prophet whose anger, as we will see below, may also be characterized as "righteous anger," "prophetic rage," and "holy indignation." In the final chapter of the book of Jonah, Jonah is depicted as being outside the city of Nineveh, facing the center of imperial subjugation, whose cruelty has made yet another community to be unable to breathe.

Jonah's Anger

In Jonah 4, God asks Jonah twice whether it is "right," or one could also say "good," for him to be angry. God asks Jonah this, the first time, in response to the prophet's rant regarding God's failure to act in anger against the Ninevites (Jonah 4:4). Jonah is thus angry because he knew all this time that God is "slow to anger," as evident in the well-known theological axiom he references that God is "a gracious God and merciful, slow to anger, and abounding in steadfast love, and ready to relent from punishing" (John 4:2; cf. also Exod 34:6–7; Num 14:18–19; Neh 9:17; Pss 86:15; 103:8; 145:8; Joel 2:13; Green 2005, 144–45). As Carey Walsh (2015, 270) says, "Jonah is angry that YHWH is who tradition claims he is!"

The second time God asks Jonah whether it is "right" or "good" for him to be angry is in Jonah 4:9. Barbara Green notes that Jonah is livid when a plant inexplicably comes up in the night only to disappear again without any warning (Green 2005, 143). The reader here knows more than Jonah does, as we are told that it is God who provides the plant as shelter for Jonah in the scorching heat, and the same God who appoints a worm "to attack" or "wage war" against the plant, much the same way in which an invading army attacks a defenseless city (Sherwood 1998, 49).

Many of Jonah's readers do not think that it is good or right for Jonah to be angry. Thomas M. Bolin (1997, 59) writes that Jonah's anger has been interpreted often as painting a picture of the prophet as petty, narrow minded, and resentful (cf. also Graybill 2019, 95). Moreover, Serge Frolov (1999, 87) gathers evidence of the various ways in which Jonah again and again has been the subject of "character scanning" by scholars and preachers who paint Jonah, for example, as a "petulant and peevish prophet whose anger is irrationally aroused by God's act of mercy," exhibiting a "narrow outlook," and engaging in "petty hatefulness."

However, viewed through a different lens that takes into consideration the importance of the reader's context, a different meaning emerges. For instance, one should note that Jonah's anger is in direct response to the lack of consequences for the unjust actions inflicted by this epicenter of the Assyrian Empire, which has come to represent empires since then to date (Downs 2009, 40; Fischer 2018, 309). For instance, Chesung Ryu (2009, 209) who writes in his South Korean context, which continues to deal with the wounds of its imperial past under Japan, argues that "Jonah's anger would have been reasonable to a colonized audience," which would have serious reservations about whether this God who sides with the oppressor still may be "called the God of Israel or the God of the oppressed."

Also, the second reference in Jonah 4:9 to Jonah's anger may be drawing on this connection between anger and injustice. The fact that the verb "to smite" (נכה), which is typically found in the context of military invasion, is used to describe the destruction of the plant suggests that Jonah's anger may not primarily be focused on his own discomfort in the scorching heat. Rather, this story of a vulnerable plant being violently attacked by a militarized worm may also be read as a symbol of the profound precarity associated with the aftermath of imperial invasion in which individuals are left vulnerable without adequate shelter and protection (Sherwood 2000, 279–80; Green 2005, 140).

In this regard, Jione Havea (2013, 49) is one of the postcolonial biblical interpreters who views Jonah's anger in terms of what has been described above as "righteous anger." He argues as follows:

> I begin with the obvious: a colonial power (read: Nineveh) should not be let off the hook but called to account for its past and ongoing violent actions. This is the implied reason in 4:2 for why Jonah "went on strike." Jonah knew that G*d's mercy would let Nineveh off the hook, even if only in the story world, and Jonah fumes not because he hates Nineveh but because G*d spares Nineveh.

Thus, it is precisely *because* God's anger recedes that Jonah becomes even more furious. Jonah is angry because God is *not* angry (4:2). With the ongoing effects of colonization in his context of Oceania clearly in mind, Havea (2013, 50) vents his own frustration at the lack of anger displayed by God:

> The thorn in my side is not that i do not want a merciful G*d, but that it rubs salt into my native eyes when mercy trumps justice for desperate and colonized peoples. The poor and downtrodden obviously need mercy. But [in God's decision to relent from punishing Nineveh] mercy benefits those who have done wrong more than those who are desperate. If i have to choose between mercy and justice, i pick justice because it benefits those who have been wronged and with whom i am in solidarity.

Rihannon Graybill is another scholar who offers a sympathetic reading of Jonah's anger. She reads the book of Jonah in conversation with Sarah Ahmed's (2010) compelling book, *The Promise of Happiness*. Graybill (2019, 105–6) views Jonah's refusal to be happy in terms of Ahmed's (2010, 121–59) notion of the "melancholic migrant," who resembles the nonwhite migrant in her own context of Britain. Typically, from the former British colonies, the melancholic migrant refuses to be happy in order to comply with the empire's insistence just to be happy, to let go of the wounds inflicted by colonialism, as well as the ongoing suffering caused by systemic racism. Read through this lens, Jonah is expected to just get over it; to let go of the hurt inflicted by empires past and present and to embrace happy memories of "a universal God who shows mercy to all" (Graybill 2019, 107). However, as a melancholic migrant, Jonah is claiming the right to be unhappy—his anger described in terms of the prophetic critique as "the practice of unhappiness" (109). As Graybill argues, "Unhappiness may do the work of critique; it may also open the possibility of imagining other ways of being" (105–6; cf. also Bolin 1997, 173–75).

Furthermore, one sees in the book of Jonah signs that Jonah's anger may cause him to fall into despair. Tzvi Abusch (2013, 149) argues that given the distinct downward trajectory evident throughout this book, as represented in the repeated use of the verb ירד ("go down"), Jonah may indeed be viewed as depressed. As Elizabeth Boase and Sarah Agnew (2016, 17) also argue, "Jonah's flight, behaviour on the ship, then descent into the sea and the belly of the great fish are described in terms of depression, the outside world reflecting the inner state of the central character, or indeed, Jonah himself seeking death right from the beginning of the story." Jonah is literally sinking deeper and deeper into despair, mirrored in his descent into the hull of the boat, into a deep sleep, plunging to the bottom of the sea after being thrown overboard, and going down, even further down into the depths of Sheol. Moreover, coupled with Jonah's repeated death wish in Jonah 4:8–9, Abusch (2013, 148) may be right that Jonah only seems to be able to "express his anger in a self-destructive fashion."

Also, Graybill (2019, 108) makes a case for the way in which anger and melancholia are deeply entrenched in the book of Jonah in that Jonah's anger may not be connected to the demise of the plant after all, but rather pertains to an inability "to mourn what cannot be admitted as lost." In this regard, Fiona Black (2019, 82) offers some insight into this question of what it is that may be lost for the angry prophet. In her essay on depression in the Psalms, Black employs the work of Ann Cvetkovich (2012, 115), who describes depression not as the consequence of "biochemical imbalances," but rather, of "colonialism, genocide, slavery, legal exclusion, and everyday segregation and isolation that haunt all of our lives." In the context of Ps 137, for example, it may be the loss of land, the failed Israelite dream, as well as the "threats against stability and integrity" that induce the psalmist's experience of depression (Black 2019, 83). Likewise, reading Jonah in light of Ahmed's notion of the melancholic migrant, one could argue that Jonah's unhappiness may thus be connected to "suffering the pain of dislocation, which can never be salved," as well as the ongoing hardships associated with imperial invasion and ongoing forms of subjugation (Black 2019, 88; cf. also Havea 2016, 99).

For Black (2019, 90), the poetic portrayal of depression in the individual and collective psalms of lament attests to the fact that "psalmic depression" has become "a type of *lingua franca* for exilic times." What is more, this public profession of unhappiness, fulfills a political purpose, as it publicly makes the case that there is something seriously wrong. In this regard, the expression of unhappiness in these psalms fulfills, as Black (2019, 91) has argued, the following function: "To open up pain and grief could mean an opportunity to pry apart the biblical colonial narrative and insert or explore the voices of dissent." Viewed in this way, one could say that in the case of Jonah's lament, "I am angry enough to die," it *is* good for Jonah to be angry. This is the case because affective language, such as the expression of anger and deep sadness, is as Black attests, "generative—of cultures of transformation and therapeutic or healing spaces" (91).

Havea (2013, 52) also supports Jonah's courage to stay angry. He imagines an "angry *and* calm Jonah" who continues to engage God (and the colonizer) with passion in a way that "privileges the voices of dissent and opens the path for justice." As he contends, "The Wrath of Jonah does not add up to hatred and discrimination but to the weaving of justice into mercy and peace" (54). Similarly, Green (2005, 140) argues that "anger has its positive place as an energy, as an apt reaction to something that is seriously wrong. Anger is often an authentic response we do best to recognize, acknowledge, channel, and transform." In these scholars' appropriation of Jonah's anger in the context of ongoing forms of injustice caused by old empires in new guises, it is evident that what is necessary for Jonah's anger to be good, or right(eous), is that it constitutes a productive form of anger in order to have any hope to usher in much needed change.

Conclusion

In this essay, we have seen how recent engagements on the important role of anger in black liberation theology may help us to rethink the portrayal of divine and human anger in the book of Jonah. It was shown how, particularly in the context of (South) Africa, a context that has been a primary research focus of Holter throughout his ongoing illustrious career, anger in the face of injustice may propel into action also "socially concerned biblical scholars," whom as Holter (2016; cf. also 1998; 2006a; 2006b; 2008) has so eloquently argued, "claim a right to participate," applying the best of their "insights and tools of their particular academic discipline," to fight ongoing manifestations of injustice as evident, for instance, in the ongoing forms of oppression attributable to systemic racism, sexism, homophobia, as well as the slow violence of poverty.

As we bring to a close this essay on anger and the book of Jonah in celebration of the life and legacy of Holter, one should note that there is a thin line between anger and despair. In an insightful article on feminism and anger, Jilly Boyce Kay and Sarah Banet-Weiser write in the context of the #MeToo movement, that "when anger is mobilised for feminist ends and still appears incapable of cracking the edifice of patriarchal and misogynistic power, it leaves a way for deep despair to set in."[3] Indeed, in this "Age

---

3. Kay and Banet-Weiser (2019, 606) specifically refer to the 2019 case of the controversial confirmation hearings of US Supreme Court justice, Bret Kavanaugh, that saw the measured testimony of Christine Blasey Ford who accused Kavanaugh

of Anger," to cite the title of Pankaj Mishra's book, *Age of Anger: A History of the Present* (2017), Kay and Banet-Weiser (2019, 603) highlight the very real possibility that anger may cause people to become resentful and bitter. Particularly when anger goes unheeded and injustice continues, people may fall into despair, and without much hope for change, anger may thrive and grow in its impotence, turning destructive. One sees evidence of such despair when property is destroyed or stores looted. Conversely, despair finds expression in inaction, causing people to disengage, fail to vote, losing all hope for any sort of meaningful future.

In the South African context in which I live and write and which is near and dear to Holter, as evident in his many publications in *Old Testament Essays* (*OTE*), as well as his deep scholarly and professional ties to this country, the suffocating reality of systemic racism, sexism, homophobia, and the dehumanization caused by poverty in many instances prevail, which may have the effect of anger turning into despair.

There is, though, a compelling alternative to despair that may be helpful for our thinking about what constitutes productive anger in our respective contexts today that offer fruitful possibilities for socially concerned biblical scholarship. In their article on feminism and anger, Kay and Banet-Weiser (2019, 607) invoke an archaic fifthteenth-century word, namely, "respair," which can be defined as "fresh hope; a recovery from despair." In terms of this understanding, hope and despair coexist, as "it is only by embracing anger and despair—and recognising them as legitimate aspects of our politics—that we can hope for genuine, transformative change." As they argue:

> The despair of respair, after all, is what has given us the bleak illumination we need to allow for any meaningful political work to take place. Things are worse than we thought; the task is so much greater than we knew—this can be mobilising rather than immobilising, if we try to rethink despair as something to be worked with rather than against. Respair is a hope that comes out of brokenness, but which does not mandate optimism or insist on happiness as an antidote or cure. (608)

---

of sexual assault when they were students, but which had no effect whatsoever. These televised proceedings caused many feminists to experience a "sense of overwhelming despair," rooted in "the realisation that the anger of #MeToo had not been enough; that what had felt like the unprecedented power of women's rage could not, in the end, batter down the doors of white male entitlement; that misogyny, after all those deeply painful and traumatic disclosures—after everything—had still won" (606).

In terms of this understanding, repair may help forge the type of productive anger that can be said to be "mobilising rather than immobilising" and that is able to work for change from within the very experience of despair. In our (South) African context, concepts such as the therapeutic and transformative potential of anger, as well as Kay and Banet-Weiser's notion of repair could be further developed in terms of how uniquely African responses of anger to injustice may enhance and perhaps challenge Western notions of anger. One could consider what impact such specifically African understandings of anger have on the portrayal of divine and human anger in the book of Jonah. But this is the topic of another essay!

Viewing Jonah's anger amid his experience of despair as a productive anger, in terms of Pierce's designation of "righteous anger," "prophetic rage," and "holy indignation," Jonah finds himself in the frontlines of the protesters, fist in the air, screaming and shouting at Nineveh, and the God who sides with the oppressor as current and future interpreters join in the struggle of holding, as a way to continue holding the feet of empires, old and new, to the fire.

Works Cited

Abusch, Tzvi. 2013. "Jonah and God: Plants, Beasts, and Humans in the Book of Jonah: An Essay in Interpretation." *JANER* 13:146–52.

Ahmed, Sara. 2010. *The Promise of Happiness*. Durham, NC: Duke University Press.

Anderson, Monica. 2016. "The Hashtag #BlackLivesMatter Emerges: Social Activism on Twitter." Social Media Conversations about Race, Pew Research Center, 15 August. https://tinyurl.com/SBL3817e.

Black, Fiona. 2019. "Public Suffering? Affect and the Lament Psalms as Forms of Private-Political Depression." Pages 71–94 in *Reading with Feeling: Affect Theory and the Bible*. Edited by Fiona. C. Black and Jennifer L. Koosed. SemeiaSt 95. Atlanta: SBL Press.

Boase, Elizabeth, and Sarah Agnew. 2016. "'Whispered in the Sound of Silence:' Traumatizing the Book of Jonah." *Bible and Critical Theory* 12:4–22.

Bolin, Thomas M. 1997. *Freedom beyond Forgiveness: The Book of Jonah Re-examined*. Sheffield: Sheffield Academic.

Cvetkovich, Ann. 2012. *Depression: A Public Feeling*. Durham, NC: Duke University Press.

Dentliger, Lindsay. 2018. "#FeesMustFall Damage Costs Soar to Nearly R800m." https://tinyurl.com/SBL3817f.

Downs, David J. 2009. "The Specter of Exile in the Story of Jonah." *HBT* 31:27–44.

Fischer, Irmtraud. 2018. "'Alles andere als zum Lachen': Das Jonabuch als Anleitung zur Traumatisierungsbewältigung." Pages 305–15 in *The Books of the Twelve Prophets*. Edited by Heinz-Josef Fabry. Leuven: Peeters.

Frolov, Serge. 1999. "Returning the Ticket: God and His Prophet in the Book of Jonah." *JSOT* 86:85–105.

Graybill, Rhiannon. 2019. "Prophecy and the Problem of Happiness: The Case of Jonah." Pages 95–112 in *Reading with Feeling, Affect Theory and the Bible*. Edited by Fiona C. Black and Jennifer L. Koosed. SemeiaSt 95. Atlanta: SBL Press.

Green, Barbara. 2005. *Jonah's Journey*. Collegeville, MN: Liturgical Press.

Havea, Jione. 2013. "Adjusting Jonah." *IRM* 102:44–55.

———. 2016. "Sitting Jonah with Job: Resailing Intertextuality." *Bible and Critical Theory* 12:94–108.

Holter, Knut. 1998. "It's Not Only a Question of Money: African Old Testament Scholarship between the Myths and Meanings of the South and the Money and Methods of the North." *OTE* 11:240–54.

———. 2006a. "Interpreting Solomon in Colonial and Post-colonial Africa." *OTE* 19:851–62.

———. 2006b. "Let My People Stay! Introduction to a Research Project on Africanization of Old Testament Studies." *OTE* 19:377–92.

———. 2008. "'A Negro, Naturally a Slave.'" *OTE* 21:373–82.

———. 2016. "The 'Poor' in Ancient Israel—and in Contemporary African Biblical Studies." *MS* 33:209–21.

Kacela, Xolani. 2005. "Towards a More Liberating Black Liberation Theology." *Black Theology* 3.2:200–214.

Kay, Jilly Boyce, and Sarah Banet-Weiser. 2019. "Feminist Anger and Feminist Respair." *Feminist Media Studies* 19:603–9.

Lorde, Audre. 1981. "The Uses of Anger: Women Responding to Racism." *National Women's Studies Association Conference*. June. https://tinyurl.com/SBL3817g.

Maluleke, Tinyiko S. 2015. "Between Pretoria and George Goch Hostel: God in South Africa in 2015." *New Agenda* 59:35–39.

Mishra, Pankaj. 2017. *Age of Anger: A History of the Present*. New York: Farrar, Straus & Giroux.

Nicolson, Greg D. 2016. "Student Protests: Only the Start of Greater Pain." *Daily Maverick.* 28 September. https://tinyurl.com/SBL3817s.

Pierce, Yolanda. 2018. "Righteous Anger, Black Lives Matter, and the Legacy of King." *Berkley Center for Religion, Peace and World Affairs.* 16 January. https://tinyurl.com/SBL3817h.

Ryu, Chesung Justin. 2009. "Silence as Resistance: A Postcolonial Reading of the Silence of Jonah in Jonah 4.1–11." *JSOT* 34:195–218.

Sherwood, Yvonne. 1998. "Cross-Currents in the Book of Jonah: Some Jewish and Cultural Midrashim on a Traditional Text." *BibInt* 6:49–79.

———. 2000. *A Biblical Text and Its Afterlives: The Survival of Jonah in Western Culture.* Cambridge: Cambridge University Press.

Urbaniak, Jakub. 2017. "Theologians and Anger in the Age of Fallism: Towards a Revolution of African Love." *Black Theology* 15.2:87–111.

Walsh, Carey. 2015. "The Metaprophetic God of Jonah." Pages 259–74 in *History, Memory, Hebrew Scriptures: A Festschrift for Ehud Ben Zvi.* Edited by Diane Gersoni-Edelman and Ian Douglas Wilson. Winona Lake, IN: Eisenbrauns.

Part 4
Ecology in Context

A Wandering Aramean and the Wandering Maasai: An Intercultural, Ecotheological Dialogue

Beth E. Elness-Hanson

Introduction

In December 1999, I was in Tanzania on the verge of the next millennium. While the Western world was anxious about Y2K, the turning was insignificant for the Maasai, a pastoralist people group in Kenya and Tanzania. While not all Maasai continue in ancestral ways, many still live with their cattle and goats, and thus they are inherently dependent upon grazing lands, very similar to the days of their ancient ancestors.[1] In contrast, in my urban context, I am distanced from a dependence upon the land for life. Thus, this examination begins with an exegetical dialogue with Maasai Christian theologians in Tanzania, where contexts matter for shaping our respective interpretations.[2] Together, we read Deut 26:1–15 and discussed our relationships to God and the land, recognizing that our understandings are influenced by our contexts, which provided opportunities to learn from each other.[3]

---

1. The term *traditional* refers to the Maasai worldview, and *ancestral* refers to the pastoralist lifestyle practiced by Maasai of different faiths. There is a danger of reductionism when reflecting upon the ancestral ways. While many Maasai continue in them, there is increasing diversity, with many choosing contemporary lifestyles.
2. Richter (2020, 18–19) also gathers biblical insights from contemporary cattle and sheep ranchers.
3. Holter (2008, 18, 38–39) makes a distinction between "Letting the Old Testament interpret Africa" and "Letting Africa interpret the Old Testament." Both approaches are factors here. I also clarify that this is not a reading of Deut 26 *through* a Maasai lens. I am not Maasai. I am in dialogue with the Maasai, which creates opportunities to learn from each other.

First, I identify an interpretive framework of triangulated shalom, developed from the ontological structure of the Maasai worldview that is correlated with the ecological triangle model, as described by Hilary Marlow. Marlow (2015, 110–11, 275–78) draws on Christopher J. H. Wright's (2004, 19) "creation triangle." Then, my exegesis of Deut 26:1–15 interlaces classic historical-critical analysis with an intercultural dialogical approach (Elness-Hanson 2017, 31), enfolding content gathered through qualitative research methods, specifically, the conversations with Maasai Christian theologians.[4] This approach was originally developed for my PhD research—under the excellent supervision of the honoree, Professor Knut Holter, for a project that was part of the Norwegian Research Council grant, "Potentials and Problems of Popular Inculturation Hermeneutics in Maasai Biblical Interpretation" (Holter, 2018). I write this essay in honor of Holter, who also directed that research. Finally, this essay includes ecotheological considerations drawn from the anthropological research by Sara de Wit (2018) on issues of climate change among the Maasai. This discussion integrates the holistic aspects of the UN's Sustainable Development Goals (SDGs) that include both human and nonhuman factors in creation care (Nilsen 2020b; Nilsen and Solevåg 2016, 665–83; United Nations n.d.).[5] The analysis of Deut 26:1–15 demonstrates that the church's ontological relationship with God, humans, and the environment makes it a strategic agent for ecological teaching and praxis in Maasailand (Elness-Hanson 2022).[6]

Interpretive Framework: Triangulated Shalom

Over the past few hundred years, this Nilotic people group immigrated south to a region in East Africa, stretching from central Kenya to south-central Tanzania (Spear 1993, 1; Sutton 1993, 38). Historically, the Maasai were exclusively pastoralists, where life centered around and was sustained

---

4. The Norwegian Centre for Research Data (NSD) approved the research (ms-509301). The interviews occurred in February 2020. Fictionalized names meet the anonymization regulations of the Norwegian Centre for Research Data (NSD).

5. I affirm Nilsen's rationale for using the SGDs, contra the Earth Bible Project. See Nilsen and Solevåg 2016.

6. This paper was developed into a successful Marie Skłodowska-Curie Postdoctoral Fellowship, Ontological Bridge-building for Climate Change Mitigation in Maasailand, granted in May 2022 and beginning Aug 2023 with Holter as supervisor.

by cattle.[7] Believing in a monotheistic creator, Engai, is symbolized by a three-legged wooden stool, "olorika," found in every family settlement (boma), according to research participant R. "Lemayian" (interview, 19 February 2020). Blessings in life are contingent upon three core relationships: Engai, others, and the environment. Principally, this worldview holds that the harmony of these relationships is maintained by faithfully following the traditions that Engai has made known through divinations by traditional shaman, "laiboni" (Elness-Hanson 2017, 77–95). These oracles are implemented through the collective wisdom of the male elders in alignment with their traditions. As three points determine a plane, the three legs of this Maasai stool form a triangle for the first stage of the triangulated-shalom framework.

The Ecological Triangle

The Maasai worldview triangle correlates to the triangle that Arthur Waskow describes as an "organic whole." Waskow (2000, 81) writes, "For the 'eco-Judaism' of the Bible, spiritual [God] enrichment is profoundly connected with limiting the society's exploitation of the earth [creation], and both of these are intimately intertwined with limiting the mastery of the rich and powerful over the poor [humans]." Thus, ecological well-being includes peace with God, creation, and others. Correspondingly, Wright (2004, 103, 106, 117) develops a "creation triangle" of God, humanity, and the earth, recognizing that the earth holds the tension of divine ownership and divine gift. Marlow (2015, 110) appropriates Wright's "creation triangle" in the description of how the eighth-century prophets' proclamations represent an environmental ethic. Marlow's cogent exegesis undergirds her paradigm of the ecological triangle with the three dimensions of God, humanity, and all nonhuman creation.

Thus, this examination applies the ecological triangle and develops an interpretive framework of triangulated shalom. Shalom—with a meaning that encompasses wholeness, health, and completeness—carries an understanding beyond "peace" when understood as the "absence of war" or conflict (Healey 1992, 206). More so, shalom includes freedom from all conflicts resulting from injustice, violence, or any other abuse of power and thus, the fullness of life. As Cornelius Plantinga Jr. (n.d.) rightly

---

7. The traditional Maasai claim that Engai gave all the cattle in the world to them.

summarizes, "the webbing together of God, humans, and all creation in justice, fulfillment, and delight is what the Old Testament prophets called shalom.... In the Bible shalom means universal flourishing, wholeness, and delight." Here, the multidimensional flourishing of triangulated shalom combines the Maasai worldview's ontological structure with the ecological triangle following Wright's and Marlow's exegesis.

Delimitations

The following exegetical portion presents a dialogue between historical-critical exegesis and Maasai contextual content. This is an ethical attempt not to privilege Western perspectives by setting a standard interpretation with which to compare the Other perspective (Elness-Hanson 2017, 31). However, this dialogue creates a zigzagging, like when sailing and tacking back and forth at angles into the headwind.[8] In addition, this is not a Maasai reading, neither is it coauthored. Rather, this is my analysis, as a Western exegete engaging an intercultural-comparative-ecotheological approach. My findings are informed by the biblical text and shaped by dialogues with the Maasai.[9]

Furthermore, this exploration engages a comparative approach, an approach that is dominant in African biblical hermeneutics (Holter 2002, 88; West 2008, 37–64). Often, the predominant bipolar approaches (engaging text and context) foreground similarities and have less critical engagement with contrastive aspects. However, tripolar approaches (engaging text, context, and a hermeneutical framework) are fruitful to avoid flattened bipolar comparisons while affirming readings that integrate contextual content (Elness-Hanson 2021; cf. Grenholm and Patte 2000). The hermeneutical framework here is the ecotheological triangulated shalom.

Finally, Jonathan A. Draper (2015, 9) notes that fuller interpretations integrate a "'moment of autonomy for the text' over against the reader ... so that we may be transformed by the experience of an-*other*." Unfortu-

---

8. To delineate, the Maasai content is italicized.

9. The complete transcribed material is edited to match the scope of this essay. Some gaps are evident in the Maasai contextual content, as I seek to include as many significant comments as possible that were made when discussing the text. I have added other Maasai ethnographic and theological content to guide any readers who are not familiar with the Maasai worldview.

nately, the contextual content below is not more contrastive due to word limits. Nevertheless, the goal of "reading with" (West 2013, 44) Maasai theologians provides opportunities to expand understandings.

Intercultural Dialogue on Deut 26:1–15

In the literary context where Moses is equipping the ancient Israelites for entering the promised land, this text comes at the end of the Deuteronomic Law Code (Deut 12–26).[10] It serves as the hinge, turning from the code and toward covenant renewal, in preparation for the two covenant ceremonies—one with Moses on the plains of Moab and the future ritual at Shechem with Joshua (Christensen 2002, 626).[11]

The traditional Maasai believe that they have a covenant-like relationship with Engai *(Kimirei 1973, 71; Donovan 2003, 33). Some Maasai Christian theologians believe that they are one of the lost tribes of Israel (Holter 2020, 143; cf. Sankan 1973, viii; Spencer 2009, 255).*[12] *Even if not descendants of Abraham, the special relationship that the Maasai have with* Engai *shapes a worldview that is intimately connected with the divine. This relationship with* Engai *permeates life, their interpersonal relationships, their sense of land, and—among the traditional Maasai—their understanding of the cause of climate change.*

In addition, *the Maasai are regarded as highly ethical in relation to their ancestral law codes, and they hold the execution of justice as a core value (Elness-Hanson 2017, 121; cf. Sankan 1973, xxiv). This traditional system*

---

10. Cf. Walton (2012, 116). Walton (2012, 116) identifies that 287 out of 331 verses of Deut 12–26 can be categorized as Decalogue exposition.
11. Christensen identifies:
    A. Public worship at the annual festivals in the promised land 26:1–19
    B. The renewal of the covenant at Shechem 27:1–26
      X. Blessings and curses of covenant renewal in Moab 28:1–69
    B'. Appeal for covenant faithfulness in the future 29:1–28
    A'. Call to decision: life and blessing or death and cursing 30:1–20
12. Holter identifies the first documented correlation of the Maasai with ancient Israel/Semitic roots as Moritz Merker's (1910) study of the Maasai. Four contrasts help develop a critical distance from simple parallels. The Maasai have: (1) no Sabbath; (2) no food laws requiring draining blood, while they do not combine meat and dairy; (3) circumcision done during adolescence as a rite of passage to warrior status without connection to divine covenant; and (4) no written scriptures or emphasis on studying Torah (Elness-Hanson 2017, 114).

has a strong resonance with the Decalogue, which is used in Christian education and liturgies in Maasailand (Elness-Hanson 2017, 121).

In a concentric structure, the correlating content of Deut 26:1–11 focuses on the vital decision to choose life and the blessings from covenant obedience (paralleling with 30:1–20). Thus, the identified curses and calamity—the central text (28:1–69) of these five chapters—are avoided.

The traditional Maasai worldview holds that Engai *is free to give both life and death, blessings and curses (Payne and Ole-Kotikash 2006).* Engai *is described as black when imparting blessings, and when misfortune is wielded, this angry side of* Engai *is referred to as red (Donovan 2003, 33). Thus, when the traditional Maasai hear of the biblical accounts of blessings and cursing or good and evil, they see a continuity with their worldview and their understanding of* Engai *(Elness-Hanson 2017, 130). The blessings in life, such as children and even rain, are seen as coming from* Engai.

Life sustaining rain is seen as a manifestation of Engai, *so when it rains, according to research participant R. Miterienanka (interview, 24 February 2020), "the Maasai say, 'God has come.'" The opposite is also understood, such that droughts are seen as evidence of broken relationships with God, others, and the environment. Anthropologist de Wit (2018, 35) writes, "The climate serves as a mirror between God and His people, a way to mediate morality and communicate both gratification as well as discontent."*

Focusing on the liturgy of firstfruits at the central sanctuary (26:1–11), this text prepares for the possession of the land of promise and includes language that all were to recite as individuals in a liturgical, ceremonial context, addressing "YHWH your God" (26:5, 13) and bringing offerings of the first fruits of the land (Tigay 1996, 240). This "First Fruits Recitation" (26:5–10) is only one of two prescribed orations for the laity in the Torah (also 21:7–9; cf. Tigay 1996, 237). The land—twice identified as "flowing with milk and honey"—is viewed as a gift from YHWH in fulfillment of the covenantal promise.

Every morning, a traditional Maasai woman will say a prayer to Engai *and give an offering of first "fruits"—literally, first milk—when milking the cows. For the Maasai, milk comprises a majority staple in their diet. With one hand, a woman will milk directly into a gourd* (calabash). *M. S. Ndapukai (personal communication, 19 May 2020) describes this offering: "A woman squirts just a little milk from each of four teats of the first cow to be milked into the gourd," and then, she stands and tosses a little milk from the gourd in the four directions of the earth as an offering to* Engai. *While offering the milk, the woman's prayer begins, "Ashe Engai inchoo iyook kuna kule" meaning, "Thank you, God, for giving us this milk" (N. "Nailegeleg," personal communication, 13 June 2020).*

In Deut 26:1–11, the center of the structure is what Gerhard von Rad called the "small historical credo" (cited in Christensen 2002, 632). The historical recital starts with "a wandering Aramean [was] my father" (v. 5). Here, ארמי אבד is typically translated a "wandering" Aramean; however, according to Benedikt Otzen (1974, 20), אבד, as a *qal* masculine singular participle, combines the principal meanings of "to perish" and "wander off." In this distinctive occurrence, Otzen identifies a sense of "an Aramean on the point of destruction." Jeffrey H. Tigay (1996, 240) translates this as "fugitive," though he notes that the meaning is uncertain. As Walter Brueggemann (2001, 246) summarizes, "The past of Israel is rooted in an at-risk ('wandering') Aramean semi-nomad." The risk is compounded at this juncture when Israel transitions from pastoralist semi-nomadism to settled agriculturalists. Waskow (2000, 71) identifies "a crisis of Israelite society" when this transition fundamentally shifted the ancient Israelite relationship with the earth, transitioning from semi-nomadic herders to a landed agricultural society.

The Maasai are also pastoralists and their lifestyle resonates with the biblical nomadic motifs (Nkesela 2020, 72). While much of the ancestral grazing land is not suitable for agriculture, some Maasai are making efforts to cultivate the land as a way to sustain claims to indigenous lands (Meindertsma and Kessler 1997, 13, 38, 46). Land is vital for the Maasai, and the loss of land through the development of national parks and agricultural encroachment highlights the at-risk nature of pastoralists (de Wit 2018, 30).

The text's recital continues to describe the sojourning in Egypt, where they became a great nation that was subsequently humiliated and put into harsh servitude. Yet, YHWH heard their voice; saw their affliction, suffering, and oppression; and brought them out from Egypt with signs and wonders.

Reflecting on the text, Miterienanka (interview, 24 February 2020) identified with the concept of humiliation, "The Maasai people really have been facing humiliation. Because, how can they continue on as a people without land?" Lemayian (interview, 19 February 2020) held the Maasai understanding that the land belongs to God, and that Engai *gave them their grazing lands.*

The culmination of YHWH's providence to ancient Israel is manifested in giving the bounteous land. The seven-fold repetition of the root "to give" (נתן) forms a concentric structure with a six-fold pulsation, confirming that YHWH (named fourteen times in eleven verses) is the giver of the land (Christensen 2002, 634). The concentric focus connects the offering of the firstfruits with the mighty acts of deliverance from slavery and being brought to this promised land. The land, while given to Israel to dwell in, still belongs to YHWH (Christensen 2002, 636). Sandra Richter (2020, 17) describes YHWH as the landlord and the people of Israel as renters. Richter also identifies the role of humankind that was delegated by the Creator as caretaking tenants in the creation (21).

"The Maasai are very friendly with the environment," states Miterienanka (interview, 24 February 2020), because "the Maasai people love the land and they don't really cause any purposely intended destruction of the land." The Maasai do not cut trees but rather harvest the dead branches for their biofuel (Lemayian, interview, 19 February 2020; Meindertsma and Kessler 1997, 49). Grasslands are typically not burned, except in limited efforts to kill disease-causing ticks and protect their cattle (Lemayian, interview, 19 February 2020).[13] The seasonal migrations of cattle both abates overgrazing and restores nutrients to the soil with organic manure fertilizer (Miterienanka, interview, 24 February 2020). The Maasai do not hunt wild animals for food, as they only eat the meat of cows, goats, and sheep. A lion is killed only if it has invaded the boma (settlement) and killed a cow. Lemayian (interview, 19 February 2020) notes that where the Maasai lived, there were so many wild animals because they were not hunted. So, these were the places where several national parks and conservation areas were established, including the Serengeti and Tarangire National Parks, as well as the UNESCO World Heritage Site, the Ngorongoro Crater. With tourism contributing 17 percent of the country's gross domestic product (Mirondo 2019), and 10.77 percent of the nation's employment (Knoema 2019), Lemayian (interview, 19 February 2020) exclaims, "Today, in this country, if not for the Maasai, I think … we'd be poor."

Land is a pillar of the Abrahamic covenant (Gen 12:7; 15:5) and a central theme within the Pentateuch (Clines 1997, 29). Deuteronomy 26:1–15 is a credo that is a cornerstone for the connection of ancient Israel's identity with the promised land (Holter 2014, 64). However, land tenure is conditioned on covenant faithfulness, as stated within this text, while disobedience is identified as the rationale for the exile (Lev 26:14–33; 2

---

13. It is now known that burning grasslands releases carbon into the environment and endangers fauna.

Kgs 17:7–23; Neh 9:30). Brueggemann (2001, 250) writes, "The thrust of Deuteronomy makes clear that this relationship of mutual fidelity is conditional. It depends upon Israel's readiness to honor its vow of obedience, for obedience is the condition of YHWH's devotion to Israel."

The traditional Maasai do not see continuation of dwelling in the land as contingent upon obedience, as they believe that Engai gave them the land without condition. However, the Maasai do see their sustained flourishing within the land as contingent upon obedience. So, catastrophes are the consequences for broken relationships with God, others, and the environment, such that blessings and calamities are a mirror that mediates morality. Lemayian (interview, 19 February 2020) sums up the relationship of the Maasai with Engai's gift of land, saying, "Land is very important for the life of the Maasai.... Without land, no life. Exactly. Without land, there is no life."

Reflections and Conclusion

The intercultural dialogue of Deut 26:1–15 identifies connections between the pastoralists of wandering, Aramean descent and the contemporary Maasai. Both have triangulated ontological worldviews with the interdependent relationships of God, humans, and nonhuman creation, and a special focus on land. Both demonstrate a livelihood that is intimately dependent upon the land. With a recognition that the land is a gift from God, both ancient Israelites and traditional Maasai give offerings to God of their first harvests—whether seasonal fruit or daily milk. While there are innumerable differences, both the biblical ecological triangle and the Maasai ontological worldview recognize the interconnectedness of God, humans, and nonhuman creation for flourishing. Where harmonious relationships with God, others, and the environment result in holistic well-being, there is triangulated shalom.

However, the environmental challenges for the contemporary pastoralist Maasai are tremendous and have jeopardized their shalom. First, since colonial times, the Maasai have seen great reductions of ancestral grazing areas. The establishment of national parks and conservation areas as well as agricultural encroachment on the best lands with stable water sources have reduced the grazing lands, especially during dry seasons. The early years of independence included forced relocation into Ujamaa villages (Hodgson 2001, 161). While the scope of this essay cannot deal with all the complex issues around land rights (Gastorn 2016, 181; Meindertsma and Kessler 1997, 30), it is important to acknowledge that government's pressures on the Maasai include the "ideological hijacking" of the concept of "carrying capacity" of the land, which serves the government's rationale to reduce Maasai herd size (de Wit 2018, 30). Anthropologist Dorothy L. Hodgson's (2001, 8, 203) work among the Maasai recognized that so-called development is "central to the establishment, exercise, and expansion of state power," which integrally relates to increasing tax revenue.

Second, the land reduction is exacerbated by seasonal irregularity and changing rainfall patterns—connected with anthropogenic climate change—that magnify the effects of these drought prone areas (de Wit 2018, 25, 28; Meindertsma and Kessler 1997, 13). Thus, the Maasai describe an "increasing unpredictability" of the climate (de Wit 2018, 36). While the Maasai recognize the aberrations of the seasonal cycles, the government's educational efforts have resulted in a "confusing 'ontological incompatibility'" with the Maasai worldview (35). De Wit documents that the climate change discourse was met with "great suspicion" as the Maasai heard the message from the scientists of "stop praying to God for He has nothing to do with [the lack of rain], but plant trees instead" (35). Even Leboi—a specifically chosen "climate change witness" who was one of the few who could discuss anthropogenic climate change—ended up abandoning the scientific "metacode." This he says is

> Because we are aware that these changes are coming from God, and nobody knows the secret of God. And in our locality the climate knows a lot of fluctuations. One year you might expect rain and there will be no rain, in another year you expect drought but there is enough rainfall. And because of these fluctuations nobody knows the secret of God. And that is why also we cannot trust these men who are telling us about climate change (de Wit 2018, 26, 35).

Thus, there is a unique opportunity for the church, as indigenous leadership has a more trusted role in the community. The church shares an ontological worldview of triangulated shalom, with the interconnectedness of God, humankind, and the creation. The church's holistic message holds the tension of the wellbeing of the people and the environment that resonates with SDGs (Nilsen 2020b, 1). Environmental efforts that do not address the human aspects, especially that of the poor, are not holistic (Marlow 2015, 18; Nilsen 2020a, 316–38). Indeed, the church is committed to the people it serves, as the pastors and priests live among the Maasai. They have skin in the game, sharing a message that is grounded in the Scriptures, informed with broader knowledge, and sensitive to the context for shared stronger outcomes. The church can be a reliable agent to address climate change education and restorative praxis—like the Lutheran Church in Tanzania did in response to the HIV/AIDS crisis (Jacobson 2017; personal communication, 6 July 2020). The church can rise as a critical agent for the health of God's creation.

Even more so, the church knows how to engage transformation. Gus Speth, Chairman of the Council on Environmental Quality under President Carter states:

> I used to think that top environmental problems were biodiversity loss, ecosystem collapse and climate change. I thought that thirty years of good science could address these problems. I was wrong. The top environmental problems are selfishness, greed and apathy, and to deal with these we need a cultural and spiritual transformation. And we scientists don't know how to do that. (Curwood and Speth 2016)

Similarly, Marlow (2015, 253) states that secular environmentalists identified "the change in human ethics with regard to land will only take place if there is an internal change in human emphases and convictions—and this will not happen until philosophy and religion enter the debate."

Clearly, the church has a strategic role in the biblically grounded commission of creation care in order to address the ecological challenges of the contemporary pastoralist Maasai. The harmony of the triangulated shalom ontologies holds together the relationships with God, humanity, and nonhuman creation. The church's more trusted presence with indigenous leadership in the midst of shared community can further develop environmental education and practices that integrate human and ecological well-being, aligning with many of the SDGs. Moreover, as witnessed throughout history, the church can be an instrument of transformation.

Works Cited

Brueggemann, Walter. 2001. *Deuteronomy*. Nashville: Abingdon.
Christensen, Duane. 2002. *Deuteronomy 21:10–34:12*. WBC 6B. Grand Rapids: Zondervan.
Clines, David J. A. 1997. *The Theme of the Pentateuch*. 2nd ed. Sheffield: Sheffield Academic.

Curwood, Steve, and J. Gus Speth. 2015. "We Scientists Don't Know How to Do That." Wine and Water Watch. 13 February. https://tinyurl.com/SBL3817i.

De Wit, Sara. 2018. "Victims or Masters of Adaptation? How the Idea of Adaptation to Climate Change Travels Up and Down to a Village in Simanjiro, Maasailand Northern Tanzania." *Sociologus* 68:21–41.

Donovan, Vincent J. 2003. *Christianity Rediscovered*. Maryknoll, NY: Orbis.

Draper, Jonathan A. 2015. "African Contextual Hermeneutics: Readers, Reading Communities, and Their Options between Text and Context." *R&T* 22: 3–22.

Elness-Hanson, Beth E. 2017. *Generational Curses in the Pentateuch: An American and Maasai Intercultural Analysis*. New York: Lang.

———. 2021. "Twin Stories of Brothers: A Comparative Analysis of Jacob and Esau with the Maasai Legend of Senteu and Olonana." Annual Meeting of the Society of Biblical Literature. San Antonio, Texas. 20 November.

———. 2022. "Ontological Bridge-Building for Climate Change Mitigation in Maasailand." Unpublished Marie Skłodowska-Curie Postdoctoral Fellowship Proposal.

Gastorn, Kennedy. 2016. "The Emerging Constitutional Indigenous Peoples Land Rights in Tanzania." *Journal of Law, Property, and Society* 2:181–221.

Grenholm, Cristina, and Daniel Patte. 2000. "Overture: Receptions, Critical Interpretation, and Scriptural Criticism." Pages 1–54 in *Reading Israel in Romans: Legitimacy and Plausibility of Divergent Interpretations*. Edited by Cristina Grenholm and Daniel Patte. Harrisburg, PA: Trinity Press International.

Healey, Joseph P. 1992. "Peace: Old Testament." *ABD* 5:206–7.

Hodgson, Dorothy L. 2001. *Once Intrepid Warriors: Gender, Ethnicity and the Cultural Politics of Maasai Development*. Bloomington: Indiana University Press.

Holter, Knut. 2002. *Old Testament Research for Africa: A Critical Analysis and Annotated Bibliography of African Old Testament Dissertations 1967–2000*. New York: Lang.

———. 2008. *Contextualized Old Testament Scholarship in Africa*. Nairobi: Acton.

———. 2014. "My Father Was a Migrant Aramean: Old Testament Motifs for a Theology of Migration." Pages 57–70 in *Global Diasporas and

Mission 23. Edited by Chandler H. Im and Amos Yong. Oxford: Regnum Books International.

———. 2018. "Potentials and Problems of Popular Inculturation Hermeneutics in Maasai Biblical Interpretation." Stavanger. https://tinyurl.com/SBLPress3817a2.

———. 2020. "Maasai and Ancient Israelites: Religio-cultural Parallels." Pages 107–19 in *Maasai Encounters with the Bible*. Edited by Knut Holter and Lemburis Justo. Nairobi: Acton.

Jacobson, Mark. 2017. *Arusha Lutheran Medical Centre Annual Report 2017*.

Kimirei, G. 1973. "Reconciliation among the Maasae in Comparison with Reconciliation in the Old Testament." Master's thesis. Wartburg Theological Seminary.

Knoema. "World Travel and Tourism Council Data." Knoema.com. 2019. https://knoema.com//WTTC2019/world-travel-and-tourism-council-data.

Marlow, Hilary. 2015. *Biblical Prophets and Contemporary Environmental Ethics*. Repr., Oxford: Oxford University Press.

Meindertsma, J. D., and J. J. Kessler, eds. 1997. *Planning for a Better Environment in Monduli District*. Rotterdam: Netherlands Economic Institute.

Merker, Moritz. 1910. *Die Masai: Ethnographische Monographie eines Ostafrikanischen Semitenvolkes*. 2nd ed. Berlin: Reimer.

Mirondo, R. 2019. "Number of Tourists Visiting Tanzania Rises to 1.5million." The Citizen. 27 July. https://tinyurl.com/SBL3817j.

Nilsen, Tina Dykesteen. 2020a. "Ecology and Economy of Shmita (Exod. 23.10–11; Lev. 25.1–7; Deut. 15.1–6): Biblical Texts and Contemporary Judaism." Pages 316–38 in *The Bible and Money: Issues of Economy and Socioeconomic Ethics in the Bible*. Edited by Markus Zehnder and Hakkvard Hagelia. Sheffield: Sheffield Phoenix.

———. 2020b. "Green Goals: The SDGs in Ecological Hermeneutics." *BibInt* 1:1–15.

Nilsen, Tina Dykesteen, and Anna Rebecca Solevåg. 2016. "Expending Ecological Hermeneutics: The Case for Ecolonialism." *JBL* 135:665–83.

Nkesela, Zephania Shila. 2020. *A Maasai Encounter with the Bible: Nomadic Lifestyle as a Hermeneutic Question*. New York: Lang.

Otzen, Benedikt. "אָבַד." *TDOT* 1:9–23.

Payne, Doris L., and Leonard Ole-Kotikash. 2006. "Ɛnk-áí." In *Maa (Maasai) Dictionary*. University of Oregon. https://tinyurl.com/SBLPress3817a3.

Plantinga , Cornelius, Jr. n.d. "Our Calling." Calvin University. https://tinyurl.com/SBL3817k.

Richter, Sandra L. 2020. *Stewards of Eden: What Scripture Says about the Environment and Why It Matters*. Downers Grove, IL: IVP Academic.

Sankan, S. S. Ole. 1973. *The Maasai*. Nairobi: East African Literature Bureau.

Spear, Thomas. 1993. Introduction to *Being Maasai: Ethnicity and Identity in EastAfrica*. Edited by Thomas. Spear and Richard Waller. Athens: Ohio University Press.

Spencer, Paul. 2009. *Time, Space and the Unknown: Maasai Configurations of Power and Providence*. London: Routledge.

Sutton, J. E. G. 1993. "Becoming Maasailand." Pages 38–60 in *Being Maasai: Ethnicity and Identity in East Africa*. Edited by Thomas Spear and Richard Waller. Athens: Ohio University Press.

Tigay, Jeffrey H. *Deuteronomy*. 1996. The JPS Torah Commentary. Philadelphia: The Jewish Publication Society.

United Nations. n.d. "The 17 Goals." United Nations: Department of Economic and Social Affairs. https://tinyurl.com/SBL3817m.

Walton, John H. 2012. "The Decalogue Structure of the Deuteronomic Law." Pages 93–117 in *Interpreting Deuteronomy: Issues and Approaches*. Edited by David G. Firth and Philip S. Johnston. Downers Grove, IL: IVP Academic.

Waskow, Arthur Ocean. 2000. "Earth, Social Justice, and Social Transformation: The Spirals of Sabbatical Release." Pages 70–83 in *Torah of the Earth: Exploring 4,000 Years of Ecology in Jewish Thought*. Edited by Arthur Ocean Waskow. Vol. 1. Woodstock, VT: Jewish Lights.

West, Gerald O. 2008. "Interrogating the Comparative Paradigm in African Biblical Scholarship." Pages 37–64 in *African and European Readers of the Bible in Dialogue: In Quest of a Shared Meaning*. Edited by Gerald O. West and Hans de Wit. Leiden: Brill.

———. 2013. "Locating Contextual Bible Study within Praxis." *Diaconia* 4:43–48.

Wright, Christopher J. H. 2004. *Old Testament Ethics for the People of God*. Downers Grove, IL: IVP Academic.

From Eurocentrism in South Africa to Ecological Universalism in Amos: An African Ecological Reading of Amos 9:7

Ntozakhe Simon Cezula and Tina Dykesteen Nilsen

Introduction

While the Hebrew Bible often portrays Israel's privileged position with Yahweh over against other nations—a position frequently connected to the exodus from Egypt—Amos 9:7 presents a different stance:

> Are you not like the children of Cushites to me,
> children of Israel?—statement by Yahweh—
> Did I not bring Israel up from the land of Egypt,
> and Philistines from Caphtor, and Aram from Kir?[1]

In this essay, we celebrate our good friend and colleague Professor Knut Holter by analyzing the preceding text in conversation with two of his publications (Holter 2000, 2015).[2] The article follows Holter's (2000) structure, as it considers first the interpreters' contexts, then, the text and its literary context. Finally, we transform Holter's historical context into a reading influenced by a contemporary context. In our approach, we combine African and ecological hermeneutics.

---

1. All biblical translations in English are our own.
2. In this essay we engage the book of Amos as the end product of a redactional process; that is, we treat the whole book as a unit.

Interpreters' Contexts

In two articles on Amos 9:7, Holter (2000, 115–18; 2015) discusses the history of the interpretation of the verse. Holter (2000, 115–16; 2015, 306–13) shows how Western scholars interpreted Amos 9:7 negatively as a threat that the Israelites may be brought down to the level of the Cushites. Such an interpretation, Holter argues, is influenced by the interpreters' own contexts—a culture in which black Africans and African Americans had recently been slaves and in which they were regarded as inferior. Holter goes on to show that, contemporaneous with the abolition of the European colonies in Africa (and sometimes even earlier), a more positive interpretation of Amos 9:7 also appeared in Western biblical scholarship. The verse is seen as a promise that Israel would be lifted up to the high level of Cush. Holter (2000, 116–18; 2015, 313–17) notes that African biblical scholars such as David Tuesday Adamo argue for a positive interpretation of Amos 9:7. Holter traces this to the postindependence era in which African universities partook in national developments by focusing on African questions and identity, among others. In biblical scholarship, Africa in the Bible (and the Bible in Africa) became an important topic.

Holter (2015, 318) shows not only that the interpreters' own contexts matter in interpretation, but also that the interpretative contexts should matter. We should, he claims, be open about our own concerns. In many conversations, Holter situates himself as a white European scholar who engages in African biblical scholarship. It is the opinion of the authors of this essay that on the continuum where Western hermeneutics is at the one end and African hermeneutics at the other, Holter would certainly be closer to the African end of the axis, with all its varieties. In line with Holter's call for openness, we include a few words about ourselves.

As authors, we come from two different contexts. One is a black Xhosa man in South Africa engaging in African hermeneutics, and the other is a white Norwegian woman in Norway engaging in ecological hermeneutics. Yet we share an agenda: to provide an interpretation of Amos 9:7 in this essay that counters Eurocentrism and that combines insights from African and ecological hermeneutics. Through our encounters, we learn from each other's hermeneutical stance. It is a dialogue between an African scholar and a European scholar, inspired by Holter (e.g., 2008b).

Africa is one of the Bible's hermeneutical cradles; yet during colonial times, it was Western hermeneutics that characterized biblical interpretations on the continent (Holter 2008a, 83–92; 2008b; Ukpong 2006). While colonizers used the Bible as an instrument to subject Africans to Europeans, the Bible was not passively received but engaged with through active interpretation, paving way for African biblical hermeneutics—the Bible interpreting African contexts, and African contexts interpreting the Bible (Holter 2008a, 92–115; 2008b; Ukpong 2006; West 2008a).

Ecological hermeneutics is the interpretation of texts or a study of the interpretation of texts that focuses on ecology, that is, on the interrelationships between living organisms and/or between the latter and their habitats (Nilsen and Solevåg 2016, 672). In biblical studies, many different approaches to ecological hermeneutics exist (Nilsen 2020; Nilsen and Solevåg 2016). Some scholars use their African contexts to interpret biblical texts ecologically (Gitau 2000; Kebaneilwe 2015; Kavusa 2021). Bigger projects that involve several scholars also contribute to the dialogue, notably, the 2008 forum of the Nigerian Association for Biblical Studies (NABIS), Western Zone, focused on the Bible and ecology, particularly, in relation to environmental issues which affect Africa (Manus 2009).

The United Nation's "2030 Agenda" states that all seventeen Sustainable Development Goals (SDGs), whether they concern social justice or ecology, are indivisible; one cannot achieve one without achieving the others (see United Nations 2020; for application in biblical hermeneutics, see Nilsen 2020). Our analysis is ecological because interrelationships between living organisms and their habitats are the focus, but it is also located in African hermeneutics in that our interpretation allows the biblical text and a specific contemporary African context to communicate with each other. We use a comparative approach, presenting a paradigmatic reading in which we find parallels between the contemporary South African context and the ancient text of Amos. The former allows us to pose certain questions to the latter, while the latter also may present pointers to the former.

Literary Context

Holter (2000, 118–23) argues that the poetic devices in Amos 9:7 underline the mutual relationship of Israel and Cush to Yahweh. Not least is this emphasized by making Israel's major salvific experience as one example among many. Holter analyzes the reference to Cush in Amos 9:7 in the context of the role of the nations in the book of Amos. Cush illustrates the point that Yahweh has a relationship not only with Israel, but also with other nations. Holter then identifies Cush in biblical texts outside of Amos.

While Holter (2000, 123–25) concludes his article on the historical context of Amos 9:7, this essay transforms the analysis of the historical context into an analysis rooted in our own contemporary context. Thus, we return to our own contexts as interpreters, and engage in a literary analysis of Amos 9:7 in the light of these contexts.

A Contemporary Context

As interpreters, we come from different contexts, but for this study we have chosen a context to which one of us is an insider and the other an outsider: South Africa. We will focus on Eurocentrism, which has deep social and economic impacts, as its presupposed superiority leads to discrimination and racism in that context. We will discuss language perspectives as one example of such an impact on the ecological reality.

The institutionalized racial discrimination in South Africa created deep racial fault lines characterized by mistrust among different racial groups. Therefore, the postamble of the Constitution of the Republic of South Africa Act 200 of 1993 states:

> This Constitution provides a historic bridge between the past of a deeply divided society … and a future founded on … peaceful co-existence and development opportunities for all South Africans.… The pursuit of national unity, the well-being of all South African citizens and peace require reconciliation between the people of South Africa and the reconstruction of society. (Republic of South Africa 1993)

Reconciliation is thus intertwined with national unity. Describing the consequent Promotion of National Unity and Reconciliation Act, Tinyiko S. Maluleke (1997, 61) says it "must itself be understood in the context of the underlying project, to achieve national unity and national reconciliation." National unity acknowledges diversity and encourages tolerance. However, many South Africans have to forgo their cultures to take up Eurocentric notions of what constitutes proper "business culture" (Kwenda 2003, 69–71). Some cultures eventually become more equal than others. Postapartheid South Africa is built on a modern system that is shaped by nineteenth-century modernity.[3] These Eurocentric notions are

---

3. The concept of modernity is the collation of European sociocultural norms, attitudes, and practices, emanating from the European Renaissance and hegemonically imposed on other contexts.

the product of that modernity, which continues to operate as an invisible power matrix that is shaping and sustaining asymmetrical power relations between the Western and the African cultures in South Africa. Since modernity and Christianity were twin processes, the perceived superiority of Western culture and its explicit or implicit racism were also justified through the Bible.

F. A. Oborji (2003, 323–24) refers to a Hamitic theology that "perceived Africans as the children of the cursed" son of Noah, Ham (cf. Gen 6:2; 9:20–27). Similarly, Holter (2008a, 5) asserts that, in the nineteenth and twentieth centuries, "the so-called curse of Ham in Genesis 9:20–27 … gained particular attention … to justify slave trade and colonialism versus Africa." Thus, in a way, the idea of Eurocentrism, racism, and the theology of apartheid were "built upon the heresy of the superiority of the White race and the curse of the Black people" (Adeyemo 1997, 15). The consequent widespread condemnation of African religion and culture by the Christian missionaries of the nineteenth and twentieth centuries led to the origin of modern biblical studies in sub-Saharan Africa (Ukpong 2006, 62). Holter (2008a, 5–6) views this development as a valuable addition that challenges the above stereotypes.

In this spirit, Adeyemo invalidates the Hamitic theology. He reveals that in Gen 9:1, God blessed Noah and his sons, including Ham. Noah could therefore not curse whom God has blessed. Noah could also not curse Cush, Ham's firstborn son, because he was protected by the law of the firstborn (Gen 27:1–37; Deut 21:17). However, referring to Num 12:1 and Jer 13:27, Holter (2008a, 5) observes that "whenever a Cushite appears in Old Testament, there has been a tendency to interpret the Cushite as slave." Adeyemo (1997, 17) further contends that "according to the biblical law of succession, a double portion of Ham's blessing should go to his first son who is Cush, the Ethiopian or African." Noah did not curse Ham; neither did he curse Cush (Ethiopia), Mizraim (Egypt), or Put (Libya). He cursed Canaan, the last born. The sons that can be associated with (North) Africa are the first three; Canaan's location is not Africa. The association of Africa with Noah's curse is thus *eisegesis* (Holter 2008a, 5–6).

Despite the legislative interventions for cultural equality in South Africa, ratification at school, workplace, and institutions endorses English or Afrikaans cultures, especially English and/or Afrikaans languages. Bemoaning this state of affairs, Thobeka V. Mda (2015, 19) writes that

> African politicians display no interest in pushing the development and uplifting of the African languages. There seems to be a need by African language-speakers generally, including government officials, to impress others that they have mastered English (the symbol of civilization and sophistication) and that they have outgrown African languages, the symbol of the "linguistic and cultural ghetto" to which they were assigned.

Because of the humiliation that accompany these circumstances, many Africans in South Africa wish they were English or Afrikaans speaking. Despite the policies, there is a growing attitude that African languages are not relevant in ascending the socioeconomic ladder. According to the research conducted by Steven Gordon and Jacqueline Harvey (2019), 55 percent of black parents in 2003 preferred English as medium of instruction for their children at all levels of education. In 2016, the number increased to 65 percent. The general view is that English is superior to other official languages. Mda (2015, 18) thus concludes that "African languages seem to be inevitably destined for extinction."

This threat raises a question about the fate of plants and animals that are protected by clans that hold them as their totems. A well-known example is in the novel *Ingqumbo Yeminyanya* (*The Wrath of the Ancestors*) by Archibald C. Jordan. A westernized bride killed a snake regarded as the ancestor of the clan, thus, arousing the wrath of the ancestors. Because languages are the media for transmitting this valuable knowledge, their extinction means losing this knowledge. As is already evident, some westernized Africans treat African beliefs as superstition, and they do not hesitate to hurt these totems when they feel threatened. But the extinction of these languages also means the vulnerability of the plants and animals. The situation highlights the United Nation's SDGs and their emphasis on connections between social justice and ecology, in particular, SDG 4.7, which speaks, among others, about "appreciation of cultural diversity and of culture's contribution to sustainable development" (see United Nations 2020).

Eurocentrism is a form of cultural centrism, even ethnocentrism, with deep consequences for socioeconomic as well as ecological matters. In the Hebrew Bible, we do not find Eurocentrism, but we do find another form of cultural centrism in some of the texts that deal with particularism. In these texts, Israel is presented as an elected nation that is superior to others, but with consequences for both socioeconomic and ecological matters. The parallels between the two forms of cultural centrism—Eurocentrism and particularism—have been explored on the African continent. During colonization, Europeans adopted biblical particularism, seeing themselves as elect and consequently superior to others whom they set out to civilize. The stories about leaving Egypt and conquering Canaan served as paradigms for civilizing the "barbaric" natives into a "superior" culture—an idea that has mutated in different political contexts in South Africa and elsewhere (Akenson 1992, 45–96; cf. Buthelezi 1975; West 2008a; 2015), leading to discrimination and racism.

Seeking a paradigmatic reading, the South African context makes us ask three questions about the text of Amos: (1) In the light of the Eurocentrism in South Africa, what is the stance on cultural centrism in Amos 9:7 and its literary context? (2) Due to Eurocentric negative effects on social justice issues, we ask: How does Amos 9:7 and its literary context outbalance cultural centrism? (3) One of the effects of Eurocentrism is ecological denigration, and so we ask: What is the connection between cultural centrism and ecology in Amos?

As Holter (2000, 121) argues, in the book of Amos, particularism and universalism—the idea that Yahweh is the god of the whole world—exist side by side. We argue that the book of Amos uses universalism to outbalance particularism. We need to seek answers to our first two questions simultaneously. Holter (2000, 121) uses Amos 3:1–2 as an example of particularism, and we wish to expand on his analysis. Amos 3:1–2a couples the exodus from Egypt with a declaration by Yahweh that "only you I know of all the families on earth." However, while particularism elsewhere in the Hebrew Bible is frequently connected to privileges, in the book of Amos, the consequence of Israel's special status is punishment, as shown by על־כן ("therefore," 3:2b): "*therefore* I will visit upon you all your iniquities." In its most explicit statement of particularism, the book overturns a traditional understanding of particularism.

As mentioned above, Holter (2000, 118–19) shows that Amos 9:7 compares Israel's major salvific event with similar events among other nations. Among other poetic devices, Holter points out the use of geographical orientation, with Cushites in the South, Philistines in the West, Arameans in the North, and Edom in the East in verse 12. Though Holter does not say so, this presupposes a geographical centrism—Israel as the center of the cardinal directions. Unlike the common (mis)conception that "center" means "importance," we argue here that Amos 9:7 unties this connection. In Amos 9:7, the geographical outskirts and the center are equal in their relationship to Yahweh. Thus, a geographical centrism does not legitimate cultural centrism.

The idea that particularism gives special privileges is also transmuted by 6:1–3. Here we find a dirge for Israel's notables (or pierced ones?)—a funeral lament for thinking they may be secure in Zion; undoubtedly a reference to the Zion traditions. In mocking mimicry of the notables, Israel is termed "the first of the nations." Though the Hebrew of the following verse is difficult, it seems to reveal that the particularism of the notables is a misconception—they are not better than other peoples. The verses triply echo 9:7. First, there is a series of rhetorical questions which compare Israel to other nations. Second, these nations are placed along the axis of cardinal directions—Calneh to the east, Hamath to the north, and Gath to the west. Third, the inhabitants associated with two of the cities are also found in 9:7—Arameans in Hamath and Philistines in Gath. The verses thus ridicule any lofty thoughts on the part of the Israelites; they intertwine particularism and universalism and, in doing so, overturn any form of cultural centrism.

The dirge in 6:1–3 continues in verse 4 and following, where those lamented for are the rich and powerful in Israelite society. They are considered dead because of the lack of social justice (6:12). The juxtaposition of 6:1–3 and 6:4–14 draws connections between traditional particularism and social injustice: The rich and powerful close their eyes, hands, and hearts to the poor and powerless. Cultural centrism has led to social injustice, just as Eurocentrism has done in our own time.

In relation to particularism and universalism, Holter (2000, 121) analyzes the chiastic echo at the end and the beginning of the book of Amos—Israel, the Philistines, and the Arameans (9:7) in the salvation oracles at the end of the book mirror the Arameans (1:3–5), the Philistines (1:6–8), and Judah/Israel (2:4–5/6–16) in the judgment oracles at the beginning of the book. Even though Edom breaks the pattern, it is present both at the beginning (1:11–12) and the end (9:12). Holter argues that these texts convey the idea that Yahweh is responsible for the history of all nations, and all nations are responsible to Yahweh.

We think that the connection between the opening and the ending of the book is strengthened by the role of exile in these texts. In the judgment oracles in chapter 1, exile is mentioned explicitly or implicitly, either as a cause for punishment (1:6.9) or as the content of punishment (1:5, 15) for other peoples. Exile as punishment for Israel appears later in the text (5:27; 6:7; 7:11). Again, the book of Amos transforms particularism, both by outbalancing it with universalism (all nations are judged equally) and by twisting what particularism means (punishment, not privilege). Particularism is also found in other books in the Hebrew Bible, and, in some texts, this entails dreams of an imperial future in which Israel rules the world (e.g., Isa 60:3–16; 61:5–7; 66:12; Ps 68:29–36). In Amos, where particularism means punishment (3:1–2), there is no place for imperial dreams of greatness, but, rather, we find nightmares of defeat and exile (e.g., 5:27; 6:7; 7:11).[4] In transmuting the dream of particularism into a nightmare, the book is deeply universalistic, as judgment befalls other nations as well as Judah and Israel alike. A transformed particularism overturns cultural centrism.

In his analysis of the literary context of Amos 9:7, Holter (2000, 121) views the doxologies in 4:13; 5:8–9; 9:5–6 as universalistic texts. The doxologies have in common the representation of Yahweh as master of the universe. While Holter does not say so, this implies that Yahweh is also master of all nations. If Yahweh rules the world, Yahweh also rules every nation on the earth—that is why Yahweh can punish all nations. However, the universalistic aspects also carry ecological bearings, so we now turn to our third and final question—the connection to ecology.

In our analysis, the doxology of Amos 4:13 is linked to Yahweh's ongoing activity in creating features of the earth and to meteorological events as well as diurnal cycles—phenomena that are universalistic and to which all nations equally relate. Two aspects are particularly noteworthy. First, Yahweh turns morning into darkness (reading with the Masoretes). This is echoed in the oracle in 8:9–10, where Yahweh's reversal of the diurnal cycle coincides with judgment and mourning; in the book of Amos, even doxologies proclaim universal doom. Second, the phrase which proclaims that Yahweh tells Yahweh's thoughts to human beings is noteworthy. "Human beings" are expressed in the generic form אדם ("human being"); that is, Yahweh communicates with human beings as human beings, whether or not they are Israelites.

The doxologies in 5:8–9; 9:5–6 reflect some of the same points— Yahweh controls astronomical phenomena, diurnal cycles, and features of the earth. In both doxologies, Yahweh calls the waters, as if these were a conscious agent. In both, Yahweh's control over natural phenomena is explicitly linked to Yahweh's power to destroy. Like the doxology in 4:13, also the one in 9:5–6 is linked to the oracles in chapter 8 and this time to verses 7–8. In both texts, the earth will undergo dramatic changes,

---

4. Or is Amos 9:12 perhaps imperialistic?

and all inhabitants will mourn. Again, we see that the doxologies are linked to judgment and that this is universalistic; it includes all of earth's inhabitants.

We consider that the mourning of the inhabitants in the doxology in 9:5 and in the oracle in 8:8 echoes the opening statement of the book (1:2): "Yahweh roars from Zion, and from Jerusalem he gives his voice; and the pastures of the shepherds mourn, and the head of Carmel dries up." The use of the verb שאג ("to roar") presents Yahweh as a lion roaring out in his speech (cf. 3:4.8). It is a message to which nature immediately responds by a change in ecosystems, as the fertile areas become dry. The word אבל, which means both "to wither" and "to mourn" (cf. Hos 4:3), refers to both the pastures in 1:2 and earth's inhabitants in 8:8; 9:5, thus linking together the saddened state of earth and its inhabitants.

In the book of Amos, this relation between ecology and human beings is subtle. In the opening statement of the book (1:2), the ecosystems respond immediately to Yahweh's roar. The cause of Yahweh's roar is the social injustice (2:6–8; 4:1; 5:7, 10–15; 6:12; 8:4–6); this is the reason for judgment. There is a delicate connection between human behavior in matters of injustice, on the one hand, and ecological systems, on the other hand. It is not clear from 1:2 what the connection is, but other texts in the book of Amos draw it out, as we shall see below.

In the doxologies, Yahweh's power over the elements of nature implies Yahweh's power also over human history. This is a destructive power, and diurnal disturbances (4:13; 5:8; 8:9) and earthquakes (8:8; 9:5) may both be warnings of as well as parts of judgment. Such events befall Israel and the nations alike. In 4:7–10, ecological disasters caused by rain, blight, mildew, locusts, and pests are used in vain to push Israel into returning to Yahweh but are not part of the judgment. The lack of response on the part of human beings contrasts the immediate response to Yahweh's roar or call by the changes of ecosystems from wet to dry or dry to wet (1:2; 5:8; 9:6). Changes in ecosystems are warnings for human beings caused by Yahweh, but they may also be one of the consequences of judgment—judgment as punishment for social injustice.[5]

---

5. Marlow (2008, 75–83) argues that, in the book of Amos, earth (in its broadest, Earth Bible Project meaning) cooperates with and speaks for Yahweh by providing a vehicle for metaphors and visions; revealing the creator; and being means of judgment and punishment. See also Marlow (2009, 120–57), which applies a hermeneutical triangle (relations between God, humanity, nonhuman creation) to Amos.

In the book of Amos, a misconceived cultural centrism leads to attitudes that lie at the heart of social injustice, with consequences for elements of nature and for ecosystems of the earth. While the earth dries and mourns with its inhabitants (Amos 1:2; 8:8; 9:5), justice itself is compared to rolling waters and an ever-flowing torrent (5:24). In the oracle at the end of the book of Amos, salvation itself is imagined as a restoration of that which has been destroyed in judgment: architecture and ecological wellbeing (9:11–15).

Conclusion

Eurocentrism in South Africa today is detrimental to local cultures and has consequences for ecological matters, as we have exemplified through a discussion of language discrimination. Particularism in ancient Israel resembles Eurocentrism and racism in South Africa, thus forming a continuity between the two contexts. Informed by the South African context, we asked three questions about the book of Amos and discussed how the book overturns traditional cultural centrism by transforming the understanding of particularism and by coupling it with a universalism that destabilizes the center. Further, the book of Amos draws subtle connections between traditional cultural centrism, questions of social justice, and functioning ecological systems. However, there are also some differences. In South Africa, the resultant ecological disaster badly affects the victims of Eurocentrism, but in the case of ancient Israel, it is punishment to the perpetrators of particularism. Either way, the resultant ecological disaster is not welcome. Amos 9:7 outbalances particularism with universalism. Likewise, Eurocentrism needs to be overturned, and all peoples, cultures and languages in South Africa and beyond, need to be valued for their equal worth. With this comes the possibility of reaching the SDG target 4.7, ensuring "appreciation of cultural diversity and of culture's contribution to sustainable development" (the United Nations 2020).

Works Cited

Adeyemo, Tokunboh. 1997. "Is Africa Cursed?" Nairobi: Christian Learning Materials Centre.

Akenson, Donald Harman. 1992. *God's Peoples: Covenant and Land in South Africa, Israel, and Ulster*. Ithaca, NY: Cornell University Press.

Buthelezi, Manas. 1975. "Reconciliation and Liberation in Southern Africa." Pages 43–49 in *African Challenge*. Edited by Kenneth Y. Best. Nairobi: Transafrica.

Gitau, Samson K. 2000. *The Environmental Crisis: A Challenge for African Christianity*. African Christianity Series. Nairobi: Acton.

Gordon, Steven, and Jacqueline Harvey. 2019. "South Africans Prefer Their Children to Be Taught in English." *The Conversation*. https://tinyurl.com/SBL3817n.

Holter, Knut. 2000. "Is Israel Worth More to God than Cush? An Interpretation of Amos 9:7." Pages 115–25 in *Yahweh in Africa: Essays on Africa and the Old Testament*. Edited by Knut Holter. New York: Lang.

———. 2008a. *Contextualized Old Testament Scholarship in Africa*. Nairobi: Acton.

———. 2008b. "Does a Dialogue between Africa and Europe Make Sense?" Pages 69–80 in *African and European Readers of the Bible in Dialogue: In Quest of a Shared Meaning*. Edited by Hans de Wit and Gerald O. West. Leiden: Brill.

———. 2015. "Being Like the Cushites: Some Western and African Interpretations of Amos 9:7." Pages 306–18 in *New Perspectives on Old Testament Prophecy and History: Essays in Honour of Hans M. Barstad*. Edited by Rannfrid I. Thelle, Terje Stordalen, and Mervyn E. J. Richardson. Leiden: Brill.

Jordan, Archibald C. 1980. *The Wrath of the Ancestors*. Alice: Lovedale Press.

Kavusa, Kivatsi J. 2021. "Towards a Hermeneutics of Sustainability in Africa: Engaging Indigenous Knowledge in Dialogue with Christianity." *Verbum et Ecclesia* 42:http://dx.doi.org/10.4102/ve.v42i1.2263.

Kebaneilwe, Mmapula Diana. 2015. "The Good Creation: An Ecowomanist Reading of Genesis 1–2." *OTE* 28:694–703.

Kwenda, Chirevo V. 2003. "Cultural Justice: The Pathway to Reconciliation and Social Cohesion." Pages 67–80 in *What Holds Us Together: Social Cohesion in South Africa*. Edited by David Chidester, Philip Dexter, and Wilmot James. Cape Town: HSRC Press.

Maluleke, Tinyiko S. 1997. "Truth, National Unity and Reconciliation in South Africa: Aspects of the Emerging Agenda." *Missionalia* 25:59–86.

Manus, Chris Ukachukwu, ed. 2009. *Biblical Studies and Environmental Issues in Africa*. NABIS West Biblical Studies. Ibadan: Nigerian Association of Biblical Studies.

Marlow, Hilary. 2008. "The Other Prophet! The Voice of Earth in the Book of Amos." Pages 75–83 in *Exploring Ecological Hermeneutics*. Edited by Norman C. Habel and Peter Trudinger. SymS 46. Atlanta: Society of Biblical Literature.

———. 2009. *Biblical Prophets and Contemporary Environmental Ethics: Re-reading Amos, Hosea, and First Isaiah*. Oxford: Oxford University Press.

Mda, Thobeka V. 2010. "Politics of Dominance: The Suppression and Rejection of African Languages in South Africa." Paper presented at the World Council of Comparative Education Societies (WCCES) 14th World Congress. Boğaziçi University, Istanbul, Turkey. 14–18 June.

Nilsen, Tina Dykesteen. 2020. "Green Goals: The SDGs in Ecological Hermeneutics." *BibInt* 1:1–15.

Nilsen, Tina Dykesteen, and Anna Rebecca Solevåg. 2016. "Expending Ecological Hermeneutics: The Case for Ecolonialism." *JBL* 135:665–83.

Oborji, F. A. 2003. "Missiology in an African Context: Toward a New Language." *Missiology* 31:321–38.

Republic of South Africa. 1993. "National Unity and Reconciliation." Provision 15.251 in *Constitution of the Republic of South Africa Act 200 of 1993*. https://tinyurl.com/SBL3817o.

Ukpong, Justin S. 2006. "Developments in Biblical Interpretation in Africa: Historical and Hermeneutical Directions." Pages 49–63 in *Voices from the Margin: Interpreting the Bible in the Third World*. Edited by R. S. Sugirtharajah. Maryknoll, NY: Orbis.

United Nations. 2020. "Transforming Our World: The 2030 Agenda for Sustainable Development." United Nations: Department of Economic and Social Affairs. https://tinyurl.com/SBL3817p.

West, Gerald O. 2008a. "Contending with the Bible: Biblical Interpretation as a Site of Struggle in South Africa." Pages 101–16 in *The Bible in the Public Square: Reading the Signs of the Times*. Edited by Cynthia Briggs Kittredge, Ellen Bradshaw Aitken, and Jonathan A. Draper. Minneapolis: Fortress.

———. 2008b. "Interrogating the Comparative Paradigm in African Biblical Scholarship." Pages 37–64 in *African and European Readers of the Bible in Dialogue: In Quest of a Shared Meaning*. Edited by Hans de Wit and Gerald O. West. Leiden: Brill.

———. 2015. "Contending for Dignity in the Bible and the Post-Apartheid South African Public Realm." Pages 76–96 in *Restorative Readings: The Old Testament, Ethics and Human Dignity*. Edited by L. Juliana Claassens and Bruce C. Birch. Eugene, OR: Pickwick.

Part 5
Contexts beyond Africa?

"Our Grandfather Made the Earth for His Grandchildren": Biblical Scholarship Traveling to the Heart of the Andes; An Exercise in Intercultural Indigenous Hermeneutics

Hans de Wit

Introduction

It is a privilege to contribute to this volume in honor of the extraordinary contribution to (African) biblical scholarship by our colleague Knut Holter. It seems to me that there is no publication on the topic of the Bible in Africa in which Holter was not involved or mentioned. In Grant LeMarquand's (2000) "A Bibliography of the Bible in Africa," the Holter's name is mentioned 241 times, and the harvest of the last twenty years should be added to that number.

In addition to our shared interest in a number of topics in the field of biblical scholarship, we also share a remarkable, almost biographical parallel. Both of us, the African Norwegian and the Dutch Latino, fell in love with the analysis of how the Bible is read outside our own countries.

One of the questions that has strongly preoccupied Holter is that of dialogue in biblical scholarship. Over a decade ago, Holter (2008, 61) expressed himself in rather pessimistic words about the possibility of a real dialogue between European and African biblical scholars, saying, "the colonial past continues to cast its shadows and unless we do something with this situation, there will hardly be any dialogue." But there is hope, he maintains: "Having said this, I still believe that something can actually be done. African and European biblical scholars should develop research projects together" (61).

The title draws from Guaraya mythology (Bolivia): "Nuestro Abuelo hizo la tierra para sus nietos." All translations from Spanish to English are mine.

I want to respond to this challenge by traveling to another continent in order to offer the vistas that Bible reading in the high Andes portrays and to show how much the fulfillment of Holter's dream resonates with the project reviewed here. It is a project located within the field of empirical hermeneutics, which engages in dialogue between marginalized, mostly, extremely poor, indigenous communities[1] in Latin and Central America. It is a dialogue between *nonprofessional* readers promoted by biblical scholarship—something that also has had the heart of Holter (2015a, 355–68; 2015b, 31–40).

First, I wish to make clear my personal motives for initiating and carrying out, together with many colleagues, the project we analyze here. Second, I will review briefly what happened when the Book came to Latin America in the colonial period. The objectives of the project and the theological and hermeneutical importance of some of its results are shown in the next step. I will end with a word of hope.

My Personal Voice

The atmosphere is serene. With great dedication and devotion, participants read the story of Tamar and Amnon (2 Sam 13), and a few sessions later, they read the story of the prodigal son (Luke 15). There are seven participants in my small group, all Mexican, but the total number of participants is about sixty. The group consists of men and women from different church denominations and with different life experiences. They gathered in Mexico City for a course in contextual reading of the Bible. The central question of the course is: what do you see when you use trauma and trauma processing as keys to reading the Bible? Before me, in the circle of my small group is a young indigenous woman, a mother who comes from a small peasant village in the interior of Chiapas. She is Maya. Her two-year-old son is on the floor playing in the middle of the small circle of participants. After a few sessions, her shyness dissipates, and the mother tells in a soft voice how everyone in her Mayan village is busy with drug trafficking. Everyone is planting

---

1. The concept indigenous (communities, Bible reading, hermeneutics, etc.), which we use in this essay, refers to what in Spanish literature is defined as "Indian" or "indígena." Both concepts are used by indigenous scientists and theologians without much distinction and refer to non-Spanish people and practices, that is, the original population of the continent.

poppies, which are used for opium cultivation. She says that she and her husband are the only ones who plant corn, which means threat and exclusion for them. The villagers wonder how they earn their money if not from poppy cultivation. When asked which Bible text she would choose to share with her villagers and to connect to the problems they are both experiencing, she says she would like to read the parable of the sower (Mark 4:3–20).

There was a considerable number of Mayans and representatives of other indigenous groups among the participants in this course on contextual reading of the Bible. They had never met one another and were from different parts of the country. What they discovered, however, was how fertile and enriching it is to share experiences with people from previously unknown places of struggle and resistance. At the end of the course, the indigenous participants themselves, many of them members of one of the Christian churches in Mexico, asked us, the facilitators, to consider the possibility of starting a project of communitarian, inter-contextual Bible reading among indigenous communities in Latin and Central America.

This request brought about mixed feelings of hesitation and embarrassment. Is a European Bible scholar, despite many years of experience with Bible reading and living in Latin America, able to participate in such a project with integrity and without prejudice and colonial bias (de Wit et al. 2004; de Wit 2010; 2012; de Wit and Dyk 2015)? What finally made me decide to embark on the project was not only our long experience with this hermeneutics of hospitality, but also the ethics of interpretation—I began to see the invitation as an assignment and a matter of commitment and responsibility. By this I mean, if in the history of Christianity and Christian theology, colonialism and empire are somewhere present, then, that would be in the history of the discovery of the Americas.

Dutch scholar Mieke Bal (1991, 14) once expressed her view of the Bible in strong words, words that apply to the whole colonial history of the Book: "The Bible, of all books, is the most dangerous one, the one that has been endowed with the power to kill."

Chilean biblical scholar Pablo Richard (1997, 46), representing many voices, writes about this history: "The Bible was read and interpreted in a colonial and Western hermeneutics of domination. Even today, the Indians of Latin America or Abya Yala [*Earth in full maturity*, translation added] are experiencing a trauma with the Bible."

The Bible in Colonial Abya Yala: Three Perspectives

"The discovery of the New World could have meant a Copernican revolution for Western thinking," says Dutch philosopher Ton Lemaire (1986, 48). That several factors account for the unique hermeneutical challenge of the encounter with the indigenous Other, which became a failure and resulted in the worst genocide human history has ever known, is not in doubt. An important factor is that among the "visitors" (conquistadores) were many exsoldiers, impoverished, adventurers, criminals, convicts, and many peasants without future, without land (Herren 1997, 20–37). They came from a completely hierarchical Spain. What was plebe in Spain became hidalgo in America, now on the backs of the Indians.

What also makes dialogue impossible with highly developed religious systems such as the religions of the Maya, the Aztecs, and the Incas was the religious mental programming of the visitors, that is, of the Reconquista and Counterreformation. The religious Other is the enemy and should convert or will perish. What happened in five centuries of European history, a history of (holy) war, of crusades, was prolonged in the Americas (Herren 1997, 34).

As in all colonial historiography, the views about the colonial history of the Americas vary widely. I would like to mention three viewpoints very briefly that will help us to locate our project of intercultural indigenous Bible reading.

The Conquest Is Called "the Pink Legend"

It is the perspective of Roman Catholic triumphalism in which the term *spiritual* is added to the term *conquest*, and it is believed that the spiritual conquest was a completely successful enterprise and that the fruit of the surrender and conversion of the Indian people was led by the teachings of the friars. This way of telling the history of the conquest has been called la leyenda rosa (the pink legend). It has also been called the myth of the tabula rasa—the indigenous people supposedly accepted the Christian beliefs and practices without modifying them (Broseghini 1989, 43; Rubial García 2002, 42–44).

Like many other perceptions of the history of the conquest, it has become clear also that the pink legend (la leyenda rosa) is indeed a legend and that, as we shall see, the role of the indigenous people in the encounter with Christianity was much more active and assertive than has been suggested.

The Black Perspective

On the other hand, we see the utterly negative appreciation of that so-called spiritual conquest as the eradication of all ancestral beliefs (Broseghini 1989, 20). This perception of the history of the conquest has erroneously been called la leyenda negra (the black legend). Puertorican historian and theologian Luis Rivera Pagán (1991, 285, 289) criticizes the use of the term thus:

> It is difficult to sustain the perverse thesis that the stories of their humiliations are nothing more than a 'black legend'.... The contemporary testimonies that closely link the death of the natives and the violent greed of the newcomers are innumerable and overwhelming.

Dutch historian B. H. Slicher van Bath (1992, 105) estimates that by the time of consolidation (1650), "only 10% of the original inhabitants remained." A frequent expression used for the tragedy is "a process of genocide not deliberately intended, but incredibly effective" (291).

In the conquest of the Americas, as elsewhere (Holter 2008, 71–72), the perception of the Other was fueled by European superiority and the well-known colonial white mythologies. That one should recognize "Jesus of Nazareth, the Christ, in the tortured and scourged natives of the Indies," as in the case of Bartolomé de las Casas (Gutiérrez 1993, 18), is hastily debunked by many.

To give just one example, all the colonial myths of the time are found in the exposition of the Dominican friar that Tomás Ortiz presented in 1524 to the Royal Council of the Indies to defend the enslavement of the Indians:

> The Indians eat as many snakes and lizards and spiders and worms as are found on the ground.... Their bestiality is greater than that of any beast in the world.... The men of the mainland eat human flesh and are more sodomist than any generation.... They are cruel and revengeful, never forgiving. (quoted in Rivera Pagán 1991, 227)

This reference to sodomy and cannibalism does not represent a rare allegory; it was used a thousand times before and a thousand times afterward.

Because the existing ancestral religions were seen as devilish and demonic, dialogue was impossible—the Indians must convert. The most important motive for the indigenous people to convert to Christianity was the need to save themselves from the pains of hell with which the infidels and bad Christians would be punished and to obtain the perpetual enjoyment that God reserved for his friends (Broseghini 1989, 52). What the indigenous people had to know to be baptized was not the Bible but the sign of the cross, the creed, the Our Father, the Ave Maria, the Salve Regina, the fourteen articles of faith, and the seven deadly sins (54).

In vain does one look for moments of careful, communal reading of Scripture in those first decades of the conquest. The place of the Bible is an ambiguous one. On the one hand, it was the "Great Unread Book"; on the other, the Bible was used to legitimize the conquest. The Indians sacrifice the hearts and flesh of men to their gods. And does not Scripture teach us that this was the reason for the flood? Were not sodomy and sexual licentiousness so practiced among the Indians and the reason God rained brimstone and fire on Sodom and Gomorrah? The indigenous inhabitants are sodomites; it is Amalek that must be destroyed.

All this means that "a profound spiritual and hermeneutic perversion in the heart of Christianity itself" has accompanied colonial readings of Scripture (Richard 1997, 46).

The Third Perspective

Between pink and black perceptions, there is a third, more recent one. In recent decades, scholars have argued for the construction of a decolonial history of Christianity in las Américas. It is believed that both previous positions are the fruit of a too massive positive *and* negative view of the hegemony and predominance of the Spanish missionaries and their conversion practices. As part of this more nuanced position, at least two things can be mentioned. First, as Jennifer Scheper Hughes (2019) argues, Las Casas and the other protest voices were no exceptions. The lament for a ruined land and a lost people was a permanent element of Spanish theological narratives. Second, the role of the Indians in the evangelization process has been greatly underestimated.

Both the pink and the black paradigms rehearse colonialist categories and narratives inherited from the Spanish missionaries themselves. "Many Mesoamerican chronicles contradict the spiritual conquest discourse" (Scheper Hughes 2019, 93), and many texts testify to an active role of indigenous experts in all kinds of construction (temples) and of creative rereadings of passages from the Bible (Christensen 2014). Scheper Hughes (2019, 104) states that "Christianity proliferated because surviving indigenous communities decided that it would and should survive." Also, "indigenous communities throughout New Spain came to regard the new religion as their own," and did not represent themselves as "vanquished and annihilated" (96).

Reflecting on this double transformation of Christianity and Andean religions, Swiss Philosopher Josef Estermann (2008, 179–80) writes: "The Christian religion has undergone a strong re-interpretation from Andean thought itself, not only in ritual and social manifestations, but also in theological conceptions."

The mention of this third perspective is important because we think that, hermeneutically speaking, the groups participating in our project should be considered heirs of those who, despite all the horror of the conquest, creatively and constructively embraced important notions of Christianity as early as the first phase of the conquest, simply because they coincided with several of their own convictions.

Postcolonial Dimension of Empirical Hermeneutics

I mentioned above the rationale for starting the intercultural reading project: a request from the indígena world itself.

A postcolonial or rather an anticolonial approach was explicitly adopted for both the collection of data and the analysis of how participants read the text. The empirical material and reading reports came from the target group itself—the subaltern spoke! The qualitative research method that guides empirical hermeneutics focuses heavily on what participants themselves say and not on theories or insights of "Great Men" (de Wit 2004, 395–436). The careful analysis of this empirical material reveals the contours of what Margaret Kovach in her book on *Indigenous Methodologies* has called "the indigenous perspective" (Kovach 2010, 110). In our analysis, we carefully listened to narrative, to ritual, to references to ancestral tradition, to indigenous appropriation of the biblical text. We discovered that the term indígena covers a multitude of expressions, habits, experiences, and languages and that we rather should speak of indigenous perspectives.

Participants were invited to put their own prejudices and positions into perspective by reading the text twice, including through the eyes of another. The central question of the project focused on what form liberating indigenous Bible pastorate can take. The beneficiaries were the indigenous communities.

A last but important objective of the project was that there has been a great deal of reflection by indigenous theologians on teologías and hermenéuticas indígenas (both in the plural) in the past few decades. Much is top-down, and one sees few examples of indigenous reading of biblical texts and much less of an intercultural sharing of them. This fact and the fact that there is very little empirical material available presented a tremendous challenge for us. We believe that the academy and biblical scholarship in Latin America, and elsewhere, would also benefit greatly from listening to and learning from the encounters between Native American communities and the Bible.

The Project

More than twenty small, very diverse groups of indigenous readers from Chile to Mexico, guided by indigenous facilitators, read the same biblical text, made a report of their experiences, and started to exchange their experiences with other indigenous communities.

On the images that all groups sent along, we see grooved faces, nowhere obese, many still in their traditional costumes. The women weaving, quietly, modestly, the little round hats in Peru and Bolivia, the berets in Colombia. These are the little beloved ones of God. Some groups live in areas where public transport passes only once a day. What all participants share is pride in being indigenous. Most of the groups belong to one of the Christian churches. Most participants did not speak Spanish; the dialogue about the text was mostly in their own language. Sometimes official translations existed. If that was not the case, facilitators used a Spanish translation and translated the Spanish into the first language of the community.

We chose the text of Gen 2:4–25 because it is a foundational story, and it would give participants the opportunity to connect it with their own ancestral creation stories. At the level of the narrative lines that Gen 2 offers—the story is about the intimate relation between the Creator, the earth, the animals, and man/woman—the relation man-woman gets attention and may offer the opportunity to discuss gender in the proper context of the participants. Themes like water-rivers-fertility, man/woman-animals, man/woman-earth (Mother Earth–Pacha Mama) seem to offer many possibilities for appropriation and exchange.

Results

The results of the project have been overwhelmingly rich and unexpected. I must confine myself to the most essential and give only some examples of the hundreds we recollected. I will do so asking three questions: (1) what did readers do with the text, (2) what did the text do with its readers, and (3) what did readers do with their fellow readers from other contexts and communities?

What Did Readers Do with the Text?

For some participants, the text was new. Consequently, there were many questions. A participant from one of the Mexican groups asks: "If to make the man God used mud and for the woman a rib, what does that mean? Because a bone is very little to make a complete woman."

Participants read with dedication, reverence, and joy. There was not only a willingness but even an eagerness to take part in the process. This raises the question of the traumatic relationship between indigenous readers and the Bible text, as Richard (1997) defines it. At first glance, aside from visceral social memories of colonialism and past extermination, we see few traces of a traumatic relationship. Until we listened more carefully to our empirical data, what helped us to reconsider this relationship was that all groups so eagerly embraced the method of communitarian, contextual reading. And it was there that we discovered trauma and liberation at the same time.

The trauma is in the forced silence. A Colombian group, reading in the high Andes, makes a tremendously important observation in which we hear the echo of many centuries of colonial and imperial use of the Bible. They say, "This is a new methodology. It is the first time that a study of the Bible is done *taking into account what the participants say*" (emphasis added). The liberative dimension is seen in what a participant of the Guatemalan group says: "We will do our reading in an indigenous way, because if we do it like other churches, then I prefer not to do it. *I want to learn, I want to talk, I want to share*" (emphasis added).

Here, the indigenous perspective is manifested. What participants of our groups want is not to give the Bible back to the colonizers, as happened in Peru; what they want is a *new* Bible, a Bible liberated from colonial interests. In this embrace of the new method, we find resistance. A hermeneutics of hospitality, of sharing, is taking shape. The communitarian aspect of indigenous culture is being made fruitful. We see trauma processing and posttraumatic growth.

The Interpretation of the Text Itself

There is a wide variety of interpretations. But when we look at parallels, what is particularly striking is the ethical-ecological tone of the interpretations. Many communities relate to verse 8 about the garden as very much theirs, very indigenous. "God behaves like a peasant father of a family. Before bringing his family to dwell with him, he prepares a house for them and sets about the task of planting a garden; then, as if it were a present, he places the man in the finished garden built for him," says an Ecuadorian participant.

The following three themes are connected in many reading reports and given much attention. They are interpreted in an ethical, existential manner: (1) the relationship between man/woman—earth; (2) the question of good and evil (both trees); and (3) the gender question.

(1) The San Cristobal group from Mexico comments: "We all agree that Gen 2, rather than speaking of the origin of Adam and Eve, as we have been taught for many years, speaks of the earth that must be cared for, respected, honored, and of equitable relations between man and woman, and with the animals, since we are all related."

(2) Groups found the metaphor of the two trees, the question of good and evil, difficult to understand. Only some readers connected the prohibition to eat from the tree of knowledge with power, wanting to be like God. One of the Chilean participants remarked: "We have to accept our human nature; we always want to be like God."

(3) The gender question is one of the preferred themes for discussion by the groups. The beautiful comments on the equality and importance of women cannot hide the fact that, in some cases, the practice is different. Much machismo can still be found among indigenous communities—the wife's task is to "contribute to the complete enjoyment of the man" (Colombia), "make him a family" (Chile), and "give him his food and treat him with affection" (Bolivia).

What Did the Text Do with Its Readers?

Some of the most important outcomes of the project were that participants were able to unburden themselves, talk about their sufferings, express their pain, and share their experiences. We did not see *any* example of the *use* and *utilitarian reading* of the Bible, as is so frequently done (de Wit 2012, 14).

The example Obvious Vengeyi (2013, 86) gives of the context of Zimbabwe can be multiplied by thousands: "The Bible is our aunt; whoever does not listen to the aunt does everything wrong. Whatever problem we have the aunt is always there.... Just take your Bible and read.... Do this you will get all your answers!"

Another important aspect of the findings was the participants' return to their ancestral traditions and roots. Who are we? The grandfathers and grandmothers—the ancestors—what did they do; what did they practice; what did they believe? A Mexican group builds an indigenous altar with fruits of the earth before the session begins and then prays: "Dear Mother, take care of us well, well. And may it never occur to us to sell you."

The return to the ancestral tradition was not only a romantic exercise, but it did also stir up visceral memories, memories that turned the interpretation process into an act of commemoration of the dead, of the martyrs. This process of reading in memory of the dead produced for many readers much sighing because the grandparents no longer answer; the tradition is disappearing. But the sighs and the feelings of great loss do not have the last word. Groups wanted to renew their encounter with their ancestral tradition, and the Bible helps them do this. What we see in our project is that reading the Bible does not imply rupture; it can also imply reawakening, renaissance, rebirth. One of the urban groups from Ecuador writes to its partner group high in the Colombian mountains: "you have encouraged us to return more to our customs and not let ourselves be trapped by what the city determines."

And the Other Reader?

Important was the social and hermeneutical dimension of the encounter with the Other reader. The desire to get to know the Other is burning. It is impressive to see the care and attention with which the groups approach the encounter with the partner group. A Bolivian group writes to its Colombian partner group: "Everyone joyfully and attentively listened to the words that our brothers and sisters from Colombia sent us through this document, reading it over and over again aloud."

For several groups, it is the first time to relate with people outside their context. A Bolivian group writes: "A lot of joy was shown because it is the first experience of relating with different brothers and sisters." The exchange is perceived almost as a real trip abroad. Those factors constitutive of successful intercultural encounter abound—admiration ("We congratulate you for your work with the land and for being so careful with the creation"), gratitude, vulnerability, openness, shared reciprocal learning, tolerance, and respect.

Participants also discover places of struggle previously unknown. The facilitator of a Bolivian group writes to her Chilean colleague: "Thank you for this sharing [of your struggles concerning the land] that leads us to expand our hearts to unite as peoples in the struggle for the dignity of lands and territories." In addition to this struggle, countless other battles are shared—against alcoholism, machismo, poverty, racism and discrimination, the neocolonialism of certain churches, and so forth.

On the hermeneutical level, we see that readers start to see themselves as more competent interpreters. The Peruvian group comments to its Guatemalan partner group: "We do a traditional reading of Genesis 2; our focus is centered on sin, the woman, and the serpent, while you talk to us about water, healing plants and nature. You have a different and in that sense liberating reading."

Groups also learn from the method of the other groups. The same group writes: "Reading the text horizontally and distancing ourselves from interpretative hierarchies has an incomparable richness."

Final Word

I promised to end this contribution with a word of hope and optimism for Knut, for us all. Let this then be a last quote from our empirical data. Groups desire to know each other better, visit their partner group to continue their dialogue, and now shared struggle.

One of the groups from Ecuador blesses its Colombian partner group with the following words: "Thank you for your company in this process; if we do not see each other on this earth, perhaps in heaven we will meet to give each other a hug." I believe that if professional readers of the Bible, in addition to their mostly historically oriented reading practice, are willing to elicit these kinds of moments of encounter, of new alliances, of transformation among nonprofessional readers, then there is reason for hope and optimism.

Works Cited

Bal, Mieke. 1991. *On Story-Telling: Essays in Narratology*. Sonoma, CA: Polebridge.

Broseghini, P. S. 1989. "Historia y métodos de la Evangelización en América." Pages 5–66 in *500 Años de Evangelización en América: Aportes para la reflexión*. Autores Varios. Quito: Ed. Abya-Yala.

Christensen, Mark Z. 2014. *Christianities: Nahuatl and Maya Religious Texts*. Latin American Originals 8. University Park, PA: Pennsylvania State University Press.

De Wit, Hans. 2004. "Codes and Coding." Pages 395–434 in *Through the Eyes of Another: Intercultural Reading of the Bible*. Edited by Hans de Wit, Louis Jonker, Marleen Kool, and Daniel Schipani. Amsterdam: Institute of Mennonite Studies.

———. 2010. *Por un solo gesto de amor: Lectura de la Biblia desde una práctica intercultural*. Buenos Aires: ISEDET.

———. 2012. *Empirical Hermeneutics, Interculturality, and Holy Scripture*. Intercultural Biblical Hermeneutics Series 1. Elkhart, IN: Institute of Mennonite Studies.

De Wit, Hans, and Janet Dyk, eds. 2015. *Bible and Transformation: The Promise of Intercultural Bible Reading*. SemeiaSt 81. Atlanta: SBL Press.

De Wit, Hans, Louis Jonker, Marleen Kool, and Daniel Schipani, eds. 2004. *Through the Eyes of Another: Intercultural Reading of the Bible*. Amsterdam: Institute of Mennonite Studies.

Estermann, Josef. 2008. *Si el Sur fuera el Norte. Chakanas interculturales entre Andes y Occidente*. Colección Teología y Filosofía Andinas 5. La Paz: ISEAT.

Gutiérrez, Gustavo. 1993. *Las Casas: In Search of the Poor of Jesus Christ*. Maryknoll, NY: Orbis.

Herren, Ricardo. 1997. *La Conquista erótica de las Indias*. Barcelona: Editorial Planeta-De Agostini.

Holter, Knut. 2008. "Does a Dialogue between Africa and Europe Make Sense?" Pages 69–80 in *African and European Readers of the Bible in Dialogue: In Quest of a Shared Meaning*. Edited by Hans de Wit and Gerald O. West. Leiden: Brill.

———. 2015a. "Am I My Brother's Keeper? Justice and Transformation in a Malagasy-Norwegian Dialogue (Genesis 4)." Pages 355–68 in *Bible and Transformation: The Promise of Intercultural Reading of the Bible*. Edited by Hans de Wit and Janet Dyk. SemeiaSt 81. Atlanta: SBL Press.

———. 2015b. "'My Punishment Is Greater than I Can Bear': Malagasy and Norwegian Ordinary Readers on Genesis 4:13." Pages 31–40 in *In Love with the Bible and Its Ordinary Readers: Hans de Wit and the Intercultural Bible Reading Project*. Edited by Hans Snoek. Elkhart, IN: Institute of Mennonite Studies.

Kovach, Margaret. 2010. *Indigenous Methodologies: Characteristics, Conversations, and Contexts*. Toronto: University of Toronto Press.

Lemaire, Ton. 1986. *De Indiaan in ons Bewustzijn: De ontmoeting van de Oude met de Nieuwe Wereld*. Baarn: Ambo.

LeMarquand, Grant. 2000. "A Bibliography of the Bible in Africa." Pages 633–800 in *The Bible in Africa: Transactions, Trajectories, and Trends*. Edited by Gerald O. West and Musa W. Dube. Leiden: Brill.

Richard, Pablo. 1997. "Interpretación bíblica desde las culturas indígenas." Pages 45–59 in *Revista de Interpretación Bíblica Latinoamericana*. Vol. 26. San José: Editorial DEI.

Rivera Pagán, Luis. 1991. *Evangelización y Violencia: La Conquista de América*. San Juan: Editorial CEMI.

Rubial García, Antonio. 2002. "Ángeles en carne mortal: Viejos y nuevos mitos sobre la evangelización de Mesoamérica." Pages 19–51 in *Signos históricos*. Vol. 7. México: Universidad Autónoma Metropolitana, Unidad Iztapalapa.

Scheper Hughes, Jennifer. 2019. "Mapping the Autochthonous Indigenous Church: Toward a Decolonial History of Christianity in las Américas." Pages 91–106 in *Decolonial Christianities: Latinx and Latin American Perspectives*. Edited by Raimundo Barreto and Roberto Sirvent. New Approaches to Religion and Power. Cham: Palgrave-McMillan.

Slicher van Bath, B. H. 1992. *Indianen en Spanjaarden: Latijns Amerika 1500–1800*. Amsterdam: Uitgeverij Bert Bakker.

Vengeyi, Obvious. 2013. "'The Bible Equals Gona': An Analysis of the Indigenous Pentecostal Churches of Zimbabwe's Magical Conception of the Bible." Pages 78–105 in *From Text to Practice: The Role of the Bible in Daily Living of African People Today*. Edited by Joachim Kügler and Masiiwa Ragies Gunda. Bamberg: University of Bamberg Press.

Reading the Bible in Present-Day Norwegian Contexts: The Case of Cancer Patients

Marta Høyland Lavik

Introduction

The present contribution investigates how people living with incurable cancer in Norway relate to the Bible. It is not an understatement to say that much of Western biblical scholarship has focused on the biblical text and its past, whereas much of African biblical scholarship has focused on the biblical text and its present readers. Although empirically based research in Western biblical scholarship is scarce, there is a growing interest in the reader's context (Malley 2004; de Wit et al. 2004; Village 2007; Lavik 2013, 2014, 2015, 2019; Autero 2016; Lavik and Braut 2016). Many of Knut Holter's works document such an interest by investigating biblical interpretation in a global context (cf. Holter 2019). His invitation of younger scholars into a worldwide scholarly network, together with his awareness of how essential our contexts are for our understanding of the Bible, has probably affected me more than I am able to comprehend. I hereby express sincere gratitude for the way Holter has made the world smaller and opened up the avenue for a potential widening of my Eurocentric horizon of understanding.

Facing Death in a Secularized Society

Biblical empirical hermeneutics investigates "ordinary people's reading habits and interpretative practices" (Autero 2016, 49). Some years ago, I

This essay is written with grateful acknowledgment of the fourteen participants who coproduced the qualitative data.

was honored to discuss the potential significance of the Bible individually with fourteen adults (ten men and four women) who were all diagnosed with incurable cancer and who were not trained in theological studies. I have no experience with cancer in my own body, but I am interested in how people relate to the Bible in various situations in life and especially when life is shortened by disease. Most of the participants belonged to the Lutheran Church of Norway, but a few were members of lay church organizations or Pentecostal-Charismatic congregations. My core question was: Is the Bible significant in the context of living with incurable cancer? This question goes straight into the sphere of meaning making and spirituality. For centuries, the term *spirituality* was applied to human experiences of the sacred. Gradually, however, spirituality has become a term used for a range of subjective experiences relating to meaningfulness (Koenig, King, and Carson 2012, 37–38; Victor, Chitra, and Treschuk 2020, 108; see also the definition of "spiritual care" by European Association for Palliative Care).

A pertinent question is: How do we define spirituality and meaning making in the Norwegian context? It can be argued that meaning making, both on a societal level and on individual levels, has gradually become more and more detached from religious norms and authorities due to the process of secularization (Schmidt 2010b). Despite secularization, religion plays an integral part in many people's lives (Botvar 2010, 23–24). In addition to the secularization process, in the last fifty years Norway has become a more multireligious state on account of migration (Schmidt 2010a, 32; Lavik et al. 2021).

In the study conducted, I had expected participants of various backgrounds, but only people from the majority population of Norway were available when the enrollment was done. When it comes to dying and death in Norway, nursing homes and hospitals do for the most part provide care for the dying (Thoresen 2017, 276–77). At the time of the interviews, all participants still lived in their homes but received palliative care from the National Health Service. Although healthcare personnel in Norway are obliged to provide for the physical, psychosocial, and spiritual needs of a patient (see Medås, Blystad, and Giske 2017, 274; Giske and Cone 2015, 2927), there are indications that spiritual needs are not sufficiently covered (The Norwegian Directorate of Health 2019, 34–35, 37–42).

Research questions about religion are regarded as sensitive in Norway ("Sensitive Research Topics." n.d.). The interviews presented here thus give a glimpse into a sphere that is not often talked about publicly in the Norwegian society. By bringing an interpretation of the participants' insights into the public, I hope to promote respect for a wide range of experiences with the Bible in my contemporary secularized society.

Theory and Method

The overall analytic approach is hermeneutical. According to the German philosopher Hans-Georg Gadamer (2011), interpretation is a universally constitutive factor of human behavior and of the human search for understanding. From the interviews, it is striking how the participants, in their search for understanding, relate their personal narratives to the broader biblical narrative and the other way round. This resonates with the French philosopher Paul Ricoeur's (1984–1988) view of narrative as a fundamental form of human existence. In and through narratives, human beings can create meaning and coherence.

In the data collection, research ethical principles were followed, namely, respect, protection from harm, informed and voluntary consent, anonymity, and proper data storage (National Research Ethics Committees n.d.). The project was approved by the regional committee for medical and health research ethics. The fourteen participants who were aged between thirty-two and seventy-eight had received palliative care for between six weeks and ten years at the time of the interview. When the informed consent was obtained, all participants were assured that they could withdraw from the project at any time without any consequence. To protect their identities, they are given fictitious names.

Empirical hermeneutics employs various approaches, and here it is combined with thematic analysis in the earlier stages of systematizing the data. Thematic analysis aims at identifying essential themes which form the data (Braun and Clarke 2006). The essential themes that have emerged in this process have assisted me to further probe the research question: how do people living with incurable cancer relate to the Bible?

Various Experiences with the Bible When Approaching Death

The main theme shows a wide range of experiences with the Bible when the participants try to make sense of the situation of approaching death. This main theme is explicated in the following four subthemes.

The first subtheme deals with what the participants read from the Bible.

"I prefer such words of comfort"—Not Everything in the Bible Is Significant

All participants expose themselves to the biblical message, but their choice of texts was different from what I expected. My prejudice, in Gadamer's words, was that people who are approaching death would have reason to lament and would prefer biblical texts about illness, suffering, and death. But Elisabeth summarizes what all fourteen said: "I prefer such words of comfort ... not words of lament."

Kristin avoids Ps 23, as it reminds her that she is facing death: "There is a Psalm I do not like [v. 4]: through the darkest valley....Then I think that God is with me in the death process. I don't like thinking of that [the death process]." Rather, Kristin reads texts that support her hope of being miraculously healed:

> It says in Isaiah 53:5: But he was wounded for our transgressions, crushed for our iniquities; upon him was the punishment that made us whole, and by his bruises we are healed. Those words have become very dear to me.... I read words [in the Bible] about hope, about healing.

Other texts mentioned by the participants are Exod 15:26; Num 6:24–26; Deut 31:8; 33:25; Josh 1:9; Job 35:14; Pss 31:15; 55:22; 91; 118:17; 139; Isa 41:10; 49:16; Jer 29:11; 30:16; Mark 11:23; John 7:38; Eph 6:13–17; Phil 1:6; 4:7; 1 Pet 2:24; 1 John 5:12; and Rev 21–22. Many of the participants mentioned Old Testament texts, but only Simon explains why:

> In earlier times I read mostly in the New Testament, but after this [the cancer diagnosis] I read for the most part in the Old Testament ... because there is much talk about the enemy in the Old Testament ... and I know who the enemy is.... It is the cancer ... and I have read in Jeremiah [30:16]: Therefore all who devour you shall be devoured, and all your foes, every one of them, shall go into captivity—and I have many tumours, and he will take them into captivity—those who plunder you shall be plundered, and all who prey on you I will make a prey.

Kristian appreciates short verses, which go to the core of the biblical message of mercy and care: "My times are in your hand [Ps 31:15]. And then it means both past, present and future times."

For the participants, reading the Bible functions as a way of getting relief from worries and hard work. In Simon's words, "I experience that I can let go of the striving." This leads to the second subtheme, which deals with how the texts are experienced.

"It is like the printing ink jumps up into the face"—The Bible Is Read Existentially

Simon claims that some texts speak directly into his contemporary situation:

> The phenomenal thing with the Old Testament, especially the prophecies, is that suddenly there are some verses which are just as if they were written to me! Then it is like the printing ink jumps up into the face. It [the text] becomes so much alive that it is amazing ... but it is also true that I realise that much is irrelevant [in the Old Testament], it does not speak to me. In that sense, I need to read many chapters.

Once, after receiving chemotherapy, Simon and his wife stop at a restaurant. When they unexpectedly find Ps 23 in the menu book, Simon reacts thus:

> I had to lie down over the table and my tears flooded. I experienced that I walk through the darkest valley, and I fear no evil [v. 4].... There we sit, in the restaurant, completely dejected—read, open up the menu book, and in the menu book we are met with Psalm 23—fantastic!

Also, Rita believes that the texts resonate with her situation:

> It was a little hard earlier this year. I received the same Bible verse from six different places. I felt it was unbelievable—it cannot be accidental! It was from Deuteronomy 31:8: It is the Lord who goes before you. He will be with you; he will not fail you or forsake you. Do not fear or be dismayed. This I received from different contexts. This was enormously great to experience!... It shows me that he [God] is before me.

The third subtheme shows embodied interactions with the Bible.

"The words have in a way come alive"—The Bible as a Subject to Relate To

The participants share how the Bible became more distinctive after they became ill. Georg says, "When I read the word of God now it is more concrete to me.... The Bible has a greater meaning now than before." This distinctiveness is explained in metaphorical terms:

> It [the Bible] is my wailing wall. (Liv)
>
> Reading the Bible is like taking medicine. (Rita)
>
> If I do not make time for reading [the Bible], it is as if the body does not get water or bread. (Otto)
>
> It [the Bible] is the anchor of my life now. (Johannes)

Two of the participants describe how their bodies react when they expose themselves to biblical texts. Simon reports: "Then I experience a form of heat flow … through my body. In several minutes … I experience the divine presence as unbelievably strong."

Johannes describes his bodily reaction as:

> a very strong warmness which is full of love.... And when I read it fits with what I experience. He [God] has promised us help and support, and I receive that.... When we read in the Bible it is as if the warmth speaks.... The words have in a way become alive.

The Bible as a material entity is understood as an active subject to relate to:

> The word of God is the most important. It is this [shows the Bible] which I carry with me everywhere.... You know, I have put Bible verses on the fridge, in the bathroom—all places in the house there are Bible verses on which I meditate. (Rita)
>
> I bring it [the Bible] with me at work—I bring it with me everywhere.... When I go to bed I have to have it with me on the pillow.... I have to hold it [he cries]. I get comfort, I get support, I get help. (Otto)

The last subtheme shows how the Bible is used to fight the situation.

"I am not going to be part of that statistics"—The Bible Is Used to Resist Disease and Death

Three participants, Kristin, Simon, and Rita, use texts to resist the disease and to hope for miraculous healings. Kristin visualizes how the armor described in Eph 6:13–17 can protect her from fear and help her fight the disease. She says, "I have a protection in me. The fear can come, but it is not going to crush me!" Kristin puts her trust in the biblical texts and reasons that, "If Jesus could resurrect … and could wake up dead people, if this is true, then a tumor, a cancer and a disease are peanuts."

After she became ill, Rita soon found a verse which helped her to fight the disease:

> When I started reading the Bible, before I was acquainted with it, it was a Psalm which came to be mine, so to say: Psalm 118:17. I proclaim it every day: I shall not die, but I shall live, and recount the deeds of the Lord … what it gives to me is that I shall live [laughs]!

Like Kristin, Rita also is armed: "It [the Bible] became my weapon straight away."

Shortly after Simon was diagnosed with incurable cancer, he read Ps 118 as part of the cycle of daily Bible readings, and he experienced a striking inner and outer change as he read verse 17:

> When I read that the whole situation altered. My wife said I changed color within five minutes, from being pale and dejected to being in good spirits.… Yes, it is obvious that it [Ps 118] is written about something completely different … but we experienced that God spoke directly into the situation [he is moved to tears].… I have never cried over my own situation … but it moves me immensely when I refer to situations where God spoke.

Simon thinks God can heal through medicine, but he puts more trust in Ps 118:17. He is aware that this unreserved trust in God can make people in the secularized Norwegian society wonder: "Some might think … how stupid can you be? Then I say I have chosen to believe it. There are no side effects by believing this."

Rita rejects the bad news from the hospital by quoting Bible verses, whereas her husband reads the reports:

> You have two reports, you have the hospital's medical report and you have God's report. And the hospital report is and has been negative. I call it the evil report, and that one I throw into the sea [she paraphrases Mark 11:23]: say this to this mountain, 'Be taken up and thrown into the sea'. So this I throw into the sea.… My husband is occupied with all the reports that come. I am like this: No, thank you!… I use Psalm 91:7 where it says: A thousand may fall at your side, ten thousand at your

right hand, but it will not come near you ... and I dismiss them [the reports]. I am not going to be part of that statistics!

Rita shares how their different strategies make it difficult for them to talk about the frightening situation of approaching death:

> It [the Bible] is alpha and omega. For sure, I have changed a lot. My husband notices that, and it can be too much sometimes.... All over the house there are Bible verses on which I meditate.... If he has a lot of fear and anxiety I feel it will be difficult for me to carry that. I feel downhearted by it—the thoughts he carries—and I ask him sometimes to talk to others about it.

How can these experiences be interpreted?

The context of facing death is pivotal for what the participants read from the Bible and how they interpret and use it. The way they relate to the Bible can be understood in the following three ways.

Bible Reading as a Coping Strategy

From previous interpretations of the same data, it was concluded that: (1) people who are living with incurable cancer connect their own personal life story to the broader biblical story and that (2) Bible reading is an important religious coping strategy that helps an individual to attain a sense of coherence (Lavik 2014; 2019).

The field of psychology of religion has developed a theory of how human beings use so-called religious coping strategies in difficult times (Pargament 1997; Pargament, Koenig, and Perez 2000; Pargament, Ano, and Wachholtz 2005). Seen as a dynamic process, coping is individual and contextual, as human beings interpret and relate to similar situations in various ways. Coping is also functional, as it is a means of establishing meaning (Dalaker 2012) and gaining some sense of vicarious control (Doka 2017, 69). A considerable body of research suggests that religious involvement can be beneficial to health (for numerous references, see Pargament 1997; Doka 2011, 101–3; Koenig, King, and Carson 2012, 94–120; Page et al. 2020, 91–95), but there are also studies which indicate that religious involvement can undermine psychological wellbeing (see Doka 2011, 102–3; Koenig, King, and Carson 2012, 53–93; Page et al. 2020, 95). The present study adds mostly to the first body of knowledge, as it shows how the Bible is experienced as a constituent element in the participants' ability to cope with their illness. However, the interview with Rita especially indicates that she and her husband experience problems due to their different coping strategies.

Communities as Interpretative Horizons

As human beings, we orientate ourselves according to our horizons of understanding, which also consist of all our prejudices. In every encounter between human beings, different horizons of understanding meet (Gadamer 2011, 305). Understanding is an ongoing and never-ending process (Gadamer 2011, 293–94; Porter and Robinson 2011, 86–87, 91; Elness-Hanson 2017, 36). This is also true for what happens in Christian communities.

It can be difficult to detect factors that influence individuals' interpretation of the Bible, but the findings of this essay suggest that church affiliation plays an important role (Conradie and Jonker 2001). What the participants share mirrors the theology preached in their congregations. Most participants belong to the Church of Norway, and they are taught that illness is an unfortunate aspect of the human condition. Some participants who belong to lay church organizations experience their disease as a blessing and God's dealing with them now. A few are taught that illness at a younger age is a curse (see Rita and Kristin). They found a Charismatic-Pentecostal congregation influenced by the American faith movement when they were diagnosed. Their hope for miraculous healing takes the form of a prediction, and their choice of Bible texts reflects this expectation (Doka 2017, 69). In this context, Kristin finds Ps 23 upsetting, whereas Simon—who also trusts he will be healed—does not. The Bible verses that Rita puts up throughout her house help to strengthen her expectations and to defend her against the disease and, ultimately, against death.

Existential Bible Reading

Whereas analytical exegesis often concentrates on past suffering, existential reading concentrates on present suffering, as the latter relates directly to the reader's experiences and contextual challenges (de Wit 2009, 6). Reading the Bible is one of several spiritual practices that can serve as a tangible sign that a patient is not facing the suffering alone (Doka 2017, 74). In the fear-inspiring situation of approaching death, the participants experience the Bible as a personal subject to relate to, and their own narrative is intertwined with the biblical one. Especially, the participants from lay church organizations and Charismatic-Pentecostal congregations revealed how the materiality of the Bible had come to hold special meaning for them after they were diagnosed with cancer.

The mind tends to seek elements in the biblical text that are experienced as relevant (Malley 2004, 105–8). In a situation of living with a lethal disease, the participants chose to expose themselves to texts that portray the deity as an active agent and the human being in a personal relationship with this agent. When biblical texts are read in present day contexts, there is a never-ending hermeneutical exchange between text and context (Patte 1995, 56–58). This interaction is a dynamic relationship between text and reader where the self can be "nourished, recognised, consoled, and reaffirmed by the text" (de Wit 2009, 5–6). Although Simon shows awareness of the hermeneutical gap between ancient and contemporary contexts, he and the others experience how the ancient words resonate with their situations and provide them with a language of interpreting the situations. This resonance is possible as the Bible itself was "formed in the context of centuries of catastrophic suffering" (Carr 2014, 2).

The phenomenon of reinterpreting biblical texts into new contexts is not a recent invention. It exists within the biblical corpus itself (Holter 2003). When the context is urgent, trained readers also can relate to biblical texts as if these were written to them (see Kugel 2011, 89–114; Lavik 2014, 168–71). The scholar's task is to be aware of experiences and concerns that form the analysis—whether the reading is pursued by trained or nontrained readers (Holter 2011, 179–80). The scholar should allow also the "then" and the "now" to meet and interact with each other (Holter 2011, 179–80). Present-day Bible readers may generate questions that can be investigated further by scholars who are acquainted with the historical understanding of the texts (Malley 2004, 10–11). Trained and nontrained readings can serve as mutual sources of inspiration and correction (cf. Holter 2019).

Conclusion

This essay contributes to the understanding of the various meanings that the Bible can hold for people who approach death in a secularized society. In searching for coherence and meaning, both the contents as well as the materiality of the Bible are vital. The horizons of understanding that the participants reveal in their encounter with the Bible are linked to their interpretative communities. Akin to what inner-biblical reception did in ancient times, contemporary Bible readings provide readers with a language for interpreting the Bible as they navigate a traumatic context.

Works Cited

Autero, Esa J. 2016. *Reading the Bible across Contexts: Luke's Gospel, Socioeconomic Marginality, and Latin-American Biblical Hermeneutics.* BibInt 145. Leiden: Brill.

Botvar, Pål K. 2010. "Endringer i nordmenns religiøse liv—teorier om religiøs endring." Pages 11–24 in *Religion i dagens Norge—mellom sekularisering og sakralisering.* Edited by Pål K. Botvar and Ulla Schmidt. Oslo: Universitetsforlaget.

Braun, Virginia, and Victoria Clarke. 2006. "Using Thematic Analysis in Psychology." *Qualitative Research in Psychology* 3:77–101.

Carr, David M. 2014. *Holy Resilience: The Bible's Traumatic Origins.* New Haven: Yale University Press.

Conradie, Ernst M., and Louis C. Jonker. 2001. "Bible Study within Established Bible Study Groups: Results of an Empirical Research Project." *Scriptura* 78:381–98.

Dalaker, Anna. 2012. "Tro—en kilde til livsmot: Erfaringen med å leve med kronisk sykdom sett i lys av Kenneth Pargaments teori om religiøs coping." *Tidsskrift for praktisk teologi* 1:14–26.

De Wit, Hans. 2009. "Exegesis and Contextuality: Happy Marriage, Divorce or Living (Apart) Together?" Pages 3–30 in *African and European Readers of the Bible in Dialogue: In Quest of a Shared Meaning.* Edited by Hans de Wit and Gerald O. West. Studies of Religion in Africa 32. Pietermaritzburg: Cluster.

De Wit, Hans, Louis Jonker, Marleen Kool, and Daniel Schipani, eds. 2004. *Through the Eyes of Another: Intercultural Reading of the Bible.* Amsterdam: Institute of Mennonite Studies.

Doka, Kenneth J. 2011. "Religion and Spirituality: Assessment and Intervention." *Journal of Social Work in End-of-Life and Palliative Care* 7:99–109.

———. 2017. "Spiritual Care: An Essential Aspect of Cancer Care." Pages 67–76 in *Dying and Death in Oncology.* Edited by Lawrence Berk. Cham: Springer.

Elness-Hanson, Beth E. 2017. *Generational Curses in the Pentateuch: An American and Maasai Intercultural Analysis*. Bible and Theology in Africa 24. New York: Lang.

European Association for Palliative Care. n.d. "Spiritual Care." https://tinyurl.com/SBL3817q.

Gadamer, Hans-Georg. 2011. *Truth and Method*. Translation revised by Joel Weinsheimer and Donald G. Marshall. 2nd rev ed. New York: Continuum.

Giske, Tove, and Pamela H. Cone. 2015. "Discerning the Healing Path: How Nurses Assist Patient Spirituality in Diverse Health Settings." *Journal of Clinical Nursing* 24:2926–35.

Holter, Knut. 2003. *Deuteronomy 4 and the Second Commandment*. StBibLit 60. New York: Lang.

———. 2011. "Hva i all verden skal vi bruke Jesaja 41,8–13 til? Noen refleksjoner om bibeltolkning og bibelbruk." Pages 171–81 in *Jerusalem, Samaria og jordens ender: Bibeltolkninger tilegnet Magnar Kartveit, 65 år, 7. oktober 2011*. Edited by Knut Holter and Jostein Ådna. Trondheim: Tapir.

———. 2019. "Malagasy, Thai, and Norwegian Youths Reading Luke 15 Together." Pages 139–52 in *A Critical Study of Classical Religious Texts in Global Contexts: Challenges of a Changing World*. Edited by Beth Elness-Hanson and Jon Skarpeid. New York: Lang.

Koenig, Harold G., Dana E. King, and Verna B. Carson. 2012. *Handbook of Religion and Health*. 2nd ed. Oxford: Oxford University Press.

Kugel, James L. 2011. *In the Valley of the Shadow: On the Foundations of Religious Belief (and Their Connection to a Certain, Fleeting State of Mind)*. New York: Free Press.

Lavik, Marta H. 2013. "Palliative pasientars forhold til bibeltekstar." *Omsorg* 4:39–42.

———. 2014. "'Do Not Fear, for I Am with You': The Use of Isaiah 41:10 in Times of Incurable Illness." Pages 157–81 in *New Studies in the Book of Isaiah: Essays in Honor of Hallvard Hagelia; Perspectives on Hebrew Scriptures and Its Contexts 21*. Edited by Markus Zehnder. Piscataway, NJ: Gorgias.

———. 2015. "'Forsvinn i Jesu namn!'—sjukdom, bibelbruk og impulsar frå global trusteologi." Pages 192–210 in *Levende religion: Globalt perspektiv—lokal praksis*. Edited by Anne Kalvig and Anna R. Solevåg. Stavanger: Hertervig Akademisk.

———. 2019. "'I Bring It with Me Everywhere': The Materiality of the Bible in Critical Illness." Pages 69–83 in *A Critical Study of Classical Religious Texts in Global Contexts: Challenges of a Changing World*. Edited by Beth Elness-Hanson and Jon Skarpeid. New York: Lang.

Lavik, Marta H., and Geir S. Braut. 2016. "Tru og bibelbruk som meistring ved alvorleg sjukdom." *Omsorg* 1:15–19.

Lavik, Marta Høyland, Birgitta Haga Gripsrud, and Ellen Ramvi. 2021. "How Do Migrant Nursing Home Staff Relate to Religion in Their Work with Patients Who Are Approaching Death?" *Journal for Holistic Nursing* 29:254–69.

Malley, Brian. 2004. *How the Bible Works: An Anthropological Study of Evangelical Biblicism*. Walnut Creek, CA: Altamira.

Medås, Kaja M., Astrid Blystad, and Tove Giske. 2017. "Åndelighet i psykisk helseomsorg: Et sammensatt og vanskelig tema" [Spirituality in Mental Health Care: A Complex and Difficult Topic]. *Klinisk sygepleje* 4:273–86.

National Research Ethics Committees. n.d. "General Guidelines for Research Ethics." https://tinyurl.com/SBLPress3817a4.

The Norwegian Directorate of Health. 2019. "Nasjonalt handlingsprogram for palliasjon i kreftomsorgen." October. https://tinyurl.com/SBLPress3817a6.

Page, Robin L., Jill N. Peltzer, Amy M. Burdette, and Terrence D. Hill. 2020. "Religiosity and Health: A Holistic Biopsycosocial Perspective." *Journal of Holistic Nursing* 38:89–101.

Pargament, Kenneth I. 1997. *The Psychology of Religion and Coping: Theory, Research, Practice*. New York: Guilford.

Pargament, Kenneth I., Harold G. Koenig, and Lisa M. Perez. 2000. "The Many Methods of Religious Coping: Development and Initial Validation of the RCOPE." *Journal of Clinical Psychology* 56:519–43.

Pargament, Kenneth I., Gene G. Ano, and Amy B. Wachholtz. 2005. "The Religious Dimension of Coping: Advances in Theory, Research and Practice." Pages 479–95 in *Handbook of the Psychology of Religion and Spirituality*. Edited by Raymond F. Paloutzian, and Crystal L. Park. New York: Guildford.

Patte, Daniel. 1995. *Ethics of Biblical Interpretation. A Reevaluation*. Louisville: Westminster John Knox.

Porter, Stanley E., and Jason C. Robinson. 2011. *Hermeneutics: An Introduction to Interpretive Theory*. Grand Rapids: Eerdmans.

Ricoeur, Paul. 1984–1988. *Time and Narrative*. Chicago: Chicago University Press.

Schmidt, Ulla. 2010a. "Norge: Et religiøst pluralistisk samfunn?" Pages 25–43 in *Religion i dagens Norge—mellom sekularisering og sakralisering*. Edited by Pål K. Botvar and Ulla Schmidt. Oslo: Universitetsforlaget.

———. 2010b. "Religion i dagens Norge: sekularisert? privatisert? pluralisert?" Pages 196–204 in *Religion i dagens Norge—mellom sekularisering og sakralisering*. Edited by Pål K. Botvar and Ulla Schmidt. Oslo: Universitetsforlaget.

"Sensitive Research Topics." n.d. Datatilsynet. https://tinyurl.com/SBLPress3817r1.

Thoresen, Lisbeth. 2017. "Døden på nordiske sykehjem—medikalisert?" Pages 263–287 in *Snart er vi alle pasienter. Medikalisering i Norden*. Edited by Hilde Bondevik, Ole J. Madsen, and Kari N. Solbrække. Oslo: Scandinavian Academic Press.

Victor, Paul, G. Chitra, and Judith V. Treschuk. 2020. "Critical Literature Review on the Definition Clarity of the Concept of Faith, Religion, and Spirituality." *Journal of Holistic Nursing* 38:107–13.

Village, Andrew. 2007. *The Bible and Lay People: An Empirical Approach to Ordinary Hermeneutics*. Aldershot: Ashgate.

Part 6
Other Forms of Context

Contextual Interpretation, Then and Now: Overhearing Inner-Biblical Discourses to Enrich Contemporary Contextual Interpretations

Louis C. Jonker

Introduction

I vividly remember a day in 1995 that I sat in a bus transporting congress attendees for the meeting of the International Organization for the Study of the Old Testament (IOSOT) around Cambridge, United Kingdom. During that bus ride, I met a shy, soft-spoken Norwegian man with a very good sense of humor—plus a vast knowledge of the Old Testament *and* of the African continent. I did not know at all that such a species existed on earth. In our conversation, I pretended to have heard of such a species, and I bit my tongue not to make an ignorant remark about him not fitting my caricature of Viking descendants. This man (obviously) was Knut Holter. Very soon, he became not only a highly appreciated colleague but also a friend, discussion partner, vast resource on African experiences, fellow Rooibos tea and red wine drinker, fellow hiker (together with our spouses) in the Norwegian mountains, and even fellow game spotter in the Maasai Mara. I once had the privilege of joining him and other colleagues at the (original) "hytta," but never did I smoke a cigar with him. Holter is not only an excellent scholar but also a remarkable human being.

One of the themes that we have discussed on many occasions is our shared hybrid identities. He is a European, Western scholar, who values contextual Bible interpretations from the African continent (north of the Limpopo and sub-Saharan—as he tends to define this concept). I am a scholar born and bred on the African continent, but with a Western upbringing and education. He wants to bring Europe and Africa nearer to each other (see, e.g., Holter 2008b; 2011a; Holter and Jonker 2010); I want to bring Africa and Europe nearer to each other in biblical interpretation. Such an in-between position brings many challenges, of which Holter surely can witness after a long career in the field. For example, he often had (and has) to endure criticism in his European context for not spending his energy on so-called real biblical scholarship. Why bother spending months and years on compiling an inventory of African Old Testament scholarship (Holter 1996; 2002)? Why bother going to all those African conferences (even with the danger of contracting malaria) and not go to so-called solid scholarly spaces in Europe or the United States (Getui, Holter and Zinkuratire 2001; Holter 2007)?

In contrast, on the African continent, his work is appreciated and valued. He is highly respected in the Old Testament guild across the continent, and he has (co)supervised many postgraduate students from this part of the world. Also, he has written many publications on Africa in the Old Testament and the Old Testament in Africa (Holter 2000). Holter is revered for taking African contextualization of the Old Testament seriously and for engaging with those contexts (Holter 2008a).

However, in the reception of Holter's work on the African continent, a highly significant aspect of his hermeneutical work on biblical texts is overlooked. I would like to state that the sophistication of his exegetical and hermeneutical engagement with biblical texts has never been acknowledged sufficiently in African biblical scholarship. He has rightly been praised for his taking seriously the contextualization of the continent. However, it is not sufficiently acknowledged that his sensitivity to inner-biblical reception and discourses guides his sensitivity to biblical reception in modern day African contexts.

The present contribution is therefore an attempt to highlight that specific feature of Holter's work. I will do so through a critical engagement with his work on Deut 4 and Isa 40–55. The aim of my contribution is to call for a more thorough reception of and engagement with his work in African biblical scholarship.

Inner-Biblical Interpretation and Hermeneutics

The phenomenon of inner-biblical interpretation has been studied widely in Old Testament scholarship for some time (Fishbane 1985; Levinson 1997, 2005, 2008a, 2008b; Otto 1999; Schmid 2000; Jonker 2013a). However, not many studies make a connection between inner-biblical interpretation and (contemporary) hermeneutics. In a number of publications, I have attempted to show how a study of the hermeneutics that brought about the biblical literature could enrich our understanding of the dynamic of (contemporary) biblical hermeneutics (Jonker 2007, 2011, 2018).

Holter (2002, 88) has rightly indicated that a comparative paradigm mostly dominates biblical interpretation on the African continent. He defines this paradigm as follows:

> [It] facilitates a parallel interpretation of certain Old Testament [and New Testament] texts or motifs and supposed African parallels, letting the two illuminate one another. Traditional exegetical methodology is of course found here, too; however, the Old Testament [and/or New Testament] is approached from a perspective where African comparative material is the major dialogue partner and traditional exegetical methodology is subordinated to this perspective.

This description has been appropriated in the self-understanding of African biblical scholarship.

Further interrogation of this paradigm has happened since Holter's 2002 publication, however. Gerald West (2008, 47), for example, indicates that "African biblical scholarship has a predilection for socio-historical textual analysis in dialogue with the socio-economic and religio-cultural realities of African contexts." However, West is also of the opinion that this predilection, which resonates with the life interests of African scholars, cuts in two directions. On the one hand, it tries to validate everything in the African sociocultural world that is similar to the sociohistorical world behind the text. On the other hand, this predilection is also evaluative and critical of African phenomena. According to West, the conclusion is often drawn that the comparative approach is not primarily interested in doing exegesis of biblical texts but wants to apply the results of exegesis to the life interests of the African context. He argues:

> What characterizes African biblical scholarship is that we are overt about why we come to the bible and what life interests drive our dialogue with it. In other words, we acknowledge the contexts out of which we interpret and for which we interpret. This does not make African biblical scholarship uncritical or un-exegetical. (54)

In a response to the discussion between West and Holter, I have gone one step further in interrogating the comparative paradigm:

> My contribution fully acknowledges the rightful place of African biblical scholarship in the hugely varied landscape of global biblical interpretation. It does not merely acknowledge this kind of scholarship as another "variation" that has to be "tolerated" due to the commitment to variety, but is deeply convinced that African biblical scholarship makes (and should make) a valuable contribution in a discursive hermeneutical model (such as propagated by West via Gadamer). (Jonker 2018, 76)

I have criticized this paradigm by indicating that

> the comparative paradigm often establishes a direct relationship between biblical texts and African contexts, or to be more precise, between the worlds constructed in the biblical texts and different African contexts.... Often African biblical scholars do not take into account the fact that the biblical texts are constructed realities that wanted to engage in dialogue with those socio-historical circumstances within which they were written.... In short, the comparative paradigm in African biblical scholarship often falls prey—at least in my opinion—to a lack of historical consciousness. (77)

Such a lack of historical consciousness normally translates into little or no understanding of the fact that biblical texts were communicated in very concrete sociohistorical circumstances where certain life interests also drove the processes of reinterpretation and discourse. No communication, oral or written, ever takes place in a sociohistorical vacuum. Biblical texts were always produced (orally or in written form) with some commitment to a discourse of the time which was considered to be (theologically) important. Biblical texts are therefore never contextless. Although this point is so obvious, it is often neglected in biblical interpretation. Historical consciousness assists us to relate the worlds-behind-the-texts with our contemporary realities—not directly, but rather analogically. I have put it as follows in a publication which emphasized why history matters: "Historical consciousness is … the reader- or context-oriented appreciation of the contexts of textual production and of textual reception (from ancient times, throughout the ages, up to modern-day receptions in various and differing circumstances)" (Jonker 2013b, 6).

At this point, Holter's analyses of texts related to the second commandment in the Old Testament come to mind. The next section will provide a short overview of his arguments, particularly as expressed in his article which explains the potential of reflecting on the notion of human dignity in Africa from these texts (Holter 2011b).

Contextual Interpretation: Then

Holter's keen interest in African biblical interpretation does not make him a dissident of the Western exegetical traditions or of historical criticism. In his own work, as will be illustrated below, he makes use of historical-critical analyses and results in his discussions on human dignity in African contexts. On the role of historical criticism in African Old Testament studies, he states his point of view clearly:

> My basic premise for defending the use of historical-critical methodology is a fear that any version of Old Testament studies—whether they are localized in Africa or in the West—that totally reject such a methodology, for dogmatic or other reasons, easily will face the danger of throwing the baby out with the bath water. In spite of all its problems … I find that historical-critical methodology addresses topics that are of vital importance to all Old Testament interpretation, also in its African versions. (Holter 2011a, 386)

Holter (1995, 2003) illustrates his use of historical-critical methodologies quite well in his exegetical studies of the idol passages in Isa 40–50 and in his study of the reinterpretation of the Decalogue's second commandment in Deut 4. He brings these two studies together when reflecting on how these passages could inform the discourse on human dignity on the African continent (Holter 2011b). He starts the discussion by expressing his astonishment that the second commandment has gained very little attention in African biblical scholarship.

Taking his cue from the German study on the second commandment by Werner H. Schmidt (1993), Holter (2011b, 52) indicates that this commandment is the Decalogue version of "a widely attested Old Testament prohibition of cultic images, documented throughout various historical epochs and literary genres of the Old Testament." The prohibition is normally stated in short sentences or orders, and few biblical texts engage more deeply with the issue. However, Holter does find in Deut 4:9–31 and in some texts of Deutero-Isaiah (40:19–20; 41:6–7; 44:9–20; 46:6–7) more elaborate engagements with the theme. Whereas the first-mentioned "relates the prohibition of images to the verbal mode of the Horeb theophany and then to the concept of Yahweh as creator," the Deutero-Isaiah texts "relate the prohibition of images to the concept of Yahweh as creator" (Holter 2011b, 52). Holter accepts the historical-critical indications that both these texts are relatively younger than the idol prohibitions in the two versions of the Decalogue. He therefore focuses on how Deut 4 and the idol passages of Deutero-Isaiah engage—each in its own unique ways—with the earlier (and shorter) forms of the idolatry prohibition.

The engagement with the theme of idolatry in these two textual versions not only opens for Holter interesting avenues to investigate the unique hermeneutical dynamic in each, but by relating these two processes of engagement with each other, he shows convincingly how these processes of inner-biblical interpretation can supply guidelines for contemporary appropriations of these same texts in the discussion of human dignity.

Being part of the Deuteronomistic layer in the book of Deuteronomy, chapter 4 shows a very negative attitude towards cultic images in general and thereby tunes into the sentiment which is expressed elsewhere in Deuteronomistic History (2 Kgs 23:24) that the Babylonian exile was actually the punishment for Judah and Jerusalem's submission to idolatry. Following Eckart Otto (1996), Holter indicates that Deut 4 belongs to some of the youngest material in Deuteronomistic literature. He sees two tendencies in this passage. First, the banning of images is linked to the theophany at Horeb, particularly through "a wordplay on the expression כל־תמונה…. The people did not see any 'form' when Yahweh revealed himself, and they should therefore not make cultic images in any 'form'" (Holter 2011b, 52). The second tendency in verses 16b–18 "link[s] the commandment to another central aspect of the same, that is, Yahweh as creator. Whereas v.16a … forbids production of 'any form' of cultic images, vv. 16b–18 offers a systematic survey of what kind of images are possible to imagine" (52–53). Holter sees in this section clear terminological links not only to the second commandment in Deut 5:8–9 (אשר + localization),[1] but also to the Priestly creation tradition of Gen 1:26–28 (list of creatures mentioned). With reference to the Deut 4 text, Holter (2011b, 53) thus concludes:

---

1. Although Eckart Otto (2012, 528; see also 2006) concurs with Holter's literary-critical analysis and with his point of view that Deut 4 explicates the ban on idol images in Deut 5:8–9, he is critical of Holter's too exclusive emphasis on Deut 5, which, according to Otto, blends out the allusions to other Pentateuchal texts.

When Deuteronomy 4:16a/b–18 reads the Decalogue version of the Second commandment together with Genesis 1, the result is that the commandment is given a theological rationale based on the concept of Yahweh as creator. Yahweh is creator of everything, and he can as such not be portrayed in any form of what he has created. This includes all creatures on earth, in the sky, and in the waters below the earth. But above all it includes the human beings, who are not allowed to make images of themselves, or of any of the other creatures they were created to rule over.

In Holter's (2011b, 55) discussion of the idol passages in Isa 40–55, he emphasizes that these chapters do not refer explicitly to the second commandment at any stage. However, he observes that

> the idol-fabricators [are] ironically portrayed according to a pattern that elsewhere is used to portray Yahweh, such as when they "form" the idol (Isaiah 44:9), like Yahweh "forms" Israel (44:21) or the history (46:11), or when they "stretch out a measuring line" on the piece of wood (44:13), like Yahweh in the creation "stretched out" the heavens (44:24). The result of this rhetoric ... serve[s] to point out fabrication of idols as wrong and to be rejected. The idol-fabricators are thereby portrayed as making themselves like Yahweh, that is the ultimate hubris of any human being.

Taking as point of departure the diachronic assumption that both Deut 4 and the idol passages of Deutero-Isaiah come from a fairly late period,[2] Holter concludes that these texts reflect a creation-theological discourse which was triggered by the second commandment. On account of the uneven structure of the Exod 20 and Deut 5 versions of the Decalogue, Holter argues that the commandments in both reflect literary historical phases when the individual commandments were still not cemented into the tradition but were part of an ongoing interpretive process. This process continued in texts outside (and those later than) the discourses incorporated in the two versions of the Decalogue. On the role of Deut 4 and Isa

---

2. I am critical of this vague indication of Holter's and suppose that he could have gone further in his placing of the studied texts in their contexts of origin and growth. More recent scholarship (such as Tiemeyer 2010, 13–51; Otto 2012, 231–57) has indeed brought light in this regard. However, the point that I wish to appreciate, here, is that Holter accounts for the historical contexts of the origin and growth of the biblical literature in his analyses.

40–50 in the creation-theological discourse, Holter (2011b, 57) therefore concludes:

> In a sum … when Deuteronomy 4 and Isaiah 40–55 interpret the Second commandment and its prohibition of cultic images from a creation-theological perspective, the result is a discourse … where the act of making such images is conceptualized as a perversion of the key anthropological concept of the Old Testament, the creation of the human being in the image of God. When human beings engage in the making of cultic images, when they even make such images in their own likeness or in the likeness of the creatures they were to rule over, they actually reverse God's creation. The result is an anthropology expressing the ultimate hubris, an anthropology where the human beings have lost their accountability to God, an anthropology where the human beings have become their own referees as a kind of perverted יהיו אשר יהיו: "they are who they are" (cf. Exodus 3:14).

The present discussion does not aim at interacting with Holter on the detailed exegesis of the mentioned text, but rather to illustrate how his exegetical analyses highlight the inner-biblical dynamics of reinterpretation. The hermeneutical value of such an analysis is clear. Biblical texts cannot simply be read by directly appropriating the contents of each text, but the exegete should also be alert to the discourses within which the texts took part in their contexts of first communication. This can only be uncovered if a diachronic perspective is taken on the texts. Without having the assumption that certain texts are younger than others, and that texts grew over time, the inner dynamic of the biblical textual corpus will simply be missed. In my view, the preceding point confirms the importance of a historical consciousness in reading Old Testament texts.

One could criticize Holter's (2011a, 386) reluctance to try to situate these texts in approximate sociohistorical contexts, as his words betray:

> In spite of all its problems, and then not only its western contextuality, but also its far too optimistic views with regard to the scholar's possibilities of reconstructing "original contexts," I find that historical-critical methodology addresses topics that are of vital importance to all Old Testament interpretation, also in its African versions.

Although I agree with him that some of these views are indeed too optimistic, one cannot deny that we know much more today about these contexts and the literary history of the biblical texts (particularly the exilic and postexilic periods) and that such contextualizations indeed bring greater insight into the ancient discourses that Holter tries to highlight.[3]

Our discussion can now move to Holter's hermeneutical strategy of using these texts for engaging in the discourse on human dignity on the African continent.

Contextual Interpretation—Now

Holter acknowledges that the Bible has been used for centuries in Western contexts for power purposes. However, he continues:

> But it is also a valid point in Africa, I would tend to argue, as African churches and their theologies—as well as African states and their ideologies—may face some of the same temptations and challenges. There is no innocent interpretation of the Bible, not even in a bible-embracing continent as Africa. Celebrated liberation hermeneutical models may become state ideology, when one political regime is exchanged with another. Radical inculturation hermeneutical models may end up as cementing traditional—and oppressing—cultural and political structures and practices. And much needed reconstruction hermeneutical models may eventually serve to legitimize one particular segment of the political spectrum, a segment that soon proves to be lacking its supposed socio-ethical qualities. Church and society are therefore in deep need, I would say, of an academic Old Testament studies that is able to express critical concerns vis-à-vis all those Old Testament interpretations that just mirror current religious, cultural and political power structures. (Holter 2011a, 386–87)

In his discussion of how human dignity is appropriated on the African continent, Holter therefore returns to the dynamic of the ancient discourse, which is reflected in Deut 4 and the idol-passages of Deutero-Isaiah. He first acknowledges that the concept of human dignity is in itself "a culturally and contextually dependent construct" (Holter 2011b, 58). But, precisely for this reason, it can interact with classical texts and discourses such as those embodied in the creation-theological reflections discussed above. In such a modern-day discourse, one might be tempted to latch onto the Gen 1:26–28 confirmation that human beings are created in

---

3. For a further discussion of this point, see Jonker 2015, 239–55.

God's image. However, Holter reminds us that the second commandment expresses a more pessimistic anthropology and that the appropriations of this commandment in Deut 4 and Isa 40–55 would recommend that it should balance the very positive anthropology of Gen 1. Holter (2011b, 58) puts it clearly thus:

> It [i.e., the second commandment] is a text, they [i.e., Deut 4 and the Deutero-Isa texts] might argue, that demonstrates the destructive potential of the human beings, when they turn their role as God's image-bearers around and—in their ultimate hubris—reject their God-given equality vis-à-vis each other, as well as their accountability to God. According to the interpretation of Deuteronomy 4 and Isaiah 40–55, the Second commandment is a text focusing on the potential of the human beings to destroy a key aspect of being a human being, and as such it is a text that is able to challenge concepts of "human dignity" in all cultures and contexts.

Holter thus indicates that the critical engagement with the second commandment in Deut 4 and the idol passages of Deutero-Isaiah, which was uncovered through his historical-critical analysis, holds great potential for our contemporary discourses on human dignity. Instead of merely latching onto one specific text (such as Gen 1:26–28), one should, through a historical consciousness, first become aware of the inner-biblical discourses before jumping directly to our own contemporary contexts. Holter (2011b, 59) concludes beautifully:

> Having looked at how Deuteronomy 4 and Isaiah 40–55 interpret the Second commandment, I would tend to think that the two may provide a model also for contemporary interpreters of, for example, the Decalogue and the question of human dignity in Africa. From a general perspective, I am sure that we can learn from our two interpretative predecessors when they relate the text that is to be interpreted to other, core texts and core concerns of the Old Testament, thereby being able to demonstrate a relevance that goes far beyond what a mere paraphrasing of the text would do.

In my estimation, the reception of Holter's work should even be deepened within African contexts. His serious engagement with African Old Testament scholarship, with all its life interests, should surely continue to be valued and respected. However, African interpreters of the Old Testament can still learn more from him—his historical consciousness allows him to build analogical bridges (Jonker 2018) between the theological discourses in ancient times and those of today.

Conclusion

I have shown in this contribution that Holter does not work with an either-or hermeneutics. He does not engage with *either* the contexts of origin of the biblical texts *or* contemporary (African) contexts but with *both*. Understandably, it is his receptions of the Bible in contemporary African contexts that have attracted most attention on this continent. However, I tried to show that those receptions are embedded in his analyses of the receptions in ancient times when the Bible gradually grew.

Let me close with another anecdote about the honoree of this volume, Holter. At an Annual Meeting of the Society of Biblical Literature in the United States, Holter was part of a team that hosted a reception in which a group of Nordic universities were introduced to conference attendees. Each participating institution had a stand with information pamphlets, but also with some of the publications of scholars based at these respective institutions. Holter represented the School of Mission and Theology in Stavanger (which later merged into VID Specialized University), and he had a few monographs from a number of his colleagues on exhibition, but also two or three of his own. While he was conversing with interested persons and good friends, he did not give full attention to his exhibition table, and someone took a few of the books on display and never brought them back. When Knut noticed that some of the books had disappeared, he looked somewhat disappointed. "None of my books was taken," he responded with a wry smile.

I hereby honor an excellent scholar who has remained humble and kept a sense of humor all through these years—indeed a rare species!

Works Cited

Fishbane, Michael. 1985. *Biblical Interpretation in Ancient Israel*. Oxford: Clarendon.

Getui, Mary N., Knut Holter, and Victor Zinkuratire, eds. 2001. *Interpreting the Old Testament in Africa: Papers from the International Symposium on Africa and the Old Testament in Nairobi, October 1999*. New York: Lang.

Holter, Knut. 1995. *Second Isaiah's Idol-Fabrication Passages*. BBET 28. Frankfurt am Main: Lang.
———. 1996. *Tropical Africa and the Old Testament*. New York: Lang.
———. 2000. *Yahweh in Africa: Essays on Africa and Old Testament*. New York: Lang.
———. 2002. *Old Testament Research for Africa: A Critical Analysis and Annotated Bibliography of African Old Testament Dissertations, 1967–2000*. Bible and Theology in Africa 3. New York: Lang.
———. 2003. *Deuteronomy 4 and the Second Commandment*. StBibLit 60. New York: Lang.
———. 2007. *Interpreting Classical Religious Texts in Contemporary Africa*. Nairobi: Acton.
———. 2008a. *Contextualized Old Testament Scholarship in Africa*. Nairobi: Acton.
———. 2008b. "Does a Dialogue between Africa and Europe Make Sense?" Pages 69–80 in *African and European Readers of the Bible in Dialogue: In Quest of a Shared Meaning*. Edited by Hans de Wit and Gerald O. West. Leiden: Brill.
———. 2011a. "The Role of Historical-Critical Methodology in African Old Testament Studies." *OTE* 24:377–89.
———. 2011b. "The Second Commandment and the Question of Human Dignity in Africa: A Creation-Theological Perspective." *Scriptura* 106:51–60.
Holter, Knut, and Louis C. Jonker, eds. 2010. *Global Hermeneutics? Reflections and Consequences*. IVBS 1. Atlanta: Society of Biblical Literature.
Jonker, Louis C. 2007. "Reforming History: The Hermeneutical Significance of the Books of Chronicles." *VT* 57:21–44.
———. 2011. "'Lewend en Kragtig'? Die Hermeneutiese Dinamika en Implikasies van (Her)Interpretasie in die Ou Testament." *NGTT* 52:128–47.
———. 2013a. "Introduction." *HeBAI* 3:275–86.
———. 2013b. "Why History Matters: The Place of Historical Consciousness in a Multidimensional Approach towards Biblical Interpretation." *VE* 34:1–7.
———. 2015. "Of Writers and Readers: Facilitating the Intercultural Encounter between (Ancient) Texts and (Contemporary) Readers." Pages 239–55 in *New Perspectives on Intercultural Bible Reading: Hermeneutical Explorations in Honor of Hans de Wit*. Edited by Daniel S. Schipani et al. Amsterdam: Vrije Universiteit Amsterdam.

———. 2018. "Further Interrogation of the Comparative Paradigm in African Biblical Scholarship: Towards an Analogical Hermeneutics for Interpreting the Old Testament in Africa." Pages 73–97 in *Reading, Writing Right: Festschrift for Elna Mouton*. Edited by Jeremy Punt and Marius J. Nel. Stellenbosch: African Sun Media.

Levinson, Bernard M. 1997. *Deuteronomy and the Hermeneutics of Legal Innovation*. Oxford: Oxford University Press.

———. 2005. "The Birth of the Lemma: The Restrictive Reinterpretation of the Covenant Code's Manumission Law by the Holiness Code (Leviticus 25:44–46)." *JBL* 124:617–39.

———. 2008a. *Legal Revision and Religious Renewal in Ancient Israel*. Cambridge: Cambridge University Press.

———. 2008b. *"The Right Chorale": Studies in Biblical Law and Interpretation*. Tübingen: Mohr Siebeck.

Otto, Eckart. 1996. "Deuteronomium 4: Die Pentateuchredaktion im Deuteronomiumsrahmen." Pages 196–222 in *Das Deuteronomium und seine Querbeziehungen*. Edited by Timo Veijola. Göttingen: Vandenhoeck & Ruprecht.

———. 1999. "Innerbiblische Exegese im Heiligkeitsgesetz Levitikus 17–26." Pages 125–96 in *Levitikus als Buch*. Edited by Heinz-Josef Fabry and Hans-Winfried Jüngling. BBB 119. Berlin: Philo.

———. 2006. "Review of Deuteronomy 4 and the Second Commandment." *ZABR* 12:397–400.

———. 2012. *Deuteronomium 1,1–4,43*. Freiburg: Herder.

Schmid, Konrad. 2000. "Innerbiblische Schriftauslegung: Aspekte der Forschungsgeschichte." Pages 1–22 in *Schriftauslegung in der Schrift: Festschrift for Odil Hannes Steck zu seinem 65. Geburtstag*. Edited by Reinhard Kratz, Thomas Krüger, and Konrad Schmid. BZAW 300. Berlin: De Gruyter.

Schmidt, Werner H. 1993. *Die Zehn Gebote im Rahmen alttestamentlicher Ethik*. Erträge der Forschung 281. Darmstadt: Wissenschaft Buchgesellschaft.

Tiemeyer, Lena-Sofia. 2010. *For the Comfort of Zion: The Geographical and Theological Location of Isaiah 40–55*. VTSup 139. Leiden: Brill.

West, Gerald O. 2008. "Interrogating the Comparative Paradigm in African Biblical Scholarship." Pages 37–64 in *African and European Readers of the Bible in Dialogue*. Edited by Hans de Wit and Gerald O. West. Leiden: Brill.

The Production and Worship of Idols in Biblical Tradition

Jostein Ådna

Introduction

The exclusive worship of YWHW alone, accompanied by the abhorrence of any other gods represented by idols, is the most outstanding characteristic of the Old Testament. Relevant examples are, inter alia, the first two commandments in the Decalogue (Exod 20:3–6; Deut 5:7–10, cf. 27:15) and the major criterion of the Deuteronomistic historian(s) for evaluating the Israelite and Judean kings, namely, whether they did what was right or what was evil in the sight of the Lord (e.g., 1 Kgs 13:33–34; 15:15, 26, 34; 16:25–26). Other examples are the scathing criticism of idolatry found in many of the prophetic writings (e.g., Jer 2; 7:9–11, 16–20, 30–31; Ezek 6:1–7; 8:5–18; 20:27–31; Hos 2:4–15 [ET 2:2–13]; 4:12–19; 8:4–14; 13:1–4). The commitment to worship the God of Israel alone and to reject all other gods continued throughout the era of early Judaism—then not only perceived as an obligation to monolatry, but as a monotheistic conviction and confession—and was taken over by the early Christians.

Polemics against Idolatry in Second Isaiah

Second Isaiah (Isa 40–55) contains more texts with polemics against idolatry than any other Old Testament book. Such polemics appear in Isa 40:19–20; 41:6–7, 21–29; 42:8, 17; 43:8–13; 44:9–20; 45:14–17, 18–25; 46:1–7; 47:1–15; and 48:3–5. For his doctoral dissertation, Knut Holter

---

Thanks to John Goldie MA for helpful suggestions for linguistic corrections and improvements.

selected the passages among these texts that describe the very production of idols, namely, Isa 40:19–20; 41:6–7; 44:9–20; and 46:6–7, and he subjected them to meticulous investigation. The revised version of Holter's dissertation was published in 1995 as a monograph entitled *Second Isaiah's Idol-Fabrication Passages*. This Festschrift offers a welcome opportunity to direct the attention of readers to the first major scholarly contribution of the honored recipient of the present volume.[1]

Analysis of Second Isaiah's Idol Production Passages

The production of idols is depicted elsewhere in the Old Testament (see especially Jer 10:4, 9; Hab 2:19; Pss 115:4; 135:15). "Nevertheless, Second Isaiah's emphasizing of this aspect holds a unique position. Nowhere else in the Old Testament is idol-fabrication depicted in more gloomy colours, and nowhere else its consequences are pointed out more negatively" (Holter 1995, 16).

Second Isaiah presents statements to his listeners and readers such as,

> [6] Those who pour out gold from the bag
> and weigh out silver on the scales,
> they hire a goldsmith who makes it to a god,
> and they bow down, yea, they worship.
> [7] They bear it upon the shoulder, they carry it,
> they set it in its place and it stands there,
> from its place it cannot move.
> Yea, although one cries to it,
> it does not answer,
> it cannot save him from his trouble. (Isa 46:6–7)[2]

---

1. I joined the faculty of the School of Mission and Theology (*Misjonshøgskolen*, MHS) in Stavanger in August 1993, and one of the academic events I experienced during my first term there in the autumn of 1993 was Knut Holter's defense of his doctoral dissertation at the University of Oslo. We were colleagues in biblical studies until my retirement in 2022, first at MHS, then, after MHS merged in 2016 with other church-oriented academic institutions in Norway, at the Faculty of Theology, Diakonia and Leadership Studies in VID Specialized University.

2. All quotations in English of the idol production passages will follow Holter's translations (see Holter 1995, 33, 91, 130, 147–48, 181, 213). All other biblical texts, including the apocryphal or deuterocanonical books, are quoted from the NRSV.

In his monograph, Holter subjects the selected passages to a structural analysis and a detailed exegesis of their content as well as an analysis of how they relate to their immediate contexts.[3] Holter observes, albeit with some minor variations, that the common denominator of all four passages is not an emphasis on the idols per se, but on the humans that make or produce them.[4] Regarding 40:19–20, Holter (1995, 78–79) shows that "the two verses … open with a presentation of the idol.… After this initial presentation, however, both verses then turn their attention from the idols and towards the idol-fabricators, thereby concentrating the polemics more specifically on these." Regarding 44:9–20, Holter observes that, "The third idol-fabrication passage … follows the lead of the two previous ones. It follows their special focusing upon the idol-fabricators rather than the idols" (202).

Other conclusions drawn by Holter (1995) from his analysis of the four selected passages within their textual contexts are that the idol fabricators appear as representatives of the nations (78, 122, 196–99, 225) and that they are contrasted with YHWH (53–59, 122, 139–40, 152–56, 175, 219–20, 224). Hence, in these passages, Second Isaiah does not primarily compare the gods of the nations or the idols as their representations to YHWH and contrast them with him as his adversaries but puts the idol manufacturers in this role.[5] In this respect, there is a difference between the idol production passages in Second Isaiah and other Old Testament idol production passages, that is, Jer 10:1–16; Hab 2:18–19; Pss 115:4–8; and 135:15–18.[6] According to Holter's (1995, 236) well-written and nuanced

---

3. Chapter 2: Isa 40:19–20 is analyzed within the context of 40:12–31 (Holter 1995, 33–79); chapter 3: Isa 41:6–7 within the context of 41:1–16 (pp. 91–122); chapter 4: Isa 44:9–20 within the context of 44:6–23 (pp. 127–202); chapter 5: Isa 46:6–7 within the context of 46:1–13 (pp. 213–31).

4. As representative examples of Holter's concluding characterizations of the four passages, I quote his statements on the first and the third passage. For corresponding statements on the second and the fourth passage, see Holter (1995, 122, 230).

5. This does not imply, however, that Holter (1995, 30) rejects the notion that Second Isaiah also undertakes a "rhetorical contrasting of Yahweh with the gods or idols." In a footnote, he refers to Isa 45:20–21 as an example and to his own article on wordplay in Isa 45 (Holter 1993) in which he has pointed out how the "god that cannot save" is rhetorically contrasted with the "God and Saviour" in these verses (cited in Holter 1995, 30, n. 32).

6. See "Excursus 5: Other Idol-Fabrication Passages in the Old Testament" (Holter 1995, 231–36). Whereas the motif of contrasting the idol manufacturers as represen-

analysis, in Second Isaiah we encounter a specific variant of the broad tradition of mocking idolatry in which he focuses on the idol manufacturers.

Guided by Holter's study, I wish to address some aspects of Second Isaiah's idol production passages that are of particular theological interest.

The true character of the idols is efficiently displayed by the emphasis on their manufacturers. This can be observed both in the first and the fourth passages (40:19-20; 46:6-7), but the effect of focusing on the craftsmen comes particularly to the fore in the long third passage in Isa 44:9-20. Verses 13-17 describe in detail how the skilled carpenter uses different types of wood as his material, both for producing the idol (vv. 13, 15b, 17a) and for food preparation and warmth (vv. 15a, 16). The obvious implication is that the idols appear as "nothing but a piece of the tree they are made of" and that they, made כתבנית איש כתפארת אדם ("after the figure of a male, according to the glory of a man"), "somehow, resemble the idol-fabricator" (Holter 1995, 158, 164).[7] Stripped of their artistic beauty and revealed to be composed of mere physical materials that are used by their manufacturers for the mundane activities of daily life such as for firewood, the idols are seen as weak and futile.[8] The idols are fastened with nails, resulting in their immobility (Isa 41:7bβ; cf. 40:20bβ); they cannot walk but are carried by human beings who put them down in the shrines from where they cannot move (see Isa 46:7a).

Further, in the idol production passages, Second Isaiah also describes the idol craftsmen and their employers, who hire them as artisans, as being involved in the worship of the idols. They carry them in religious processions (46:7a); they prostrate and bow down before them as their gods (44:15b, 17bα), and they pray and say: "Save me, for you are my god" (44:17bβγ). However, in spite of the committed efforts of the worshipers, the idol cannot help: "Yea, although one cries to it, it does not answer, it cannot save him from his trouble" (46:7b). The idol producers should be

---

tatives of the nations with YHWH also seems to appear in these texts (cf. Jer 10:2-4, 6-7), the dominating viewpoint of the idol production passages elsewhere in the Old Testament is "the more traditional contrastive pattern, that between Yahweh and the idols" (p. 234).

7. The translation of the Hebrew phrases is taken from Holter (1995, 147), who also discusses in detail the implications of the two expressions, כתבנית איש and כתפארת אדם, on pp. 163-69.

8. This description also applies to the idols of gold, silver, and other metals crafted by smiths (cf. Isa 40:19; 41:7; 44:12; 46:6).

able to consider that they use the same wood to produce idols and also for the basics of everyday life (see above) and draw appropriate conclusions. However, because they fail to do so (see 44:18), Second Isaiah utters a strong accusation against them in 44:19–20:

> ¹⁹ He does not consider in his heart, and he has neither knowledge nor understanding to say: "Half of it I burned in the fire, yea, I baked bread upon its coals, I roasted meat and ate. Shall I make the rest into an abomination, shall I bow down before a piece of firewood?" ²⁰ He feeds on ashes, a deceived heart has turned him aside. Neither can he save himself, nor does he say: "Is there not a deception in my right hand?"[9]

Instead of enthusiasm and mutual assistance among the idol craftsmen (41:6–7), they should rather realize that their whole undertaking is futile and that what they make of the remaining wood after burning half of it is an abomination (תועבה). In 44:19, this term "is obviously used as a designation of a pagan god, corresponding with the אל in vv. 15 and 17," with "polemical connotations" even "stronger than those of אל" (Holter 1995, 186).

The long idol production passage in Isa 44:9–20 is structured in three sections: (1) an accusatory introduction (vv. 9–11), (2) a description (vv. 12–17), and (3) an accusatory conclusion (see Holter 1995, 127–30). Above, I have drawn extensively from the description section and quoted most of the conclusion. The introductory accusation contains an outright condemnation of the idol manufacturers. As noted above, the idols can neither answer nor save, they can neither see nor understand, and they cannot do any good. With this background, Second Isaiah asks rhetorically: "Who fashions a god and casts an idol that does not profit?" (44:10). There is no profit to be acquired from manufacturing idols and worshiping them. Therefore, the idol producers, who are mere men themselves (וחרשים המה מאדם, v. 11aβ), "shall be put to shame" (v. 11aα).[10]

---

9. See the comments on the noun שקר, rendered "deception," in Holter (1995, 189). It is also appropriate to refer to 46:7 here, where "the total impotence of the god" (218) is expressed in the triple negation that he cannot move, answer or save the one who turns to him for help. "This is, basically, a synthesis of Second Isaiah's concept of the gods and idols of the nations; they cannot save" (219).

10. See also Isa 44:11b: "Let them all assemble, let them come forward, they shall be terrified and put to shame together." The "description of the idol-fabricators as *men*

Theologically, contrasting the idol manufacturers with YHWH relates both to creation and redemption. Whereas YHWH is the one "who has measured the waters in the hollow of his hand and marked off the heavens with a span" and the one "who stretches out the heavens like a curtain, and spreads them like a tent to live in" (Isa 40:12a, 22b), the idol maker only "stretches a line, and marks it [the idol] out with a stylus. He makes it with planes, and with compasses he marks it out" (Is 44:13a). The ironic contrast between the stretching of the Creator of the universe, on the one hand, and of the creator of the idol, on the other hand, is noteworthy (see Holter 1995, 159–61). The same applies to the activity of the Lord in history as one with the task of saving his elect people, Israel. He is the one "who has roused a victor from the east, summoned him to his service" (Isa 41:2a), saying to Israel,

> [8] my servant, Jacob, whom I have chosen, the offspring of Abraham, my friend; [9] you whom I took from the ends of the earth, and called from its farthest corners, saying to you, "You are my servant, I have chosen you and not cast you off"; [10] do not fear, for I am with you, do not be afraid, for I am your God; I will strengthen you, I will help you, I will uphold you with my victorious hand. (Isa 41:8–10)

Compared with YHWH, the idol manufacturers are as weak as the nations they represent and without any capacity to rescue Israel (e.g., Isa 44:11–12).[11] Hence, the demonstration of YHWH's incomparability is a major point in Second Isaiah's theology: "To whom will you liken me and make me equal, and compare me, as though we were alike?" (Isa 46:5).[12]

Some of the most appreciable merits of Knut Holter's monograph, from which further research will profit, are his meticulous analyses of significant nouns and verbs in the idol production passages that carry theological weight with regard to creation and redemption.[13]

---

is of course in ironical contrast with the concept expressed elsewhere in Is 40–55, that Yahweh is the creator—also of man, cf. 45:12" (Holter 1995, 145).

11. In v. 12bβγ, Second Isaiah recalls the description of YHWH in Isa 40:28–31 as "the everlasting God, the Creator of the ends of the earth," who "does not faint or grow weary" and "gives power to the faint, and strengthens the powerless." See Holter 1995, 155–56.

12. See Isa 40:25 and Holter 1995, 29. Various strong expressions of YHWH's incomparability are numerous in Second Isaiah (e.g., Isa 43:10b–11; 44:6–8; 46:9).

13. Inter alia, this applies to the four verbs in Isa 40:19–20, רקע, צרף, בחר, and כון, which, elsewhere in Second Isaiah and in the Old Testament, are used with the Lord as

Criticism of Idol Production and Worship in Early Judaism and in the New Testament

Numerous echoes of Second Isaiah's ridiculing and scathing polemics against the idol manufacturers and the idols produced by them occur in early Judaism and in the New Testament. The rejection of any divine rivals to the God of Israel is a necessary consequence of the Jewish monotheistic faith, but there are multiform variations of how this rejection of idols is expressed. In this later tradition, I am aware of only one example of mockery of idol manufacturers that equals the detailed portrayal of them in Second Isaiah (see below). In general, the emphasis lies on the condemnation of the idols themselves and on the incompatibility of paying any kind of respect to them while believing in the one and only true God.

Early Judaism

The challenges of pagan cults and international culture to Jews in Hellenistic times were manifold. Whereas some Jewish diaspora communities accommodated and were assimilated into their surroundings, other Jewish communities, which were heavily pressurized to participate in religious activities considered idolatrous, resisted and developed a deepened commitment to a religious practice that opposed any kind of syncretism.[14]

Criticism of idol production and worship is a frequent element in the extant Jewish literature from this period. One example is the book of Jubilees, which backdates the criticism of idols to Abraham, who already as a child "separated from his father so that he might not worship idols with him" (Jub. 11.16; trans. O. S. Wintermute, *OTP* 2:79). After unsuccessfully trying to convince his father to refrain from idolatry and burning down the house of the idols (see 12.1–14), Abraham leaves for the promised land.[15]

---

subject (Holter 1995, 54–59), to יצר and יעל in 44:9, 10 (Holter 1995, 132–42), and, as a third example, to פעל and זרוע כח in 44:12 (Holter 1995, 152–55).

14. Fascination with Hellenistic culture was not a phenomenon limited to distant regions; it was felt in Jerusalem, even among the priests (see 2 Macc 4:12–17). The paradigmatic example of resistance is the persecution of the Seleucid king Antiochus IV Epiphanes and the Maccabean revolt, as recounted in 1 and 2 Maccabees.

15. Polemics against idolatry also plays a significant role in the pseudepigraphon Apocalypse of Abraham (see the text of Apoc. Ab. 1–6 in *OTP* 1:689–91).

The deceptive character of idols is disclosed in amusing narratives and admonishing instructions. A clear example is the story of the Babylonian god Bel (together with Nebo, another Babylonian god, referred to in Isa 46:1-2) in the additions to Daniel in the Septuagint (LXX Dan 14). In the so-called Epistle of Jeremiah, a treatise or a sermon based on the idol production passage in Jer 10:1-16, we also encounter satirical criticism that resembles the polemics of Second Isaiah:

> [4] Now in Babylon you will see gods made of silver and gold and wood, which people carry on their shoulders, and which cause the heathen to fear.... [8] Their tongues are smoothed by the carpenter ... but they are false and cannot speak.... [45] They are made by carpenters and goldsmiths; they can be nothing but what the artisans wish them to be. [46] Those who make them will certainly not live very long themselves; [47] how then can the things that are made by them be gods? They have left only lies and reproach for those who come after. (Ep Jer [Bar 6] 4, 8, 45-47)

The book of Wisdom, presumably originating from the Jewish community in Alexandria, offers the most sophisticated treatment of the issue of idolatry in early Judaism in the section 13:1-15:19.[16] First, the fact that people mistake tremendous manifestations of nature for the Creator and that, consequently, they turn to idol worship is exposed (13:1-9). Then a passage about idols follows in which a scathing criticism of their manufacturers, resembling the idol production passages in Second Isaiah, takes a prominent position (13:10-14:11):

> [11] A skilled woodcutter may saw down a tree easy to handle and ... make a useful vessel that serves life's needs, [12] and burn the cast-off pieces of his work to prepare his food, and eat his fill. [13] But a cast-off piece from among them, useful for nothing ... he takes and carves with care in his leisure.... he forms it in the likeness of a human being [14] ... covering every blemish in it with paint; [15] then he makes a suitable niche for it, and sets it in the wall, and fastens it there with iron.... [17] When he prays about possessions and his marriage and children, he is not ashamed to address a lifeless thing. [18] For health he appeals to a thing that is weak; for life he prays to a thing that is dead. (Wis 13:11-18*)

---

16. For the following exposition, I have benefited from Hübner 1999.

The parallel to Second Isaiah's portrayal in Isa 44:13–17 is apparent. Here we read of the carpenter collecting wood both to burn in the fire for food preparation and warmth and for making a god whom he invokes for protection and life. Further, this passage parallels Second Isaiah's description of how the crafted idols must be fastened in order not to topple and, as a consequence, that they cannot move by themselves (see Isa 40:20b; 41:7bβ; 46:7a).

The third passage, Wis 14:12–31, describes how idolatry has perverted and driven humankind to immorality throughout history: "For the worship of idols not to be named is the beginning and cause and end of every evil" (v. 27). Finally, Wis 15 combines a confession to the one true God (15:1–6), a description of the activity of a potter paralleling that of the carpenter in chapter 13 (15:7–13), and a description of the worshipers of idols (15:14–19).

The New Testament

The most powerful statement about idols in the New Testament appears in Rev 9:20: "The rest of humankind, who were not killed by these plagues, did not repent of the works of their hands or give up worshiping demons and idols of gold and silver and bronze and stone and wood, which cannot see or hear or walk."[17] This description of the idols as products of five different materials incapable of seeing, hearing, or walking clearly echoes the two psalms that speak about idol production, namely, Pss 115 and 135, but it does not echo any of Second Isaiah's idol production passages.

It seems that the closest to any equivalent of Second Isaiah's idol production passages in the New Testament is Paul's speech in Athens (Acts 17:22b–31). The body of this speech concentrates on God as the Creator of the world (vv. 24–25) and of humankind (vv. 26–29). Connecting to the preceding citation from the Greek poet Aratus in verse 28 ("For we too are his offspring"; Phaenomena 5), verse 29 reads:

γένος οὖν ὑπάρχοντες τοῦ θεοῦ οὐκ ὀφείλομεν νομίζειν χρυσῷ ἢ ἀργύρῳ ἢ λίθῳ, χαράγματι τέχνης καὶ ἐνθυμήσεως ἀνθρώπου, τὸ θεῖον εἶναι ὅμοιον.

---

17. This verse belongs to the account of the sixth trumpet (Rev 9:13–21; cf. 8:2–9:21; 11:15–19) and describes the religious practice of the survivors after a third of humankind has been killed.

Since we are God's offspring, we ought not to think that the deity is like gold, or silver, or stone, an image formed by the art and imagination of mortals. (Acts 17:29)

We might suggest a connection between the reference to the idols as artistic products of the imagination and skill of mortal human beings and certain statements throughout Second Isaiah's idol production passages (e.g., Isa 40:19; 44:12).[18] Here, too, as in Rev 9:20, the link to the Septuagint version of the two psalm verses speaking of idol production seems closer (LXX Pss 113:12 = MT 115:4; 134:15 = MT 135:15).[19] However, what is most obvious as a tradition-historical background is an implied connection to the argument developed in Wis 13–15 (see above).[20]

Turning to the textual evidence from the apostle Paul in his letters, we begin with a textual unit that is generally considered to have a special affinity with ideas typical of Qumran, 2 Cor 6:14–7:1, where Paul rhetorically asks, "What agreement does Christ have with Beliar.... What agreement has the temple of God with idols?" (2 Cor 6:15a, 16a). From his First Letter to the Thessalonians, it is apparent that Paul considered the rejection of idols and turning to the one true God the fundamental step to be taken by gentiles who convert to God and join his church. Retrospectively, he tells the Thessalonians that there are reports of how they "turned to God from idols, to serve a living and true God, and to wait for his Son from heaven, whom he raised from the dead—Jesus, who rescues us from the wrath that is coming" (1 Thess 1:9b–10). A corresponding statement appears in 1 Cor 12:2: "You know that when you were pagans, you were enticed and led astray to idols that could not speak." There are four more occurrences of the term εἴδωλον/εἴδωλα (idol/idols) in Paul's writings. Three of them appear in 1 Corinthians within Paul's extensive exposition of the issue of how believers should relate to food sacrificed to

---

18. The flimsy direct connection between the idol production passages in Second Isaiah with their emphasis on the manufacturers and the New Testament finds an indirect confirmation in the fact that the only reference to these passages in the outer margin of the Greek text in NA[28] appears in Acts 17:29; it is a global reference to the whole third passage, Isa 44:9–20.

19. The identical text of these two verses runs thus: τὰ εἴδωλα τῶν ἐθνῶν ἀργύριον καὶ χρυσίον, ἔργα χειρῶν ἀνθρώπων ("the idols of the nations are silver and gold, works of human hands"; NETS).

20. Hence, the outer margin of NA[28], in addition to Isa 44:9–20, lists Deut 4:28, Isa 40:18 and Wis 13:10–19 as parallels to Acts 17:29.

idols (1 Cor 8:1–11:1, see 8:4, 7; 10:19).²¹ The last occurrence of the term εἴδωλον/εἴδωλα appears within the textual unit of Rom 2:17–29, where Paul notes the guilt of the Jews, addressing them with a chain of accusatory rhetorical questions in verses 21–24, among which is: "You that abhor idols, do you rob temples?" (2:22b).

Paul's most extensive exposition of the topic of idol worship is found in Rom 1:18–32. He portrays the contemporary Greco-Roman culture as idolatrous and in moral decline. In a similar way to Wis 13:1–5, he starts from creation and accuses humans of not recognizing God from the things he has made (vv. 19–20); on the contrary, they have "worshiped and served the creature rather than the Creator" (v. 25). Failing to honor and give thanks to God, "their senseless minds were darkened" (v. 21), and "they became fools" (v. 22),

> ²³ and they exchanged the glory of the immortal God for images resembling a mortal human being [ἤλλαξαν τὴν δόξαν τοῦ ἀφθάρτου θεοῦ ἐν ὁμοιώματι εἰκόνος φθαρτοῦ ἀνθρώπου] or birds or four-footed animals or reptiles. ²⁴ Therefore God gave them up in the lusts of their hearts to impurity, to the degrading of their bodies among themselves.

In addition to accusing the gentiles of having substituted idols for the true God, Paul further reproaches them for having turned to homosexual practices, contrary to nature (vv. 26–27; see Wis 14:26) and for complete moral havoc (vv. 29–31; see Wis 14:22–31). As the references to Wisdom demonstrate, Paul concurs with the critical evaluation of Greco-Roman culture typical of Jewish diaspora communities. By perceiving idol worship and moral collapse not only as sins that will lead to condemnation in the final judgement but as effects of God's wrath operating already now,²² Paul even intensifies the theological assessment of idolatry and the vices that accompany it.

Although there is no reference in Rom 1:18–32 to idol manufacturers, some agreement is noticeable between Paul and Second Isaiah about the

---

21. Additionally, see the four different cognates in 1 Cor 8:1, 4, 7, 10 [2x]; 10:7, 14, 19.

22. See the recurring phrase, παρέδωκεν αὐτοὺς ὁ θεός, "God gave them up," in verses 24, 26 and 28. God's wrath is implemented in the way that he has simply confirmed humanity's choice of idols instead of God's glory, and lies instead of God's truth, by giving them up to the effects of that which they themselves desire to do in their ungodliness and wickedness.

abandonment of the only true and living God as the fundamental human sin. The gravity of the idol manufacturers' appeal to the idol they have produced, "Save me, for you are my god" (Isa 44:17), is clearly exposed based on the background of Second Isaiah's monotheistic core statement, "Before me no god was formed, nor shall there be any after me" (Isa 43:10bβγ). As Holter (1995, 179) notes, "both הצילני, 'save me,' and כי אלי אתה, 'you are my god,' are fixed expressions in Israel's prayer."[23] It is this appalling exchange of God for a human-made idol, produced in the image of man, that Second Isaiah displays in his mockery of idolatry with the emphasis on the idol craftsmen and their guilt and which Paul expounds in his documentation of universal sinfulness in Rom 1:18–32.

However, neither Second Isaiah nor Paul considers the exposure of sin, guilt, and judgement to be the final words. On the contrary, they were both commissioned to proclaim a message of redemption and justification. The disclosure of humankind's state of guilt serves to demonstrate that the one and only God, the Creator, is about to accomplish salvation and redemption, both for his elect people Israel, as told by Second Isaiah and, ultimately, in "the fullness of time" (Gal 4:4), for all humankind as told in the gospel. This is the gospel of which Paul is not ashamed, because "it is the power of God for salvation of everyone who has faith, to the Jew first and also to the Greek" (Rom 1:16).

Conclusion

We can trace an uninterrupted tradition of unequivocally rejecting idols and any worship of them from the Old Testament through early Judaism to the New Testament. Within this tradition, Second Isaiah focuses on the idol manufacturers in some central passages (Isa 40:19–20; 41:6–7; 44:9–20; 46:6–7), directing his criticism, which is rich in irony and mockery, toward them. It remains the scholarly merit of Holter that he exposed the specific character of these passages in Second Isaiah, proving them to hold a unique position within the biblical tradition of the production and worship of idols.

---

23. Holter provides due references in n. 123 and n. 124.

Works Cited

Holter, Knut. 1993. "The Wordplay on אֵל ('God') in Isaiah 45,20–21." *SJOT* 7: 88–98.

———. 1995. *Second Isaiah's Idol-Fabrication Passages*. BBET 28. Frankfurt am Main: Lang.

Hübner, Hans. 1999. *Die Weisheit Salomons*. ATD Apokryphen 4. Göttingen: Vandenhoeck & Ruprecht.

Structural Differences between the Source Languages and the Target Languages in Bible Translation

Magnar Kartveit

Introduction

Knut Holter has been instrumental in founding and supporting the Bible Translator Study Program at The School of Mission and Theology, now part of VID Specialized University. Facing numerous difficulties, he has adamantly kept the program running and carried the largest burden of teaching and planning. This is the only professional training program for Bible translators in Norway, and he is rightly praised for his efforts and results. This article is only a small token of gratitude for his work in this field—one of his many engagements and commitments. I would like to address a topic of relevance for Bible translation, but also for translation in general, that is, grammatical structural differences between languages.

The present volume is entitled *Context Matters*, an expression that refers to an important topic in itself but is also an appropriate title for a volume honoring Holter. Context can describe cultural phenomena such as habits, rituals, environmental issues, thinking, ideas, and presuppositions in our lives. The purpose of this essay is to demonstrate that language is part of the context for the content of the Bible and its addressees. Words and sentences are carriers of meaning, and this is readily recognized in semantics. Less studied, if at all, is the notion that grammar—that is, forms and syntax—is part of this context. Language enables authors to express their views and, at the same time, limits their range of possibilities for doing it. This essay is a contribution to setting the topic on the agenda of Bible translators—those educated by Holter and by others (cf. Holter 2000).

I will try to demonstrate that grammatical structures in morphology and syntax are part of context. The study limits itself to the biblical languages and some European languages, but the observations made here apply to every translation process in every language. African languages have their own structures and systems, but the fact that they are structured is the important point here. There is, therefore, a possibility for transferring general observations of European languages to any language or set of languages. Translation is loss, and translation is gain. This general comment may be repeated also here. I hope that readers from other contexts will appreciate studying the examples offered here, transferring the insights to their own context.

When Bible translations are planned and discussed, a great deal of effort goes into semantic questions. How should we render the Hebrew word נפש? Is it "soul," "breath," or "life"? And what about the Greek σάρξ? Does it mean "flesh," "body," "human nature," or something else? Such discussions may end in controversy between people who subscribe to literal translations and those who opt for contextual renderings. Eugene A. Nida (1964) launched the principle of "dynamic equivalence," which is an attempt at recreating in the target language the dynamic impact a word has in the source language. By this suggestion, he added another method to the existing ones, and today one may find an array of approaches to semantic questions in Bible translation. These discussions are important and interesting, and they deserve our full attention.

Nida also discusses many instances where languages have different structures, and the present article will focus on one part. It will deal with a topic that is both important and interesting and that has gone under the radar in many discussions. This is the question of grammatical structural differences between the source languages and the target languages.

A Neglected Field

The Bible is written in three languages: Hebrew, Aramaic, and Greek. These languages have survived until today but in versions different from the biblical ones. Even in the contexts where Ivrit (Modern Hebrew), the Syriac version of Aramaic, or Modern Greek are known and used, the biblical languages are not easily understood. An example of this situation is the translation of the Hebrew Bible into Ivrit (Ahuvya 2010), a project that has been welcomed by school children and their parents and heavily criticized by rabbis and orthodox Jews. Even in this project, with its emphasis on vocabulary, structural differences are evident. The consecutive imperfect in biblical Hebrew has been replaced with perfect forms, which is the current way of expressing the past tense. There is not much loss of meaning in this replacement, but it shows that change in grammatical structure has to be dealt with in a context where the biblical language has developed into a new form.

The quotations from the Old Testament/Hebrew Bible in the New Testament are rendered in Greek—a process often involving changes in meaning, affecting both semantics and structural differences. This, however, is a special field of study, and space constraints do not allow me to engage this field here.

Remarkably, grammatical, structural differences are rarely emphasized in scholarly discussions. In a fairly recent treatment of translation questions, for example, one cannot find anything on this subject (De Waard 2015). In the section on source culture and problems of translation, De Waard (2015, 682–84) comes close to structural differences. Here, he mentions "joy," "heart," "beating his breast," "treasures on earth," "father," "mother," "spirit," and Today's English Version (TEV)'s choices in these cases and further mentions "anoint," "shoe," and a few more words. In his discussion, he stays with semantic and cultural questions and does not approach grammatical structures, which would have required attention to these phenomena in the different languages. De Waard is no exception in this respect, as he typifies discussions of Bible translation, which regularly concentrate on semantics and cultural differences between old Israel and current contexts.

Structural Differences

A word about what I define as structural differences will now be in order. I do not aim at the broader field of structuralism, as this expression is associated with Ferdinand de Saussure (1916) and other linguists. The basic idea for these linguists is that of a linguistic structure, a linguistic system that prioritizes senses and meanings of words. Each language may have its own system and structure that may or may not correspond to those of other languages. As noted, I will not veer into semantics but present some examples of grammatical categories in the biblical languages that are not found in a language such as English. Still, I find it helpful to speak of structure, because grammar is the scaffolding used by languages to create utterances and written texts. This structure of morphology and syntax is the form in which lexemes are forged (Lyons 1995, 69). This means that the borders between grammar and lexicon in one language may be different from those in another language. Differences between languages on the morphological level, grammaticalized phenomena, may be lexicalized in another language. A language without cases, for example, would use prepositions to express the same meaning as cases do. The effect may be a different syntax.

The Lord's Prayer

One of the structural differences I wish to address can be exemplified by the Lord's Prayer in Matt 6:9–13. The translation of this text is widely discussed, and one of the reasons for disagreements on the translations is that the Greek uses the third-person imperative, a grammatical form that many languages lack. Additionally, some of the imperatives are in aorist form, for which many languages have no equivalent, and some of the sentences are passive, while many languages employ active expressions. In the following discussion, all translations are mine unless otherwise stated. The *BHS* edition of the Hebrew text and the Nestle-Aland edition of the Greek text are used.

The first sentence is ἁγιασθήτω τὸ ὄνομά σου ("hallowed be your name"; NRSV). The verb is third-person passive aorist imperative, whose equivalents is hard to find in some target languages. Many languages can match the passive expression, here, the so-called divine passive, in NRSV translated as "hallowed be." If the passive form is not used in target languages, an active voice may be used; "God" will be introduced as subject. Aorist forms basically indicate punctuality (Blass 1965, § 318), and some languages have corresponding forms that others do not have. It may thus be very hard to find third-person imperatives in target languages. The NRSV uses a form that indicates a divine passive with "name" as the grammatical subject and would have to add "by you" if the logical subject should be expressed. But "hallowed be" is a wish form, a kind of subjunctive, and it misses the command element in an imperative. A total transformation of this sentence and the following ones might end up in "God! Make sure you sanctify your name!," but this would miss the enigma of the prayer, where humans are involved in the sanctification.

The second sentence is ἐλθέτω ἡ βασιλεία σου ("Your kingdom come"; NRSV). The verb here is third-person active aorist imperative, which does not present us with the conundrum of the divine passive, but the other problems are the same as in the first prayer. "Come" in the NRSV is a subjunctive and not an imperative, but "kingdom" as the grammatical subject corresponds to the source language.

In the third sentence, γενηθήτω τὸ θέλημά σου ("Your will be done"; NRSV), we again have the third-person passive aorist imperative. The passive voice is used in the translation as well as in the source, and "will" is the grammatical subject, but the verb is subjunctive and not imperative.

According to Friedrich Blass (1965, 208), the use of the aorist form in the Lord's Prayer is "complex," meaning that it refers to absolute, categorical prohibitions, and prayers. The use of the aorist may explain the use of the third-person. The grammatical subjects "name," "kingdom," and "will" require the third-person, and the absoluteness of the prayer requires the aorist form. This absoluteness is difficult to render in many target languages, unless translators turn to lexicalization of the expression, which involves using more words.

In the following prayers, second-person imperatives are used: δὸς, ("give!"), ἄφες ("forgive!"), and ῥῦσαι ("deliver!"), but also a subjunctive εἰσενέγκῃς ("bring into"). They are all aorist forms, and this punctual aspect cannot be rendered in English.

We encounter a similar situation in the story of the Canaanite woman in Matt 15:28: γενηθήτω σοι ὡς θέλεις ("Let it be done for you as you wish"; NRSV). The verb here is also third-person passive aorist imperative, and English has the same challenges as with the Lord's Prayer. The translation uses an imperative and adds "it" as subject in order to express the third-person. "Be it unto thee even as thou wilt" in the KJV also introduces a subject for the imperative, whereas *Dir geschehe, wie du willst* in Luther's 1912 version ("may it happen to you as you wish"), uses a subjunctive and not an imperative.

Duration and Punctuality

When Paul and Barnabas arrived at Salamis in Cyprus, they "proclaimed the word" in the synagogues (Acts 13:5). It must have been for some time, as the imperfect form, κατήγγελλον, is used. Similarly, the lame man in Lystra, had been sitting down all his life, as shown by the imperfect ἐκάθητο (Acts 14:8). When he was healed, he sprang up (aorist) and walked around (imperfect), καὶ ἥλατο καὶ περιεπάτει (v.10). After the first missionary journey, Paul and Barnabas returned to Antioch and reported their activities, and "they stayed [imperfect] there for not a short time with the disciples" (διέτριβον δὲ χρόνον οὐκ ὀλίγον σὺν τοῖς μαθηταῖς) (Acts 14:28).

The Great Commission

The Great Commission may illustrate another feature of the Greek language—the use of participles. The text is well known, and this is the section with participles: πορευθέντες οὖν μαθητεύσατε πάντα τὰ ἔθνη, βαπτίζοντες αὐτοὺς εἰς τὸ ὄνομα τοῦ πατρὸς καὶ τοῦ υἱοῦ καὶ τοῦ ἁγίου πνεύματος, διδάσκοντες αὐτοὺς τηρεῖν πάντα ὅσα ἐνετειλάμην ὑμῖν: "As you go out, make all nations disciples, by baptizing them to the name of the Father, the Son, and the Holy Spirit, as you teach them to keep everything that I have commanded you" (Matt 28:19–20a).

Here, the three participles rendered by "go out," "baptizing," and "teach" all depend on the imperative "make disciples." Usually, a participle would refer to actions that are concomitant to the main action of the main verb, but in the preceding case, they seem to serve different functions. The first participle, πορευθέντες ("having gone out"), in aorist, would refer to the action needed before reaching all nations, that is, the presupposition for making disciples. A translator may here use a participle, if the receptor language has this in the grammatical repertoire, or move to lexicalization, as I have done in the translation given above.

The second participle, βαπτίζοντες ("baptizing"), present tense, may refer to an activity following the going out or happening simultaneously with the discipling or the way in which all nations are made disciples (cf. Blass 1965, 260). If a translator uses a participle here, the different possibilities in the Greek can perhaps also be transmitted in the translation; if lexicalization is needed, the ambiguity may be lost.

Also the third participle, διδάσκοντες ("teaching"), which is cast in the present tense, is ambiguous. It may refer to concomitant action, but also to the act of making the discipling more precise—the apostles shall make disciples by baptizing and teaching them. Translations that choose dividing the sentence into several sentences, like the Norwegian Bibel (2011), risk making the Great Commission into three commissions.

Double Genitive

Koine Greek has five cases, that is, nominative, vocative, accusative, genitive, and dative. This grammaticalization of syntactical functions may pose problems for translation into languages that do not have corresponding phenomena. Usually, translators can remedy the situation by lexicalization, through prepositions, or in other ways.

A particular phenomenon in Greek is the double genitive. It means that two words occur in the genitive case and are syntactically related to each other, often a noun or a pronoun plus a participle. An example is found in the Mark version of the story of John the Baptist: καὶ εἰσελθούσης τῆς θυγατρὸς αὐτοῦ Ἡρῳδιάδος καὶ ὀρχησαμένης ἤρεσεν τῷ Ἡρῴδῃ καὶ τοῖς συνανακειμένοις, "and Herodias his daughter having come in and danced, she/it was pleasing to Herod and his co-diners" (Mark 6:22). The expression ἀρέσκω with the dative, meaning "please somebody," is here rendered literally (with a preposition), since it illustrates the use of cases in general and the possibility or need for circumventing such expressions in languages where there are no cases, or where cases are used sparingly.

The two aorist participles, εἰσελθούσης and ὀρχησαμένης, are genitive, corresponding to the genitive forms τῆς θυγατρὸς and Ἡρῳδιάδος. Together, the four words form a unit, which may express past or contemporaneous action with the main verb. This is ἤρεσεν, which is aorist also, and the question then is whether the double genitive expresses previous action, the reason for the pleasing, or another part of the scene (Blass 1975, 263). A translator would have to make a choice here in order to avoid a rather wooden translation like the one offered above.

A more complicated instance of this construction is found in the opening sentence of Sirach: Πολλῶν καὶ μεγάλων ἡμῖν διὰ τοῦ νόμου καὶ τῶν προφητῶν καὶ τῶν ἄλλων τῶν κατ' αὐτοὺς ἠκολουθηκότων δεδομένων, "Many and great things having been delivered unto us by the Law and the Prophets, and by the others that have followed them." This part of speech should depend on a finite verb, which is not easy to find in the following complex set of genitives, participles, and accusatives. One phrase with a finite verb is δέον ἐστὶν, "it is necessary [to praise Israel for instruction and wisdom because of these]," in the following sentence. If this is the main verb of the sentence, the question then is: what is the meaning of the opening double genitive? Does it refer to past action, to the existence of Holy Scriptures, to the giving of Scriptures, or to some other circumstance? The double genitive in many instances is ambiguous, and such ambiguity may be lost in translation.

The Hebrew Verbal System

The Hebrew and Aramaic verbal systems are fundamentally different from Greek grammar and from many modern languages. For example, a standard way of expressing past tense in biblical Hebrew is through the use of the consecutive imperfect. Since it is formed by adding a *waw* to the imperfect form, it looks like a conjunctive form, as if it should be read as, "and he went and he said and they listened," and so on. In many instances, there is coordination in sentences with the consecutive imperfect, but subordination may be intended in other instances.

The Decalogue

The Decalogue is found in Exod 20 and Deut 5. Some of the commandments use second-person masculine singular verb forms. Verbs are gendered in most instances in Hebrew, and this is so also here. This means that the Decalogue is directed to a male recipient, in the singular.

The third commandment is לא תשא את שם יהוה אלהיך לשוא, "You shall not lift the name of Yahweh your God to vanity" (Exod 20:7). Here the masculine form (תשא) is impossible to render in English and in many other languages, so this information is lost. The same goes for כבד את אביך ואת אמך, "Honor your father and mother" (Exod 20:12), and for the following commandments: לא תרצח, "You shall not murder" (v. 13), לא תנאף, "You shall not commit adultery" (v. 14), לא תגנב, "You shall not steal" (v. 15), לא תענה ברעך עד שקר, "You shall not answer as a false witness against your neighbor" (v. 16), and לא תחמד, "You shall not covet" (v. 17), with the different objects specified. The male addressee is also evident in the tenth commandment, where the objects for coveting include the neighbor's wife. The last case is telling; here the translator does not need to add or subtract anything, but in the instances with second-person masculine forms, the gender of the recipient is lost in translation.

Hebrew and Aramaic have gender specification for verbs and suffixes, while target languages may not have such. This can hardly be remedied by lexicalization instead of grammaticalization.

Gender

Hebrew and Aramaic employ only two grammatical genders, but Greek has three. This sometimes has been used to the effect that nouns in the feminine are thought to be of a feminine nature, as is the case with "wisdom" in Hebrew, חכמה. The Greek noun for wisdom, σοφία, is also feminine, which would point in the direction of a feminine element in "wisdom," associated with the divine, as "wisdom" is often associated with God. To further advance a feminine element in the divine, the feminine gender of "spirit" may also be emphasized in the Hebrew רוח. This line of thinking runs into trouble when one considers the Greek word for "spirit," πνεῦμα. This word is neuter in Greek (so in the expression "the Holy Spirit"). This example should warn translators and theologians against putting more into grammatical genders than grammar. We are probably mistaken if we think of a bifurcation of the world in Hebrew and a triple division in Greek.

One can widen the perspective and include words in languages with two genders, such as Hebrew, Italian, Spanish, and French, compared to languages with three genders, such as Greek, German, and Norwegian. To look at the gender in German and Norwegian, both with three genders, is instructive. The standard word for "knife" is neuter in German but masculine in Norwegian, "spoon" is masculine in German but feminine in Norwegian, and "fork" is feminine in German but masculine in Norwegian. It is hardly advisable to read more from these cases than grammar, as a gendering of words and, in this case, objects produced may lead to strange results.

The Construct State in Hebrew

Hebrew has no cases, as opposed to Akkadian, Arabic, Ugaritic, and Greek, and many modern languages. A traditional way of seeing this phenomenon is expressed by Paul Joüon S.J. and Takamitsu Muraoka (2000, 237) in their grammar.

Because the Hebrew noun has lost the final vowels that indicated *cases* (nominative, accusative, genitive, §93b), there is, properly speaking, no declension. The logical relations expressed by the nominative, the accusative, and the genitive are shown by the position of the noun in the phrase or sentence. For the genitive, however, the first noun (*nomen regens*), which *governs* the second noun (*nomen rectum*), often has a special form called the *construct state*, as opposed to the ordinary form, which is called the *absolute state* (§92a). The changes in the vocalization of the noun in the construct state and those changes that occur when a noun is lengthened by the addition of the plural, dual, and feminine endings and of the pronominal suffices are due to stress shift. All these changes in the vocalization constitute the *inflection* of the noun, §95a.

Joüon, Muraoka, and other grammarians rest on a tradition from Gesenius (2006, 247), whose grammar opens the morphological treatment of the construct state thus:

> The Hebrew language no longer makes a living use of *case-endings*, but either has no external indication of case (this is so for the *nominative*, generally also for the *accusative*) or expresses the relation by means of prepositions (§119), while the *genitive* is mostly indicated by a close connexion (or interdependence) of the *Nomen regens* and the *Nomen rectum*.

In a study of the Hebrew construct state, Magnar Kartveit (2013) compares the Semitic languages to each other for this question. The result can be summarized in the following way: there is every reason to compare languages, but what is the effect of doing it? Otto Hintze (1964, 251) suggests that we compare for two reasons, first to comprehend generalities and then to see individualities more clearly ("ein Allgemeines zu finden, das dem Verglichenen zugrunde liegt" and "[den historischen Gegenstand] in seiner Individualität schärfer zu erfassen und von dem anderen abzuheben"). It seems that the first point has been exaggerated in Hebrew grammar for the construct state, and it is time to bring also the second point to the fore.

Like Akkadian, classical Arabic, and Ugaritic, Hebrew has construct morphemes, a specific modification of the word seen against the basic form. When this is viewed against the background of the lack of genitive forms in Hebrew, unlike in other languages, there is reason to focus on the construct form in Hebrew and study its syntactical possibilities. The nouns in biblical Hebrew are inflected for the morphosyntactic features of the construct state. Of the different morphemes, the allomorph zero is an option, but this should not obscure the fact that all nouns are inflected for the construct state.

These deliberations make relevant the long-standing discussion of the general understanding of languages. Are they separate, self-contained entities, or can we see patterns and common phenomena across language boundaries? As with many problems, a mix of theory and empirical data may provide for a reasonable attitude to the topic under discussion. For the genitive and the construct state, I find it useful to concentrate on the data we see in Hebrew without recurring to explanations cultivated on foreign soil.

Genitive, as a morphological category, is found in other Semitic languages, but not in Hebrew. The expression "genitive" is to be avoided for Hebrew, without any loss in precision. For the morphology, "construct state" and "absolute state" can be used. The construct state is found in Hebrew with the same usages as in other Semitic languages. These usages include ownership, belonging, and possession, as in many instances where genitive is used in other languages (for instance, "the king's house," "God's name"). But the construct phrase may also be used for characterization ("unclean lips," Isa 6:5; "beautiful appearance," Gen 12:11). Sometimes, a metaphor is found in the *nomen rectum* ("rulers of Sodom" = Sodom-type rulers, as in Isa 1:9; "people of Gomorrah" = Gomorrah-type people, as in Isa 1:9). In other instances, a metaphor is found in the *nomen regens* (בת ציון, "daughter of Zion" = dear Zion, בת ירושלם, "daughter of Jerusalem" = dear Jerusalem in Zech 9:9, בתולת ישראל, "virgin of Israel" = poor, innocent Israel in Amos 5:2).

Translators will have to find ways of expressing the meanings of such phrases, but genitive has often been used. Languages without cases must find other ways. For characterization, adjectives are often employed. In the case of "daughter of Zion" and similar phrases, the genitive is often employed, giving the impression that Zion has a daughter. This is, of course, not the case, leading to a change in translation, "Daughter Zion." But, again, what is the meaning of this phrase? Is Zion a daughter? Is it daughter-like in some respects? Kartveit's (2013) suggestion is to find the metaphorical sense of "daughter," "virgin," and some more words and use the metaphorical sense as a guide to translation, as in the phrase "dear Zion." This works well with this phrase in many instances. And it recommends itself for phrases such as בת עמי, "daughter of my people," which can be rendered "my dear people" (cf. also Jer 4:11, 13). Translators sometimes render this phrase "my beloved people" or "my poor people," realizing that there is a metaphor in "daughter." In other instances, the sense of בת might be "poor," even in an ironical way—"poor Babylon!" This seems to make sense in Ps 137:8: "Poor Babylon! You devastator! Blessed are the people who pay you back the deeds you have done to us!" This may seem a daring rendering in some eyes, but translators who work with languages distant from the culture of old Israel, often have to make more radical choices than this one.

Nominal Sentences

A phenomenon found in some languages is the nominal sentence, which is a sentence that lacks a finite verb. This is very common in Hebrew and may lead to difficult translational decisions. One example is Deut 6:4: שמע ישראל יהוה אלהינו יהוה אחד, which may be rendered: "Hear, O Israel: The Lord is our God, the Lord alone," (NRSV, NJPS), or "Hear, O Israel: The

Lord our God is one Lord." The first sentence is an imperative and a vocative and pose few problems: "Hear, O Israel." But the next expressions lack a verb and therefore may be understood as two sentences or as one sentence. The translator will then have to decide where to place the verb in the translation, as in English. Even in English, nominal clauses are used, for instance, in abbreviated utterances like superscriptions in newspapers, journals, and books, or in everyday speech ("Your car?" "Your turn next!"). Still, it would not be appropriate to translate Deut 6:4 as, "Hear, O Israel: The Lord our God the Lord alone." A reader would at the very least want some punctuation to clarify the meaning of the verse.

Another example is the song of the seraphim in Isa 6:3: קדוש קדוש קדוש יהוה צבאות מלא כל הארץ כבודו ("Holy, holy, holy is the Lord of Hosts! What fills all the earth is his glory"). In this translation, מלא כל הארץ is viewed as the subject of the second sentence and כבודו as its predicate. More common is the translation, "the whole earth is full of his glory" (NRSV). It is also possible to reverse the roles as "His presence fills all the earth!" (NJPS). The first sentence does not present similar problems; יהוה צבאות is the subject, and קדוש קדוש קדוש is the predicate. There is no way of turning this around; only the Lord is holy in the Bible.

Conclusion

This essay has presented some examples of grammatical, systematic differences between source languages and target languages in Bible translation. There is nothing like a complete list here; only some of the cases that translators have to struggle with, are foregrounded.

The idea is to guide the awareness of translators and readers. When surprise, questions, or irritation arise over a specific translation of the Lord's Prayer or the Decalogue, it may be helpful to consider the systemic differences between the languages involved. Translation may be compared to the problems of cooking Asiatic food without the necessary ingredients or giving a presentation to students without a classroom. The food will taste Asian to a certain degree, and the teaching will lack the information of body language. If we turn it around, a Norwegian meal prepared with all the ingredients of Africa will be different from the traditional taste, and a presentation will be much more enjoyable when people meet than when done virtually.

The systemic differences between the grammar of a source language and that of a target language in translation can be profitably explored further. What has been presented in the form of examples in this essay applies to whole translation projects as well as other languages than those mentioned here.

Holter has done Bible translation a great service by starting and running the teaching program for prospective translators. We can only honor his efforts in this field with the Jewish birthday greeting, based on Gen 6:3: Until 120! (עד מאה ועשרים!)

Works Cited

Ahuvya, Avraham, trans. 2010. *Tanakh Ram*. Herzliya: RAM.
Blass, Friedrich. 1965. *Grammatik des neutestamentlichen Griechisch*. Bearbeitet von Albert Debrunner. 12. Auflage. Göttinger theologische Lehrbücher. Göttingen: Vandenhoeck & Ruprecht.
De Saussure, Ferdinand. 1916. *Cours de linguistique générale*. Paris: Éditions Payot & Rivages.
De Waard, Jan. 2015. "Modern Theories of Translation with Special Regard to Recent Bible Translations." Pages 674–703 in *The Twentieth Century: From Modernism to Post-modernism*. Edited by Magne Sæbø. Hebrew Bible/Old Testament: The History of Its Interpretation 2. Göttingen: Vandenhoeck & Ruprecht.
Gesenius, Friedrich Wilhelm et al. 2006. *Gesenius' Hebrew Grammar*. Repr., Mineola, NY: Dover.
Hintze, Otto. 1964. *Soziologie und Geschichte, Gesammelte Abhandlungen*. Vol. 2.2. Göttingen: Vandenhoeck & Ruprecht.
Holter, Knut. 2000. "Should Old Testament Cush Be Rendered 'Africa'?" Pages 107–25 in *Yahweh in Africa: Essays on Africa and the Old Testament*. Edited by Knut Holter. New York: Lang.
Joüon, Paul S.J., and Takamitsu Muraoka. 2000. *A Grammar of Biblical Hebrew*. Rome: Pontifical Biblical Institute.
Kartveit, Magnar. 2013. *Rejoice, Dear Zion! Hebrew Construct Phrases with "Daughter" and "Virgin" as Nomen Regens*. BZAW 447. Berlin: De Gruyter.
Lyons, John. 1995. *Linguistic Semantics: An Introduction*. Cambridge: University Press.
Nida, Eugene A. 1964. *Toward a Science of Translating: With Special Reference to Principles and Procedures Involved in Bible Translating*. Leiden: Brill.

Part 7
Context Indeed Matters in Biblical Studies:
The Legacy of Knut Holter

Global Biblical Criticism:
Toward a Dialogical Hermeneutics

Fernando F. Segovia

Introduction

Over the course of thirty years, from 1993 to 2023, Knut Holter has played a distinguished role in the field of Old Testament studies. This he has done in an expansive variety of contexts—the critical circles of his native Kingdom of Norway, the academic-professional trajectories of Western Europe, and the global stage through immersion in the critical paths of sub-Saharan Africa. I take 1993 as point of origins on two counts—the bestowal of his doctoral degree by the University of Oslo and his appointment as associate professor in the School of Mission and Theology at Stavenger, Norway.[1]

For this volume, I have been graciously asked by the editors, all close colleagues or students of his, to write a reflection on his life and work as a biblical critic. This invitation, which I accepted forthwith and for which I am most grateful, represents for me a distinct honor as well as a great pleasure. Not only do I regard Holter as an ally in the sempiternal struggle for a better world for all, especially the marginalized, but I also hold his work in great esteem, given his engagement with the Other of the theological-hermeneutical periphery. I shall pursue my task with the notion of context foremost in mind. In so doing, I take my inspiration from the title of the volume, *Context Matters*. Neither transparent nor determinate, this concept can encompass the whole of any temporal-historical and spatial-geographical framework and can thus be deployed to refer to any

---

1. Holter's relationship with the School of Mission and Theology in Stavanger, Norway, goes back a good ten years further. It was there he obtained an MTheol degree in 1985 and served as Research Fellow from 1987 through 1993.

dimension(s) thereof. Consequently, it can be constructed in any number of ways, and any such circumscription should always be explained. For this reflection, it is the trajectory of biblical criticism during the years in question—times of far-reaching and ever-expanding changes—that I take as primary framework of reference.

This I do because I see his tightly knit combination of personal journey and academic path as a keen reflection of such times in the field. Indeed, the shifts in question had begun almost two decades earlier, in the middle to late 1970s, and had thus become by 1993 a widely acknowledged, broadly accepted, and thoroughly ongoing feature of the field. Holter may be described as both a child and a force in that process of transformation—a sign of the times. To the extent that his life and career take place within the orbit of European criticism, I would describe this role as discursive signifier as played in a contrarian key. I do so on two grounds: openness to diversity in critical approaches as well as commitment to critical exchange.

Regarding diversity, mainline European criticism does not prove, by and large, as receptive to such developments. Its reaction is to keep to a historical approach focused on the world of production and sustained by an empiricist-objectivist framework. Holter does, however—indeed, decidedly so and in sundry ways. Most prominent, without question, is his inclusion of the world of reception, through the lens of sub-Saharan Africa, its lines and contexts of criticism. Regarding exchange, traditional European criticism approaches border-crossing with its Others, by and large, along dialectical lines. Its aim is to bring enlightenment to realms of ignorance and superstition through the flow and impartation of knowledge and science from the West. Holter deviates from this norm, in fact, altogether so, by pursuing border-crossing along dialogical lines. His goal is to seek mutual enlightenment with the Other by way of a joint academic-intellectual endeavor, driven by a spirit of learning and engagement alongside conscientization and solidarity.

A Point of Entry

With this background in mind, I turn to his curriculum vitae as a point of entry for my reflection. I find therein a distinct division in mode of approach, for which the year 1997 serves as a turning point. From 1986 to 1996, a period encompassing his position as research fellow and his early years as associate professor, Holter's output developed along two lines of research: historical-literary analysis and theological-missiological reflection. In 1997, a triad of articles appear that focus on matters of context—the problematic of context in criticism and the question of Africa in interpretation. From 1998 through 2023, a period comprising the height of his career as associate professor and then professor, Holter's production pursued the question of context in two directions: sustained attention to Africa from a variety of perspectives and initial reflection on the problematic of doing global criticism.

The first phase (1986–1996) reveals a variety of topics in largely unrelated fashion. Some publications relate to the production of the text—traditional historical pursuits as well as recent literary analysis. Others address a religious-theological concern—the relation between biblical texts and missiological practices. Most weighty is the revised version of his doctoral dissertation, *Second Isaiah's Idol-Fabrication Passages* (Holter 1995), where both aspects come to light: analysis of the passages in their narrative context and ideological interrogations of deity constructions and group identity.[2] While the former angle reflects the advent of literary criticism in the field in the mid-1970s, the latter shows the missiological tradition behind the School of Mission and Theology.[3]

The turning point in 1997 revolves solely around context, with Africa as focus. The range is broad—an institutional overview of contextualized programmes in Old Testament study (1997a), a textual point regarding translation (1997b), and a scholarly overview of Old Testament research in sub-Saharan Africa north of the Zambesi River (1997c). What lies behind such a turn in research? In general terms, the 1990s bring a formal problematization of the relation between context and criticism in interpretation (Segovia and Tolbert 1995). In concrete terms, Holter himself provides an answer, as he takes up, in late 1996, the editorial task of publishing a biannual *Newsletter on African Old Testament Research*. In the introduction to

---

2. The review in the *Catholic Biblical Quarterly* (Dick 1997), quite complimentary, proves insightful. While foregrounding the careful interpretation of the passages along the lines of literary criticism, the reviewer regrets how certain issues raised regarding theological implications—monotheism versus monoyahwehism and universalism versus nationalism—were not more extensively developed. Here the influence of missiology is evident.

3. This focus is highlighted in the historical account of the School on the VID University web page: "The School of Mission and Theology (Stavenger) was founded in 1843 by the Norwegian Mission Society, with the purpose of training ministers and teachers for missionary service in other parts of the world on behalf of the Church of Norway." See https://www.vid.no/en/about-us/history/misjonshogskolen/.

the first issue (Holter 1996b), he cites ongoing work on African scholarship on his part and highlights three dimensions thereof—bibliographical interest in the production of African scholars, travels to Africa to attend scholarly conferences and visits to theological institutions, and the discovery of new and valuable questions and approaches for the study of the Old Testament from Africa.[4] In fact, the newsletter is envisioned as a place of encounter for scholars throughout the world with an interest in Africa as well as for African scholars scattered throughout the continent.[5]

The second phase (1998–2023) presents a concentrated focus on context. The vast majority of publications center on Africa from a rich variety of concerns. These involve both the production and the reception of texts, with decided emphasis on the latter. A number of publications move beyond the African axis. They either draw on other spatial-geographical contexts or problematize the project of global criticism. With regard to the focus on Africa, such paths of research include matters of critical approach and issues of translation, overviews of professional scholarship, reports on institutional frameworks, analyses of popular readings in context, comparative studies of biblical and African parallels, and comparative analyses of Western and African interpretations of texts. With respect to the focus beyond Africa, such concerns are tied to other endeavors—the project of intercultural criticism spearheaded by Hans de Wit and a project on global biblical studies by the Society of Biblical Literature.

In relation to Africa, the record of publications provides a multidirectional mapping of biblical interpretation in sub-Saharan Africa from the start of the contextual movement. Quite valuable is Holter's (2008) *Contextualized Old Testament Scholarship in Africa*, a scholarly account of textual references to and academic interpretations in Africa; this volume

---

4. Such questions and approaches have, he states, "enriched my own understanding of the Old Testament as such, but also of what Old Testament scholarship is all about" (1996b, 1). The work on African bibliography came to fruition in the publication of a "select and annotated" bibliography that year (Holter 1996a).

5. "As a Westerner interested in African Old Testament scholarship," Holter (1996b, 1) writes, "it is my impression that the present contact between African and Western Old Testament scholarship is at a minimum. I regret this, as I belive [sic] both parts would benefit from a closer interaction." He adds, "However ... even the contact between African Old Testament scholars themselves is rare and often accidental" (2). The newsletter would thus serve as a valuable source of information, including presentations and overviews as well as conference reports and research announcements from all over the continent.

brings together much of his work over the years. Beyond Africa, new lines of research emerge. The first, inspired by the vision of de Wit, concerns studies on comparative readings of texts undertaken by ordinary readers in different global contexts and in dialogue with one another.[6] These bring together communities of readers in Madagascar and Norway (Holter 2015a; 2015b).[7] The second, responding to professional ventures, involves a collaborative exercise of theoretical reflection on a global key.[8] This brings together scholars from around the world by way of a coedited volume, *Global Hermeneutics?* (Holter and Jonker 2017), in which his own contributions adress the dynamics and mechanics of such an undertaking (Holter 2010a; 2010b).

In the light of this exposition on his personal-professional and academic-intellectual path, I would like to proceed by examining key aspects of his career. I begin by describing the course of biblical studies from the mid-1970s through the present, thus providing the overall context for Holter's life and work as a biblical critic. I do so by way of a series of criti-

---

6. Intercultural empirical criticism was a hermeneutical project launched by Hans de Wit, then, professor and Dom Hélder Câmera Chair at the Free University of Amsterdam, with a sharp methodological-theoretical grounding and a strong religious-theological objective. In a world where Christian communities find themselves distant from one another, materially and discursively alike, de Wit envisioned the Bible as a way of bringing Christians together, as a common denominator, for religious-theological and social-cultural reflection and action. Such interchange he promoted by having any number of reading groups throughout the world discussing the same text. The process would always involve two groups from different regions in conversation. See, e.g., de Wit et al. (2004).

7. Years later, Holter would return to intercultural hermeneutics by way of another project on global readings of classical religious texts, now bringing three groups together from Madagascar, Norway, and Thailand (Holter 2019).

8. In the introduction, Holter and Jonker (2019, vii–viii) describe the twofold origin of the volume. On the one hand, it is tied to the International Organization for the Study of the Old Testament. In 2007, for only the second time in its history, its 19th Annual Meeting was held outside Western Europe, in Ljubljana, Slovenia. The president at the time, Jože Krašovec from the Theological Faculty in Ljubljana, asked Holter to put together a special session on "Global Biblical Hermeneutics." The aim was to reflect on the impact of the global world on interpretation. It was also tied to the Society of Biblical Literature. In 2010, a number of the papers were published as the inaugural volume in a new series, International Voices in Biblical Studies, as part of its International Cooperation Initiative. The aim was to reflect on biblical hermeneutics on a global scale.

cal turns that set the field of studies on a broad variety of new directions. I go on to situate the course of Holter's career from 1983 to 2023, within this ongoing transition regarding all parameters of the field (concerns and approaches, objectives and practitioners). This I do by showing his stance on such turns, a disposition that I would describe as decidedly creative. Above all, I concentrate on his pursuit of the global turn through sustained engagement with the Other of Africa and his call for a global criticism. I conclude with a set of reflections on his proposal regarding the meaning and implications of such criticism. I do so by casting his comments and suggestions against the background of broader discursive developments.

Biblical Studies: Critical Trajectory from 1970s to 2020s

For many years now, I have sought to delineate the historical trajectory of biblical criticism. This I have done in terms of three major stages: (1) from the established tradition of interpretation since the nineteenth century, encompassing an array of constitutive variations; (2) through the fundamental reconceptualization that begins to take place around the middle 1970s, with the presence of new faces and voices and the corresponding genesis of novel orientations and approaches; (3) to the situation of diversity that comes about as a result of manifold developments, not only along such early lines, but also in new directions altogether. Such a mapping of the field I have had to revise from time to time, on two counts, by no means unrelated. On the one hand, reconfiguration has been dictated by the swift and ongoing emergence of new models of interpretation. On the other hand, readjustment has been rendered imperative in the wake of significant and recurring shifts in my own understanding of the process. The result has been an evolving trail of cartographies, each one a reflection of the state of affairs in the field as perceived at the time of remapping.

In the past, I have done remapping by way of grand models of interpretations—large-scale discursive frameworks that represent a fairly distinctive approach to the critical task. Such models comprise a variety of critical movements and are thus complex and conflictive. Indeed, while such movements share certain theoretical and methodological features in common, each bears a particular stamp of its own—orientation, objective, and repertoire. More recently, I have approached the trajectory by way of critical turns, targeted discursive foci that set the critical task in different directions (Segovia forthcoming). Such turns encompass a variety of critical emphases and hence prove no less convoluted or disputed. The emphases revolve around a threefold set of factors: (1) the status of the critical agent—professional or alternative; (2) the focus of the inquiry—the past of antiquity or the present of interpretation; and (3) the angle of reading—the array of discursive frameworks. Such factors affect the full range of the interpretive enterprise, from the realm of production to the realm of reception.

So far, I have pointed to seven such turns since the 1970s, namely, discursive and materialist, contextual and ideological, popular and culturalist, and interdisciplinary. These I have listed, as reflected above, in sets of two, with one exception. Previously, I had identified seven models as well—historical, literary, sociocultural, ideological, social-cultural, religious-theological, and global-systemic. These I have always outlined individually. The two typologies are by no means radically dissimilar. To the contrary, they have much in common, since, after all, they describe the same phenomenon. The difference is one of accentuation. On the one hand, the recourse to grand models reflects a fairly sequential pattern, with certain paradigms setting the stage for others to follow. The use of critical turns proves looser in this regard, less attentive to logical or causal development. On the other hand, the deployment of grand models leads to analysis of each paradigm by itself—overall configuration and internal dynamics. The invocation of critical turns is more flexible, allowing for a bringing together of foci for joint consideration—shared emphases involving reading agents, temporal foci, and reading foundations.

Both typologies have a central element, the point of departure, in common—the long-established tradition of historicist-contextualist criticism in place, formally as well as practically, until the middle 1970s. Each of the typologies also represents, in one way or another, a reaction to its driving principles and operative practices, which reflected, in turn, the project of modern science since the seventeenth century.[9] In the grand-models typology, this tradition stands as the first grand model of interpretation. It is against this paradigm that all subsequent grand models seek to move, adopting different theoretical principles and methodological practices. Such reaction varies with time—at first, quite direct; then, as the years

---

9. What the tradition sought, in the spirit of the scientific project of modernity, was a role of the critic as intermediary between antiquity and modernity. Its principles followed those at the core of epistemologies of the Global North; a realist-empiricist view of history alongside an objectivist-disinterested view of historiography. On the nature and consequences of such principles, see de Sousa Santos (2018, 1–16).

pass and new grand models arise, less so. In the critical-turns typology, this tradition stands not as a turn—although it is very much so, given its own reaction to ecclesial concerns and controls—but rather as the norm of interpretation. It is away from this rule that all turns to come seek to deviate, opting for different foci of attention. This reaction changes with time as well—quite pointed, to begin with; more remote, as the years elapse and the turns multiply.

A succinct description of the critical turns is in order, whereupon I shall argue that another such shift is in order. All of this is essential for a proper placement of the figure and work of Holter within the field.

1. Discursive-Materialist

The first set of turns has to do with the realm of professional scholarship and the world of the past, the texts and contexts of antiquity. The discursive turn problematizes questions of meaning and representation regarding texts, moving away from set notions of determinacy and mimeticism. The materialist turn problematizes questions of construction and organization regarding contexts, including texts as social and cultural products in their own right, leaving aside set notions of naturalness and looseness.

2. Contextual-Ideological

The second set also attends to the realm of professional criticism but with a focus on the present, the agents and contexts of modernity. The contextual turn foregrounds the local and limited nature of agents—against any sense of universality and unfetteredness. This demands close analysis of such contexts. The ideological turn highlights the active and partisan role of the agent, against any conception of passivity and distantiation. This requires detailed scrutiny of power relations in all dimensions of identity.

3. Popular-Culturalist

The third set of turns switches to the realm of alternative interpretations, with a wideranging temporal focus. The popular turn problematizes questions of critical privilege, valorizing the interpretation of ordinary readers, individuals and groups alike. The culturalist turn problematizes questions of religious-theological privilege, welcoming interpretations advanced in the social as well as the cultural arenas.

4. Interdisciplinary

The final turn also involves the realm of professional criticism and a focus on the present, the agents and contexts of modernity. It arises from and impacts upon all other turns. The interdisciplinary turn entails an imperative recourse to any number of fields of study, depending on the angle of vision applied to the analysis of texts and contexts of the past as well as of agents and contexts of the present. It demands sophisticated acquaintance with and proper critique of trajectories and discussions in such discursive frameworks. The turn also calls for knowledge of and interaction with ongoing trajectories along such interdisciplinary lines within biblical criticism itself.

Holter's Locus and Call in Critical Trajectory of Biblical Studies

The exposition of Holter's curriculum vitae has shown that he has subscribed to several of these critical turns. In so doing, he may be said to stand as both a product of and an agent in the reaction to the established tradition of interpretation. Four such lines of engagement can be discerned. These are largely sequential in appropriation but not altogether so, for one critical turn is, to one degree or another, present throughout. In addition, Holter embodies and presses yet another turn not listed above, one that has been quite prominent in this period of transition for the field and that he regards as imperative for the future. It is indeed a turn that must be included in any critical trajectory of the field and that does bear close and sustained attention.

Embracing the Critical Turns

Early on, Holter follows the discursive turn. In his doctoral study, he pursues a project along the lines of the vibrant literary criticism of the times, with a focus on narrative sequence and context. Subsequently, leaving that initial focus behind, he veers toward the contextual turn. His critical gaze turns to the pursuit of interpretation within particular spatial-geographical designations. Such work, which he pursues in wholehearted fashion for the remainder of his academic-intellectual career, he carries out in two ways. On the one hand, he does so directly through a focus on Africa, delving into all aspects of interpretation on the continent, material and discursive alike. On the other hand, he does so indirectly with a focus on Europe, given the comparative element at the heart of such work. In other words, his primary aim is to examine the ways and means of interpretation in Africa in relation to the European tradition of criticism. Consequently, the former lens I would describe as far more intense and comprehensive than the latter.

In time, Holter pursues the popular turn as well. He shifts his critical gaze from the circles of professional critics to the world of ordinary readers in interpretation. In so doing, the influence of the contextual turn is palpable, as he brings together groups of everyday readers from widely different spatial-geographical and spatial-national contexts in dialogue. In such work, Africa is always present. Throughout, as he takes up these different turns, he integrates the intercultural turn, engaging with other fields of study as well as with ongoing scholarship along such lines within biblical criticism itself. Most significantly in this regard, I find, is the surfacing of global criticism as a problematic. Thereby he brings up the field of global studies as a discursive framework and problematizes the relation between global studies and biblical studies. His approach to this turn may be described, by and large, as broad rather than detailed.

In this account of Holter's locus within biblical studies, I have foregrounded the turns that he has embraced. Those that he has not, however, prove just as important: the materialist, ideological, and cultural turns. Most intriguing in this regard, given the focus on context, is the relative absence of ideological criticism: trenchant analysis of the differential formations and relations of power in society and culture, which are always at work in all contexts as well as between/among contexts. To be sure, there is keen awareness, at one level, of imperial-colonial relations in Africa and, at another level, of relations between the Global North and the Global South in general. The analysis of such relations, however, remains, on the whole, subdued.

Toward a Global Turn

In setting forth the critical turns that have marked the field since the 1970s, I stated that the naming of another such turn was in order. This reflection on Holter has pressed such a move upon me. What I have in mind is a global turn, which, while closely related to the contextual turn, is worth distinguishing in its own right. This turn has been there from the beginning of the transition, given the influx of new faces and voices, a development that has only grown exponentially with the years. It is increasingly emphasized with the proliferation of ideological approaches through the 1980s into the 1990s. It is appropriated by Holter toward the late 1990s and becomes the driving force of his work from that point on.

How is it to be defined? It is a critical turn that emphasizes the spatial-geographical and spatial-geopolitical location of reading agents throughout the world—against any sense of Western centeredness or mimeticism. How does it compare to the other turns? It could be joined to the intercultural turn as a set. First, both attend to the realm of professional critics and focus on the present, the agents and contexts of modernity. Second, both bring about significant expansion of the field. While the intercultural turn does so by way of fields of study outside the traditional boundaries of the field, the global turn proceeds by way of reading agents outside the traditional membership of the guild. Holter addresses this global turn in his introduction to the volume *Global Hermeneutics?* (2010a).

Reflecting on the question of what impact global hermeneutics might have on the academic study of the Old Testament, from within the context of the International Organisation for the Study of the Old Testament (IOSOT), Holter sets forth the material dimensions behind such a development prior to laying out its discursive implications. This exposition he casts against a fundamental historical-ecclesial transformation—the massive shift of Christianity from the Global North to the Global South. This Holter traces, writing in 2010, from 1900 to 2025. Looking back, he describes the shift as unfolding steadily through the whole of the twentieth century and into the first decade of the twenty-first century. Looking ahead, he projects the shift as continuing apace through the first quarter of the century. With this gradual and ongoing shift, he notes, major transformations take place in the material conditions and discursive parameters of the theological curriculum, including the study of the Old Testament.

The material conditions are presented in numerical-geographical and institutional-academic fashion. The numerical account is done by way of global regions (Africa, Asia, Europe, South America, North America, Oceania) and nation-states (top ten countries). These figures are charted as follows: (1) four temporal points of reference—1900, 1970, 2005, 2025; and (2) three approaches to church members—absolute number; percentage within the region; and percentage worldwide. The latter I find most revealing. In 1900, 68 percent percent of all church members lived in Europe and 17 percent in the Global South; by 2005, the percentage in Europe had decreased to 26 percent, while in the Global South it had surged to 60 percent.[10] The other approaches bear out the same process, as does the list of top ten countries throughout. The institutional account is carried out in terms of three academic-professional categories, all of which record a sharp increase—universities and seminaries, doctoral programs and dissertations, and professional venues and outlets (organizations, conferences, journals). The trajectory laid out for sub-Saharan Africa, extending from the end of the colonial era to the turn of the century, I find most telling. Whereas in 1960 there were six universities and a few dozen seminaries in the region, by 2010 one finds two hundred universities and several hundred seminaries. The other categories confirm the same trend. "In the same way as Christianity … is gradually becoming a religion of the Global South," concludes Holter (2010a, 4), "so too are theological and biblical studies gradually becoming southern academic enterprises."

The discursive parameters are approached from the point of view of relations between southern hermeneutics and northern hermeneutics within such transformed conditions. This interaction is pursued, with a focus on sub-Saharan Africa throughout, from two angles—the issue of dependence and the question of vision. With regard to dependence, most southern critics of the Old Testament have been trained in northern institutions, following traditional links—political as well as ecclesial—with former imperial contexts. As a result, the traditional inequality set between northern and southern critics remains largely in place in all realms, including the academic-intellectual—the southern critic as a child alongside the northern critic as a parent. With respect to vision, most southern critics emphasize the question of relevance for contemporary contexts. As a result, the traditional concepts of northern critics fail to take root in them—the northern critic as universal alongside the southern critic as contextual. As a result, Holter (2010a, 4) concludes, "our traditional northern concepts of Old Testament studies will eventually have to be balanced by more southern concepts, as we are heading toward a more global Old Testament studies."

It is this question of northern-southern interaction that the reflection on the advent of global hermeneutics, its meaning and impact, takes up. This it does through analysis of the name assumed by IOSOT since

---

10. The total percentage provided for the Global South is broken down by geographical region. In 1900, the 17 percent cited includes Africa (2 percent), Asia (4 percent), and South America (11 percent). In 2025, the 60 percent cited includes Africa (19 percent), Asia (17 percent), and South America (24 percent).

its founding (1950). The focus is on two components regarded as problematic in the wake of the shift. The first involves the use of the adjective *international* to describe its membership. Since most members have been northerners, hailing from the North Atlantic or the North Mediterranean of Europe, this term can only be understood in terms of "northern internationalisation" and the association itself as a "European organisation" (Holter 2010a, 3). In light of the shift, however, this traditional context for the academic study of the Old Testament no longer applies. The second has to do with the use of the designation *Old Testament* to describe the field of study. Since most members have been based in theological faculties within Christian ecclesial frameworks, this designation has survived to this day (3). In light of the shift, this traditional context for the academic study of the Old Testament does still apply.

In both regards, therefore, the new southern context has to be integrated into the study of the Old Testament. On the one hand, the geographical signification of the term international has to be pursued on a different key—as a global enterprise, bringing together northern and southern hermeneutics. On the other hand, the theological signification of the designation Old Testament cannot be bypassed: as a call for contemporary relevance, keeping in mind this driving concern of southern hermeneutics. In sum, for Holter (2010a, 14), there is urgent need to envision "what it means to interpret the Old Testament in today's global world," hence undertaking "a new and global Old Testament studies in relation to its traditional northern location" (4).

This question of meaning and impact, which calls for reconceptualization and restructuring of the field, Holter (2010b) unfolds at greater length in his concluding piece for *Global Hermeneutics*. This he does by problematizing the use of the term *global* to define the new hermeneutical context, placing it within the broader scenario of modern globalization. Thus, he brings closely together the Western process of globalization and the Christian phenomenon of globalization—the geographical and numerical expansion of the latter in tandem with the economic and geopolitical expansion of the former. Then, he foregrounds a key dimension of this parallel development—the hegemony of the West secured through the process of globalization brings hegemony in matters theological in general and hermeneutical in particular, duly reinforced by economic and institutional hegemony in matters ecclesial.

This contradiction at the core of theological-hermeneutical globalization has been resolved along two contrasting lines. While many critics detect no problem at all, as they continue to "underestimate the role of the interpretive context," others see it as quite problematic, troubled by any type of claim to "universality, principally and practically detached from the socio-cultural context of the interpreter" (Holter 2010b, 87). While the former continue the task of interpretation along traditional lines, the latter, in ever growing fashion, seek to develop alternative and resistant projects of interpretation. These opt for a different path by rejecting any presumption of universality and by adopting a nonconformist strategy, using the contexts of the marginalized, along any number of axes, as a platform for interpretation. Given their diversity, Holter (2010b, 88) classifies the sum of such projects as global in their own right, insofar as "they grow out of experiences of 'every nation, tribe, people, and language.'"

At the same time, attempts to integrate the global dimension in the crafting of a new hermeneutic must be duly compared and evaluated. Toward this end, Holter analyzes a developing tradition of works, edited collections of articles, that draw on global participation and use the term global in the title.[11] While such works attend to the element of the geographical-numerical expansion of Christianity, seeking representation from a broad variety of faces and voices throughout the world, they tend not to explore further the meaning of the term global or to address the broader context of Western globalization. As a result, the specter of Western hegemony, which permeates all aspects of global society and culture, including the theological-hermeneutical realm, fails to be exposed and analyzed, much less transcended.

There are some who do, however, and it is with these that Holter situates his work. Thus, he places himself in a line leading from the call by Elisabeth Schüssler Fiorenza (1988) to decenter the discipline, expanded in a discussion on reading the Bible in the "global village" (2000), to a discussion of the same topic between Justin Ukpong and Musa Dube (Ukpong et al. 2002).[12] In effect, for the dialogical northern-southern hermeneutics

---

11. The volumes in question are, in chronological order: Levison and Pope-Levinson (1999); Räisänen et al. (2000); and Patte (2004). Here Holter points to an important vacuum in scholarship: a comprehensive analysis, historical and ideological, of this tradition of edited collections on global criticism that begins toward the 1990s.

12. The point of departure is represented by the presidential address of Elisabeth Schüssler Fiorenza in 1987 (published Schüssler Fiorenza 1988). Its expansion (Schüssler Fiorenza 2000) formed part of a panel session at 1999 International Meeting of the Society of Biblical Literature in Helsinki, Finland, later published as

envisioned, no omission of the process of modern globalization is possible. While the geographical-numerical element of Christian globalization is of the essence and disruptive in its own right, no less so is the economic-geopolitical element of Western globalization and its repercussions and far more disruptive. Both dimensions of globalization must play a role in a radically reconceptualized and restructured academic study of the Old Testament, if it is to qualify, as it must, as a global undertaking.

Reflections on Meaning and Implications of Global Criticism

I have argued that Holter stands as a signifier of the transformation in biblical criticism as a field of studies that began in the 1970s—doing so in discursive as well as material fashion. I have further argued that he thus stands in contrarian and creative fashion—deviating in manifold ways from the path of traditional criticism and embracing in innovative ways a variety of new critical directions. A reading of his scholarly trajectory and his alternative proposal for the field—forged within the ambit of Old Testament studies—more than justifies such an assessment. At this point, I should like to offer a concluding reflection on this overall critical stance of his by way of its three central components—the overriding concern with context, the clarion call for a dialogical hermeneutics, and the pointed attention to globalization. I shall place each within the context of broader discursive developments, analyzing how they fit within their respective trajectories and addressing what remains to be done for the future. In the process, these components emerge as signifiers of the wherefrom, the wherein, and the whereto of the field.

Overriding Concern for Context: Holter's insistence on taking context into account in interpretation arises relatively early in his academic-professional career and then turns forthwith into the driving force behind the whole of his work. Such a move can be readily set in the context of the times—the decade of the 1990s. On the one hand, it occurs at a time of initial and formal attention to the relation between context and interpretation in the field. In the problematization of this relation, the expression

---

the inaugural volume in a new series, Global Perspectives on Biblical Scholarship (Räisänen et al. 2000). The final discussion involving Ukpong (2002) and Dube (2002) also goes back to a panel session at the 2000 International Meeting of the Society of Biblical Literature in Cape Town, South Africa, subsequently published in the same series (Ukpong et al. 2002).

social location begins to be used as a common designation for the aspect of context. Its scope proves quite expansive, encompassing both the social-material and the cultural-discursive dimensions of context. On the other hand, the move takes place in the light of direct and wide contact on his part with the world of interpretation in Africa. Such experience is quite broad as well. It bears a social-material dimension, comprising extensive travel in sub-Saharan Africa, as well as a cultural-discursive one, involving close attention to critical voices and production across sub-Saharan Africa.

The move expands the scope of the critical task: from analysis of social-cultural context in the production of the texts, a foundational element of traditional criticism, to analysis of social-cultural context in the reception of the texts. In the eyes of traditional criticism, such a move would be regarded as anathema, opening the way for the advent of eisegesis—the intromission of the critic. Yet, it is a move that is demanded by a turn in historiography from empiricism to constructivism and from objectivism to perspectivism. What engagement with sub-Saharan Africa, undertaken against a background of growing discussion about the role of critical context, brings across to Holter is the immense value of marshalling context in the interpretation of the writings. Such conscientization leads him to cast aside the presumption of universality that he had inherited and imbibed from his context in northern Europe.

In such an approach to interpretation, the context of the present would be used to shed light on the context of the past, just as the context of the past would be used to shed light on the context of the present. This relationship could be approached in any number of ways, but it would always include a pivotal point, or set of points, for the exercise in transhistorical analogy. The recognition of the inherent contextualization of interpretation, however, proves quite a challenge. Contextualization cannot be reduced to a mere recitation of status sets or to a general account of group customs and values. Problematization calls for theorization. It demands detailed and sophisticated analysis of context in macrostructural as well as microstructural terms, with attention to and mapping of historical-political as well as social-cultural circumstances. While much work has been done with regard to the realm of production, precious little has been carried out with regard to that of reception. In this regard, a recourse to social theory proves imperative, yet social theory is complex, conflicted, ever-shifting.

Here I speak to the contemporary context, putting aside the use of social theory with respect to antiquity, in itself a most important question. The trajectory offered by Steven Seidman, Professor of Sociology at the State of University of New York, Albany, provides a useful point of departure (Seidman 2013, 157–58). In describing the reaction against the classical tradition of social theory that follows the Second World War, Seidman points to three overall critiques and revisions of the modernist vision and project. Each movement comprises a variety of theorists and proposals—the postmodern turn (on teleological vision), identity politics and theory (on unitary vision), and theories of world order (on political vision). While all are important, the last one, in particular, proves most relevant, insofar as its adherents diagnose the global order of postmodernity. In sum, what Holter's overriding concern for context demands is close scrutiny of the geopolitical and economic context of the world, with special attention to sub-Saharan Africa, in the light of the various critical models offered by social theory. Such a theorized situation of ourselves as critics has, alas, barely begun.

Clarion Call for Dialogical Hermeneutics: Holter's emphasis on crafting a dialogical approach in interpretation between northern hermeneutics and southern hermeneutics surfaces at a later point in his career, whereupon it turns into a key component behind the theoretical culmination of his work. This move can also be readily placed against the context of the times—the decade of the 2000s. From a general perspective, these were years in which such exchanges were being formally developed. Two lines can be distinguished—(1) direct and guided interaction between groups of ordinary readers from different regions of the world and (2) indirect and topical interaction by way of participation of professional critics from around the world in editorial projects. From a personal perspective, these are years that follow sustained and systematic attention on his part to the dynamics and mechanics of interpretation around the sub-Saharan African scene and that have demonstrated for him the wisdom to be gained by appealing to context in criticism.

This move amplifies the mode of the critical task—from sole analysis of the social-cultural context of production from a disengaged and universalist standpoint, a mainstay of northern hermeneutics, to additional analysis of the social-cultural context of reception from an engaged and particularist standpoint, a core element of southern hermeneutics. In northern hermeneutics, such a move would be viewed as incomprehensible, tantamount to an abandonment of knowledge and science—a surrender to ignorance and superstition. However, it is a move necessitated by the critique lodged against the Western project of modernity and its strategy of dialectical hermeneutics. What experience with the world of sub-Saharan Africa, pursued in a context of growing experimentation with dialogical interchanges, has taught Holter is profound respect for the knowledge and science signified by southern hermeneutics. The awareness brings about a ready rejection of such an attitude of dismissiveness at the heart of his own context in northern Europe.

In this approach to interpretation, it would be incumbent upon practitioners of northern hermeneutics to look outside their circles by entering into conversation with critics throughout the world of the South, just as it would be imperative for practitioners of southern hermeneutics to look beyond their northern orientation by attending to their own world of the South as well as to the many other worlds of the South. Such a dialogical frame of mind would require both sets of critics to change their habitual performance in a radical fashion. That shift of vision represents no small challenge. Critics from the North would have to read widely in the production and about the contexts of southern criticism, while critics from the South would have to do likewise, not only in their own particular production and about their own context, but also across the whole range of production and contexts from the South. In such a fundamental redirection, neither set of critics would be called upon to abandon altogether its former practices; to the contrary, both would be required to expand their existing borders through integration of new fields of vision. Northern critics would do so by engaging with its Others, while southern critics would cease to mimic their northern counterparts by looking at themselves and others in the South, without turning the North into a new Other.

Beyond such mutual engagement, the shift of vision would also require theorization of the dialectical hermeneutics long in place and for this task, analysis in the light of social theory would be in order. Two lines of research suggest themselves. The first focuses on the concept of the Global South, which is neither self-evident nor stable. It calls for analysis along such lines as historical trajectory dating back to the era of the Cold War and its emergence as the Third World, defining characteristics as attributed by the scholarly literature, and representation in our own times. In recent times, such concern with the meaning and import of the term has come to the fore, as evidenced by the work on constructing the Global South by Sinah Theres Kloß (2017) and Nina Schneider (2017), among many others. The second approach centers on the fundamental difference posited, emanating from the North, between the epistemologies of the North and the epistemologies of the South. This calls for attention to such lines as the close analysis of such knowledges and their differential separation, overhauling in the light of the failure of the modern project, and a search for alternatives from the South. In this regard, the work of Boaventura de Sousa Santos (2018), among many others, on the epistemological abyss sundering the world is to the point in confronting the present world crisis. In conclusion, Holter's clarion call for dialogical hermeneutics requires close scrutiny of the epistemological chasm that separates the West from its Others alongside creative attention to the ways and means of such a different hermeneutics. Unfortunately, such a theorized situation of ourselves as critics remains distinctly absent.

Pointed Attention to Globalization: Holter's insistence on approaching the dialogical hermeneutics envisioned as a distinct critical model in its own right, identified as global criticism, and on specifying the semantic parameters of this nomenclature through recourse to the phenomenon of globalization also appears at a later time in his career, whereupon it becomes another central component behind the theoretical culmination of his work. The move can be readily set as well in the context of the times—the beginning of the 2010s. On the one hand, it takes place at a time when the project of globalization, as espoused by the model of neoliberal economics, has been underway for about three decades, since the early 1980s. Indeed, the move comes at a crucial time: after its implosion with the economic collapse of 2008 and following a series of warning bubbles in the global economy. On the other hand, it takes place at a time when the quest for a global approach to biblical criticism has been underway for some fifteen years, since the middle 1990s. In effect, the move occurs at a pointed time: after the development of a scholarly movement that seeks to integrate global representation at all levels and that views all such efforts as exercises in global criticism.

Such a move expands the agents of the critical task—from critics inside the West, the geopolitical-economic center of globalization and the long-standing religious-theological center of Christianity, whose base lies in institutional circles and critical traditions of the North; to critics outside the West, the geopolitical-economic periphery of globalization and the newly-emerging religious-theological center of Christianity, whose base lies in a multitude of institutional circles and critical traditions throughout the South. In the eyes of Western centrism, such a move would be regarded as misdirected, upsetting the rightful flow of globalization—allowing the marginal to stand alongside the center. Yet it is a move demanded by two developments, namely, the disastrous failure of the globalization project undertaken by the North and the massive shift of Christianity to all corners of the South. What immersion in the world of sub-Saharan Africa, filtered through the reality of globalization patterns and consequences, has made clear to Holter is the immense value of working with such global developments in mind and on a global key. That conscientization leads him to undo the differential reality of core and periphery that he had received and learned as part and parcel of his northern, European tradition.

In such an approach to interpretation, a particular dimension of the present context would need to be thoroughly addressed, that is, the phenomenon of globalization. One aspect of this inquiry would attend to the geopolitical-economic project advanced by the neoliberal model, launched in reaction to the crisis of capitalism in the 1970s and pressed on the world as the sole path forward. Another aspect would deal with the religious-theological diffusion of Christianity throughout the South, the result of the ongoing outreach of ecclesial bodies riding upon the crest of imperialism. Such recognition of globalization as a defining feature of the times, presents a severe challenge as well. It requires theorization in both respects. It calls for close study of the neoliberal project as a whole: ideological foundation, strategic platform, and actual development. This would also demand a long-range historical perspective regarding the path of political economy. It again calls for close scrutiny of global criticism as a critical model that reflects the reality of a mostly-southern Christianity—scholarly representation, driving objectives, and relation to globalization. This would also demand a long-range understanding of the center-periphery relation in ecclesial relations and theological-critical thinking.

The literature on geopolitical-economic globalization is enormous. Two approaches come readily to mind. First, the world-systems analysis developed by Immanuel Wallerstein (2004) would be most helpful in this endeavor. He traces the world-economy of capitalism from its beginnings in the period 1600–1750, through its successive formations up to the emergence of the United States as hegemonic power in 1945–1975, to the crisis of relative decline during 1975–2000 and keen decline over 2000–2025, given the utter failure of the neoliberal project. In so doing, Wallerstein clearly outlines the geopolitical, economic, and ideological framework of the world-system leading up to and including our days. Just as valuable would be Ankie Hoogvelt's (2011) analysis of globalization during the various phases of capitalism. The literature on academic-scholarly globalization is ever expanding. For a focus on Christianity, the recent account of theological production in the South by Juan José Tamayo (2017) is essential, as is, on a broader scale, the analysis of Lynn Hunt (2014) (on the relation between the forces of globalization and the writing of history). In sum, what Holter's pointed attention to globalization demands is sophisticated scrutiny of the phenomenon of globalization, geopolitical-economic and religious-theological alike, certainly with attention to sub-Saharan Africa, but beyond to the South as a whole. Such a theorized situation of ourselves as global critics finds itself, regrettably, at a very early stage.

Concluding Word

I have proposed that Holter stands as a signifier of the manifold and profound changes at work over the course of the last fifty years, critical turns that reflect similar shifts across the full range of the academic-intellectual spectrum in the human and social sciences. I would submit that the preceding triad of components stand in their own right as signifiers of the immense task ahead, of proper conceptualization and elaboration of biblical criticism as a global undertaking. Such is the case for him personally, as he no doubt continues to pursue his wanderings along such paths. It is also the case for all critics, in principle, given the undeniable and ineluctable global dimensions of the field, even if they should choose to look away or askance. It is especially the case for like-minded critics in practice, as the challenge of the task makes itself felt upon us. At this point, a word on borders and crossings is in order.

Ours is a world in which the appropriation and asseveration of identity, along all axes of status, have intensified and become the norm. That is as it should be. Such critical movements and knowledges are indispensable, welcome, and irreversible. In the face of a universalist representation of humanity, which has led to the advantage of some and the detriment of many, the latter have every right to mobilize and represent themselves. Ours is also a world in which such identity affirmation has not infrequently resulted in the exclusion of Others, explicitly or implicitly. These Others are various. They include, most prominently, those who are seen as representing the ways of the past, the traditions of domination and dismissal, who have long excluded their Others. They also include those who are taken to embody the ways of other marginalized formations, traditions that lie outside a group. Sometimes, that too is as it should be, if exclusion is deployed for the sake of strategic goals. At other times, it is not, when exclusion is portrayed in stereotypical terms for the sake of rejection or sidelining. Far too often, it would seem, it is this latter posture of deliberate and alienating exclusion that rules the day.

In religious-theological circles, as in academic-intellectual circles in general, the awakening of the Others of Western modernity has tended to yield a repression of the Selves of such modernity. The figure of Holter calls for a rethinking of any such epistemological reversal. Thoroughly from the North as he was, he opted for immersion in the South, through the lens of sub-Saharan Africa, and he did so with a disposition of dialogical enlightenment and integration. I should like to share a story that he once shared with me. Upon embarking on such work, he was warned by a senior colleague of his in Norway that such a path would exact a heavy price on his academic-professional development in both field and guild. This prospect did not deter him. From a critical perspective, this verdict was altogether wrong; crossing borders did bring breadth and sophistication as well as recognition and distinction. Unfortunately, even today, not enough critics from the North have followed his example, for whatever reason. The loss, alas, is entirely theirs.

Crossing borders in the other direction, from the South, also yields similar academic-professional enrichment. To be sure, such an option has to be exercised not as in the past, immersion through assimilation, but rather with a parallel attitude of dialogical enlightenment and integration, immersion through critical interaction. Such crossings, however, are oftentimes dismissed or condemned as utterly and damnably passé—enough, enough from the realm of white males, dead or alive, from the West! It is a posture easily understandable, to be sure, in the light of an inglorious past. Such a prospect should not deter us. From my critical standpoint, any such banishment is decidedly wrong as well. Crossing borders is imperative, but it must focus on the how, not the who or the where, and thus place ideological critique at the heart of a dialogical hermeneutics. Not to do so would be, alas, quite a loss.

In sum, a global model of criticism, grounded in a project of dialogical hermeneutics, such as Holter and others are clamoring for, would demand border crossings—from South to North and from North to South, but also in all directions within both the North and the South. The present volume in honor of his sixty-fifth birthday and in celebration of his service to the guild and the field alike is a splendid testimony to this vision and mission of his. Context does indeed matter, as the title would have it, as does the critical interaction across contexts advocated by the dialogical hermeneutics of global criticism. *Ad multos annos.*

Works Cited

De Sousa Santos, Bonaventura. 2018. "Introduction: Why the Epistemologies of the South? Artisanal Paths for Artisanal Futures." Pages 1–14 in *The End of the Cognitive Empire: The Coming of Age of Epistemologies of the South*. Edited by Boaventura de Sousa Santos. Durham, NC: Duke University Press.

De Wit, Hans, et al., eds. 2004. *Through the Eyes of Another: Intercultural Reading of the Bible*. Elkhart, IN: Institute of Mennonite Studies.

Dick, Michael B. 1997. Review of *Second Isaiah's Idol-Fabrication Passages*, by Knut Holter. *CBQ* 59:542–43.

Dube, Musa. 2002. "Villagizing, Globalizing, and Biblical Studies." Pages 41–63 in *Reading the Bible in the Global Village: Cape Town*. Edited by Justin K. Ukpong et al. GPBS 3. Atlanta: Society of Biblical Literature.

Holter, Knut. 1995. *Second Isaiah's Idol-Fabrication Passages*. New York: Lang.

———. 1996a. *Tropical Africa and the Old Testament*. Oslo: University of Olso.

———. 1996b. "Not Another Journal?!" *NAOTS* 1:1–3.

———. 1997a. "Contextualized Old Testament Programmes?" *Newsletter on African Old Testament Scholarship* 2:3–7.

———. 1997b. "Gammeltestamentlig Forskning mellom Sahara og Zambesi." *TTKi* 68:135–46.

———. 1997c. "Should Old Testament 'Cush' Be Rendered 'Africa'?" *BT* 48:331–36.

———. 2008. *Contextualized Old Testament Scholarship in Africa*. Nairobi: Acton.

———. 2010a. "Geographical and Institutional Aspects of Global Old Testament Studies." Pages 3–14 in *Global Hermeneutics? Reflections and Consequences*. Edited by Knut Holter and Louis C. Jonker. IVBS 1. Atlanta: Society of Biblical Literature.

———. 2010b. "When Biblical Scholars Talk about 'Global' Biblical Interpretation." Pages 85–93 in *Global Hermeneutics? Reflections and Consequences*. Edited by Knut Holter and Louis C. Jonker. IVBS 1. Atlanta: Society of Biblical Literature.

———. 2015a. "Am I My Brother's Keeper? Justice and Transformation in a Malagasy-Norwegian Dialogue (Genesis 4)." Pages 355–68 in *Bible and Transformation: The Promise of Intercultural Reading*. Edited by Hans de Wit and Janet Dyk. SemeiaSt 81. Atlanta: SBL Press.

———. 2015b. "'My Punishment Is Greater that I Can Bear': Malagasy and Norwegian Ordinary Readers on Genesis 4:13." Pages 31–39 in *In Love with the Bible and Its Ordinary Readers: Hans de Wit and the Intercultural Bible Reading Project*. Edited by Hans Snoek. Elkhard, IN: Institute of Mennonite Studies.

———. 2019. "Malagasy, Thai, and Norwegian Youths Reading Luke 15 Together." Pages 139–52 in *A Critical Study of Classical Religious Texts in Global Contexts: Challenges of a Changing World*. Edited by Beth E. Elness-Hanson and Jon Skarpeid. New York: Lang.

Holter, Knut, and Louis C. Jonker, eds. 2010. *Global Hermeneutics? Reflections and Consequences*. IVBS 1. Atlanta: Society of Biblical Literature.

Hoogvelt, Ankie. 2011 *Globalization and the Postcolonial World: The New Political Economy of Development*. 2nd ed. Baltimore: Johns Hopkins University Press.

Hunt, Lynn. 2014. *Writing History in the Global Era*. New York: Norton.

Kloß, Theres Sinah. 2017. "The Global South as Subversive Practice: Challenges and Potentials of a Heuristic Concept." *The Global South* 11.2: 1–17.

Levinson, J. R., and Priscilla Pope-Levinson, eds. 1999. *Return to Babel: Global Perspectives on the Bible*. Louisville: Westminster John Knox.

Patte, Daniel, ed. 2004. *Global Bible Commentary*. Nashville: Abingdon.

Räisänen, H., et al., eds. 2000. *Reading the Bible in the Global Village: Helsinki*. GPBS 1. Atlanta: Society of Biblical Literature.

Schneider, Nina. 2017. "Between Promise and Skepticism: The Global South and Our Role as Engaged Intellectuals." *The Global South* 11.2:18–37.

Schüssler Fiorenza, Elisabeth. 1988. "The Ethics of Biblical Interpretation: Decentering Biblical Scholarship." *JBL* 107:3–17.

———. 2000. "Defending the Center, Trivializing the Margins." Pages 29–48 in *Reading the Bible in the Global Village: Helsinki*. GPBS 1. Edited by H. Räisänen et al. Atlanta: Society of Biblical Literature.

Segovia, Fernando F. Forthcoming. "Reading in These Times: Contexts of Minoritized Biblical Criticism." In *Reading in These Times: Purposes and Practices of Minoritized Biblical Criticism*. Edited by Tat-siong Benny Liew and Fernando F. Segovia. SemeiaSt 98. Atlanta: SBL Press.

Segovia, Fernando F., and Mary Ann Tolbert, eds. 1995. *Reading from This Place*. Social Location and Biblical Interpretation in Global Perspective 1. Minneapolis: Fortress.

Seidman, Steven. 2013. *Contested Knowledge: Social Theory Today.* 5th ed. Malden, MA: Wiley-Blackwell.
Tamayo, Juan José. 2017. *Teologías del Sur. El giro descolonizador.* Colección Estructuras y Procesos: Religión. Madrid: Editorial Trotta.
Ukpong, Justin S. 2002. "Reading the Bible in a Global Village: Issues and Challenges from African Reading." Pages 9–39 in *Reading the Bible in the Global Village: Cape Town.* Edited by Justin K. Ukpong et al. GPBS 3. Atlanta: Society of Biblical Literature.
Ukpong, Justin S., et al., eds. 2002. *Reading the Bible in the Global Village: Cape Town.* GPBS 3. Atlanta: Society of Biblical Literature.
Wallerstein, Immanuel. 2004. *World-Systems Analysis: An Introduction.* Durham, NC: Duke University Press.

Knut Holter's Life and Work

A Short Biography

Knut Holter was born in Norway on October 12, 1958. He graduated from the theology program (cand.theol.) at the School of Mission and Theology (MHS) in Stavanger in 1985, but his interest in the Old Testament led him to study Hebrew at the University of Oslo alongside the theology degree. In 1990–1993, Holter was a research fellow at the MHS, and he was awarded the Doctor of Theology degree from the University of Oslo in 1993. By then, Holter's engagement with the MHS was well established, and he continued his employment there first as an associate professor of the Old Testament (1993–2002) and then as professor (2002–2022). Between 2004 and 2010, he was the rector of the MHS. During his tenure as rector, the institution gained accreditation as a specialized university. Holter continued as professor at MSH even after MSH merged with other institutions and changed to VID Specialized University in 2016. In August 2022, Holter was appointed full professor at NLA University College, Norway and professor II at VID Specialized University. Holter is also an extraordinary professor at the University of Stellenbosch, South Africa.

While Holter's research contributions span topics such as idol fabrication in the book of Isaiah, relations between Deuteronomy and the book of Isaiah, Bible translation, and development of intercultural hermeneutics, he is especially acclaimed for his work on African biblical hermeneutics in terms of documentation, networking, facilitation, and analysis of the various interpretation strategies vis-à-vis the Bible in Africa. For the latter, the list of publications below speaks on its own. On several occasions, Holter has received external funding, for example, from the Research Council of Norway and from NUFU: Norwegian Programme for Development, Research and Education. However, Holter has also frequently paid for his work travels to Africa from his own pocket.

Holter's engagement is visible in his analysis of African Old Testament scholarship (1995–2002); his editorial responsibility for *Bulletin for the Old Testament Studies in Africa* (1996–2006); the project "The Old Testament in Africa at the Turn of the Century" in collaboration with Kenyan and other scholars (1999–2001); editorial responsibility for the Peter Lang book series Bible and Theology in Africa (2001–); oversight of the joint project by the MHS and the University of South Africa, "Africanization of Biblical Studies," involving several PhD candidates and researchers (2002–2006); involvement with the project "Reintegration of Female Ex-child Soldiers in Eastern Africa" (2007–2011); as well as development and direction of the project "Empirical and Intercultural Biblical Interpretation," involving research participants from Norway, Madagascar and Thailand (2011–2015); the major research project, "Potentials and Problems of Popular Inculturation Hermeneutics in Maasai Biblical Interpretation," with several collaborators (2014–2018); and the open access publication of textbooks in Malagasy (2018–2019). Holter has founded several research groups and networks, such as SIMBA (The Stavanger Initiative on Method, Bible and Africa; https://simb.africa/), which includes the research cluster CollECT (Colloquium on Epistemology, Context, and Text, in Biblical Interpretation), where African and Western scholars collaborate. Additionally, Holter has facilitated interactions not only between Africa and the West, but also among Africans. His wife Berly, their children, and grandchildren have sometimes accompanied Holter on his many work trips to Africa. His passion for Africa has become part of their family story, and from his extensive network, they have received countless guests in their home. On such occasions Holter has also included colleagues from MHS/VID and elsewhere, with the effect that the network has expanded and new relations have been established. Indeed, his broad network made it difficult for the editors of this volume to set a limit for contributions—several anthologies could have been made in honor of Holter.

Beyond his engagement with African biblical hermeneutics, Holter is a very popular lecturer and supervisor, a beloved colleague, and a very competent administrator. He is also an ordained minister and an active participant in media debates. Holter has taken the initiative to create evening courses for adults, and he teaches the Bible to children in his parish—including via YouTube-videos, which he made during the restrictions of COVID-19.

In everything, Holter shows excellence in competence and genuine care for the wellbeing of those around him.

Publications by Knut Holter, 1986–2022

Books

1995. *Second Isaiah's Idol-Fabrication Passages.* New York: Lang.
1996. *Tropical Africa and the Old Testament.* Lang: New York.
2000. *Yahweh in Africa: Essays on Africa and Old Testament.* Lang: New York.
Coedited with Mary Getui and Victor Zinkuratire. 2001. *Interpreting the Old Testament in Africa: Papers from the International Symposium on Africa and the Old Testament in Nairobi, October 1999.* New York: Lang. Republished as: 2001. *Interpreting the Old Testament in Africa.* Biblical Studies in African Scholarship Series. Nairobi: Acton.
2002. *Old Testament Research for Africa: A Critical Analysis and Annotated Bibliography of African Old Testament Dissertations, 1967–2000.* New York: Lang.
Deuteronomy 4 and the Second Commandment. StBibLit 60. New York: Lang.
Ed. 2006. *Let My People Stay! Researching the Old Testament in Africa; Report from a Research Project on Africanization of Old Testament Studies.* Nairobi: Acton.
Ed. 2007. *Interpreting Classical Religious Texts in Contemporary Africa.* Nairobi: Acton.
2008. *Contextualized Old Testament Scholarship in Africa.* Nairobi: Acton.
Coedited with Louis C. Jonker. 2010. *Global Hermeneutics? Reflections and Consequences.* IVBS 1. Atlanta: Society of Biblical Literature.
Coedited with Jostein Ådna. 2011. *Jerusalem, Samaria og jordens ender: Bibeltolkninger tilegnet Magnar Kartveit, 65 år, 7. oktober 2011.* Trondheim: Tapir.
2012. *La recherche en Ancien Testament dans le contexte africain.* Yaoundé: Éditions CLÉ.
2018. *Fandalinana Testamenta Taloha mihatra ami-konteksta any Afrika sy Madakasikara.* Stavanger and Antananarivo.
2019. *Moa Mpitandrina ny Rahalahiko va aho? Malagasy sy Norveziana Miara-Mandinika ny Baiboly ao amin'ny Genesisy 4 sy ny Lioka 15.* Stavanger and Antananarivo.
2019. *Nanokatra ny sain'ireo Izy: Ny Misiolojia sy ny Testamenta Taloha.* Stavanger and Antananarivo.

Coedited with Lemburis Justo. 2020. *Maasai Encounters with the Bible.* Nairobi: Acton.

Articles

1992. "Die Parallelismen in Jes 50,11ab*a*—im Hebräischen und Syrischen Text." *BN* 63:35-36.
1993. "A Note on the Old Testament Background of Rom 1, 23-27." *BN* 69:21-23.
1993. "The Wordplay on *el* ('God') in Isaiah 45, 20-21." *SJOT* 7:88-98.
1994. "Å skape guder i menneskets bilde." *Misjon og Teologi* 1:45-53.
1994. "Det gamle testamente og misjonen." Pages 23–36 in *Missiologi i dag.* Edited by Jan-Martin Berentsen et al. Oslo: Universitetsforlaget.
1995. Et al. "Å lese Hosea 2 i en santal-landsby." *Misjon og Teologi* 2:15-29.
1996. "Literary Critical Studies of Deut 4: Some Criteriological Remarks." *BN* 81:91-103.
1996. "Zur Funktion der *Städte* Judas in Jes xl 9." *VT* 46:119-21.
1997. "Contextualized Old Testament Programmes?" *Newsletter on African Old Testament Scholarship* 2:3-7.
1997. "Gammeltestamentlig Forskning mellom Sahara og Zambesi." *TTKi* 68:135-46.
1997. "Should Old Testament 'Cush' Be Rendered 'Africa'?" *BT* 48:331-36.
1998. "Afrikansk gammeltestamentlig forskning i spenning mellom Sørs myter og Nords metoder." *NTM* 52:147-59.
1998. "It's Not Only a Question of Money! African Old Testament Scholarship between the Myths and Meanings of the South and the Money and Methods of the North!" *OTE* 11:240-54.
1998. "The Institutional Context of Old Testament Scholarship in Africa." *OTE* 11:452-61.
1998. "Some Recent Studies on Postcolonialism and Biblical Scholarship." *Newsletter on African Old Testament Scholarship* 5 :20-23.
1998. "Trøst, ja, trøst mitt folk! Jesaja 40-55 og sjelesorgen." *Tidsskrift for sjelesorg* 18:241-49.
1999. "Men det er bare én bok som leser meg! Noen linjer i afrikansk tolkning av Det gamle testamente." *NTM* 53:231-40.
1999. "Old Testament Proverbs Studies." *NAOTS* 6:11-15.
1999. "Relating Africa and the Old Testament on the Polygamy Issue." Pages 61-71 in *L'eglise famille et perspectives bibliques: Actes du huitième con-*

grès de l'Association Panafricaine des Exégètes Catholiques. Edited by J.-B. Matand et al. Kinshasa: Association Panafricaine des Exegetes.

1999. "Report: Symposium in Nairobi, October 1999." *Newsletter on African Old Testament Scholarship* 7:8-9.

2000. "Africa in the Old Testament." Pages 569-81 in *The Bible in Africa.* Edited by Gerald O. West and Musa W. Dube. Leiden: Brill.

2000. "Is There a Need for a Pan-African and Non-denominational Organisation for Biblical Scholarship?" *BOTSA* 8:10-13.

2000. "Nabots vingård: En fortelling om makt, eiendom og rettferdighet i Det gamle testament." Pages 98-114 in *Makt Eiendom Rettferdighet: Bibelske moraltradisjoner i møte med vår tid.* Edited by Jan-Olav Henriksen. Oslo: Gyldendal.

2000. "New Name, Same Vision." *BOTSA* 8:1-2.

With Kari Stortsein Haug. 2000. "No Graven Image? Reading the Second Commandment in a Thai Context." *AJT* 14:20-36.

2000. "Old Testament Scholarship in Sub-Saharan African North of the Limpopo River." Pages 54-71 in *The Bible in Africa: Transactions, Trajectories, and Trends.* Edited by Gerald O. West and Musa W. Dube. Leiden: Brill.

2000. "Old Testament Researchers North of the Limpopo: A Bibliography of Doctoral Dissertations." *BOTSA* 9:6-21.

2001. "The Current State of Old Testament Scholarship in Africa: Where Are We at the Turn of the Century?" Pages 27-39 in *Interpreting the Old Testament in Africa: Papers from the International Symposium on Africa and the Old Testament, Nairobi 1999.* Mary Getui, Knut Holter, and Victor Zinkuratire. Bible and Theology in Africa 2. New York: Lang.

2002. "Is It Necessary to Be Black?" *BOTSA* 13:7-8.

2003. "The 'Africanization of Biblical Studies' Project." *BOTSA* 14:17-19.

2003. "Two Recent Research Contributions from Kinshasa." *BOTSA* 15:18-20.

2004. "The First Generation of African Old Testament Scholars: The Geographical Hermeneutics of Their Academic Training." *BOTSA* 17:2-18.

2004. "The Maasai and the Old Testament: Marking the Centennial of M. Merker's Monograph on the Maasai." *BOTSA* 16:13-16.

Coauthored with Georges Razafindrakoto. 2005. "Challenging the Christian Monopoly on the Bible: An Aspect of the Encounter between Christianity and Malegasy Traditional Religion in Contemporary

Madagascar." Pages 141-48 in *African Identities and World Christianity in the Twentieth Century: Proceedings of the Third International Munich-Freising Conference on the History of Christianity in the Non-Western World (September 15-17, 2004)*. Edited by Klaus Koschorke and Jens Holger Schjørring. Wiesdbaden: Harrassowitz.

2005. "The First Generation of African Old Testament Scholars: African Concerns and Western Influence." Pages 149-63 in *African Identities and World Christianity in the Twentieth Century: Proceedings of the Third International Munich-Freising Conference on the History of Christianity in the Non-Western World (September 15-17, 2004)*. Edited by Klaus Koschorke and Jens Holger Schjørring. Wiesdbaden: Harrassowitz.

2005. "Recent Literature on Old Testament Translation in Africa." *BOTSA* 18:20-23.

2006. "Bibeltolkning og bibeloversettelse i afrikansk akademia." *NTM* 60.2:3-15.

2006. "Bibeloversettelse som studium ved Misjonshøgskolen." *NTM* 60.2:16-26.

2006. "Interpreting Solomon in Colonial and Post-colonial Africa." *OTE* 19:851-62.

2006. "Jan-Martin Berentsen som lærer." Pages 301-7 in *Misjon og kultur: Festskrift til Jan-Martin Berentsen*. Edited by Thor Strandenæs. Stavanger: Misjonshøgskolens forlag.

2006. "Let My People Stay: Introduction to a Research Project on Africanization of Old Testament Studies." Pages 1-18 in *Let My People Stay! Researching the Old Testament in Africa; Report from a Research Project on Africanization of Old Testament Studies*. Edited by Knut Holter. Nairobi: Acton.

2006. "Let My People Stay! Introduction to a Research Project on Africanization of Old Testament Studies." *OTE* 19:377-92.

2006. "'Like Living in Old Testament Times': The Interpretation of Assumed Affinities between Traditional African Culture and the Old Testament." *Analecta Bruxellensia* 11:17-27.

2006. "Sub-Saharan African Doctoral Dissertations in Old Testament Studies, 1967-2000: Some Remarks to Their Chronology and Geography." Pages 99-116 in *Biblical Interpretation in African Perspective*. Edited by David T. Adamo Lanham, MD: University Press of America.

2007. "A Conference Volume on the Interpretation of Classical Religious Texts in Contemporary Africa." Pages 1-10 in *Interpreting Classical*

Religious Texts in Contemporary Africa. Edited by Knut Holter. Nairobi: Acton.

2007. "Religious Texts in Critical Contexts: The Interpretation of Classical Religious Texts in Contemporary African Academia." Pages 45-56 in *Interpreting Classical Religious Texts in Contemporary Africa*. Edited by Knut Holter. Nairobi: Acton.

2008. "Does a Dialogue between Africa and Europe Make Sense?" Pages 69-80 in *African and European Readers of the Bible in Dialogue: In Quest of a Shared Meaning*. Edited by Hans de Wit and Gerald O. West. Leiden: Brill.

2008. "'En neger, naturligvis en slave': En side ved kolonitidens tolkning av Det gamle testamente." Pages 183-92 in *Med Kristus til jordens ender: Festskrift til Tormod Engelsviken*. Edited by Kjell Olav Sannes et al. Trondheim: Tapir.

2008. "The Left Hand Washes the Right and the Right Hand Washes the Left: Some Remarks to the Use of African Proverbs in Old Testament Proverb Scholarship." *African Journal of Biblical Studies* 26:45-55.

2008. "'A Negro, Naturally a Slave': An Aspect of the Portrayal of Africans in Colonial Old Testament Interpretation." *OTE* 21:373-82.

2008. "Whose Book Is It, by the Way? An Aspect of Popular and Scholarly Strategies for Interpreting the Bible in Africa." Pages 205-14 in *Mission to the World: Communicating the Gospel in the Twenty-First Century; Essays in Honour of Knud Jørgensen*. Edited by Tormod Engelsviken et al. Oxford: Regnum.

2008. "Dialogue and Interpretative Power." Pages 409-16 in *African and European Readers of the Bible in Dialogue: In Quest of a Shared Meaning*. Edited by Hans de Wit and Gerald O. West. Studies of Religion in Africa 32. Leiden: Brill.

2008. "Fascination and Challenge." Pages 368-70 in *African and European Readers of the Bible: In Quest for a Shared Meaning*. Edited by Gerald O. West and Hans de Wit. Leiden: Brill.

2009. "Did Prince Cetshwayo Read the Old Testament in 1859? The Role of the Bible and the Art of Reading in the Interaction between Norwegian Missionaries and the Zulu Elite in the Mid-Nineteenth Century." *OTE* 22.3:580-88.

2009. "The Old Testament and Africa—and Malagasy Old Testament Scholarship in Relation to Some Major Interpretative Strategies of African Old Testament Scholarship." *ATJ* 32.2:21-38.

2010. "Geographical and Institutional Aspects of Global Old Testament Studies." Pages 3–14 in *Global Hermeneutics? Reflections and Consequences*. Edited by Knut Holter and Louis C. Jonker. IVBS 1. Atlanta: Society of Biblical Literature.

2010. "Old Testament Studies and Social Transformation in Africa." *African Journal of Biblical Studies* 28:32–45.

2010. "Woman and War in Northern Uganda and Ancient Israel: The Interpretative Role of Academia." Pages 207–18 in *Culture, Religion, and the Reintegration of Female Child Soldiers in Northern Uganda*. Edited by Bård Mæland. Bible and Theology in Africa 10. New York: Lang.

2010. "When Biblical Scholars Talk about 'Global' Biblical Interpretation." Pages 85–93 in *Global Hermeneutics? Reflections and Consequences*. Edited by Knut Holter and Louis C. Jonker. IVBS 1. Atlanta: Society of Biblical Literature.

2011. "Hva i all verden skal vi bruke Jesaja 41,8–13 til? Noen refleksjoner om bibeltolkning og bibelbruk." Pages 171–81 in *Jerusalem, Samaria og jordens ender: Bibeltolkninger tilegnet Magnar Kartveit, 65 år, 7. oktober 2011*. Edited by Knut Holter and Jostein Ådna. Trondheim: Tapir.

2011. "Muslim and Christian Interaction with Regard to Old Testament Interpretation in Africa." *African Journal of Biblical Studies* 29:99–112.

2011. "The Role of Historical-Critical Methodology in African Old Testament Studies." *OTE* 24:377–89.

2011. "The Second Commandment and the Question of Human Dignity in Africa: A Creation-Theological Perspective." *Scriptura* 106:51–60.

2013. "Global tekst i lokal tapning." *Kirke og Kultur* 118:146–59.

2014. "Pregnancy and Psalms: Aspects of the Healing Ministry of a Nigerian Prophet." *OTE* 27:428–43.

2015. "Am I My Brother's Keeper? Justice and Transformation in a Malagasy-Norwegian Dialogue (Genesis 4)." Pages 355–68 in *Bible and Transformation: The Promise of Intercultural Reading*. Edited by Hans de Wit and Janet Dyk. SemeiaSt 81. Atlanta: SBL Press.

2015. "Being Like the Cushites: Some Western and African Interpretations of Amos 9:7." Pages 306–18 in *New Perspectives on Old Testament Prophecy and History: Essays in Honour of Hans M. Barstad*. Edited by Rannfrid I. Thelle, Terje Stordalen, and Mervyn E. J. Richardson. Leiden: Brill.

2015. "'My Punishment Is Greater than I Can Bear': Malagasy and Norwegian Ordinary Readers on Genesis 4:13." Pages 31–40 in *In Love with the Bible and Its Ordinary Readers: Hans de Wit and the Intercultural Bible Reading Project*. Edited by Hans Snoek. Elkhart, IN: Institute of Mennonite Studies.

2016. "The 'Poor' in Ancient Israel—and in Contemporary African Biblical Studies." *Mission Studies* 33:209–21.

2017. "The Maasai and the Ancient Israelites: An Early Twentieth Century Interpretation of the Maasai in East Africa." *Scriptura* 116.2:66-74.

2017. "Presteutdanning som investering i fremtiden." Pages 225–29 in *Sendt sammen: NMS i 175 år*. Edited by Kjetil Aano. Stavanger: Hertervig.

2017. "What Shall We Do with the Canaanites? An Ethical Perspective on Genesis 12:6." *OTE* 30:337–47.

2017. "Relocating Keil and Delitzsch: Reading a Mid-Nineteenth Century Biblical Commentary from Germany with Early Twenty-First Century Theology Students from Tanzania and Norway." Pages 279–88 in *Transkulturelle Begegnungen und interreligiöser Dialog*. Edited by Uta Andrée, Ruomin Liu, and Sönke Lorberg-Fehring Hamburg: Missionshilfe Verlag.

2017. "Some Interpretive Experiences with Isaiah in Africa." Pages 181–99 in *Studies in Isaiah: History, Theology and Reception*. Edited by Tommy Wasserman, Greger Andersson, and David Willgren. London: Bloomsbury.

2018. "Sjangeren bibelkommentar—og 'Afrika.'" Pages 227–38 in *Ordet er dig mycket nära: Tolkningar av Gamla testamentet*. Edited by James Starr and Birger Olsson. Skellefteå: Artos & Norma.

2018. "Texts of Affirmation Rather than Negation: Jesse N.K. Mugambi and African Biblical Studies." Pages 17–24 in *Religion and Social Reconstruction in Africa*. Elias Kifon Bongmba. London: Routledge.

2018. "To the Question of an Ethics of Bible Translation: Some Reflections in Relation to Septuagint Isaiah 6:1 and 19:25." *OTE* 31:651–62.

2019. "'Den andre leseren' som tolkningsmessig inspirasjon og korrektiv: Noen erfaringer med interkulturell bibellesning blant ungdom." *NTM* 73.2:5–15.

2019. "Malagasy, Thai, and Norwegian Youths Reading Luke 15 Together." Pages 139–52 in *A Critical Study of Classical Religious Texts in Global Contexts: Challenges of a Changing World*. Edited by Beth E. Elness-Hanson and Jon Skarpeid. New York: Lang.

2019. "Thou Shalt Not Smoke: Content and Context in the Lord's Resistance Army's Concept of the Ten Commandments." *HvTSt* 75.3:art. 4997. https://doi.org/10.4102/hts.v75i3.4997.

2020. "Context of Contextual Project on the Maasai and the Bible." Pages 13-23 in *Maasai Encounters with the Bible*. Edited by Knut Holter and Lemburis Justo. Nairobi: Acton.

2020. "Doing Biblical Studies in Poverty Contexts: Some African Experiences and Concerns." Pages 378-92 in *The Bible and Money: Economy and Socioeconomic Ethics in the Bible*. Edited by Markus Zehnder and Hallvard Hagelia. Bible and the Modern World 76. Sheffield: Sheffield Phoenix.

2020. "Interpretive Context Matters: Isaiah and the African Context in African Study Bibles." Pages 655-69 in *The Oxford Handbook of Isaiah*. Edited by Lena-Sofia Tiemeyer. Oxford: Oxford University Press.

2020. "Isak—the Son of the Rainmaker—and the Bible: An Example of Resistance Hermeneutics in Zululand around 1870." *JTSA* 166:41-51.

2020. "The Maasai and the Ancient Israelites: Religio-cultural Parallels." Pages 107-19 in *Maasai Encounters with the Bible*. Edited by Knut Holter and Lemburis Justo. Nairobi: Acton.

2021. "Davis Tuesday Adamo's Academic Context: Nigerian Biblical Studies Navigating between African Interpretive Concerns and Western Scholarly Traditins." *OTE* 34:353-69.

2021. "'If a King Judges the Poor with Fairness, His Throne Is Established Forever': Approaching Proverbs 29:14 with African Interpretive Resources." *JSem* 30: https://doi.org/10.25159/2663-6573/9076.

2022. Coauthored with Anne Lise Matre: "Laamdo som alternativ gudsbetegnelse til Allah i bibeloversettelsen til Mali-fulani." *NTM* 76:203-16.

2022. "'Vi vet noe om Zanahary som dere ikke vet': Kristningen av afrikanske gudsbetegnelser som strategisk og etisk spørsmål." *NTM* 76:189-202.

Postscript: A Generous Move

Sigbjørn Sødal

In 2022, NLA University College, Norway was delighted to appoint Knut Holter as a fulltime professor. Throughout his academic life, Holter has crossed borders, and in the last thirty years, his main research and publishing focus has been on African interpretive strategies vis-à-vis the Bible. His networking and involvement in projects in the South and North, and between the South and North, demonstrate how dialogue can bring mutual illumination to all involved. Through his border crossing Holter has contributed to bringing more breadth, width, and recognition to the global field of biblical studies.

What institutional characteristics may encourage (or discourage) a highly qualified scholar like Holter from joining NLA, one may ask? NLA is rooted in the same Low Church or lay tradition as most of the other private university colleges in Norway with a religious clause. However, it differs from them in certain respects. This short postscript allows for some remarks on a few characteristics of this tradition.

NLA was established in Bergen in 1968, and it focused on religious studies and pedagogy based on Christian values, primarily targeting teachers within the public school system. The size and scope of study programs and research are much wider now, but teacher training remains at the core of NLA's business. Considering how Christian faith is losing ground in society today while the influence of teachers on children remains, teacher training based on Christian values may well be one of the most meaningful missions one can have in Norway today.

As the other religious colleges typically focus on theology or diaconal services, their relation to religious life and institutions often come naturally. At NLA, the portfolio of studies and research includes not only theology, pedagogy, and general teacher training, but also journalism and communication, performing music, intercultural studies, and business administration. This brings NLA closer to a *liberal arts* tradition, which implicitly creates the potential for further growth and influence, but also the risk of losing identity in a secular society. For that reason, NLA is quite explicit about its religious bias. This can create tension in academic or political settings, but NLA has overcome such tension so far. At the time of writing, NLA has close to three hundred employees and almost ten times as many students. The academic staff has higher qualifications, and more research is being published than ever before at the institution.

Finally, most religious colleges in Norway are owned either by a single church or organization (simplifying governance) or by an independent foundation (with no owner). But NLA is an intermediate case, as it is owned by seven Lutheran organizations or churches and operates in three cities from four campuses (two in Bergen, one in Oslo, and one in Kristiansand). The ownership and campus structures make NLA well positioned to expand its activities and further develop its distinctive character as an academic institution. The current strategic plan aims at doing so in cooperation with NLA's owners and other relevant partners.

The generous move by the internationally and nationally highly acclaimed Holter to join NLA University College has made the task more exciting and the overall mission more achievable.

Contributors

†**David Tuesday Adamo** (1949-2022), Professor of Old Testament Studies, Kogi State University; Research Associate, Department of Biblical and Ancient Studies, University of South Africa

Jostein Ådna, Professor Emeritus of New Testament Studies, VID Specialized University, Stavanger, Norway

Hendrik L. Bosman, Professor Emeritus of Old Testament, Faculty of Theology, Stellenbosch University, South Africa

Ntozakhe Simon Cezula, Senior Lecturer, Old and New Testament, Stellenbosch University, South Africa

L. Juliana Claassens, Professor of Old Testament and Head of the Gender Unit, Faculty of Theology, Stellenbosch University, South Africa

Hans de Wit, Professor Emeritus of Contextual Theology and Intercultural Hermeneutics and the Dom Hélder Câmara Chair, Faculty of Religion and Theology, Vrije Universiteit Amsterdam, the Netherlands

Beth E. Elness-Hanson, Postdoctor Hebrew Bible, VID Specialized University, Stavanger, Norway

Louis C. Jonker, Distinguished Professor of Old Testament, Faculty of Theology, Stellenbosch University, South Africa

Magnar Kartveit, Professor Emeritus of Old Testament, VID Specialized University, Stavanger, Norway

Contributors

Marta Høyland Lavik, Professor of Biblical Studies, The Research Group for Nursing- and Healthcare Science, Stavanger University Hospital, Norway; Research Associate, Faculty of Theology, Stellenbosch University, South Africa

Grant LeMarquand, Professor of New Testament, Trinity School for Ministry, Ambridge, PA, United States

Madipoane Masenya (Ngwan'a Mphahlele), Professor of Old Testament Studies (Hebrew Bible), Department of Biblical and Ancient Studies; Acting Executive Director, Office of the Principal and Vice-Chancellor, University of South Africa, Pretoria, South Africa

Jesse N. K. Mugambi, Professor Emeritus, Department of Philosophy and Religious Studies, the University of Nairobi, Kenya

Kenneth N. Ngwa, Professor of Hebrew Bible and the founder-cum-director of the Religion and Global Health Forum, Drew Theological School, Madison, NJ, United States

Tina Dykesteen Nilsen, Professor of Biblical Studies, Centre of Mission and Global Studies, VID Specialized University, Stavanger, Norway

Helen Nambalirwa Nkabala, Associate Professor, Department of Religion and Peace Studies, Makerere University, Kampala, Uganda

Funlọla O. Ọlọjẹde, Research Fellow, Old and New Testament, and Postgraduate Coordinator, Faculty of Theology, Stellenbosch University, South Africa

Fernando F. Segovia, Oberlin Graduate Professor of New Testament and Early Christianity, the Divinity School and the Graduate School of Religion of Vanderbilt University, TN, United States

Terje Stordalen, Professor of Hebrew Bible/Old Testament Studies, Faculty of Theology, University of Oslo; Scientific Director of the National and Trans-Disciplinary PhD School Authoritative Texts and Their Receptions

Charlene van der Walt, Professor and Head of Gender and Religion, the School of Religion, Philosophy, and Classics, University of KwaZulu-Natal, South Africa; Deputy Director of the Ujamaa Center for Biblical and Theological Community Development and Research

Gerald O. West, Professor Emeritus, the School of Religion, Philosophy, and Classics, University of KwaZulu-Natal, South Africa

Author Index

Abusch, Tzvi 169–70, 173
Adamo, David Tuesday 4, 18, 22, 63, 68, 74, 194
Adeyemo, Tokunboh 197, 203
Ådna, Jostein 7
Agnew, Sarah 169, 173
Ahmed, Sara 169–70, 173
Ahuvya, Avraham 268, 279
Akenson, Donald Harman 199, 203
Akoto-Abutiate, Dorothy BEA 20, 22
Allen, David 11, 22
Anderson, Monica 164, 173
Ano, Gene G. 230, 235
Assmann, Aleida 80–81, 85–86, 88
Assmann, Jan 80–81, 85–86, 88
Autero, Esa J. 223, 233
Aymer, Margaret 18, 22
Baines, Erin 139–40, 147
Bal, Mieke 83, 88, 211, 220
Banet-Weiser, Sarah 171–74
Baumann, W. 71, 74
Becken, Hans-Jürgen 110, 117
Bediako, Kwame 109, 117
Beebee, Thomas O. 12, 22
Bell, Catherine 140, 147
Bennett, Jane 81, 88
Berlinerblau, Jacques 79, 84, 88
Besten, Michael P. 101–2
Betchel, Lyn M. 150, 160
Beukes, Piet 101–2
Black, Fiona 170, 173
Blass, Freidrich 270–73, 279
Blenkinsopp, Joseph 64, 74
Block, Daniel I. 66, 70, 74
Blystad, Astrid 224, 235

Boadt, Lawrence 66, 74
Boase, Elizabeth 169, 173
Bodi, Daniel 71, 74
Boer, Roland 12, 22
Boezak, Willa 94–95, 97–98, 101–2
Bolin, Thomas M. 167, 169, 173
Boonzaaier, Michelle 129, 133
Bosman, Hendrik L. 4
Botvar, Pål K. 224, 233
Bourdieu, Pierre 79–80, 89
Bradley, Mary H. 100, 102
Braun, Virginia 225, 233
Braut, Geir S. 235
Brendon, Piers 101–2
Brooke, George J. 13, 22
Broome, Edwin C., Jr. 66, 74
Broseghini, P. S. 212–14, 220
Bruce, F. F. 142–43, 148
Brueggemann, Walter 185, 187, 189
Bryce, Trevor 55, 62
Burdette, Amy M. 235
Burge, Gary M. 142, 145, 147
Buthelezi, Manas 199, 204
Cabrita, Joel M. 109, 117
Cameron, Trewhella 99, 103
Campbell, John 92, 103
Carley, Keith W. 66, 74
Carr, David M. 81, 89, 232–33
Carrithers, Michael 81, 89
Carson, Verna B. 224, 230, 234
Caspi, Mishael Maswari 150, 160
Cezula, Ntozakhe Simon 6
Childs, Brevard 58, 62
Chitra, G. 224, 236
Christensen, Duane 183, 185–86, 189

Christensen, Mark Z.	214, 221	Gadamer, Hans-Georg	225–26, 231, 234
Claassens, L. Juliana	6	Gafney, Wil	43, 46
Clarke, Victoria	225, 233	Galtung, Johan	151–52, 160
Clines, David J. A.	186, 189	Galvin, Garrett	55, 57, 62
Cone, Pamela H.	224, 234	Gastorn, Kennedy	187, 190
Conradie, Ernst M.	231, 233	Gatu, John G.	27–28, 33, 35
Corral, Martin Alonso	65, 74	Gesenius, Friedrich Wilhelm	275, 279
Craige, Peter C.	19, 22	Getui, Mary N.	14, 22, 25, 35, 107, 117, 240, 249
Cranny-Francis, Anne	125, 134		
Crouch, C. L.	65, 69–70, 74	Giske, Tove	224, 234–35
Crowther, Samuel Adjayi	26	Gitau, Samson K.	195, 204
Curwood, Steve	189–90	Gordon, Steven	198, 204
Cvetkovich, Ann	170, 173	Graham, M. Patrick	64, 75
Dalaker, Anna	230, 233	Graybill, Rhiannon	168–70, 174
Darr, Katheryn P.	65, 74	Green, Barbara	167–68, 171, 174
Davids, Hanzline	124, 134	Greenberg, Moshe	64, 74
Davidson, Hilda R. Ellis	18, 27, 29, 34	Grenholm, Cristina	182, 190
Davidson, Richard M.	150, 160	Gripsrud, Brigitta H.	235
Davidson, Steed	18, 22	Gunn, David M.	44, 46
Davis, Stephen J.	60, 62	Gunner, Elizabeth	105–6, 110–15, 117
Dedering, Tilman	95, 101, 103	Gutiérrez, Gustavo	213, 221
DeHaan, Peter	32, 35	Guy, Michael R.	23
Deist, Ferdinand E.	39, 46	Habtu, Tewoldemedhin	51, 62
Dentliger, Lindsay	164, 174	Hahn, Theophilus	97, 103
De Saussure, Ferdinand	269, 279	Halford, Sameul James	94–95, 97, 103
De Sousa Santos, Bonaventura	289, 301, 305	Halperin, David J.	66, 74
		Halpern, Baruch	66, 74
De Waard, Jan	269, 279	Hamilton, Victor P.	153
Dick, Michael B.	285, 305	Hancock, W. Keith	99, 100, 103
Doka, Kenneth J.	230, 231, 233	Harlacher, Thomas	139, 147
Donovan, Vincent J.	183, 184, 190	Harvey, Jacqueline	198, 204
Downs, David J.	168, 174	Hauser, Alan J.	65, 74
Draper, Jonathan A.	109, 117, 182, 190	Havea, Jione	18, 22, 168–71, 174
Dube, Musa	297, 305	Healey, Joseph P.	181, 190
Dube, Zorodzai	22	Herren, Ricardo	212, 221
Duguid, Ian M.	67, 74	Hexham, Irvin	106, 108, 110–11, 115, 117–18
Dyk, Janet	211, 221		
Elness-Hanson, Beth E.	6, 25, 180–84, 190, 231, 234	Hill, Andrew E.	142, 145, 147
		Hill, Terrence D.	235
Estermann, Josef	215, 221	Hintze, Otto	276, 279
Festugière, A. J.	60, 62	Hodder, Ian	81, 89
Fewell, Danna N.	44, 46	Hodgson, Dorothy L.	187–88, 190
Fischer, Irmtraud	168, 174	Hoffman, Wilma	151, 160
Fishbane, Michael	240, 249	Holscher, Gustav	65
Frolov, Serge	168, 174	Hölscher, Tonio	81, 88

Author Index

Holter, Knut 1–8, 11, 14–17, 21–22, 25–26, 28, 32–35, 37–42, 46, 51, 61–63, 77–78, 80, 84–85, 87, 89, 91, 101, 103, 107, 115–17, 123, 126–27, 129, 132, 134, 138, 141, 147, 149, 160, 163, 171–72, 174, 179–80, 182–83, 186, 190, 193–97, 199–201, 204, 209–10, 213, 220–21, 223, 232, 234, 239–50, 253–59, 264–65, 267, 279, 283–88, 290–306
Honwana, Alcinda 139, 147
Hoogvelt, Ankie 302
Høyland, Marta 235
Hübner, Hans 260, 265
Hulsman, Cornelis 61–62
Hunt, Lynn 303, 306
Jacobson, Mark 189, 191
Johnstone, Ronald L. 73, 75
Jonker, Louis C. 7, 221, 231, 233, 239, 242, 247, 249–50, 287, 306
Jordan, Archibald C. 198, 204
Joüon, Paul, S.J. 275, 279
Joyce, Paul M. 67, 75
Justo, Lemburis 33, 35
Kacela, Xolani 164–65, 174
Kampen, John 12, 22
Kaoma, Kapja J. 126, 135
Karimakwenda, Nyasha 157–58, 160
Kartje, John 20, 22
Kartveit, Magnar 7, 276–77, 279
Kavusa, Kivatsi J 195, 204
Kay, Jilly Boyce 171–74
Kebaneilwe, Mmapula Diana 195, 204
Kessler, J. J. 185–88, 191
Kibobo, Kabamba J. 11, 23
Kimirei, G. 183, 191
King, Dana E. 224, 230, 234
Kirkby, Joan 134
Kloß, Theres Sinah 300, 306
Knighton, Ben 29, 35
Koenig, Harold G. 224, 230, 234–35
Köhler, Ludwig 143, 147
Kohn, Risa Levitt 66, 75
Kool, Marleen 221, 233
Kovach, Margaret 215, 221
Kugel, James L. 232, 234
Kwenda, Chivero V. 196, 204
Lavik, Marta H. 7, 223–24, 230, 232, 234–35
Lee, Lydia 65, 68–69, 71–72, 75
Lemaire, Ton 212, 222
LeMarquand, Grant 4, 209, 222
Lentin, Anthony 99, 103
Levinson, Bernard M. 240, 251
Levinson, David 151, 160
Levinson, J. R. 296, 306
Lorde, Audre 165, 174
Luc, Alex 67–68, 75
Luckenbill, Daniel David 64, 75
Lyons, John 270, 279
Magesa, Laurenti 28, 35
Malley, Brian 223, 232, 235
Maluleke, Tinyiko S. 106, 118, 166, 174, 196, 204
Manus, Chris Ukachukwu 195, 204
Marlow, Hilary 180–82, 188–89, 191, 202, 205
Maseno-Ouma, Loreen 22
Masenya (Ngwan'a Mphahlele), Madipoane 4, 11, 12, 20–21, 23, 41, 45–47 21
Matheny, Paul D. 11, 23
Matties, Gordon H. 67, 75
Matyila, Abongile 124, 134
Mays, James Luther 64, 75
Mbiti, John S. 14, 23, 26–27, 33–35, 41, 47
Mbuvi, Andrew M. 2, 8, 12, 15, 23, 39, 47, 73, 75
McGuire, Meredith B. 140, 147
McKeating, Henry 66, 75
McKendrick, Brian W. 151, 160
McKenzie, Steven L. 64, 75
Mda, Thobeka V. 197–98, 205
Mdluli, S. 110, 118
Medås, Kaja M. 224, 235
Meindertsma, J. D. 185–88, 191
Merry, Sally Engle 151, 160
Meyer, Birgit 86, 89
Mijoga, Hilary 28, 35

Miller, Carlyn R.	12, 23	Parker, Mike	82, 89
Millin, Sarah Gertrude	100, 103	Patte, Daniel	182, 190, 232, 235, 296, 306
Mirondo, R.	186, 191		
Mishra, Pankaj	172, 174	Payne, Doris L.	184, 192
Mitri, Raheb	11, 23	Peel, J. D. Y.	108, 118
Mligo, Elia Shabani	22	Peltzer, Jill N.	235
Mojola, Aloo O.	28, 35	Perez, Lisa M.	230, 235
Morier-Genoud, Eric	31, 35	Pierce, Yolanda	165–66, 173, 175
Moskala, Jiří	73	Plantinga, Cornelius, Jr.	181, 192
Motyer, Alec J.	57, 59, 62	Pope-Levinson, Priscilla	296, 306
Mpanza, Mthembeni	107, 110, 118–19	Porter, Stanley E.	231, 235
Mthethwa, Bongani	107, 119	Rad, Gerhard von	185
Mtshiselwa, Ndikho	17, 23	Räisänen, H.	296–97, 306
Mugambi, Jesse N. K.	3–4, 11, 23	Ramantswana, Hulisana	40, 47
Muller, Carol Ann	107, 118	Ramvi, Ellen	235
Muraoka, Takamitsu	275, 279	Rice, Kathleeen	157–58, 161
Mwaura, Philomena N.	142–43, 147	Richard, Pablo	211, 214, 217, 222
Naguib, Saphinaz-Amal	83, 90	Richter, Sandra L.	179, 186, 192
Ngwa, Kenneth N.	2–3, 8 12, 23	Ricoeur, Paul	225, 236
Niang, Aliou Cissé	12, 23	Rivera Pagán, Luis	213, 222
Nicolson, Greg D.	167, 175	Robbins, Vernon	26, 36
Nida, Eugene A.	268, 279	Robinson, Jason C.	231, 235
Niditch, Susan	153, 155–56, 158, 160	Rollston, Christopher A.	81, 89
Nilsen, Tina Dykesteen	6, 180, 188, 191, 195, 205	Ross, Robert	95–96, 98, 103
		Rubial García, Antonio	212, 222
Nkabala, Helen N.	77, 79–80, 84–87, 89	Ryu, Chesung Justin	168, 175
Nkesela, Zephania Shila	185, 191	Sankan, S. S. Ole	183, 192
Ntreh, B. A.	2, 8	Sarna, Nahum M.	152, 155, 161
Nussbaum, Martha C.	130, 134	Scheper Hughes, Jennifer	214, 222
Oborji, F. A.	197, 205	Schipani, Daniel	221, 233
Odell, Margaret S.	64, 75	Schmid, Konrad	240, 251
O'Donovan, Wilbur	143, 148	Schmidt, Brian B.	81, 89
Oduyoye, Mercy A.	43, 47	Schmidt, Ulla	224, 236
Ojewska, Natalia	78, 89	Schmidt, Werner H.	243, 251
Okwaro, Ferdinand	140, 148	Schneider, Nina	300, 306
Ole-Kotikash, Leonard	184, 192	Schoeman, Karel	92–96, 103
Ọlọjẹde, Funlọla O.	5, 13, 23, 151, 161	Scholz, Susanne	150, 154, 161
Oosthuizen, G. C.	108, 110, 115, 117	Schüssler Fiorenza, Elisabeth	127, 134, 296, 306
Oswalt, John N.	59, 62		
Otto, Eckart	244, 251	Segovia, Fernando F.	7, 285, 288, 306
Otzen, Benedikt	185, 191	Seidman, Steven	299, 307
Page, Robin L.	230, 235	Shanahan, Fiona	139, 148
Pandey, Vimal Nayan	151, 161	Shank, David	109, 118
Papini, Robert	110, 118	Sherwood, Yvonne	167–68, 175
Pargament, Kenneth I.	230, 235	Shorter, Aylward	28, 36

Sithole, Sindi	124, 134	Victor, Paul	153, 160, 224, 236
Skidelsky, Robert J. A.	99, 103	Vilakazi, Absalom	107, 119
Slicher van Bath, B. H.	213, 222	Village, Andrew	223, 236
Smith, Mitzi J.	11, 23	Vine, W. E.	142–43, 148
Smith, Steve	11, 22	Wachholtz, Amy B.	230, 235
Smith, Wilfred C.	79, 87, 89	Waetjen, Herman C.	111, 113, 119
Snell, Daniel C.	55, 62	Waigwa, Solomon	28, 30, 36
Solevåg, Anna Rebecca	180, 191, 195, 205	Waldman, Linda	92, 101, 103
		Walker-Jones, Arthur	19–20, 24
Spear, Thomas	180, 192	Wallerstein, Immanuel	302, 307
Spencer, Paul	183, 192	Walls, Andrew F.	26, 36
Speth, J. Gus	189–90	Walsh, Carey	167, 175
Sproul, R. C.	142, 144, 148	Walton, John H.	183, 192
Stavropoulos, Pam	134	Waring, Wendy	134
Steyn, Richard	99, 103	Waskow, Arthur Ocean	181, 185, 192
Stordalen, Terje	4, 81–83, 90	Watts, James W.	82–83, 90
Sugden, Chris	143, 148	West, Gerald O.	5, 17, 24, 39, 47, 106, 108–10, 112, 115–16, 119, 126–27, 130–31, 135, 182–83, 192, 205, 241, 301
Sutton, J. E. G.	180, 192		
Sweeney, Marvin A.	75		
Tamayo, Juan José	303, 307		
Terblanche, Judith	129, 135	Wit, Hans de	6, 24, 42, 47, 211, 215, 218, 221, 223, 231–33, 286–87, 305
Terrien, Samuel	21, 23		
Teubal, Sylvia J.	43–44, 47	Wit, Sara de	180, 184–85, 188, 190
Thatcher, Adrian	125, 134	Wright, Christopher J. H.	180–82, 192
Thesnaar, Christoffel H.	139, 148	Wünch, Hans-Georg	3, 8
Thoresen, Lisbeth	224, 236	Zimmerli, Walther	64–65, 68, 76
Tiemeyer, Lena-Sofia	245, 251	Zinkuratire, Victor	14, 22, 25, 35, 107, 117, 240, 249
Tigay, Jeffrey H.	184–85, 192		
Tolbert, Mary Ann	285, 306	Zondi-Mabizela, Phumzile	130, 135
Toorn, Karel van der	81, 90	Zwane, Sithembiso	130–31, 135
Treschuk, Judith V.	224, 236		
Truman, Emily	82, 85, 90		
Tshehla, Maarman Samuel	16–17, 23		
Tuell, Steven Shawn	67, 75		
Ukpong, Justin S.	8, 194–95, 197, 205, 296–97, 307		
Urban, Hugh B.	79, 90		
Urbaniak, Jakub	166, 175		
Van der Merwe, Hugo	151, 161		
Van der Walt, Charlene	5, 124, 126, 128–31, 133–35		
Van Huyssteen, J. Wentzel	139, 148		
Veale, Angela	139, 148		
Vengeyi, Obvious	218, 222		
Verter, Bradford	79, 90		

www.ingramcontent.com/pod-product-compliance
Lightning Source LLC
Chambersburg PA
CBHW050856300426
44111CB00010B/1275